STRATEGIC DIGITAL TRANSFORMATION

Marc K. Peter & Johan P. Lindeque

STRATEGIC DIGITAL TRANSFORMATION

Theory and Practice

Sage

Sage

1 Oliver's Yard
55 City Road
London EC1Y 1SP

2455 Teller Road
Thousand Oaks
California 91320

10th Floor, Emaar Capital Tower 2
MG Road, Sikanderpur, Sector 26
Gurugram, Haryana – 122002
India

8 Marina View Suite 43-053
Asia Square Tower 1
Singapore 018960

Editor: Amy Mitchell
Editorial assistant: Hanine Kadi
Production editor: Nicola Marshall
Copyeditor: Martin Noble
Proofreader: Anthony Green
Indexer: Gary Kirby
Marketing manager: Elena Asplen
Cover design: Bhairvi Vyas
Typeset by: C&M Digitals (P) Ltd, Chennai, India
Printed in the UK

Library of Congress Control Number: 2025936699

British Library Cataloguing in Publication data

A catalogue record for this book is available from the British Library

ISBN 978-1-5296-9156-6
ISBN 978-1-5296-9155-9 (pbk)

CONTENTS

FOREWORD

Modern advancements in the economy are characterised by a series of transformative industrial revolutions over the past three hundred years, each driven by groundbreaking technological innovations that reshaped societies, industries, businesses, and the way we live and work. The first industrial revolution, which began in the late 18th century, was driven by the mechanisation of production through steam power and the advent of factories. This era saw a dramatic increase in productivity and the rise of urban centres, fundamentally altering the social and economic landscape. The second industrial revolution in the late 19th and early 20th centuries introduced mass production and assembly lines, powered by electricity. Innovations such as the telegraph, telephone, and internal combustion engine further accelerated industrial growth and global connectivity, resulting in consumer markets.

The third industrial revolution, starting in the mid-20th century, brought automation and the digitalisation of manufacturing processes. The development of computers and the internet revolutionised industries, enabling unprecedented levels of precision and efficiency. This era laid the groundwork for the interconnected world we live in today. We are currently in the midst of the fourth industrial revolution, characterised by the fusion of digital and physical dimensions, creating smart factories and shaping digital societies. As we stand on the brink of the fifth industrial revolution, the focus shifts towards human–machine symbiosis, ethical AI, and sustainable practices. This emerging era emphasises the integration of advanced technologies with human capabilities, fostering collaboration between humans and robots, and prioritising ecological sustainability and social well-being.

In this rapidly evolving landscape, strategic digital transformation is not just an option but a necessity for organisations to remain competitive and relevant. It involves a holistic renewal of business models, processes, and organisational structures, leveraging digital technologies to create new value and drive innovation. This new textbook describes the components and provides a toolkit for strategic digital transformation, which requires a clear vision, a comprehensive digital strategy, a robust implementation plan, and a commitment to continuous learning and adaptation.

Organisations that embrace this transformation will be better positioned to navigate the complexities of the digital age, capitalise on new opportunities, and contribute to a more sustainable and inclusive future. It is an exciting time to be part of this journey and I am confident that the insights and strategies presented in this textbook will provide valuable guidance for young leaders and innovators seeking to thrive in the digital era.

Alois Zwinggi
Managing Director, World Economic Forum
www.weforum.org

Alois Zwinggi, Managing Director, WEF
© World Economic Forum/Pascal Bitz (Flickr, 2023)

ABOUT THE BOOK

BACKGROUND

This digital transformation textbook will provide students with a learning experience that is academically rigorous, integrating insights from the latest research on the strategic digital transformation of organisations, while supporting the practical application of this knowledge with the ACT (*Analyse, Create, Transform*) method and the *Digital Transformation Toolkit*.

The ACT method and toolkit are the results of the multi-year and ongoing digital transformation research agenda of both authors, involving over 12,000 participants in design science research projects between 2016 and 2025. The textbook and its *Digital Transformation Toolkit* will support students and future managers in understanding the practical realisation of digital transformation of organisations to allow the development of competitive advantages for the digital age, while enabling this to be done in a manner that reflects a sustainable approach.

Students (guided and supported by motivated lecturers) arguably have two jobs to be done while at university, namely (1) to acquire the contemporary state-of-the-art knowledge in their chosen domain of specialisation, and (2) to show that they can communicate and apply this knowledge. This textbook addresses these opportunities by actively embedding a validated and practice-oriented method for the realisation of strategic digital transformation.

In 12 chapters, students are provided with contemporary knowledge about and understanding of strategic digital transformation of organisations across seven distinct strategic action fields (SAF) of digital transformation, while developing their capability to address real world business challenges through the application of the digital toolkit.

The textbook's structure supports this integration of academic rigour and practical relevance to enable an approach to teaching strategic digital transformation that is unique and prepares students for using the knowledge and experience they will acquire in their future careers.

We wish to thank all contributors who supported the making of this textbook (see the acknowledgement section). Please visit www.strategic-digital-transformation.com for ancillary resources.

Prof. Marc K. Peter and Dr. Johan P. Lindeque
Australia/Switzerland

USING THIS TEXT IN THE CLASSROOM

Strategic Digital Transformation: Theory and Practice is a suitable textbook for a full semester (and a semester long project), with the text structured into four parts and 12 chapters:

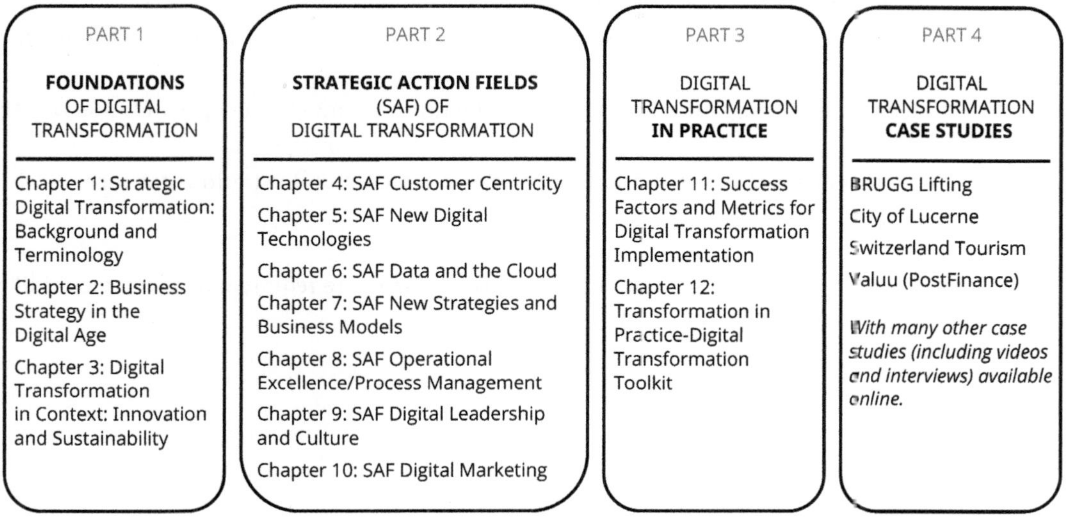

Figure 0.1 Structure of the book

Each chapter is structured as follow:

- Learning goals;
- An opening case (e.g., a pre-read) to introduce the topic in class;
- The main text with an introduction, core chapters, illustrations, tables, and information boxes;
- One or multiple case studies with student questions;
- Exercises (for individual or group-based completion, also linked back to the opening case);
- Further suggested literature; and
- References.

Lecturers have the choice to work on a single-case organisation that will be selected during the first class (for a semester long project), or to work with the recommended cases included in the text and online resources, end of chapter guidance and suggested questions/tasks/support knowledge from different chapters to be applied to cases repeatedly (and thereby incrementally deepen the understanding of the cases and the connections between topics and issues – see the Appendix for the collection of cases studies, with additional cases available online). In Chapter 12, the ACT method and the ten project steps for digital transformation will form the basis for a final project assignment/assessment (which, optionally, can be linked to group presentations on the last day in class).

The *Digital Transformation Toolkit* includes several templates and checklists which allow the transfer from theory into practice. The templates and case studies are available on the book's website: www.strategic-digital-transformation.com

Finally, ancillary online resources are available, including:

- The *Digital Transformation Toolkit* with workshop templates and checklists;
- Videos for each chapter (for instance, to prepare for class or as a summary for students who could not attend class);
- Videos from case organisations (case introductions, promotional clips, and interviews); and
- Slide decks with the most important concepts, tables, and illustrations for each chapter.

Please contact the authors if additional ancillary resources are required, or if you would like to contribute a digital transformation case study.

ABOUT THE AUTHORS

Marc K. Peter is Professor of Digital Business at the HES-SO Valais-Wallis School of Management (Switzerland) and faculty member at the University of Rochester (USA), the University of Bern's Rochester-Bern Executive Programs (Switzerland), and at Charles Sturt University (Australia).

He has over 30 years of professional experience in Swiss SMEs and large enterprises, including eBay, E*TRADE (ANZ), and LexisNexis in Europe and Asia-Pacific. Over the past decade, he supported many organisations in their pursuit of digital transformation, among others, Accenture, Amnesty International, BDO, Canon, Caritas, Lenovo, Logitech, Mayo Clinic, MSD, RUAG, Sharp, Siemens, Swisscom, and T-Systems.

Professor Peter's research interests include digital strategy, digital transformation, digital leadership, digital marketing, and cybersecurity. He studied Electronic Business Engineering at BFH (Switzerland), Corporate Finance at UC Berkeley (USA), obtained his Master of Marketing from the University of Basel (Switzerland), Executive MBA from BFH (Switzerland) / Babson College (USA) / PKU (China), and Doctor of Business Administration from CSU (Australia). He is a Fellow of Advance HE (UK), the British Computer Society (UK) and Chartered Institute of Marketing (UK).

Visit www.digitalprof.com to contact Marc K. Peter.

Johan P. Lindeque is Head of the Science.Lab and Head of the Focus Theme 'International Market Strategies for SMEs' at the FHNW School of Business (Switzerland). He has previously held the position of Assistant Professor of Strategy at the University of Amsterdam Business School (The Netherlands) and as Lecturer in International Business at Queen's University Management School, Belfast (UK).

His research interests focus on firms' strategic responses to transition processes, including digital transformation, the sustainability transition, and global economic integration processes.

Dr Lindeque obtained his Bachelor of Business Administration BSc (Hons) and PhD degrees from the University of Bath School of Management (UK). He is an editorial board member of the *Journal of World Business* and *Journal of International Business Studies*.

Visit www.nullpointventures.com to contact Johan P. Lindeque.

You can contact the authors at authors@strategic-digital-transformation.com for any enquires related to teaching, research projects, and strategy workshops.

ACKNOWLEDGEMENTS

The authors would like to express their gratitude to the research and project teams that have – over many years and in various contexts, directly and indirectly – contributed to and supported the development of the ideas and insights in this textbook, at the FHNW School of Business (Deborah von Büren, Miriam Christ, Martina Dalla Vecchia, Adele Dörner, Knut Hinkelmann, Christine Jacob, Corin Kraft, Nicole Krättli, Emanuele Laurenzi, Marco Looser, Kirsten Maier, André Niedermann, Anna V. Rozumowski, Dino Schwaferts, Danilo Siscaro, Martha Streitenberger, Tsvetana Spasova, Cécile Zachlod), at Charles Sturt University (Alain Neher, Alfred Huah-Syn Wong and Lucia Wuersch), at Gheorghe Asachi Technical University of Iaşi (Amalia Georgescu), at Griffith University (Luke Houghton and Khondker M. Zobair), at Rochester-Bern Executive Programs (Nadine Heuberger and Petra Joerg), at the Simon Business School at the University of Rochester (Jim Brickley, Wayne France, Mitch Lovett, Ravi Mantena), at the University of Amsterdam Business School (Ans Kolk, Francesca Ciulli, Corine Boone), at the University of Basel (Manfred Bruhn, Karsten Hadwich, Isabel Plüss), at the University of Maia (José Luís Reis), at the World Economic Forum (Alois Zwinggi), at Strategylab (Fred Kessler, Valerie Savoy, Angelo Seiler, Mike Tonazzi), at home (our families, children, parents, and friends); to Matthias von Lonski for the book's illustrations, the design team at Polarstern (Chantal Brülhart, Jörg Bruppacher, Susanne Loacker, and Benedikt Roth), our market research partner (Karin Mändli Lerch), the contributors of case studies (Sudip Chaudhuri, Mohamad Syazli Fathi, Michael Gaschen, Marc Heggemann, Thomas Jakob, Marius Keckeisen, Roger Lötscher, Patrick Marti, Eloy Martinez, Helene Müller, Sarah Owens, Ljubica Radoicic, Christoph Salzmann, Raphael Schifferle, Dominic Stöcklin, Urs Truttmann, Christian Zimmerli), the untold number of students across the diverse study programmes and courses we were fortunate to teach, and who contributed to the refinement and evaluation of the ideas in this textbook over the years of the underlying research agenda, and the team at Sage Publishing (Elena Asplen, Amy Douglas, Anthony Green, Charlotte Hanson, Maura Mary Joseph, Hanine Kadi, Nicola Marshall, Amy Mitchell, Martin Noble, Matthew Waters); for their energy and support to publish *Strategic Digital Transformation: Theory and Practice*.

For practitioners, the following practical textbook is recommended: Marc K. Peter (2024): *The Digital Transformation Canvas: Deveop and Implement Your Digital Strategy*. London: FT Publishing/Pearson, www.the-digital-transformation-canvas.com

The publisher and the authors accept no liability for technical implementations of the concepts and examples described in this book.

1

STRATEGIC DIGITAL TRANSFORMATION

BACKGROUND AND TERMINOLOGY

Learning Goals

By the end of this chapter, you should...

- Be able to understand how technological innovation drove (and is still driving) industrial revolutions impacting businesses, organisations, and society.
- Be able to identify and critically evaluate how technological innovation includes both opportunities and challenges.
- Be able to explain the difference between digitisation, digitalisation, and strategic digital transformation.
- Be able to explain why different digital maturity levels are observed across individual (business) organisations and countries for national context.
- Be able to critically assess why strategic digital transformation is relevant to businesses (and other organisations) for business strategy development.

The Astonishing UK Red Flag Act of 1865

The UK Red Flag Act, officially known as the Locomotive Act of 1865 (Great Britain, 1869), was a pivotal piece of legislation in the history of British transportation. This Act was part of a series of laws known as the Locomotive Acts, which aimed to regulate the use of mechanically propelled vehicles on public highways during the late 19th century. The Red Flag Act is particularly notable for its stringent restrictions on the operation of road locomotives, which included early automobiles.

One of the most significant requirements of the Red Flag Act was that any vehicle had to be preceded by a person walking at least 60 yards (55 metres) ahead, carrying a red flag or lantern to warn others of the vehicle's approach. This measure was intended to ensure the safety of pedestrians and horse-drawn carriages, which were the primary users of the roads at the time. The red flag bearer served as an early warning system, alerting people to the presence of a potentially dangerous vehicle.

Figure 1.1 The UK Red Flag Act of 1865

Source: own illustration

In addition to the red flag requirement, the Act set very low speed limits for these vehicles: 4 miles per hour (6.4 km/h) in rural areas and just 2 miles per hour (3.2 km/h) in urban areas. These restrictions were seen as necessary to prevent accidents and damage to the roads, which were not designed to handle the weight and speed of mechanically propelled vehicles. The low-speed limits effectively limited the practicality and efficiency of using road locomotives for transportation.

The Red Flag Act also mandated that vehicles be manned by a crew of three: a driver, a stoker, and the person carrying the red flag. This requirement added to the operational costs and complexity of using road locomotives, further discouraging their widespread adoption. The need for a three-person crew made it more expensive and less convenient to operate these vehicles compared to traditional horse-drawn carriages.

Managing New Technology (Automobiles) in the Nineteenth Century

The UK Red Flag Act of 1865 (Great Britain, 1869, sections 3/4) stipulated the following:

- … while any locomotive is in motion, (one person) shall precede such locomotive on foot by not less than sixty yards, *and shall carry a red flag constantly displayed, and shall warn the riders and drivers of horses of the approach of such locomotives, and shall signal the driver thereof when it shall be necessary to stop, and shall assist horses, and carriages drawn by horses, passing the same.*
- … any person in charge of any such locomotive *shall provide two efficient lights* to be affixed conspicuously, one at each side on the front of the same, between the hours of one hour after sunset and one hour before sunrise.
- … it shall not be lawful to drive any such locomotive along any turnpike road or public highway at a greater speed than four miles an hour, or *through any city, town, or village at a greater speed than two miles an hour*; and any person acting contrary thereto shall for every such offence, on summary conviction thereof, forfeit any sum not exceeding ten pounds.

The Act was influenced by various factors, including the interests of the railway industry and those who relied on horse-drawn transportation. There was significant concern that the new steam-powered vehicles would pose a threat to public safety and disrupt the existing transportation infrastructure. The railway companies were keen to limit the competition posed by road locomotives. By imposing strict regulations on road vehicles, the Act helped to protect the interests of the railways and maintain their dominance in the transportation sector.

Despite its restrictive nature, the Red Flag Act played a crucial role in shaping the early development of the automotive industry in the UK. It highlighted the need for a regulatory framework to manage the introduction of new technologies and their impact on society. However, the Act also stifled innovation and delayed the adoption of automobiles in Britain compared to other countries. The stringent regulations made it difficult for inventors and entrepreneurs to experiment with and improve upon early vehicle designs (Kyprianou, n.d.).

The limitations imposed by the Red Flag Act were eventually recognised as overly restrictive, and the Locomotives on Highways Act of 1896 repealed many of its provisions. The 1896 Act raised the speed limit to 14 miles per hour (22.5 km/h) and removed the requirement for a person to walk in front of the vehicle. This change marked the beginning of a more favourable regulatory environment for the automotive industry, paving the way for the growth and development of motor vehicles in the UK.

The repeal of the Red Flag Act's most restrictive measures allowed for significant advancements in vehicle technology. Inventors and manufacturers were able to experiment with new designs and improve the performance and safety of automobiles. The increased speed limits and reduced operational costs made motor vehicles more practical and appealing for a wider range of uses. As a result, the automotive industry began to flourish, leading to the widespread adoption of motor vehicles and the transformation of transportation in the UK.

1.0 TECHNOLOGY INNOVATION AND INDUSTRIAL REVOLUTIONS

When one looks back over 70,000 years of (modern) human efficiency enhancement, it is Frederick Taylor's 'scientific management' (Grönroos, 1994) and Henry Ford's car production on the assembly line (Wilson, 2014) that have become symbols of industrial revolution. Over two hundred years later, today's digital age with its cyber dimension and cyber-physical systems set new challenges but also presents new opportunities.

The transition to digitalisation and digital transformation was preceded by three industrial revolutions (mechanisation (~1750), mass production (~1870), and automation (~1960)), each of them driven by innovation in technology. Each affected the lives of citizens and consumers in terms of education, occupation, and health and safety. Some of the changes came very quickly and were extremely serious: for example, people lost their jobs due to productivity improvements in factories, and their lives had to be completely reorganised (Arsić, 2020; Kraft et al., 2022).

Since the start of the 2000s, organisations have been part of the fourth industrial revolution, characterised by the 'networking of everything with everything else' and enabled by digital information and communication technologies (ICT). The internet and new information technologies in general are creating a dependency on technology that society has never experienced. Education, employment, and health and safety are confronted by the fourth – this still young industrial revolution – which often results in phenomena to which politicians and businesses still do not have answers. Since the 2020s, ongoing advancements in technology (predominantly artificial intelligence (AI)) and societal transformation have triggered the notion of an emerging fifth industrial revolution that will foster ever greater humans and machines/robots interactions (see Figure 1.2).

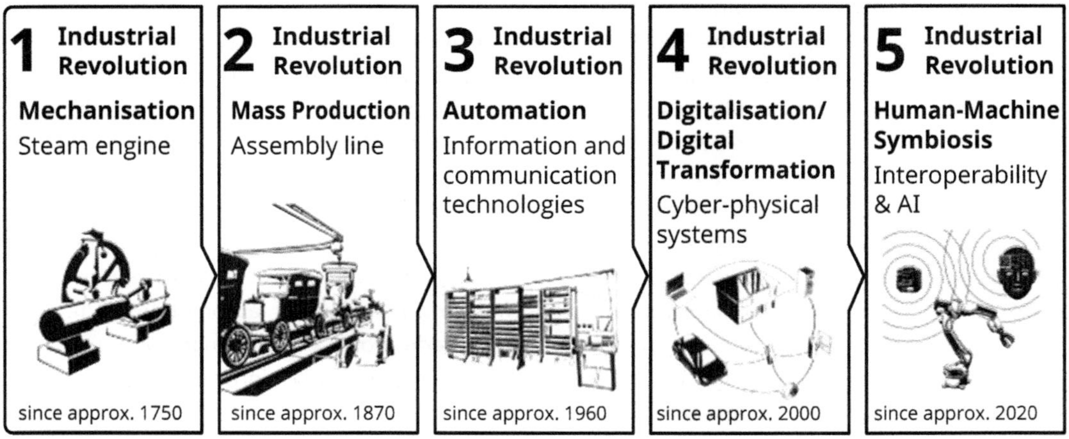

Figure 1.2 Industrial Revolutions

Source: Peter (2017, 2021, 2023, 2024)

1.1 THE FIVE INDUSTRIAL REVOLUTIONS

The concept of industrial revolutions highlights the transformative power of technological advancements over time. Each revolution has brought about significant changes in production processes, societal structures, and economic landscapes. Understanding these revolutions provides a foundation for comprehending the ongoing digital transformation and its impact on modern businesses and industries.

1.1.1 First Industrial Revolution: Mechanisation

Until the 18th century, society was dominated by agriculture. Goods were made by hand with tools and muscle power. With the use of steam power to create products in a factory, it became possible to produce many times the volume within the same timeframe (Atack et al., 2008; Sharma & Singh, 2020). People had known about steam power, but the fact that it could now be used for industrial purposes led to the greatest increase in productivity in the history of humankind. Instead of muscle power, people now used steam engines or waterpower.

Developments such as the steamship, or later the steam-powered locomotive, brought additional big changes. People and goods could now travel long distances much faster. Coal mining was accelerated and intensified in order to obtain the needed energy. The importance of banks increased, as many of the new organisations took out loans for necessary investments. The first corporations and joint-stock organisations emerged. The challenging situation faced by workers, in comparison to factory owners, led to social problems and political upheavals.

1.1.2 Second Industrial Revolution: Mass Production

The second industrial revolution began in the second half of the 19th century as a result of new discoveries and inventions, such as electricity. Electricity made refrigerators, electric motors and light bulbs possible. In Europe, development focused on electrical engineering and the chemical industries, while car production in the USA experienced a boom due to the invention of assembly-line production by Henry Ford. Previously, an entire car was assembled at one station, but now individual stations took care of individual sub-steps, as this was much faster and cheaper. The focus was on efficiency, and assembly lines made mass production possible in the second industrial revolution. The corresponding management principle is called Taylorism (see Box 1.1), in reference to Frederick Taylor's 'scientific management' (Grönroos, 1994; Taylor, 1911).

The second industrial revolution led to a boom in the growth of cities and transport. General prosperity increased and infrastructure, including leisure facilities, expanded significantly. With the expansion of aviation, shipping, and telecommunications, humankind took the first steps towards the globalisation of economic and societal activities.

Box 1.1: Frederick Taylor's 'Scientific Management'

Frederick Taylor's scientific management, developed in the early 20th century, is a management theory that emphasises efficiency and productivity through the systematic study and optimisation of work processes. Taylor believed that work could be analysed scientifically to identify the most efficient ways to perform tasks (Taylor, 1911). His approach involved breaking down tasks into smaller, simpler components and optimising each step to maximise efficiency. Key principles of scientific management include:

- Standardisation: establishing standardised methods for performing tasks to ensure consistency and efficiency.
- Time and motion studies: analysing the time and movements required to complete tasks to identify and eliminate unnecessary actions.
- Specialisation: assigning workers to specific tasks based on their skills and abilities to increase productivity.
- Incentives: implementing performance-based incentives to motivate workers to achieve higher productivity levels.
- Management control: emphasising the role of management in planning, organising, and supervising work to ensure adherence to standardised methods.

While Taylor's 'scientific management' significantly increased efficiency in manufacturing, it has been criticised for how workers were treated as a 'resource' and for neglecting their social and psychological needs. In the digital age, Grönroos (1994) argues that this approach, which emphasises specialisation, division of labour, and cost reduction, is becoming obsolete in the face of increasing service competition and changing customer expectations.

1.1.3 Third Industrial Revolution: Automation

The third industrial revolution began in the 1970s. Programmable logic controllers and computers made partial automation and digitisation possible (Haddon, 1988; Xu et al., 2018). After the development of big calculating machines, the personal computer (see Box 1.2 for impact on consumers) made its way into offices. The first large IT organisations were incorporated and, for the first time, digital data was being collected and stored. Specific areas of work were taken over by computers or robots, making many employees redundant and limiting the professional prospects of people who were less technically skilled.

In later decades, prosperity continued to increase. There was a shift away from sellers' markets to buyers' markets (Ford, 1980), as there was now an oversupply of products. As a result, organisations with technological innovations achieved a competitive advantage over other firms. The computer made automation possible in the third industrial revolution.

Box 1.2: Market Entry of Computers in Consumers' Homes

The journey of personal (home) computers began in the 1970s with the development of microprocessors, which made it possible to create smaller, more affordable computers. Initially, these microcomputers were primarily of interest to hobbyists who enjoyed the fascination of the new technology. Early personal computers were often sold as kits, requiring consumers to assemble and programme them. This hobbyist community laid the groundwork for the home computer market and was famously the origin of Apple Computer Inc.

As the technology evolved, companies began to see the potential for a broader market. The introduction of the Apple II in 1977 marked a significant shift. Apple focused on making computers more user-friendly and accessible, with an emphasis on aesthetics and ease of use. This approach helped to broaden the appeal of computers beyond the hobbyist community.

In the UK, Sinclair's ZX80 and ZX81 were instrumental in popularising home computers; in the USA (and globally), Commodore played a significant role with its VIC-20 and later the Commodore 64. Commodore's strategy was to position their computers as versatile machines that could run a variety of software, including games. This approach helped to establish the home computer as a multi-functional device, suitable for both work and play.

In hindsight, the evolution of the home computer was a complex process influenced by technological advancements, hobbyist enthusiasm, and strategic marketing. The transition from hobbyist machines to consumer electronics involved not just changes in technology but also shifts in how these devices were perceived and used by the public (Haddon, 1988).

1.1.4 Fourth Industrial Revolution: Digitalisation and Digital Transformation

At the time of writing, we are still in the middle of the fourth industrial revolution which emerged in around 2000. It is characterised by its use of the internet in everyday life and industry (aka the Internet of Things) (Sharma & Singh, 2020; Xu et al., 2018). Production plants that were already controlled by computer technology are now extended by a network connection and can communicate independently via the internet with other plants, providing information in real time (referred to as the Industrial Internet of Things (IIoT)).

The networking of all production plants led to cyber-physical (production) systems (Gunes et al., 2014; Marwedel, 2021) and thus to the intelligent factory, in which production systems, components, and people communicate with each other via a network and production almost controls itself (see Box 1.3). The cyber dimension thus takes control of the physical production systems.

Through networking, each system can access the information it needs for optimal operation and, at the same time, can make its own data available. Networking also exists in the goods that are produced. Data from the lifecycle of the product flows back into development and influences current production. Machines share their status with other production systems, which then in turn react. This inherent data generation capacity is a unique feature of all digital technologies, leading to the emergence of the data economy (see Chapter 6). At the same time, managers need to identify and implement new digital tools (apps, platforms) that enable networking and collaboration in the fourth industrial revolution (Kraft et al., 2022).

Digitalisation can be viewed both internally and externally, with the central connection between humans and machines (Hoc, 2000). The inward view shows that all processes within an organisation are affected by the digital age. Externally, digitalisation refers to the link between a company's own products and services and its customers. This interaction generates data that is collected in order to optimise the existing offer and develop new products and services. This then leads to the development of new markets, business models and market participants that are part of the holistic digital transformation. The networking of everything is at the heart of the fourth industrial revolution.

Box 1.3: Cyber-Physical Systems

Cyber-physical systems (CPS) represent a transformative approach to integrating digital technologies with the physical world. These systems are designed to monitor, coordinate, control, and integrate physical processes, across the dimensions of land, water, air, and space, by embedding computing and communication technologies into the physical world (see Figure 1.3). The concept of CPS emerged in the early 2000s and has since gained significant attention globally.

The integration of digital technologies (the cyber dimension) with the physical dimensions allows for real-time interaction and feedback between the physical processes and digital elements. The physical world in CPS refers to the tangible elements and phenomena that the system aims to monitor or control, such as machinery, vehicles, or environmental conditions. The cyber components include embedded systems, sensors, actuators, and communication networks that process information and facilitate interaction with the physical world. The design of CPS involves addressing complex challenges

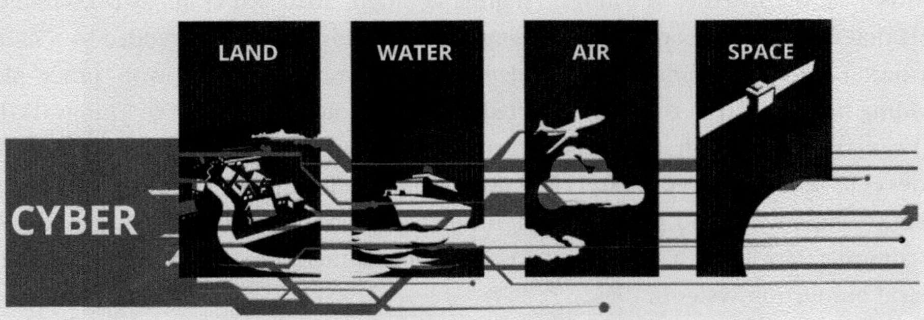

Figure 1.3 Cyber dimension and cyber-physical systems

Source: Peter (2023, 2024)

related to reliability, real-time performance, security, and interoperability. These systems must be able to operate autonomously, adapt to changing conditions, and ensure the safety and efficiency of their operations (Gunes et al., 2014; Marwedel, 2021).

CPS and its cyber dimension, which is at the core of the fourth industrial revolution, represent a significant advancement in engineering, offering the potential to revolutionise how we interact with and control the physical world through sophisticated, interconnected, and digital systems.

1.1.5 Fifth Industrial Revolution: Human–Machine Symbiosis

Since 2020/2023, the notion of a fifth industrial revolution has emerged. It aims to continue to leverage advancements of the fourth industrial revolution, with digital transformation at its core, but with an emphasis on an evolving view towards the Industrial Internet of Things (IIoT), by optimising the human–machine symbiosis (collaborative robots or cobots) (Prassida & Asfari, 2022), fostering interoperability, implementing ethical artificial intelligence models (which, in turn, trigger legal and ethical considerations), and focusing on sustainable actions. Sustainability concepts focus on ecological transformation and include recyclable products, a carbon-neutral industry, and the circular economy. Interoperability refers to the ability to connect various systems and devices so they can work together (Burns et al., 2019). This requires a common definition and understanding of open standards including data formats, interfaces, and communication protocols.

Cloud data storage and computing power (which is an action field of digital transformation from the fourth industrial revolution that was enabled through automation and ICT in the third industrial revolution) and interoperability are enablers of the current advances in AI. In addition to advancements in technology, further debate and new frameworks will emerge regarding new work, including topics such as reduced working hours, state-sponsored unconditional basic income, and well-being. This is sometimes referred to as 'Society 5.0' (Mouazen et al., 2025), which aims to integrate social issues into digital technology advancements topics and the emerging fifth industrial revolution by achieving a balanced economic development with the resolution of societal and environmental challenges.

The human–machine symbiosis is the emerging fifth industrial revolution that is driven by AI and includes notions of robots, ethics, sustainability, and the resulting impact on society and work.

1.2 CHALLENGES AND OPPORTUNITIES OF THE DIGITAL AGE

The digital age, with its dominant cyber dimension from the fourth industrial revolution, triggers many challenges within organisations (Acemoglu & Restrepo, 2019; Gunes et al., 2014; Peter, 2024; Vial, 2021). These include the following.

1.2.1 Dependence on the Internet and Electricity

The internet has become the most important resource of the digital age. Without a strong network connection (and electricity) it doesn't operate and reverts to the status it occupied before the fourth revolution. Therefore, networks must be completely and broadly protected, not only against destruction by natural forces, accidents, and human error, but also against cyberattacks, sabotage, and misuse. As the most important resource, an internet connection in an organisation must be constantly monitored to ensure a quick reaction to critical events. This requires a great deal of knowledge, capital, and resources. Those who cannot provide these resources and skills put their business at risk.

1.2.2 Complexity and Digital Skills

With data availability growing exponentially, and with it the self-optimisation of machines, machine complexity is ever increasing. Some fear that humans will one day no longer control machines but instead will be controlled by machines. Even worse, humans might not even notice, because artificial intelligence (AI) might become superior, and humans will not understand the machines' motives. Then there is the danger of a totalitarian surveillance state consisting of largely autonomous (cyber-physical) computer systems. Nonetheless, society and every individual must keep up. Lifelong learning is booming in the fourth and fifth industrial revolutions.

1.2.3 Influence on Society

With digitalisation, human workers are increasingly replaced by AI and robots. This might be a relief, especially for physically strenuous or monotonous work. Modern software solutions and smart devices also assist in intellectual work, for example with IT-based assistance systems. These are adaptable to individual abilities and needs and can, for example, enable older people to stay in the workforce longer or introduce inexperienced employees to demanding production processes.

The structural change associated with the fourth and fifth technological revolutions however also offers opportunities in terms of demographic development. Educational measures must be taken and offers must be made in response to the change in order to guarantee equal opportunities. Otherwise, as with the third industrial revolution, featured by ICT and automation, society runs the risk of excluding people and widening the digital gap. Society will polarise if these measures are not supported by politics, the state, society, and the economy. With increasing digitalisation, those who prefer an analogue life, or are unable to acquire digital skills, will be left behind. Other opportunities which balance these challenges include customer-driven new business or revenue models, increased effectiveness and efficiency, and internationalisation (see Table 1.1).

Table 1.1 Opportunities and Challenges of Digital Transformation

Opportunities of Digital Transformation	
Customer-driven new business or revenue models	The digitalisation of everything and the market-driven need for new (partly mobile and always available) applications, as well as the resulting opportunities for new business opportunities, are creating innovative business models. These include, for example: • Subscription models: monthly fee instead of individual transactions • Peer-to-peer models: customers sell directly without the involvement of intermediaries • Freemium models: the basic version is made available to a wide audience free of charge
Increased effectiveness and efficiency	One advantage of digital transformation is increased effectiveness and efficiency through digitisation. It also creates opportunities for individuals and small businesses that were previously reserved exclusively for large organisations, for example, the broad and automated communication and distribution of information.
Internationalisation	Digital transformation also plays an essential role in the internationalisation of organisations. As communication and logistics are simplified, it is easier for an organisation to expand internationally following digital transformation.
Challenges of Digital Transformation	
New leadership values and corporate culture	The use of new technologies changes corporate and work processes and, in turn, leadership behaviour and organisational values. The transformation has a direct influence on the culture and – if not planned and considered – can be a risk to the organisation's principles and values.
Cybersecurity	Increased digitalisation requires investments in the IT infrastructure. Everything is networked with everything else. With cloud-based systems, data is theoretically accessible to everyone, at all times and from everywhere. This increases the complexity and the risks of losing data or being attacked. Cybersecurity becomes increasingly important.
Changes in job profiles and redundancies	Jobs that coordinate or execute individual work or production processes are partly replaced by machines or software. At the same time, tasks and requirement profiles resulting from digital transformation require new (digital) skills. This change is demanding and may lead to job losses.

Source: Peter (2021, 2023, 2024)

It can be problematic for organisations if they do not adapt quickly to the new requirements and opportunities and, as a result, miss out on growth opportunities or fail to make consistent use of them. In addition to technical qualifications, the fourth and fifth industrial revolution requires, for example, the motivation to take responsibility for networked, cyber-physical production processes. Employees must be prepared for the change, in order for firms to adapt effectively. At the same time, countless new opportunities are emerging – especially for small businesses and start-ups – which will help them succeed in the market (see Box 1.4).

Box 1.4: Flexible Working Arrangements and Working from Home

The Covid-19 pandemic has significantly transformed the way businesses operate, particularly highlighting the importance of home offices and working from home (WFH). This shift has underscored the critical role of digital transformation in enabling remote work and maintaining business continuity during unprecedented times. WFH arrangements have demonstrated that many tasks can be effectively performed remotely, challenging traditional notions of productivity and workplace presence. The flexibility to work from home has allowed employees to balance their professional and personal lives better, leading to increased job satisfaction and overall well-being.

For businesses, providing flexible working arrangements is not just a response to a crisis but a strategic move that can yield long-term benefits. Flexibility in work arrangements can enhance employee morale and retention. When employees have the autonomy to choose their work environment, they are likely to be more motivated and committed to their roles. This flexibility also opens up opportunities to tap into a broader talent pool, as geographical constraints become less relevant. Moreover, businesses that embrace flexible working arrangements can achieve significant cost savings. Reduced need for physical office space, lower utility costs, and decreased expenditure on commuting allowances are some of the financial benefits. Additionally, the environmental impact is reduced as fewer employees commuting means lower carbon emissions.

The digital transformation of work, accelerated by the pandemic, has shown that technology adoption is crucial for enabling WFH. Companies that were early adopters of digital technologies found it easier to transition to remote work, maintaining productivity and operational efficiency. These 'technology pioneers' have set an example for others, demonstrating that investment in digital infrastructure is not just beneficial but necessary for resilience in the face of disruptions (Peter et al., 2024a, 2024b; Neher et al., 2025).

See Chapter 9 for a more detailed description of digital leadership and culture strategies/concepts.

Strategic digital transformation can be particularly worthwhile for smaller businesses (small and medium-sized enterprises), as they can benefit from new technologies. SMEs can implement digital solutions (in most cases) much quicker than large organisations. SMEs also do not generate quite as much data as large organisations, which makes data quicker and easier to handle. However, the transition into the fourth/fifth industrial revolution and the technologies of the digital age are also associated with major investments in infrastructure and further employee training, which may be more challenging for smaller firms. Of course, sufficient attention must also be paid to data and IT security in order to avoid failures.

1.3 DIGITISATION, DIGITALISATION, AND STRATEGIC DIGITAL TRANSFORMATION

Since the early 2000s digital transformation has been the central theme for business strategy development and implementation. For years now, it has been a buzzword not only used by consulting firms, but also in board meetings and management teams. With the internet and the establishment of the cyber dimension, customers can more efficiently compare and purchase products and services. New business models emerged (see Box 1.5) in the form of new organisations, such as Alibaba, Baidu, Tencent, and Xiaomi in China; and Amazon, Apple, Google, and Meta in the USA.

Box 1.5: Robot Vacuum Cleaners

A Digital Example of the New Challenges for Organisations

The first robot vacuum cleaners were developed at the beginning of the 21st century. Think about how different traditional vacuum cleaners are from vacuum cleaner robots. Some examples:

- Robot vacuum cleaners have a variety of sensors to detect objects and measure spaces.
- The data obtained is transferred via the internet to a cloud, which, in many cases, is operated by the foreign manufacturer.
- The data is evaluated using algorithms/AI and allows efficiency improvements to the product but also helps to create customer profiles.
- The findings, based on customer profiles in turn, help market further products and services by word of mouth and via digital channels.
- The most important digital channel is the app on the smartphone, which is used to control the robot.
- With the app, further (personal) data is collected from the users, transmitted, evaluated, and used.
- With the new technologies in the robot vacuum cleaners comes the risk of digital dependency on the internet, data loss, and cyberattacks, which all need to be addressed proactively.
- The development of a robot, technical infrastructures, and the associated app requires a lot of specialised knowledge developed during the fourth/fifth industrial revolutions.
- Accordingly, talented employees are needed, whom the organisation can attract with competitive working conditions and a modern working environment.

You can see from this simple example how diverse and complex the digital age has become, and thus the challenges for leaders of the strategic digital transformation of a business. One way to meet these challenges is to develop strategic partnerships with firms who can

(Continued)

provide technical expertise. Behind the development and marketing of a robot vacuum cleaner lies much that is made possible through digital transformation.

Source: Peter (2024)

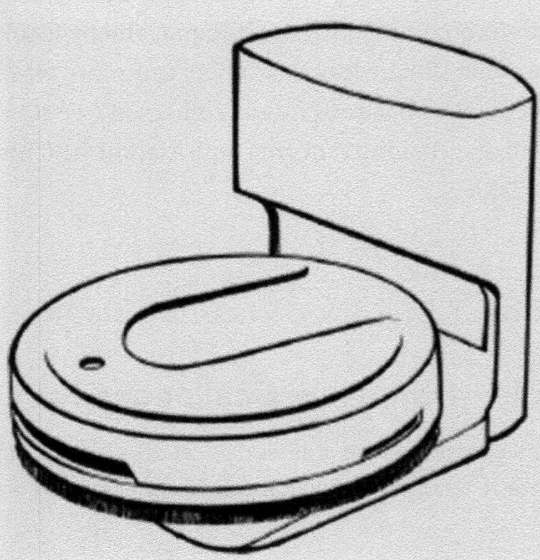

Figure 1.4 The robot vacuum cleaner demonstrates the many facets of digital transformation

Source: Peter (2023, 2024)

However, there is a difference between activities to bring the analogue into the digital, for example, to implement the paperless office (digitisation), to improve and automate processes with new technology (digitalisation), and the holistic and sustainable renewal of an organisation (strategic digital transformation). Often used as synonyms in everyday life (see also Figure 1.5), the three terms describe two fundamentally different concepts (Gradillas & Thomas (2025), Peter (2024); Peter et al. (2020)):

- **Digitisation** refers to the technical process of converting analogue or physical information into a digital form. This involves creating digital artifacts through processes such as conversion, representation, and enhancement. For example, scanning a paper document to create a digital image, or embedding sensors in physical objects to collect data, are forms of digitisation. It focuses on the transformation of information and objects into a digital format that can be easily stored, transferred, and manipulated.
- **Digitalisation** is the broader process of transforming the socioeconomic environment through the adoption, application, and utilisation of digital artifacts. This encompasses how digital technologies are integrated into organisational

processes and everyday life, leading to significant changes in industries and society. Digitalisation involves leveraging digital technologies to create new business opportunities, improve efficiency, and drive innovation, ultimately resulting in a new socioeconomic reality.

- **Strategic digital transformation** is a comprehensive process that aims to renew an organisation in the long term (strategically) through the integration of digital technologies. It is a holistic approach that impacts all areas and functions of the organisation, including business models, processes, and organisational structures. This leads to the development of new value creation paths and the transformation of business operations to remain competitive in the digital age (see Table 1.2 for various definitions). It encompasses both internal and external dimensions, affecting how businesses interact with customers, manage processes, and leverage data. The process requires overcoming organisational and cultural barriers and implementing structural changes to achieve positive outcomes.

Table 1.2 Digital Transformation Definitions

Definition	Source
'Our working definition of digital business strategy is simply that of organizational strategy formulated and executed by leveraging digital resources to create differential value.'	Bharadwaj et al. (2013), p. 472
'Whatever the end state of digital transformation turns out to be, reaching it is not simply about technology. (...) Digital maturity is the product of strategy, culture and leadership.'	Kane et al. (2015), p. 15
'A managerial perspective of digital transformation (...) is thus two-sided, including the adoption of digital technologies in managerial work and the use of digital technologies that operational employees utilize in their work, associated with the changing nature of the work to be completed.'	Kraft et al. (2022), p. 474
'... digital transformation (...) is driven by work that takes an internal perspective, i.e., a resource-based view, as well as an external perspective, i.e., one of structural change, and a change in the way value is/can be created as a result.	Kraus et al. (2022), p. 11
'... digital transformation (can be described) as a process where digital technologies create disruptions triggering strategic responses from organizations that seek to alter their value creation paths while managing the structural changes and organizational barriers that affect the positive and negative outcomes of this process.'	Vial (2021), p. 118
'... digital transformation is an ongoing process of using new digital technologies in everyday organizational life, which recognizes agility as the core mechanism for the strategic renewal of an organization's (1) business model, (2) collaborative approach, and eventually the (3) culture.'	Warner & Wäger (2019), p. 326

Source: Bharadwaj et al. (2013); Kane et al. (2015); Kraft et al. (2022); Kraus et al. (2022); Vial (2021); Warner & Wäger (2019)

However, in business practice, the two terms of digitisation and digitalisation are often used as interchangeable terms; and even digitalisation (as a verb) and digital transformation (as a noun) are used to describe the same or similar set of activities.

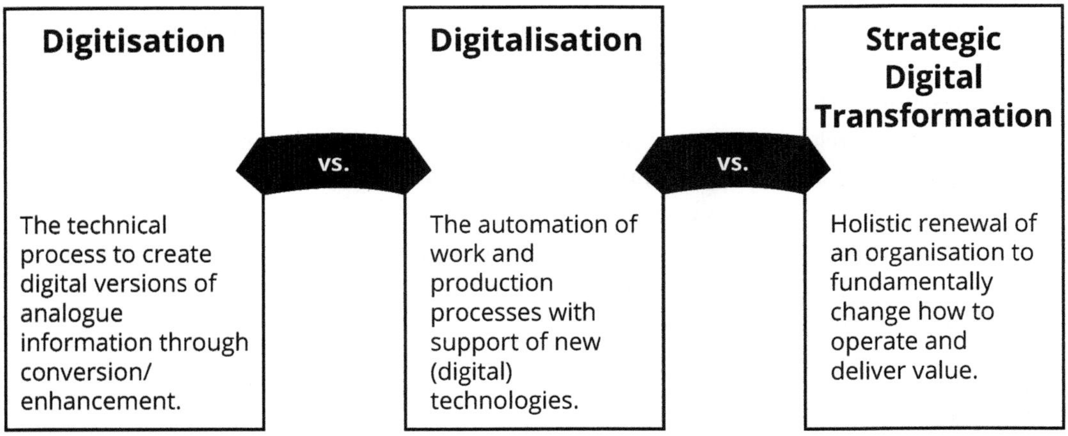

Figure 1.5 Digitisation, digitalisation, and strategic digital transformation

Source: Gradillas & Thomas (2025); Peter (2017, 2021, 2023, 2024)

Based on various factors such as competition, customer requirements, technology availability/fit, current digital maturity, and general organisational or financial urgency for transformation, organisations thus can evaluate themselves or initiate a discussion about the need for change and whether digitisation, digitalisation, or strategic digital transformation is required. There three generic phases or digital maturity levels deriving from above concepts are (see Figure 1.6):

- **Digital enablement (digitisation)**: In the first phase, processes are optimised and digitised. Examples of this are the paperless office or the use of online platforms for meetings.
- **Digital optimisation (digitalisation)**: In the second phase, technologies are assessed to determine their potential and actively used. A strategy based on digital technologies emerges. Examples are the automation of important business processes or internationalisation of an organisation via global e-commerce platforms.
- **Strategic digital transformation**: In the third phase and with the highest aspired digital maturity level, a holistic renewal of the organisation takes place by planning and implementing promising technologies and business models in existing and new markets. An example of this is an existing small and medium-sized enterprize (SME) in a traditional market that wants to enter a new, developing market with new strategic partnerships in an ecosystem.

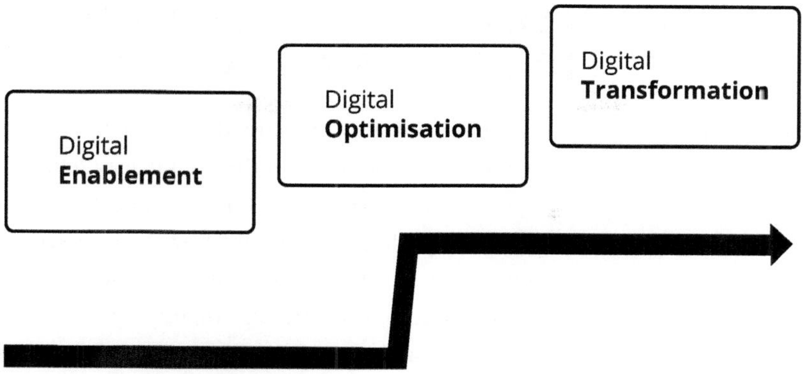

Figure 1.6 Digital maturity levels and choice of strategic investments from digital enablement (digitisation) and optimisation (digitalisation) to strategic digital transformation

Source: Peter (2023, 2024)

Even in the first phase of digitisation and second phase of digitalisation, there are numerous questions to answer about the appropriate technologies, the necessary skills of the employees, the investments, the cultural change, and the risks that are being taken. The third phase, digital transformation, brings with it many other issues. This is because new strategic partnerships and ecosystems are developed, and new business models are implemented, which increase investments and risks.

In summary, digitisation/digital enablement is about creating digital versions of analogue information; digitalisation/digital optimisation is about using these digital artifacts to improve/transform tasks and processes; and strategic digital transformation is a holistic renewal of an organisation to fundamentally change how businesses operate and deliver value, ensuring they can thrive in an increasingly digital world (see Box 1.6).

Box 1.6: Strategy – Not Technology – Drives Digital Transformation and Maturity

In a study from 2015 (the year in which the term digital transformation became popular) with 4,800 study participants, published in the American *MIT Sloan Management Review* (Kane et al., 2015), found that only 15% of organisations with low digital maturity had a digital strategy. However, 80% of digitally mature organisations had a digital strategy. The existence of a digital strategy is therefore related to the progress of digital transformation. It has also been shown that organisations with low digital maturity tend to focus on individual technologies (i.e., pushing operational digitalisation) instead of taking a broad view of technology, with a focus on holistic digital transformation. Moreover, digitally mature organisations are not only much more customer-focused, efficient, and innovative than the less digitally advanced organisations, but they also find it easier to attract motivated employees. According to the study, these employees primarily want to work for digitally progressive organisations.

1.4 THE CASE FOR STRATEGIC DIGITAL TRANSFORMATION

Studies among businesses in Switzerland but also globally show that there is need for a higher degree of strategy planning and implementation in the digital age (Peter, 2017, 2021; Peter et al., 2020), as businesses (especially SMEs) often don't have an analysis of their market and new technology, or a digital roadmap/plan that defines how to leverage new digital technology in order to compete. Only half of the surveyed SMEs conduct at least a once-a-year market analysis or have a digital strategy, even though digital competition is strong. One thing is certain: there are many good reasons to take a more active approach in strategic digital transformation (see Figure 1.7).

1.4.1 Market Analyses as a Basis for Strategic Digital Transformation

Only half of SMEs conduct a market analysis (including customer and competitor analysis) at least once a year. Almost a quarter conduct them less frequently and almost a quarter do not conduct any market analyses at all. That is too little. Small businesses are missing out on the opportunity to identify trends and opportunities.

1.4.2 Threat from Competitors' Digital Strategies

SME competitors pursuing digital strategies pose a threat to one-third of respondents. Their main fears are cheaper prices and better internal processes. SME business leaders also mention that the competition has better products/services, as well as better customer relationships, due to their digitalisation and automation of processes. However, comparing large organisations and SMEs, and whether they perceive their competitors as a threat, indicates that large organisations are more likely to perceive a competitive threat and actively react to it with a digital strategy. SMEs must therefore close the planning gaps between them and large organisations by developing strategic transformation roadmaps.

1.4.3 Change in Market Positioning

The SME market is in a state of upheaval. Slightly more than two-fifths of the respondents have changed their market positioning. This means that they have tried to stand out from the competition with new products, product features, services, or marketing campaigns. Again, this means that a strategy or at least a plan is desperately needed. Only with an analysis, a strategy discussion, and a plan should organisations move to change their market positioning, because these often require large investments and are associated with risks.

1.4.4 Availability and Need for a Digital Roadmap or Digital Strategy

Half of the SMEs surveyed do not have a digital strategy/roadmap. For the other half that have developed a digital roadmap/strategy, it is part of the business strategy for about one-third, part of the IT strategy for 12% and exists as a separate strategy for 7%. Again, the larger the company, the more likely it is to have a digital strategy. Large organisations state far more frequently that they have a digital strategy (75%) than SMEs (50%).

The progress of digitalisation efforts in SMEs is estimated to be at 56% (Peter, 2017). The CEOs see themselves just over halfway along their path of digital transformation – the larger the SME, the higher the estimated progress. In addition, SMEs report a slightly higher degree of progress in their company's transformation compared to large organisations, and the degree of satisfaction with digital transformation is significantly higher among SMEs (81% are satisfied or very satisfied) than among large organisations (50%).

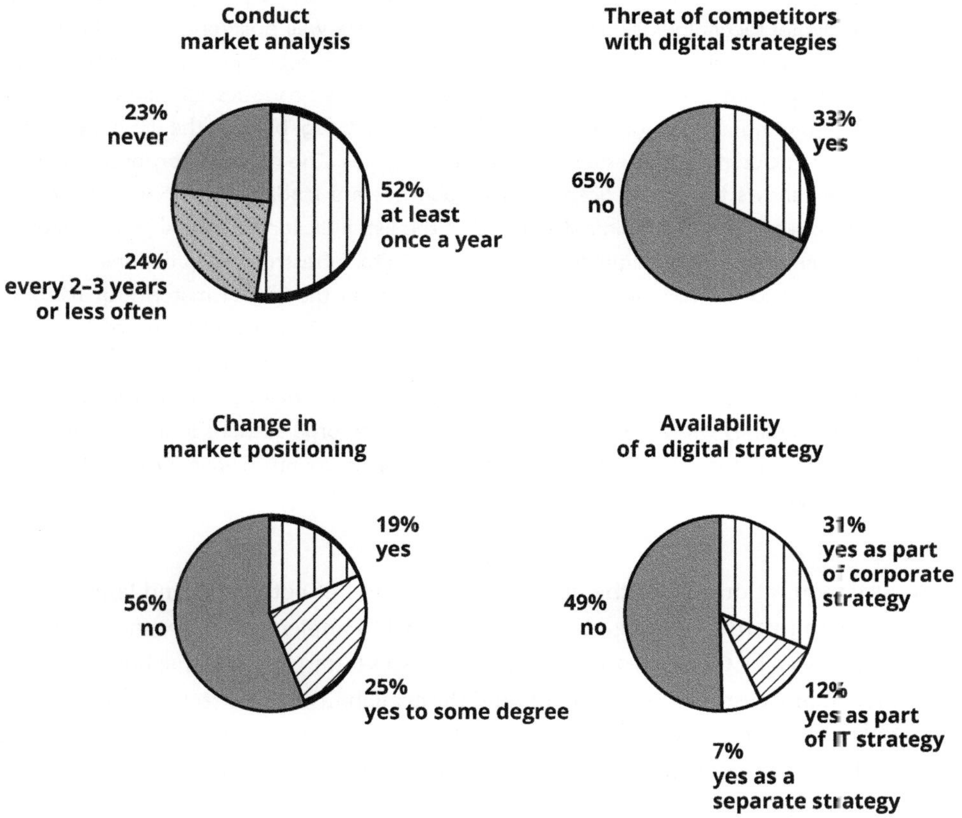

Figure 1.7 Progress of strategy work in Swiss SMEs

Source: Peter (2021, 2023, 2024)

Box 1.7: An International Comparison of Digital Transformation Maturity

IMD's world digital competitiveness ranking (2023) is based on three factors of knowledge (e.g., digital/technological skills, number of science graduates, R&D per capita), technology (e.g., scientific research legislation, IP rights, IT/media stock capitalisation, venture capital, internet users), and future readiness (e.g., internet retailing, use of big data and analytics, e-government, cybersecurity). The USA (100%), the Netherlands (98.1%), Singapore (97.4%), Denmark (96.9%), and Switzerland (96.2%) are leading the list. Japan (75.4%) and Thailand (70.5%) are in the middle; India (57.7%), Mexico (51.3%) and Brazil (49.7%), among others, are in the lower third of the ranking of reviewed nations.

Dell Technologies' Digital Transformation Index (2020) is based on a survey of 4300 executives of mid-sized to large enterprises with the aim to provide a global benchmark. India (64/100) is leading the global digital maturity benchmark (same as in 2016 and 2018), followed by Mexico (61), Brazil (60), European countries (52 to 60 each), the USA (58), China (58), Singapore (55), as well as Australia, Canada, New Zealand, and the UK (54 each), with Japan in 17th place (38).

In a recent European Union (EU) publication of the European Investment Bank (2023), it is argued that EU firms are rapidly catching up with their US peers in implementing advanced digital technologies, but European firms are not well positioned in digital innovation. In terms of digital technologies, it is assumed that European firms (compared to a US study) adopt some technologies fast, including advanced robotics, digital/online platforms, 3D printing, and augmented/virtual reality, but lag behind the USA in some technologies, including the Internet of Things and drones. The reports' corporate digitalisation index shows that many Scandinavian countries are leading the index, with many Eastern European countries being at the end of the list, indicating a digital divide among European countries and highlighting the need for digital infrastructure in nations.

The global and EU comparisons show a difference in the digital maturity of nations (IMD and EU reports) versus the executives' views of organisations (Dell report) in these countries but show that important factors to determine digital maturity are technology, data, legislation, cybersecurity, the customer experience, as well as digital skills and culture. In addition, they show that developed countries (and organisations in these countries) seem to have a higher digital maturity than developing countries (and organisations in these countries).

The most important drivers for the digital transformation of both SMEs and large organisations lie in both internal considerations (e.g., the need to implement more efficient business processes, followed by the desire to make these processes faster) and external business considerations (changing customer requirements and the availability of new technologies) (Omrani et al., 2022; Peter, 2017, 2014). Those internal and external factors cover organisational, operational, technological, and market/contextual drivers that force organisations to strategically transform (see Box 1.7) as per Tangwaragorn et al. (2024):

- **Organisational** drivers such as culture, human capital, governance, and research and development (R&D) and the need for an organisational, digital strategy.

- **Operational and management** drivers such as improvements in processes and operations, new products and services, and digital business opportunities.
- **Technological** drivers such as new digital technology, cybersecurity measures, data analytics, and strategic data management.
- **Environmental and contextual** drivers such as government/legal frameworks, collaboration and value creation in the ecosystem, digital, literary, and market factors such as economic indicators, labour market dynamics, and digital competition.

These drivers collectively form a comprehensive framework for understanding and implementing strategic digital transformation, emphasising the importance of culture human capital, governance, R&D, strategy, processes, new digital technology, data, legal frameworks, the ecosystem, and market factors.

A comprehensive/holistic and sustainable digital transformation will lead to a long-term strategic renewal of an organisation, which takes advantage of digital technology and new leadership approaches, while developing new products and services, while implementing new business models that opens a variety of growth opportunities.

1.5 CONCLUSION

This chapter provides an overview of digital transformation, emphasising its significance in the context of technological innovation and industrial revolutions. The UK Red Flag Act of 1865 illustrates the challenges and regulatory responses to new technologies in the second industrial revolution. The Act imposed stringent restrictions on early automobiles, highlighting the need for a regulatory framework to manage technological advancements, but also to strategically respond to new technology and regulation as a commercial organisation (in this case, the manufacturers of automobiles).

Each industrial revolution is characterised by significant technological advancements that transformed production processes, societal structures, and economic landscapes. The fourth industrial revolution, marked by digitalisation and the Internet of Things, drove the integration of cyber-physical systems and created our dependence on the internet. The emerging fifth industrial revolution focuses on human–machine symbiosis, the widespread use of AI for many uses cases, and sustainability. It highlights the importance of interoperability and data management for contemporary digital transformation strategies.

For strategy development, organisations should understand the differences between digitisation (digital enablement), digitalisation (digital optimisation), and strategic digital transformation, and assessing the need, urgency, and relevance of these digital maturity levels in the context of current future competition.

Case Studies

You will find a collection of case studies for *Strategic Digital Transformation* in the Appendix and additional cases online at www.strategic-digital-transformation.com

For this chapter, we recommend the following case work in addition to the exercises (see below):

Step 1: Selection of a case organisation

1 Read the Swiss retail bank case '*Valuu: a corporate start-up for digital business model innovation*' (sections 'Background' and 'The launch'), or
2 Select any other major retail bank in your country, or
3 Identify any other organisation in your country which is well documented (e.g., has a website and social media presence), and which can form the basis for future course work in Chapters 2 to 12 based on the *Digital Transformation Toolkit* present in Chapter 12.

For options 2 and 3 (if you chose to select another case organisation than *Valuu*), you should document the following:

- Name of the organisation including information about their website and social media profiles.
- Organisational facts and figures (e.g., financial metrics; number of employees, products, and services; geographical reach; as well as its office, production, and distribution locations).
- Industry information with challenges and opportunities.

Step 2: Case questions linked to this chapter

1 Describe how each industrial revolution has transformed the business and identify the technology that was the trigger point which led to the need for a new strategy, new skills and new resources (see Chapter 1.0 and Figure 1.2).
2 Select a new digital technology (e.g., the cloud, sensors as part of the Internet of Things, or AI) and describe the opportunities and challenges of this technology for the business (see also Box 1.4).
3 Describe how the organisation could utilise technology for (1) digitisation, (2) digitalisation, and (3) strategic digital transformation (see Chapter 1.3 and Figure 1.5).
4 Describe why this organisation would require a holistic, strategic digital transformation, and define the internal and external areas/functions (e.g., processes, marketing, new products and services) in which the organisation should pursue digital transformation.

Exercises

Discuss the following questions in your class, in your group, or assignment:

1 Based on the opening case (UK Red Flag Act of 1865), describe how society today might react to further advancements in AI (artificial intelligence) with new laws, impacting business strategy and operations.

2 Identify an established industry/sector that you think has been transformed by technologies and explain how each industrial revolution has transformed the business and identify the technology that was the trigger point which led to the need for a new business strategy.
3 Identify an established large company and describe how they did (or could) utilise technology for (1) digitisation, (2) digitalisation, and (3) strategic digital transformation.
4 Forming two small groups (2–4 students in each group), assign a pro and contra position to each group and debate the degree to which strategic digital transformation is required, or if digitalisation would be sufficient to compete in the digital age.
5 Select 2–3 countries and use the United Nations' (2025) Digital Development Compass on https://digitaldevelopmentcompass.undp.org to review the nations' digital readiness. Discuss the reasons and drivers for their digital maturity level.

Further Reading List

- Gradillas, M., & Thomas, L. D. (2025). Distinguishing digitization and digitalization: A systematic review and conceptual framework. *Journal of Product Innovation Management*, 42(1), 112–43.
- Peter, M. K., Kraft, C., & Lindeque, J. (2020). Strategic action fields of digital transformation: An exploration of the strategic action fields of Swiss SMEs and large enterprises. *Journal of Strategy and Management*, 13(1), 160–80.
- Tangwaragorn, P., Charoenruk, N., Viriyasitavat, W., Tangmanee, C., Kanawattanachai, P., Hoonsopon, D., Pungpapong, V., Pattanapanyasat, R.-P., Boonpatcharanon, S., & Rhuwadhana, P. (2024). Analyzing key drivers of digital transformation: A review and framework. *Journal of Industrial Information Integration*, 42, 100680.
- Vial, G. (2021). Understanding digital transformation: A review and a research agenda. Managing digital transformation, *Journal of Strategic Information Systems*, 13–66.

References

Acemoglu, D., & Restrepo, P. (2019). Automation and new tasks: How technology displaces and reinstates labor. *Journal of Economic Perspectives, 33*(2), www.aeaweb.org/articles?id=10.1257/jep.33.2.3.

Arsić, M. (2020). Impact of digitalisation on economic growth, productivity and employment. *Economic Themes, 58*(4), 431–57.

Atack, J., Bateman, F., & Margo, R. A. (2008). Steam power, establishment size, and labor productivity growth in nineteenth century American manufacturing. *Explorations in Economic History, 45*(2), 185–98.

Bharadwaj, A., El Sawy, O. A., Pavlou, P. A., & Venkatraman, N. V. (2013). Digital business strategy: Toward a next generation of insights. *MIS Quarterly*, 471–82.

Burns, T., Cosgrove, J., & Doyle, F. (2019). A review of interoperability standards for Industry 4.0. *Procedia Manufacturing, 38*, 646–53.

Dell Technologies (2020). *Digital Transformation Index 2020: Vanson Bourne Research Findings & Methodology*. Dell Technologies, www.delltechnologies.com/asset/no-no/solutions/business-solutions/briefs-summaries/dt-index-2020-executive-summary.pdf.

European Investment Bank (2023). Digitalisation in Europe 2022–2023: Evidence from the EIB Investment Survey. *European Investment Bank*, www.eib.org/economics.

Ford, D. (1980). The development of buyer–seller relationships in industrial markets. *European Journal of Marketing, 14*(5/6), 339–53.

Gradillas, M., & Thomas, L. D. (2025). Distinguishing digitization and digitalization: A systematic review and conceptual framework. *Journal of Product Innovation Management*, *42*(1), 112–43.

Great Britain (1869). *The Statutes of the United Kingdom of Great Britain and Ireland [1807-1868/69]*. His Majesty's Statute and Law Printers, p. 183, https://archive.org/details/statutesunitedk30britgoog/page/182/mode/2up (accessed 2 March 2025).

Grönroos, C. (1994). From scientific management to service management: A management perspective for the age of service competition. *International Journal of Service Industry Management*, *5*(1), 5–20.

Gunes, V., Peter, S., Givargis, T., & Vahid, F. (2014). A survey on concepts, applications, and challenges in cyber-physical systems. *KSII Transactions on Internet and Information Systems (TIIS)*, *8*(12), 4242–68.

Haddon, L. (1988). The home computer: the making of a consumer electronic. *Science as Culture*, *1*(2), 7–51.

Hoc, J. M. (2000). From human–machine interaction to human–machine cooperation. *Ergonomics*, *43*(7), 833–43.

IMD (2023). *IMD World Digital Competitiveness Ranking 2023*. IMD, www.imd.org/centers/world-competitiveness-center/rankings/world-digital-competitiveness.

Kane, G. C., Palmer, D., Phillips, A. N, Kiron, D. and Buckley, N. (2015). *Strategy, Not Technology, Drives Digital Transformation: Becoming a Digitally Mature Enterprise*. MIT Sloan Management Review and Deloitte University Press.

Kraft, C., Lindeque, J. P., & Peter, M. K. (2022). The digital transformation of Swiss small and medium-sized enterprises: Insights from digital tool adoption. *Journal of Strategy and Management*, *15*(3), 468–94.

Kraus, S., Durst, S., Ferreira, J. J., Veiga, P., Kailer, N., & Weinmann, A. (2022). Digital transformation in business and management research: An overview of the current status quo. *International Journal of Information Management*, *63*, 102466.

Kyprianou, Emilio (n.d.). *The Red Flag Act*. The Open University Law School, https://law-school.open.ac.uk/blog/red-flag-act (accessed 2 March 2025).

Marwedel, P. (2021). *Embedded System Design: Embedded Systems Foundations of Cyber-Physical Systems, and the Internet of Things*. Springer Nature.

Mouazen, A. M., Hernández-Lara, A. B., Chahine, J., & Halawi, A. (2025). Triple bottom line sustainability and Innovation 5.0 management through the lens of Industry 5.0, Society 5.0 and Digitized Value Chain 5.0. *European Journal of Innovation Management*.

Neher, A., Wuersch, L., Wong, A., & Peter, M. K. (2025). The association between technology group, working from home behaviour and preferred communication tools in disruptive times: A micro and small enterprise perspective. *European Research on Management and Business Economics*, *31*(2), 100280.

Omrani, N., Rejeb, N., Maalaoui, A., Dabić, M., & Kraus, S. (2022). Drivers of digital transformation in SMEs. *IEEE Transactions on Engineering Management, 71,* 5030–43.

Peter, M. K. (Hrsg.) (2017). *KMU-Transformation: Als KMU die Digitale Transformation erfolgreich umsetzen. Forschungsresultate und Praxisleitfaden.* FHNW Hochschule für Wirtschaft, Olten/Schweiz, www.kmu-transformation.ch.

Peter, M. K. (Hrsg.) (2021). *Strategieentwicklung im digitalen Zeitalter: Planung und Umsetzung der Digitalen Transformation.* FHNW Hochschule für Wirtschaft und Strategylab, Olten/Schweiz, www.strategische-transformation.ch.

Peter, M. K. (2023). *Digitaler Masterplan für KMU. So gelingt die digitale Transformation in Ihrem Unternehmen.* Verlag Beobachter Edition & Handelszeitung. Zürich/Schweiz, www.digitaler-masterplan.ch.

Peter, M. K. (2024). *The Digital Transformation Canvas. Develop and Implement Your Digital Strategy.* FT Publishing/Pearson, London/UK, www.the-digital-transformation-canvas.com.

Peter, M. K., Kraft, C., & Lindeque, J. (2020). Strategic action fields of digital transformation: An exploration of the strategic action fields of Swiss SMEs and large enterprises. *Journal of Strategy and Management, 13*(1), 160 – 80.

Peter, M. K., Wuersch, L., Neher, A., Lindeque, J. P., & Mändli Lerch, K. (2024a). The workplace of the future: the COVID - 19 pandemic and working from home in Swiss small businesses. *Journal of Strategy and Management, 17*(4), 707–29.

Peter, M. K., Wuersch, L., Wong, A., & Neher, A. (2024b). Digital transformation of work: Swiss MSEs working from home behaviour during COVID–19–pioneers leading the pack. *European Business Review, 36*(2), 249–70.

Prassida, G. F., & Asfari, U. (2022). A conceptual model for the acceptance of collaborative robots in industry 5.0. *Procedia Computer Science, 197,* 61–7.

Sharma, A., & Singh, B. J. (2020). Evolution of industrial revolutions: A review. *International Journal of Innovative Technology and Exploring Engineering, 9*(11), 66–73.

Tangwaragorn, P., Charoenruk, N., Viriyasitavat, W., Tangmanee, C., Kanawattanachai, P., Hoonsopon, D., Pungpapong, V., Pattanapanyasat, R.-P., Boonpatcharanon, S., & Rhuwadhana, P. (2024). Analyzing key drivers of digital transformation: A review and framework. *Journal of Industrial Information Integration, 42,* 100680.

Taylor, F.W. (1911): *The Principles of Scientific Management*: first published in 1911. Ocean of Minds Media House, River Denys.

United Nations (2025). *Digital Development Compass.* United Nations Development Programme, https://digitaldevelopmentcompass.undp.org/ (accessed on 2 March 2025).

Vial, G. (2021). Understanding digital transformation: A review and a research agenda. *Managing digital transformation, Journal of Strategic Information Systems,* 13–66.

Warner, K. S., & Wäger, M. (2019). Building dynamic capabilities for digital transformation: An ongoing process of strategic renewal. *Long Range Planning, 52*(3), 326–49.

Wilson, J. M. (2014). Henry Ford vs. assembly line balancing. *International Journal of Production Research, 52*(3), 757–65.

Xu, M., David, J. M., & Kim, S. H. (2018). The fourth industrial revolution: Opportunities and challenges. *International Journal of Financial Research, 9*(2), 90–5.

2

BUSINESS STRATEGY IN THE DIGITAL AGE

Learning Goals

By the end of this chapter, you should...

- Be able to explain how the digital age is shifting the sources of firm strategic competitive advantage.
- Be able to explain how established theories of firm strategic competitive advantage apply in the digital age.
- Be able to critically evaluate the potential of digitisation, digitalisation and digital transformation to allow firms to achieve sustained competitive advantage.
- Be able to explain the appropriate approach to the formulation of firm strategies in the digital age.
- Be able to critically assess the enablers and inhibitors of the formulation of firm strategies in the digital age.

Success Story: Adidas Storefactory and Speedfactory Concepts

Adidas designs, produces, and markets athletic and sports lifestyle products and is headquartered in Herzogenaurach, Germany. Starting in 2016 and continuing through to 2019, Adidas made some of the most public investments in experiments with new production approaches, building on the cyber-physical systems of Industry 4.0 with their Storefactory pop-up store in Berlin from 2016 to 2017 and Speedfactories located in Ansbach, Germany, and Atlanta, USA between 2015 and 2020. The insights and technologies developed from these experiments were transferred to two Asian suppliers to Adidas in 2019 and the Speedfactories closed in 2020. These examples represent two distinct real-world tests of concrete ideas about the future of manufacturing in the athletic and sports lifestyle products industry.

The Storefactory concept allowed customers to undergo a body scan by projection technology and kinetic motion sensors and then use a design station to design a woolen sweater that was then produced in the store. The Storefactory enabled up to ten pullovers a day to be designed and produced in around four hours and at a cost of about EUR 200. The concept employed all of the digital technologies associated with a cyber-physical system and Industry 4.0 in the instore experience of the brand, and associating advanced manufacturing and technology experimentation with the consumer brand. While allowing Adidas to gather data about customer preferences and willingness-to-pay for mass customised products and services.

Figure 2.1 Adidas' SpeedFactory Concept

Source: Own illustration

(Continued)

The Speedfactory was a larger scale experiment in highly automated manufacturing, employing digital technologies like 3-D printing, robotics, and computerised knitting machines. But it also adopted the emerging phenomenon of aligning machines and humans in advanced machine-human, cyber-physical systems of production, in this case reflecting the acknowledged advantage of humans, in especially dexterous physical activities compared to contemporary robots. Strategically, the Speedfactories are interesting because of their clear digital strategies, with digital technologies integral to the concept for serving local markets through local production. This provided a test of the arguments for digital technologies and manufacturing with Industry 4.0 logics as a means to shorten supply chains and increase responsiveness to market trends and changing local customer preferences. This larger-scale project was another example of mass customisation, with consumers able to design their products within limits. Once the advanced manufacturing technologies had been proven, Adidas adopted digital marketing strategies to create awareness for the project, designing a series of sneakers with input from 'running influencers' as part of a social media campaign. The project is also interesting because it was enabled by an internal incubator unit, independent of the parent firm, called Future Team, that has adopted new work practices and flexible working space principles. The project stimulated debate about automation and employment and more critical observers wondered if the Speedfactories were nothing more than a marketing campaign.

The Storefactory and Speedfactory reflect a history of innovative experimentation by Adidas, reflecting experiments that arguably respond to societal trends around personalisation and sustainability. The Speedfactories were closed in 2020 and the technology and insights transferred to Asian suppliers, with the promise to enable short production times and flexibility, continuing to allow some responsiveness to consumer demand.

Source: Adidas (2019); Müller (2017); Wiener (2017)

2.0 INTRODUCTION

Digital transformation is a strategic undertaking that improves the ability of firms to create and capture value in the digital age, by leveraging the integration of digital technologies as a central consideration of business strategising (Bharadwaj et al., 2013; Peter et al., 2020). This understanding of digital transformation draws attention to the importance of both digital strategy formulation and implementation for explaining firm performance (Bharadwaj et al., 2013; Rêgo et al., 2022; Verhoef et al., 2021). This chapter explores how established theories of strategic competitive advantage apply to strategy formulation in the digital age, and the practical implementation of these explanations are addressed with the ACT Method proposed in Chapter 12 (Analyse, Create, Transform). The necessary knowledge for this practice-oriented strategising across seven strategic action fields (SAFs) of digital transformation is covered in Chapters 4 to 10, and the implementation of digital transformation in Chapter 11.

2.1 STRATEGIES AS THEORIES OF COMPETITIVE SUCCESS

Firm strategies are theories of how to compete successfully (Barney, 1991; Porter, 1996) and research has identified a number of interconnected alternative theories which will explain the performance of a specific firm to different degrees. This chapter first discusses different understandings of firm performance as the primary outcome of successful firm strategies. Firms, however, formulate and implement their strategies within the context of the socio-technical systems in which they are embedded (Cherns, 1976; Kant, 2016) and this broader context of the firm needs to be understood before reviewing the established theories of competitive success. The first group of theories for explaining firm competitive success that are reviewed are focused on internal explanations of firm performance and include the important resources (Barney, 1991, 2001), capabilities (Barney, 2001; Porter, 1996), and dynamic capabilities (Teece et al., 1997) of firms. The other strategic theories provide explanations for firm performance based on the external competitive environment of the firm, including corporate decisions on entering specific industries (Porter, 1979; Short et al., 2007) and strategic positioning relative to competitors in an industry (Akan et al., 2006; Kim et al., 2004). The chapter closes with a discussion of how the formulation of strategies drawing on these different theories should be approached in the digital age.

2.2 ASSESSING FIRM PERFORMANCE

Firm performance from a strategic perspective is typically assessed using accounting and finance measures (Barney, 2020), but increasingly there is recognition of the necessity to integrate broader performance measures to take account of the impact of firms on stakeholders, as well as the role of stakeholders in value creation by firms. Where stakeholders are 'any group or individual who can affect or is affected by the achievement of the organization's objectives' (Freeman, 1984, p. 46), external stakeholders are argued to be increasingly important for understanding value creation by firms, as they provide resources and capabilities not owned or directly controlled by firms, but none-the-less needed by them. This phenomenon is being accelerated by the digital transformation of business and society, as in the digital age information and network effects that are increasingly determining firm performance for both traditional and digital businesses (Bharadwaj et al., 2013).

Firm performance can thus be understood in terms of (1) economic, (2) natural environmental, (3) societal, and (4) digital performance. A further important distinction is between organisational performance and organisational effectiveness. Organisational performance focuses on the financial performance, product market performance, and shareholder return performance of a firm (Richard et al., 2009). One might say that these are the traditional performance measures for firms, based around measurable quantitative indicators of economic value creation. Organisational effectiveness is a broader concept that focuses on internal performance outcomes related to more efficient and/or effective operations, but also broader internal and external performance assessments beyond those focused on economic value creation, like corporate social responsibility. To support managers, organisational performance, and organisational effectiveness indicators are implemented into balanced scorecards that provide a wholistic assessment of firm performance. The composition of organisational performance and effectiveness indicators on a balanced scorecard will reflect the perceived legitimacy of stakeholders' interest in the activities of a firm (Richard et al., 2009).

Finally, organisational performance and effectiveness can be assessed at a point in time and over time (e.g., year-on-year comparisons), but also for a single firm or in comparison to direct competitors (e.g., compared to perceived strategic group members), or firms in other industries (Short et al., 2007). Importantly, the assessment of organisational performance and effectiveness is not only compared over time and to other firms, but also in terms of expectations of both internal and external stakeholders in a firm (see Box 2.1).

Box 2.1: Comparative Firm Performance Assessment

Economic performance assessments emphasise a comparison of performance outcomes to expectations for firm performance for a given industry, but this can also be extended to strategic groups, allowing performance expectations to be assessed relative to a firm's main competitors. The logic can however be extended to between strategic group comparisons within an industry and to include competitive, environmental, societal, and digital performance measures.

- Above Normal Performance: Performance exceeds expectations for the industry and that of members of firm's strategic group
- Normal Performance: Performance meets expectations for the industry and is comparable to members of firm's strategic group
- Below Normal Performance: Performance is below expectations for the industry and members of firm's strategic group

2.2.1 Economic Performance

The economic performance of a firm assessed both in terms of its organisational performance (see Box 2.2) and organisational effectiveness (see Box 2.3) is focused on the effectiveness and efficiency with which the firm creates and captures economic value. Arguably the clearest primary stakeholders in this aspect of firm performance are firm employees, both operative and managerial; customers; suppliers and distributors; and shareholders.

The economic value that is created differs for each customer of a firms' products or services, as the perceived benefit derived from the product or service purchased will differ for each customer, and this will be reflected in the willingness-to-pay of each customer at a given point of time and set of circumstances. The economic performance of a firm is a reflection of the ability of a firm to optimise its ability to capture the value created for customers, through pricing strategies that optimally reflect customers willingness-to-pay for a single transaction and over time with repeat purchases. Firms should pursue pricing strategies that optimise for the willingness of customers to pay for the value created by products or services for the highest number of customers and purchases over time.

Economic performance is however also concerned with the effectiveness and efficiency with which the value embodied in products and services is created and delivered to customers. The lower the direct and indirect costs of a firm for developing, producing, and delivering a product or service to customers, as represented in Porter's (1985) Value Chain (see Figure 2.2), all other things being equal, the higher the profit of the firm will be. When considered at the level of the individual product or service purchase (transition) by a customer, the total net profit of a firm represents the total number of sales (volume of transactions) multiplied by the net profit per unit sold. Of course, these values will vary by product or service and so in practice this calculation will be more complex to calculate for all products and services of a firm, but using a single product or service is helpful to illustrate the logic.

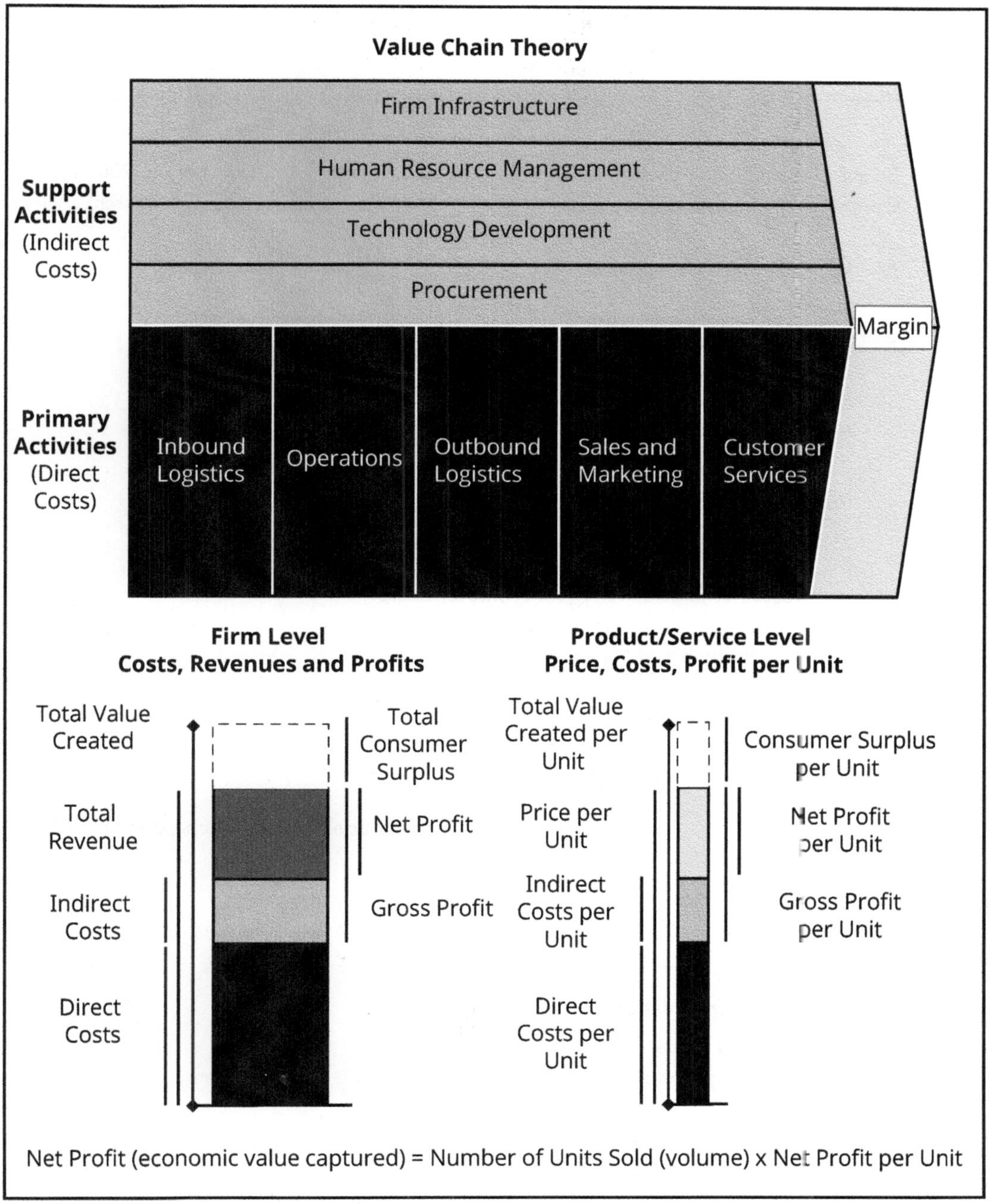

Figure 2.2 Value Chain Theory and the creation and capture of economic value

Source: adapted from Kaplinsky & Morris (2000) and Porter (1985)

Understanding how digital technologies and the digital transformation of firms, industries and society affect the costs and revenues of firms is a central goal of this text. Being able to understand the effects of digital transformation on the willingness-to-pay in terms of price and frequency of purchase (volume), as well as the cost structures of firms as a whole but also for individual products or services, allows a far more careful assessment of the potential for digital technologies to allow firms to both create and capture economic value.

Box 2.2: Organisational Performance Measures

Selected exemplary indicators (please see Tables 2, 3, and 4 in Richard et al., 2009 for a comprehensive account of operational performance measures in strategy research).

- ***General***
  - Firm Survival
- ***Financial Performance***
  - Profit Growth
  - Profit Margin
  - Return on Assets
  - Return on Investments
- ***Product Market Performance***
  - Revenue / Sales Growth
  - Growing Market Share
  - Customer Satisfaction / Net Promotor Score
  - Improving Profitability of Existing Customers
  - Gain Profitable of New Customers
- ***Shareholder Return***
  - Total Shareholder Return
  - Dividend Payments
  - Stock / Share Price Increases

Source: adaptation of Richard et al. (2009)

Box 2.3: Organisational Effectiveness Measures

- ***Operative Performance***
  - Reducing Costs
  - Improving Product and Service Quality
- ***People Performance***
  - Culture and Values
  - Employee Satisfaction
  - Employee Retention Rates

Source: adaptation of Richard et al. (2009)

2.2.2 Natural Environmental Performance

The digital transformation of business and society has both negative and positive impacts on the natural environmental sustainability of economies, industries, and firms. In terms of the natural environment, digital technologies and digital transformation are not able to escape the 'wicked problem' nature of the pursuit of sustainability goals (von Kutzschenbach & Daub, 2020). For example, a commonly referred to advantage of the digitisation of work is the reduction in use of paper in the office, but increasingly it is being recognised that an unintended consequence of this digitisation is greater e-waste, as more and more ICT equipment is used and over time replaced. Digital technologies may then contribute to enabling solutions to this problem such as recycling or even circular business models, thereby potentially encouraging ever greater use of new ICT equipment and so on, reflecting the technical and non-technical aspects of sustainability initiatives. Undeniably though, as things stand there is currently significant interest in the potential for digital technologies and digital transformation to contribute to a more sustainable impact of business on the natural environment (see Box 2.4 for a selection of potential environmentally related performance measures for firms in the digital age). The potential for digital transformation to contribute to natural environmental sustainability is addressed in Chapter 3.

Box 2.4: Natural Environmental Performance Measures in the Digital Age

- Enabling Sustainability of Other Economic Actors
- Reduced Resource Consumption
- Carbon Emissions
- Energy Use and Heat Pollution
- E-waste
- Impact on Natural Habitats

2.2.3 Societal Performance

The comprehensive impact of the digital age on economic and societal activities within countries, but also globally, is clearly fundamentally changing the way in which economies function, and people live their lives (von Kutzschenbach & Daub, 2020). The impact on and the potential for digital transformation to contribute to societal sustainability is addressed in detail in Chapter 3. For most firms, their primary societal stakeholders are their local communities, employees, and customers (Lindeque & Samuel, 2022). The digital transformation of business and society has the potential to impact these societal stakeholders in terms of employment, education, access to food and water, physical health, mental health, lifestyles, equality and inclusion, safety and crime prevention (Szalkowski & Johansen, 2023). Reflecting the fact that technologies are value neutral, and their impact is determined by how they are used, digital technologies have the potential for both positive and negative impacts. The societal performance measures (see Box 2.5), that a firm will adopt will be determined by the societal contexts in which they operate, reflecting their stakeholders' demands.

Box 2.5: Societal Performance Measures in the Digital Age

- Employment
- Education
- Physical Health
- Mental Health
- Equality and Inclusion
- Safety and Crime Prevention

Source: Szalkowski & Johansen (2023)

2.3 DIGITAL TRANSFORMATION AND FIRM PERFORMANCE

The impact of digital transformation enabled by digital strategies on firm performance can be assessed in terms of four impacts of digital technologies on the creation and capture of value by firms, including impacts on the (1) scope, (2) scale, (3) speed, and (4) sources of value creation and capture (Bharadwaj et al., 2013). The performance indicators for a digital strategy / digitally transformed firm (see Box 2.6), emphasise the need for stakeholders in a firm to understand the nature of digital technologies. The formulation and implementation of a digital strategy and associated digital transformation of a firm will, for example, lead to changes in how the scope of business activities is understood both internally and externally to the firm (Bharadwaj et al., 2013). But digital technologies not only enable, but require a different approach to, thinking about the internal and external scale of activities: for example web services allow firms to rapidly scale up and down their digital storage or computing power to reflect demand for such resources. Digital transformation also speeds up the pace of both traditional and newer business activities. Finally, the digital transformation of a firm allows new sources of value creation and capture to be identified and implement.

Box 2.6: Dimensions of Digital Technologies Impact on Firm Performance

These performance indicators in relation to digital strategy formulation are discussed in Chapter 11.

- ***Scope***
  - Cross Functional and Process Silo Activities
  - Digitisation of Products and Services

- Digitisation of Information and Knowledge
- Participation in Dynamic Ecosystems

- ***Scale***
  - Rapid Digital Scaling Up and Down
  - Network Effects for Rapid Scaling
  - Scale through Information Abundance
  - Scale through Networks and Alliances
- ***Speed of Business Activities***
  - Speed of Product Launches
  - Speed of Decision-making
  - Speed of Supply Chain Orchestration
  - Speed of Network Formation and Adaptation
- ***New Sources of Value Creation***
  - Increased Value from Information
  - Multi-sided Business Models
  - Coordinated Business Models in Networks
  - Control of Digital Industry Architecture

Source: adaptation of Bharadwaj et al. (2013)

2.4 FIRM EMBEDDEDNESS

Firms are most commonly described as being members of an industry or, put differently, they are embedded in the technological landscape and the flows of information and goods and services in a given industry. The digital age is showing that the embeddedness of firms extends beyond traditional notions of industry membership and that firms are in fact embedded in ecosystems that may incorporate multiple different industries and which we can describe as socio-technical systems.

2.4.1 Socio-Technical Systems

The socio-technical systems (STS) perspective emphasises the integration of both social (human) and technology (non-human) aspects into a system that pursues a common goal (Kant, 2016; Sony & Naik, 2020). Such integration of the social and (new) technology reflects every proceeding industrial revolution, with humans and the innovative technology of the day co-evolving as the technology was rapidly adopted by organisations and people (see Chapter 1). A socio-technical approach however emphasises that when technology is adopted without taking into consideration the behavioural consequences of the adoption, then sociological challenges are likely to emerge in a business organisation (Sony & Naik, 2020).

Box 2.7: Six Dimensions of Cyber-Physical Systems

- People
- Culture
- Infrastructure
- Technology
- Processes / Procedures
- Goals

Source: Sony & Naik (2020)

The current early stages of the digital age are featured by emerging digital socio-technical systems, within which organisations and people are rapidly adopting digital technologies to conduct specific economic and social activities, by developing processes that incorporate digital technologies to achieve business goals (see Box 2.7) for the elements of socio-technical systems. Indeed, the digital age features a complex set of evolving socio-technical systems around specific digital technologies and activities, with these alternative systems at times embedded in, overlapping with, dependent on or independent of each other. Depending on the firm and its activities, a firm can be embedded in one or more such socio-technical systems (see Figure 2.3 for a stylised visualisation of the potential for multiple embeddedness of firms in shared and separate socio-technical systems through horizontal integration (Type 2)). Firms however also have internal socio-technical sub-systems that can be vertically integrated (Type 1). It is important to remember that firms are open systems, that is they take in inputs and produce outputs, which are released into their environments, and that the internal activities of the firm will be aligned with broader external socio-technical systems, through horizontal integration (Menz et al., 2021; Sony & Naik, 2020).

Figure 2.3 further seeks to show how over the last 50 years in, broadly speaking. five phases of technology development (see 'industrial revolutions' (Figure 1.2) in Chapter 1), we have moved from physical systems increasingly supported by ICT to advanced cyber-physical systems with significant human–technology interaction in ever more complex networks. Initially these developments mostly affected managerial work, but increasingly, digital technologies also began to impact the work of operative employees. As the technologies underpinning the different socio-technical systems enabling work moved from information and communication to networking and now also controlling and sensing technologies, the complexity of the networks within and across socio-technical systems also increased in complexity, to the point today that firms rely on diverse human–human, human–technology and technology–technology networks, featuring increasing automation. The combination of humans and machines in the human technology networks are interesting, as initially the machines were assisting humans to do work and over time humans have increasing taken roles supporting machines to get work done.

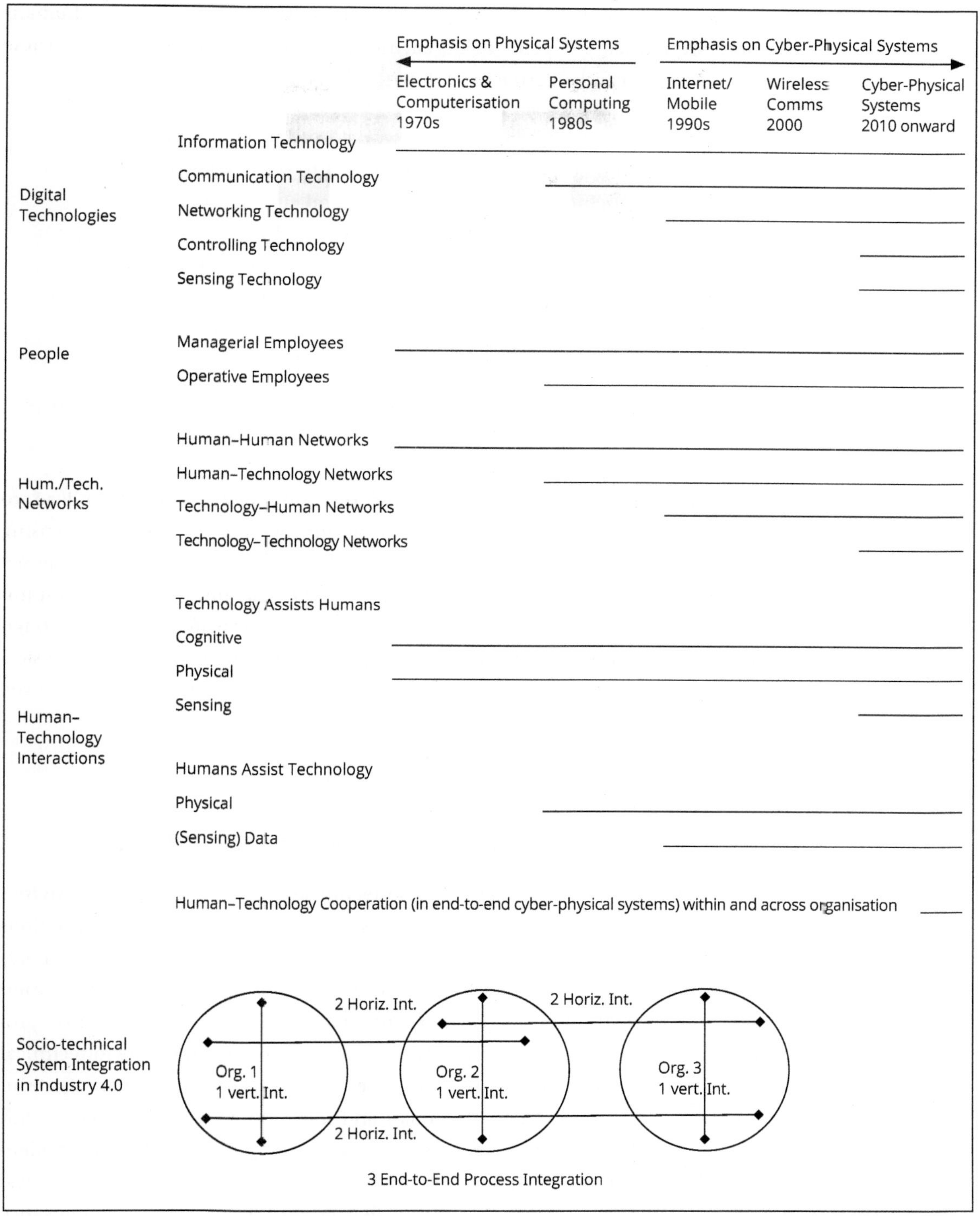

Figure 2.3 Evolving socio-technical systems in the digital age resulting in vertical (Vert.) and horizontal (Horiz.) integrations (Int.)

Source: adapted from Kant (2016); Kraft et al. (2022); and Sony & Naik (2020)

In its most advanced forms this leads to symbiotic cyber-physical systems, where humans and machines are mutually dependent on each other to achieve common goals. These cyber-physical systems can be defined as follows:

> Cyber Physical Systems (CPS) are smart networked systems with embedded sensors, processors and actuators that are designed to sense and interact with the physical world (including the human users), and support real-time, guaranteed performance in safety-critical applications. In CPS systems, the joint behaviour of the 'cyber' and 'physical' elements of the system is critical – computing, control, sensing and networking can be deeply integrated into every component, and the actions of components and systems must be safe and interoperable.
>
> Networking and Information Technology Research and Development Program of the United States Government (NITRD, 2015)

It's important to remember that digital transformation does not need to lead to cyber-physical systems; many digital transformation processes do not integrate sensing and controlling technologies into firm procedures. As can be seen it is equally possible and more likely that firms today are primarily relying on information, communication, and connectivity technologies to realise their digital transformation. Although some firms, especially in manufacturing, have begun to experiment with cyber-physical systems for production: a notable example was Adidas' Speedfactory concept (see the opening chapter case above).

2.4.2 Strategic Action Fields of Digital Transformation

Firms integrate themselves into different socio-technical systems for specific activities and goals and research has shown that this results in the emergence of strategic actions fields for the digital transformation of firms (Peter et al., 2020). The strategic action fields (SAF) of digital transformation emphasise the social aspects of the digital transformation process by focusing attention on managerial sense-making and related legitimation processes for a specific digital technology. This choice is about which socio-technical systems the firm wishes to develop internally (vertical integration) and participate in externally (horizontal integration). The human and machine networks associated with these choices will reflect one or more of seven strategic action fields that have been identified (see Box 2.8). A SAF may include all or only subsystems of a broader socio-technical system within which a firm is operating, this is dependent on the technology relevance and the perceived attractiveness of different activities (applications) that a specific digital technology enables.

A SAF approach emphasises the importance of managers and employees in the framing and sense-making of socio-technical systems as part of the digital transformation process for a firm (Peter et al., 2020). Figure 2.4 is a reminder that not only the technology networks cross firms, but so do the human networks (managers and employees) that are central to the legitimation of participating in specific socio-technical systems. Reflecting the internal (vertical) and external (horizontal) integration processes associated with the participation in a specific socio-technical system, key employees act as institutional entrepreneurs and serve to legitimise specific digital technologies, and the socio-technical systems associated with those technologies, internally and externally, as part of the technology adoption process. This is critical, as it is a reminder that firms will not all share the same understanding of the attractiveness of the diverse digital technologies and will make different choices about how to digitally transform, by deciding on which strategic action fields (socio-technical systems) are legitimate and likely to be most beneficial to firm performance.

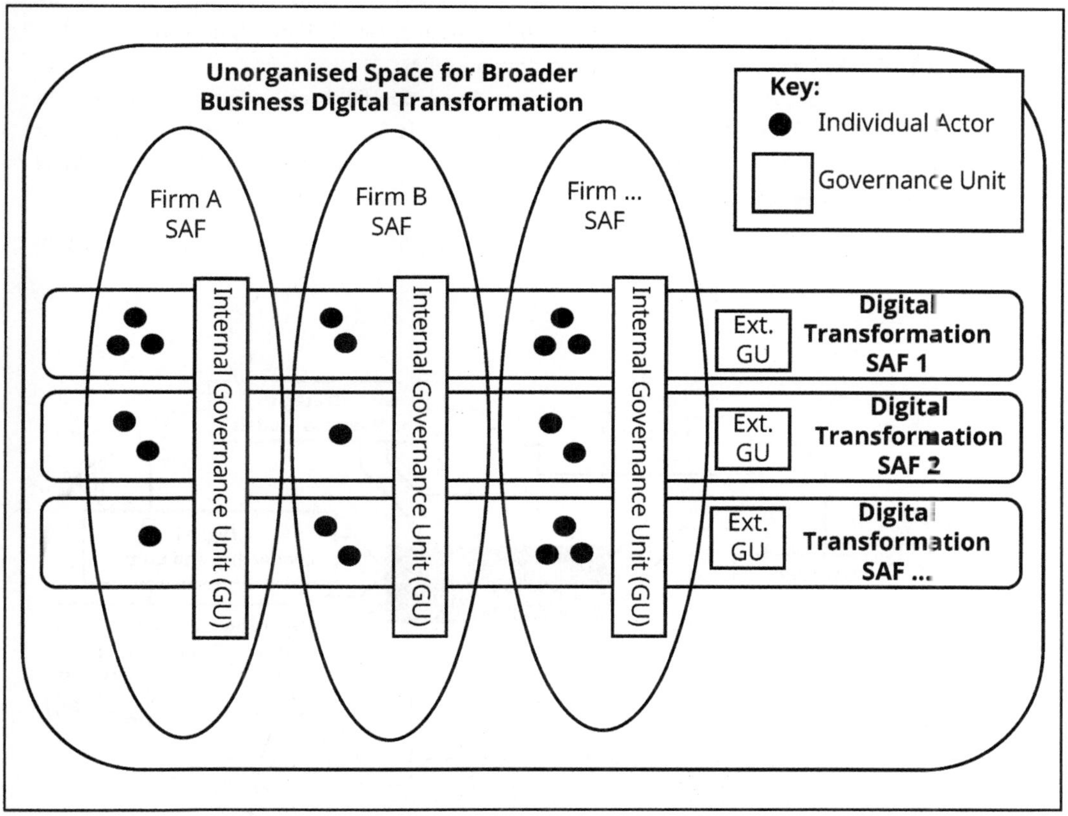

Figure 2.4 Development of strategic action fields of digital transformation

Source: Peter et al. (2020)

Box 2.8: Strategic Action Fields of Digital Transformation

The seven strategic action fields (SAF) of digital transformation are (see Figure 2.5):

1 Customer Centricity
2 New Digital Technologies
3 Data and the Cloud
4 New Strategies and Business Models
5 Operational Excellence / Process Management
6 Digital Leadership and Culture
7 Digital Marketing

Chapters 4–10 cover all seven strategic action fields of digital transformation in more detail. The SAF sequence starts market-driven, with the external perspectives of the customer (SAF no. 1) and new, available digital technologies (SAF no. 2), followed by the internal perspective of available data (SAF no. 3). These insights lead to the creation of customer, technology and data-driven new strategies (SAF no. 4), resulting in an adaptation of the internal operating model (SAF no. 5) and leadership framework (SAF no. 6). Finally, products and services are promoted in the market (SAF no. 7) and with that, the final SAF links back to the initial, market-driven SAF no. 1.

For public-sector/government organisations, the action fields are roughly the same, with the exception of SAF 4 (which for the public sector is focussed on 'digital e-government strategies') and SAF 7 (which focuses on 'digital communication', rather than digital marketing in businesses).

Source: Peter (2017, 2021, 2023, 2024); Peter et al. (2020)

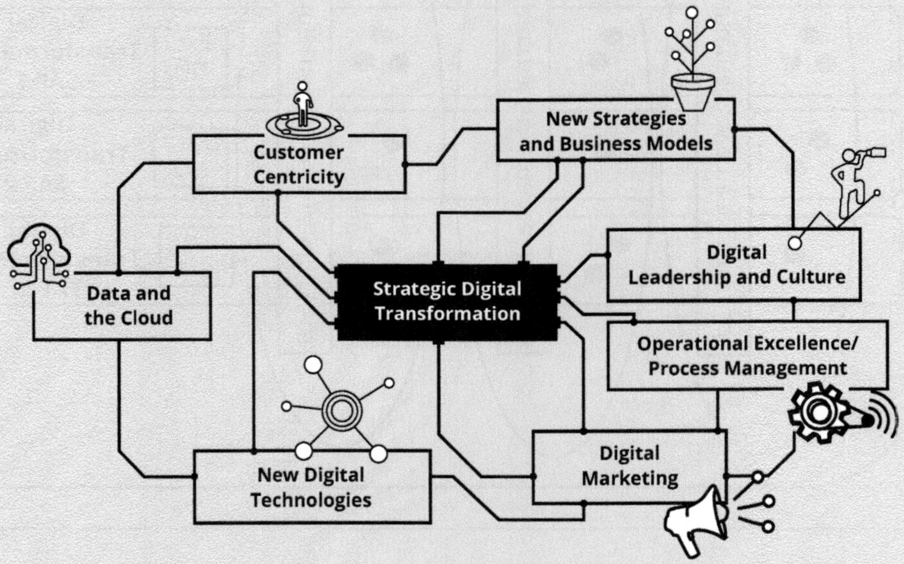

Figure 2.5 Seven strategic action fields of digital transformation

Source: Peter (2017, 2021, 2023, 2024); Peter et al. (2020)

Table 2.1 Theories of competitive advantage and the digital age

		Theory of Competitive Advantage		Implications for Value Creation in the Digital Age	
	Theory	**Core Assumptions**	**Source of Competitive Advantage**	**Generic Strategies** **Porter (1979)** **Treacy & Wiersema (1993)**	**Strategic Action Fields Perspective** **Peter et al. (2020)**
Internal Perspective	**Resources** Barney (1991a,b; 2001) Newbert (2007)	• Resources enable the production of products and services customers demand	• Acquire valuable and rare resources needed for production	• Market strategies require access and / or control over the resources needed for a specific product-market fit	• Firms must evaluate the strategic action fields that support their intended generic strategy
	Capabilities Zacharias et al. (2016) Newbert (2007)	• Capabilities are the ability to manage resources within organizational process to create value	• Capability to optimally orchestrate firm resources drives sustained competitive advantage	• While a firm may have an overarching generic strategy for value creation, it is essential to be able to respond to changing competitive conditions within that approach, to ensure the product / service offering has product market fit	• Strategic action fields that are aligned with new logics of value creation, process optimization and enable adaptability are important for supporting firm responsiveness to changing market conditions and customer preferences
	Core Competences Prahalad & Hamel (1990)	• Core competencies allow firms to respond to market opportunities	• Control over core products allows competitive advantage in different related final product markets • Inimitability sustains competitive advantage		
	Dynamic Capabilities Baía & Ferreira (2024) Newbert (2007)	• Dynamic external environments require firms be adaptable to survive • Dynamic capabilities allow firms to achieve new resource and capability configurations in response to changing external conditions	• Dynamic capabilities are not suitable for securing sustainable competitive advantage due to their imitability and substitutability • It is the new configurations of resources and capabilities that realize sustained competitive advantage	• Firms do not have to change their generic strategy if market conditions change, by reconfiguring their resources and capabilities they can deliver the same value proposition in a manner that reflects the new external conditions	• The strategic action fields within which a firm is operating is a source of sense-making that allows managers better assess how digital technologies can contribute to the process of resource and capability reconfiguration

(Continued)

Table 2.1 (Continued)

		Theory of Competitive Advantage		Implications for Value Creation in the Digital Age	
	Theory	**Core Assumptions**	**Source of Competitive Advantage**	**Generic Strategies Porter (1979) Treacy & Wiersema (1993)**	**Strategic Action Fields Perspective Peter et al. (2020)**
External Perspective	**Industry Dynamics** *Structure-Conduct-Performance* Porter (1979) Panagiotou (2006)	• The structure of an industry in terms of customers and suppliers to competing firms in an industry affects costs and revenues respectively	• Bargaining power in input or final markets • Degree of competition • Barriers to entry • Limited substitute products / services	Successful execution of generic strategies • Change bargaining power of incumbent suppliers or customers • Can create barriers to entry • Change competitive dynamics	The digital strategic action fields have the potential to • Change bargaining power of incumbent suppliers or customers • Change barriers to entry and availability of substitute products / services • Change competitive dynamics
	Strategic Groups Panagiotou (2006) Short et al. (2007)	• Unequal performance between strategic groups, depending on industry segment • Limited inter-strategic group mobility for firms • Strategic group members serve as reference group for other members affecting managerial cognition	• Managerial sense-making	• Generic strategies are the outcome of collective sense-making regarding the optimal strategy for a specific firm	• Digital transformation of a firm will reflect the collective managerial sense-making about how different strategic action fields for digital transformation are relevant to a firm given its generic strategy orientation

Source: Newbert (2007); Peter et al. (2020)

2.5 THEORIES OF (SUSTAINABLE) COMPETITIVE ADVANTAGE

This subchapter provides a concise review of the established theories for explaining competitive strategies and firm performance. In all these strategic theories the goal is to explain how firms can achieve not only competitive advantage but even sustained competitive advantage, where competitive advantage is above normal performance in the short term and sustained competitive advantage can be understood as above normal performance in the medium to long term. This performance assessment could include some or many of the economic (competitive), natural environment or societal performance.

Reflecting the open systems framing from the previous two subsections, an explanation of firm performance requires that the firm, strategic group, and industry effects on firm performance be simultaneously considered, as over time these three levels of analysis will interact and thereby drive co-evolution between firms within a specific industry. This dynamic 'systems theory view of performance suggests that firms, strategic groups, and industries are interdependent parts of a complex system that collectively influences firms' fates. Only by examining each level in the context of the others can each level's role be diagnosed' (Short et al., 2007, p. 149). This complexity has been confirmed in the mixed results of efforts to confirm to what degree firm, industry, or strategic group membership determine firm performance (McGahan & Porter, 1997; Short et al., 2007).

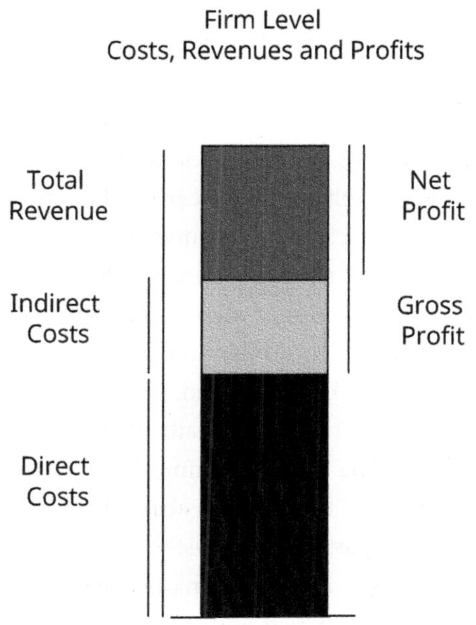

Figure 2.6 Resource-based view

The remaining sub-sections follow this complex system framing of firm performance, starting with an internal perspective (see Figure 2.6 on the evolution of the resource-based view) then covering the external perspective (see Figure 2.7 parts a, b and c on industry dynamics and strategic groups) before discussing two main typologies of 'generic' strategies (see Figure 2.9) for competitive advantage as integrative logics for linking internal and external explanations for competitive advantage.

2.5.1 Ownership and Control Over Resources

Resource-based explanations for the competitive advantage of firms are a long-established contribution to the strategic management literature; attributed to work as early as the late 1950s (Newbert, 2007). Resources are defined as 'all assets, capabilities, organisational processes, firm attributes, information, knowledge etc. controlled by a firm that enable the firm to conceive of and implement strategies to improve its efficiency and effectiveness' (Daft, 1983, cited in Barney, 1991, p. 101). The resource-based view, including all the variations that have developed over time, provides an important explanation for why there is consistent support for the primacy of firm effects on firm performance, compared to strategic group and industry membership on firm performance (McGahan & Porter, 1997; Short et al., 2007). All three are discussed in this chapter, as integral parts of an overall open system of value creation.

The formalisation of theory occurred when the link between the direct contribution of products and/or services and the indirect contribution of the resources needed to produce the products and/or services was theorised (Barney, 1991; Wernerfelt, 1984). Barney (1991) understood a firm to have a sustainable competitive advantage when it is implementing a value creation strategy that is not being implemented by current or potential competitors and when these competitors are unable to duplicate the value creation benefits of the strategy. The resource-based view has two main assumptions and a set of four necessary conditions for a sustained competitive advantage resulting in above normal returns to be achieved. The theory assumes that firms do not all have access to the same quality of value creating resources and that high value creating resources are not easily transferable from one firm to another. For the unique and immobile resources of a firm to allow a sustained competitive advantage, they must have four attributes. The resource must be valuable, in the sense that it allows opportunities to be exploited and threats to be neutralised, it must also be rare, difficult to imitate, and finally there should be limited or no strategically equivalent substitute resources that do not meet the first three criteria. The implicit assumption is that a valuable resource allows products and services to be produced that have an attractive value proposition for customers. The question of inimitability is of particular interest when thinking about digital transformation, as it relies on causal ambiguity about the link between the resource endowments of a firm and the competitiveness of its products and services. Social complexity as a result of the internal and relational capital of a firm, including for example organisational culture, is highly related to technology adoption and successful integration and contributes to the inimitability of firm resources and capabilities. These are often the barriers to effective adoption and integration of technology in general and also for digital technologies.

Box 2.9: Resources and Capabilities and Products and Service Competitives

Wernerfelt (1984)

Established the relationship between firm resources and the final product and/or services market competitiveness.

(a)

Acquisition of Critical Resources → Production of Products/ Services Demanded by Customers → Above Normal Performance

Barney (1991, 2021)

Establishes the assumptions and conditions for firm resources to lead to substained competitive advantage.

(b)

Assumptions		***Necessary Conditions***		***Goal***
Resource heterogeneity	→	Value Creating Resources	→	Sustained Competitive Advantage
Resource immobility		Rare Resources		Above Normal Performance
		Inimitability		
		Non-substitutability		

From Resources to Capabilities

It is not necessarily the ownership and or control over value creating resources that leads to competitive advantage, but rather the capability to optimally orchestrate the resources of a firms that leads to sustained competitive advantage. These capabilities place a strong emphasis on resources management and organisation processes.

Prahalad & Hamel (1990)

Provides an explanation of how capabilities and or control over value creating resources that leads to competitive advance, but rather the capability to optimally orchestrate the resources of a firms that leads sustained competitive advantage. These capablilities place a strong emphasis on resources management and organisation process

(c)

Core Competencies collective learning capability → Core Products/ Services → Portfolio of Products/ Services Demanded by Customers

Figure 2.7 (a), (b), (c) Evolution of the resource-based view of (sustained) competitive advantage

Dynamic Capabilities (Teece et al., 1997)

Provied an explanation for how firms can 'Integrate, build and reconfigure internal and external resources and competencies'/capabilities in response to rapidly changing environments (Teece at al., 1997,p. 516). Dynamic capabilities can serve diffrent purposes:

(Continued)

1 Integrate resources and capabilities (Elsenhardt and Martin, 2000; Teece et al., 1997)
2 Gain and release resources and capabilities (Elsenhardt and martin, 2000; Teece et at.,1997)
3 Reconfigure existing resources and capabilities (Elsenhardt and martin, 2000; Teece et al at.,1997)

This allows the firm to adapt to changing marker or environmental conditons and are especially important in highly dynamic markets.

Source: Newbert (2007)

2.5.2 Capabilities

It is not necessarily the ownership and/or control over value creating resources that leads to competitive advantage, but rather the capability to optimally orchestrate the resources of a firms that leads to sustained competitive advantage. These capabilities place a strong emphasis on resource management and organisation processes (Newbert, 2007).

The core competency theory of Prahalad & Hamel (1990) was arguably the first to introduce a capabilities-based explanation for how firms can achieve sustained competitive advantage across multiple final product and/or service markets. The focus on how capabilities contribute to value creation is an answer to one of the main critiques of Barney's (1991) resource-based theory, namely that the value creation process is not explained. Core competencies were defined as the 'the collective learning in the organization, especially how to coordinate diverse production skills and integrate multiple streams of technology' (Prahalad & Hamel, 1990, p. 82). Understanding the core competence of a firm allows it to focus on core products/services that it is uniquely able to produce and can be integrated into diverse final products and services, while meaningfully adding to the value proposition to customers in these offerings, thereby allowing access to a range of final markets. For the advantages in the final markets to be sustained, the core competencies and core products or services need to remain difficult for competitors to imitate. The core competences approach clearly reflects all four conditions for sustained competitive advantage according to Barney (1991), while explaining how value is created.

2.5.3 Dynamic Capabilities

Dynamic capabilities (Vial, 2019; Warner & Wäger, 2019) extended resource and capability-based thinking to explain how firms can 'integrate, build and reconfigure internal and external resources and competencies' (Teece et al., 1997, p. 516) in response to rapidly changing environments. Dynamic capabilities thus 'are the organizational and strategic routines by which firms achieve new resource configurations as markets emerge, collide, split, evolve, and die' (Eisenhardt & Martin, 2000, p. 1107). It is however important to understand that while dynamic capabilities are likely to be rare and very valuable for a firm, there are doubts about the inimitability and non-substitutability of dynamic capabilities. Dynamic capabilities are thus essential for ensure a firm can effectively orchestrate its resource and capability endowments in response to external conditions, but it is not the dynamic capabilities that will lead to sustained competitive advantage but rather the rare, valuable, inimitable, and non-substitutable resources and capabilities, which the dynamic capabilities contribute to organising and managing, that will enable a firm to achieve sustained competitive advantage (Eisenhardt & Martin, 2000).

2.5.4 Industry Dynamics

Industry characteristics have a longstanding and well supported influence on firm performance (Panagiotou, 2006; Short et al., 2007). Reflecting the open systems approach to thinking, underlying socio-technical thinking and the firm as an open system that takes in inputs to produce products and/or services to be outputted for purchase in markets, industry-based explanations of firm performance have also adopted open systems thinking for explaining industry effects on firm performance. Porter's Five Forces (Porter, 1979) model of industry attractiveness, with the related implications for firm performance, synthesises decades of economic and strategic management theorising about industry attractiveness and related firm performance (Panagiotou, 2006) (see Box 2.10). The Five Forces Model is a clear example of the Structure-Conduct-Performance (SCP) school of thought, which argues that industry characteristics (underlying structure) determine firm behaviour (conduct) and thereby determine firm performance. The SCP approach is rooted in economic thinking about industry market structures, Porter (1979) and is in essence a model that allows firms to deduce strategic implications of perfectly competitive, monopolistic, oligopolistic, and monopoly market structures. The attractiveness of an industry is determined by the concentration of firms in different roles in an industry; product or service differentiation and how open the industry is in terms of the ability for new entrants to the industry or for incumbent firms to leave (exit) an industry; this reflects an open systems approach at the industry level. There is also an emphasis on those factors that might change the structure of an industry and firms' conduct in an industry, traditionally chance, innovation/technological change, and government policy-making. Here, digital transformation is likely to have important impacts. Managers are also argued to play a critical role through their sense-making of competitive landscapes and their dynamics, as their decision-making can change industry structure and firm conduct (Panagiotou, 2006).

Box 2.10: Industry Dynamics and Competitive Performance (Five Forces Model)

1. **Competitive pressure**

   The degree of active competing by incumbent firms in an industry.

2. **Bargaining power of suppliers**

   The greater the concentration of suppliers compared to the competing firms, the greater their ability to influence the cost of inputs.

(Continued)

3 **Bargaining power of buyers**

The greater the concentration of customers (buyers) compared to the competing firms, the greater their ability to influence the price (willingness-to-pay) for goods or services offered.

4 **Threat of new entrants**

New competitors can change the bargaining dynamics by changing the relative concentration of firms in the industry.

5 **Threat of substitutes / presence of complementary products or services**

Substitute and complementary products or services change the willingness-to-pay of customers (buyers).

Source: adapted from Porter (1979, 1991)

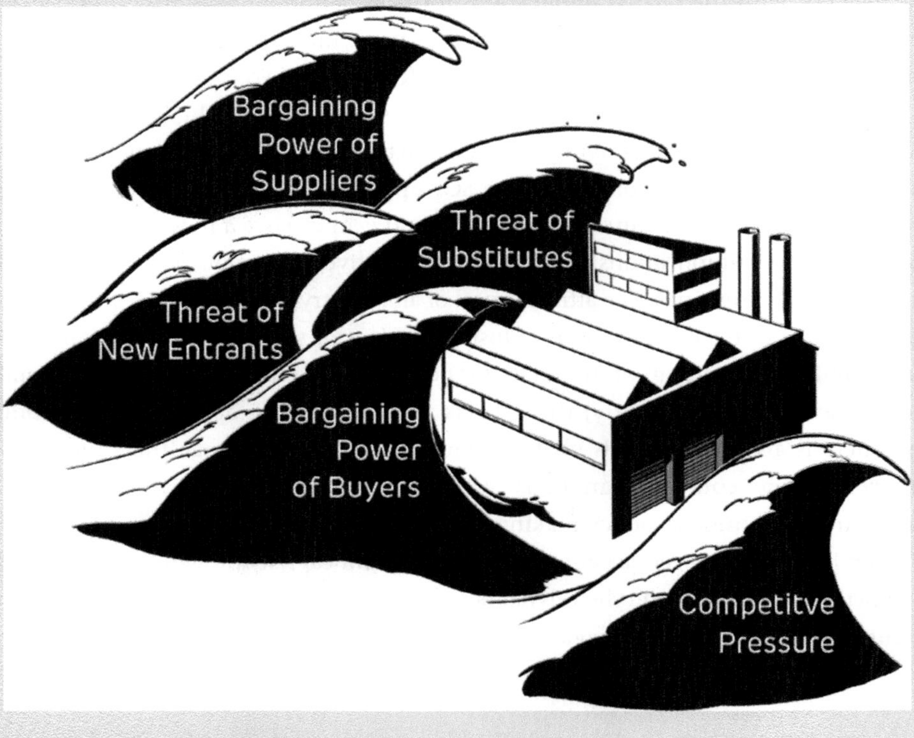

Figure 2.8 Five Forces Model

Source: own illustration following Porter (1979, 1991)

Porter's (1979) Five Forces Model (see Box 2.10) thus can provide an extremely valuable framework for organising managers analysis and sense-making of their environments, including supplier power over their costs, customer buying power as expressed in their willingness to pay, as well as the threat of new entrants or threat of substitute products or services, or complementary products and services (Panagiotou, 2006). This important role of managerial cognition and sense-making also extends to the exogenous element of the Five Forces Model, chance and government policy (Porter, 1979). The prescriptive guidance of the model is that a firm should seek out a position in an industry that minimises the bargaining power of suppliers and customers, while limiting the risk of new entrants or substitute products or services. Equally important would be aligning with complementary products or services to raise switching costs for customers and seeking out a position that limits the degree of competition between incumbents. External influence that could result in industry dynamics changing includes chance and government policy. Box 2.11 lists the mechanisms that underly the strength of the different forces and these mechanisms also represent the way that digital transformation of an industry will change its attractiveness for incumbents and new entrants.

Box 2.11: Underlying Mechanisms for Five Forces Model

It is important to understand the underlying drivers of the different elements of the Five Forces Model, as digital technologies and the digital transformation of firms and their industries has the potential to affect them and thereby they represent the underlying mechanisms through which digital technologies can change industry attractiveness for incumbents and new entrants.

- ***Competitive Intensity (Jockeying for Position)***
  - Concentration of Competing Firms
  - Industry Growth
  - Degree of Standardisation or Differentiation
  - Cost Structures of Competitors
  - Industry Capacity
  - Exit Barriers
- ***Buyer (Customer) and Supplier Power***
  - Concentration
  - Product Standardisation or Differentiation
  - Criticality of Product or Services
  - Substitutes
  - Switching Costs
  - Industry Mutual Dependencies
  - Risk of Value Chain Integration / Disintermediation
- ***Barriers Reducing Threat of New Entrants***
  - Economies of Scale
  - Product Differentiation
  - Capital Requirements
  - Cost Disadvantages Not Associated with Firm Size (e.g., learning curve)
  - Access to Distribution Channels
  - Government Policy / Regulation
- ***Substitute Products or Services***
  - (Changes in) Relative Price-Performance Trade-off

(Continued)

- ***Complementary Products or Services***
  - (Changes in) Relative Price-Performance Trade-off

Source: adapted from Porter (1979)

2.5.5 Strategic Groups

Strategic groups can be defined as 'naturally occurring subsets of firms that are more homogeneous in actions than is found across industry incumbents in general' (Short et al., 2007, p. 150). It is expected that firm performance will differ across strategic groups in an industry. Categorising firms in an industry into strategic groups relies on identifying similarities or differences in attributes of firms, that may include the strategic orientation of firms for value creation (e.g., exploitation of existing resources vs exploration for new resources), how broad or narrow a firms' scope of operations are (e.g., geographic or number of product types) and the scale of resource deployment (e.g., physical resource endowments, intangible resource endowments, financial resources, and organisational size). Short et al. (2007) found support in their analysis for strategic group membership as an influence on firm performance, when simultaneously also assessing the effect of firm characteristics and industry membership, although firm effects on performance were clearly the strongest effect, followed by industry and then strategic group membership. Given that strategic groups can be considered a subset of the firms in an industry, this is probably to be expected.

The analysis of objective data to determine the role of strategic groups in influencing firm performance, as was done by Short et al. (2007), however, is not able to capture the important role of other firms in a strategic group as a reference group for managers in a firm competing with the other firms (Panagiotou, 2006). Porter (1991) acknowledges the importance of managerial strategic decision-making over time in relation to the positional strategy and industry attractiveness at any one point in time. This is critical, as the firms in a strategic group are likely to be active in the same strategic action fields of digital transformation and are expected to be clear references for managers seeking to make sense of digital technologies and organisational transformation using those technologies. As a result, the shared belief of managers about industry structure, competitive challenges, and changing industry dynamics will result in firms adapting organisational structures and competitive strategies (Panagiotou, 2006). In essence a firm's managers will collectively be making sense of the meaning and implications of the underlying mechanisms of the Five Forces Model listed in Box 2.11 with reference to the other firms in their strategic group.

2.6 'GENERIC' STRATEGIES FOR VALUE CREATION

Two of the most well-known 'generic' strategy typologies are that of Porter (1985) and Treacy and Wiersema (1995). Both typologies articulate clear and distinct value propositions to customers of firms (see Figure 2.7), that require different resource and capability configurations to be realised. It is in these value proposition typologies that the alignment of internal resource- and

Figure 2.9 Generic strategies for value creation

Source: adapted from Akan et al. (2006) and Treacy & Wiersema (1995)

capability-based and external market position-based theories of competitive advantage becomes visible. Porter (1996, p. 38,) in a less discussed paper, indeed makes the point that 'strategic positioning means performing *different activities* from rivals' or performing *similar activities in different ways*.' The resource-based view makes the point that it is the possession of rare, value-creating resources and capabilities that are non-substitutable and inimitable, and that allow firms to be able to execute different activities or similar activities differently. Therefore, underlying each of the strategies in the typologies of both Porter (1985) and Treacy and Wiersema (1995) are a set of resources and capabilities enabling activities that create the intended value propositions for customers. As was seen in the opening sections of the chapter, though, it is not only the creation of value but also the ability to capture a meaningful proportion of the value created in net profit that will determine the performance of a firm (Jaeger et al., 2016). In the digital age, managers are challenged to actively seek to understand how digital technologies can be integrated into resource and capability bundles, to support activities that support value proposition demanded by customers in the digital age (Kim et al., 2004).

Understanding the customer (Piepponen et al., 2022; Taylor et al., 2020) is a central strategic concern for the digitally transforming firm and customer centricity has been identified as a distinct strategic action field of digital transformation (Peter et al., 2020). The strategy typologies of Porter (1985) and Treacy and Wiersema (1995) (see Figure 2.9) are not entirely aligned but can broadly be synthesised into three shared value proposition categories, firstly those focused on cost-based value for customers, secondly value propositions that address product or services attributes, and finally a relational value proposition.

Treacy and Wiersema (1995) do not frame their cost-based strategy in those terms, but rather in terms of operational excellence, but in describing the strategy, the operational excellence strategy relies on the ability to manage costs so that reliable middle market products can be offered at the best price in the market. The extended version of Porter's (1985) generic strategies includes a cost focus strategy (Akan et al., 2006), that similarly pursues outstanding customer service, operational efficiency, and actively controls product or service quality to create value for customers. Porter (1985) adds the pure cost leadership strategy focused on efficiency through vigorous pursuit of cost reductions in production, tight control of overhead costs and minimising distribution costs to allow highly competitive pricing in the market.

Treacy and Wiersema's (1995) product leadership strategy pursues a value proposition around product and service innovation to become the firm that is defining the state of the art in a particular product category over the long term. This value proposition aligns with the differentiation focus strategy (Akan et al., 2006) that offers specialty products or services at high price market segments. The differentiation strategy of Porter (1985) represents a mass market premium pricing strategy, made possible with a broad range of products and services that are associated with strong brand identification developed through innovative marketing and creative advertising.

A final strategy in the Treacy and Wiersema (1995) typology is that of customer intimacy, which can be understood as a differentiation strategy that is based on a more direct and personalised customer relationship building compared to the brand-based relationship in Porter's (1985) differentiation strategy, which focuses on a larger customer base. Customer intimacy thus extends Porter's typology on the differentiation end of the continuum in much the same way as Porter's (1985) cost leadership strategy extends the cost-based end of Treacy and Wiersema's (1995) typology continuum. The customer intimacy strategy moves differentiation from the mass market to smaller niche customer segments (see Box 2.12), offering bespoke value propositions that are total solutions which are specialised, based on the understanding of customers' needs achieved through long-term relationship building.

Box 2.12: Key Idea

Customer Segmentation Analysis

Customer segmentation is an important activity in the process of developing value propositions. A value proposition is tailored to address the needs and preferences of customers in a specific customer segment, thereby increasing the customers' willingness-to-pay in that segment. The willingness-to-pay refers not only to the price, but also how frequently a customer in a specific segment is likely to pay for a product or service.

Broadly speaking, there are three approaches that managers can take to developing an understanding of the customer segments in the market, either using previously published research, qualitative primary research (e.g., workshops or focus groups) or quantitative primary research approaches (e.g., surveying customers of a firm / in a specific market). When academically done, the literature is an important place to start but sometimes the qualitative approaches also support the development of the survey instrument for the quantitative segmentation research, in a mixed methods design.

A comparison of the results of a workshop-based approach and a customer survey-based approach to develop customer segments for two electric utilities in Switzerland showed that while the two approaches did not deliver exactly the same empirical results, they were very aligned (see Barjak et al., 2022). The key to a successful workshop-based approach to customer segmentation is a diverse stakeholder representation in the workshops. The key to a successful survey-based approach is a pre-phase of focus groups with purposefully selected customers to rigorously develop the survey instrument. Both of these approaches can benefit significantly from an initial engagement with the research literature to see if some customer segmentation has been done previously or not; this may even be sufficient for business needs.

Source: adaptation of Barjak et al. (2022)

2.7 DIGITAL BUSINESS STRATEGY FORMULATION

Digital business strategies can be defined as 'organizational strategy formulated and executed by leveraging digital resources to create differential value'. The formulation of digital strategies requires an assessment of how applicable resource-based and structure-conduct-performance (Five Forces Model) thinking, as well as established generic value creation strategies, are to strategy formulation in the digital age.

2.7.1 Digital Technologies and Strategy Formulation

Broadly speaking, the assessment of product-market position and choices about generic value creation strategies are part of the strategy formulation process, while considerations related to organisational structures, resources, and capabilities are related to strategy implementation (Henderson & Venkatraman, 1999). As with traditional strategising there is an assumption of an open system and dynamic interaction between the different actors in an industry / socio-technical system. Critically, a fit between the internal resources and capabilities and the external competitive positioning of a firm's product and services is essential for competitive success.

Thinking about the position of a firm in the socio-technical system of its industry, it is essential that firms assess the optimal scope of digital technologies for supporting business activities, the development of a digital transformation capability to support integrating the digital technologies into business activities, and digital governance for gaining access and control over required digital technologies. Internally the digital technology strategy must make choices about the IT infrastructure needed (portfolio of applications, hardware, data architectures, etc.), information systems processes, and related human skills needed from an information systems perspective (adaptation of Henderson & Venkatraman, 1999). See Box 2.13 for an exposition of the dimensions in a cyber-physical system.

Box 2.13: Digital Technology Resources and Capabilities in Cyber-Physical Systems

- Digital Technology Capability
- Information Technology (IT) Infrastructure Resources
- Computing Technology (CPT) Infrastructure Resources
- Communication Technology (CT) Infrastructure Resources
- Connectivity Technology (CNT) Infrastructure Resources
- Control Technology (CNTR) Infrastructure Resources
- Human IT Resources
- Human CPT Resources
- Human CT Resources
- Human CNT Resources
- Human CNTR Resources
- IT-enabled Intangible Resources
- CPT- enabled Intangible Resources
- CT-enabled Intangible Resources
- CNT-enabled Intangible Resources
- CNTR-enabled Intangible Resources

Source: integration of Bharadwaj (2000); Bharadwaj et al. (2013); and Sony & Naik (2020)

Today the relationship between competitive strategising and digital technology strategy needs to be more than just an alignment; the two disciplines rather need to be merged (Henderson & Venkatraman, 1999) to an integrated co-evolving digital strategy in which competitive and technological considerations are simultaneously considered. There is no longer a distinction between the competitive business strategy and the digital technology strategy (Bharadwaj et al., 2013). This approach has fundamental implications for thinking about the interaction of a firm with the socio-technical system within which it is embedded, i.e., the scope of the business (horizontal integration in Figure 2.3), as many of the digital technologies are fundamentally dependent on interacting with the broader ecosystem of the firm to create the intended value of the competitive strategy. At the same time digital technologies also raise important challenges for thinking about the digital scale of the business (vertical integration in Figure 2.3). But digital technologies also allow businesses to think more dynamically about the scale of a business, due to the potential of digital technologies to allow rapid scaling up/down in terms of storage and computing capacities, for example, as well as in terms of access to partners and information. This offers unique potential for thinking about how rescaling of the scale of the business could change competitive dynamics in an industry; think about the drivers of barriers to entry in the Five Forces Model. Digital technologies also have the potential to accelerate product/service launches and strategic decision-making, with fundamental consequences for industry competitive dynamics. Finally, digital strategising needs to consider the value creation potential in information abundance and new business models (Bharadwaj et al., 2013).

2.7.2 Implementing Digital Strategies to Create and Capture Value

As firm performance is additionally increasingly dependent on external stakeholders and the information and network effects of the digital age, the ability of firms to not only create but also capture value from the integration of digital technologies into business processes, products, and services, and leverage the associated information (Bharadwaj et al., 2013) is critical if above normal performance is to be achieved through sustained competitive advantage.

As described in Chapter 1.3, there are various ways to capture value from digitisation/digitalisation and strategic digital transformation. The seven action fields of digital transformation, as presented in Section 2.4.2, provide the topical context for value creation. Depending on the competitive pressure in the industry and the firm's individual situation (e.g., its digital maturity), these action fields (see Figure 2.10) can be considered holistically as a strategic digital transformation, as individual strategic initiatives/projects, or in the less mature form as digitalisation efforts.

From a resource-based view digital technologies in and of themselves are unlikely to lead to sustained competitive advantage due to their general availability and imitability. Instead, it is firms' dynamic capabilities to reconfigure non-digital and digital resources into capabilities (Volberda et al., 2021) that meet the criteria of being rare, value creating, non-substitutable, and inimitable that will allow firms to develop core competences that allow sustained competitive advantage (Bharadwaj, 2000). These resources and capabilities need to enable firm activities that that are either different to those of competitors or the execution of similar activities differently to support unique product/service market positional strategies. Under these conditions firms are more likely to be able to execute a generic value creation strategy that realises sustained competitive advantage.

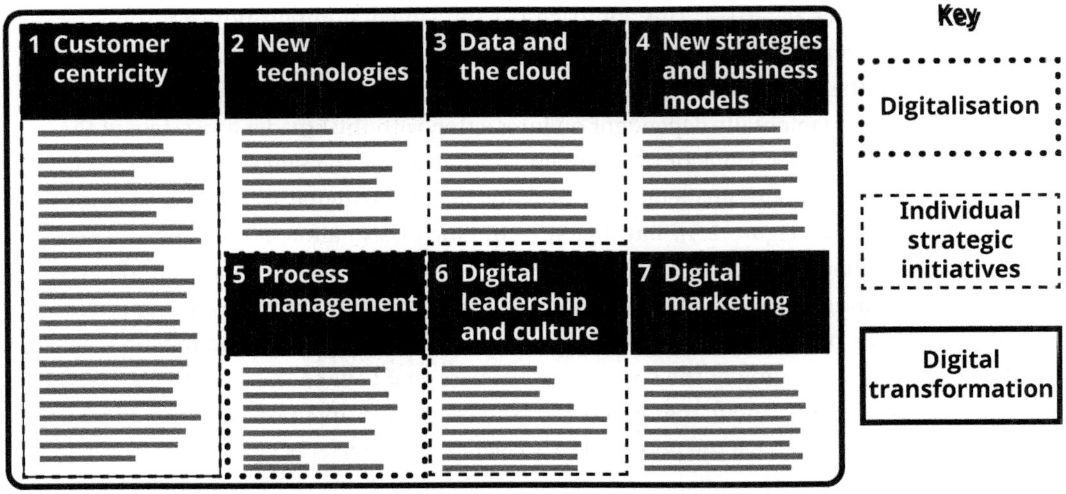

Figure 2.10 Value capture options based on the seven action fields of digital transformation

Source: Peter et al. (2020); Peter (2017, 2021, 2023, 2024)

2.8 CONCLUSION

The digital transformation of society, industries, and firms is bringing about fundamental changes in the way firms create and capture value. Digital strategies go beyond simply aligning technology and competitive strategies, instead managers are challenged to think about how digital technologies change the resources and capabilities of their firms and how the activities of the firm that allow chosen generic strategies are changed by this process. At the same time, the competitive forces that a firm is subject to are changing and there is a need to ensure that the activities of the firm are still fit for purpose in terms of realising the generic value creation strategies of the firm that underpin the market positional strategies that are being pursued.

Case Studies

Take your assigned or self-selected focal case study from week 1 (Chapter 1) or one of the cases provided with this text to complete the following tasks / answer the questions posed below.

Students should complete the following tasks:

1. Explain to what degree the case study shows evidence of the focal firm responding to changes in the socio-technical systems in which the firm is embedded (see Chapter 2.4.1).
2. Identify the stakeholders of the focal firm in the case and justify their selection.
3. Justify a set of metrics, e.g., key performance indicators (KPIs) based on the case study, that includes KPIs that account for the diverse stakeholders of the firm (see Boxes 2.2 to 2.5 for performance measures).
4. Explain which of the seven strategic action fields of digital transformation are relevant in the case study (see Box 2.8).

5 Discuss the degree to which you believe the firm in the case study is likely to be able to achieve sustained competitive advantage, from both an internal resource/capabilities-based, and external market positioning strategy perspective.
6 Given the value proposition in the case study, which other firms can you find online that would be members of the strategic group (i.e., which are strategically relevant) of the firm?
7 How similar do you consider the generic (digital) business strategies of the firms in the strategic group?

You will find the collection of case studies for strategic digital transformation in the Appendix and additional cases online at www.strategic-digital-transformation.com

Exercises

Discuss the following questions in your class, in your group or assignment:

1 What are the six dimensions of cyber-physical systems (see Box 2.7) that allowed Adidas to implement their Storefactory and Speedfactory concepts (see opening case)?
2 Identify an established industry/sector that you think has been transformed by digital technologies and explain how you believe the digital age has shifted the sources of firm strategic competitive advantage as a result.
3 Identify a firm of your choice that has achieved significant success by relying on digital technologies and discuss how well the success is explained by established theories of firm strategic competitive advantage.
4 Forming two small groups (2–4 students in each group), assign a pro and contra position to each group and debate the degree to which digital transformation allows firms to achieve sustained competitive advantage.
5 Identify a firm that is largely or entirely analogue in the way it serves its customers and formulate a strategy for the firm that is adequate for competing in the digital age.
6 Critically assess the enablers and inhibitors of the formulation of the firm strategy for the digital age developed in exercise 5.

Further Reading List

- Bharadwaj, A., El Sawy, O.A., Pavlou, P. A., & Venkatraman, N. V. (2013). Digital business strategy: Toward a next generation of insights. *MIS Quarterly*, 37(2), 471–82.
- Peter, M. K., Kraft, C., & Lindeque, J. (2020). Strategic action fields of digital transformation: An exploration of the strategic action fields of Swiss SMEs and large enterprises. *Journal of Strategy and Management*, 13(1), 160–80.
- Porter, M.E. (1979). How competitive forces shape strategy. *Harvard Business Review*, March–April, 137–45.
- Richard, P. J., Devinney, T. M., Yip, G. S., & Johnson, G. (2009). Measuring organizational performance: Towards methodological best practice. *Journal of Management*, 35(3), 718–804.

References

Adidas (2019) Adidas deploys Speedfactory technology at Asian suppliers by end of 2019. Adidas Press Release. Last accessed on 8 March 2024 from www.adidas-group.com/en/media/news-archive/press-releases/2019/adidas-deploys-speedfactory-technology-at-asian-suppliers-by-end-2019.

Akan, O., Allen, R. S., Helms, M. M., & Spralls III, S. A. (2006). Critical tactics for implementing Porter's generic strategies. *Journal of Business Strategy*, *27*(1), 43–53.

Baía, E. P., & Ferreira, J. J. (2024). Dynamic capabilities and performance: How has the relationship been assessed? *Journal of Management & Organization*, *30*(1), 188–217.

Barjak, F., Lindeque, J., Koch, J., & Soland, M. (2022). Segmenting household electricity customers with quantitative and qualitative approaches. *Renewable and Sustainable Energy Reviews*, *157*, 112014.

Barney, J. (1991). Firm resources and sustained competitive advantage. *Journal of Management*, *17*(1), 99–120.

Barney, J. B. (2001). Resource-based theories of competitive advantage: A ten-year retrospective on the resource-based view. *Journal of Management*, *27*(6), 643–50.

Barney, J. B. (2020). Measuring firm performance in a way that is consistent with strategic management theory. *Academy of Management Discoveries*, *6*(1), 5–7.

Bharadwaj, A. S. (2000). A resource-based perspective on information technology capability and firm performance: an empirical investigation. *MIS Quarterly*, *24*(1), 169–96.

Bharadwaj, A., El Sawy, O.A., Pavlou, P. A., & Venkatraman, N. V. (2013). Digital business strategy: Toward a next generation of insights. *MIS Quarterly*, *37*(2), 471–82.

Cherns, A. (1976). The principles of sociotechnical design. *Human Relations*, *29*(8), 783-792.

Eisenhardt, K. M., & Martin, J. A. (2000). Dynamic capabilities: What are they?. *Strategic Management Journal*, *21*(10–11), 1105–21.

Freeman, R. E. (1984). *Strategic Management: A Stakeholder Approach*. Boston: Pitman.

Henderson, J. C., & Venkatraman, N. (1999). Strategic alignment: A model for organizational transformation via information technology. *IBM Systems Journal*, *38*(2&3), 472–84.

Jaeger, N. A., Zacharias, N. A., & Brettel, M. (2016). Nonlinear and dynamic effects of responsive and proactive market orientation: A longitudinal investigation. *International Journal of Research in Marketing*, *33*(4), 767-779.

Kant, V. (2016). Cyber-physical systems as sociotechnical systems: a view towards human–technology interaction. *Cyber-Physical Systems*, *2*(1-4), 75-109.

Kaplinsky, R., & Morris, M. (2000). *A Handbook for Value Chain Research* (Vol. 113). Brighton: University of Sussex, Institute of Development Studies.

Kim, E., Nam, D. I., & Stimpert, J. L. (2004). The applicability of Porter's generic strategies in the digital age: Assumptions, conjectures, and suggestions. *Journal of Management*, *30*(5), 569–89.

Kraft, C., Lindeque, J. P., & Peter, M. K. (2022). The digital transformation of Swiss small and medium-sized enterprises: insights from digital tool adoption. *Journal of Strategy and Management*, *15*(3), 468–94.

Lindeque, J., & Samuel, O. (2022). The societal case for small business social responsibility: A review of the evidence of societal impact types and their relevance to stakeholders. In Kudlak, R., Barkmeyer, R., Preuss, L., & Heikkinen, A. (eds.) *The Impact of Corporate Social Responsibility* (44–69). New York: Routledge.

McGahan, A. M., & Porter, M. E. (1997). How much does industry matter, really?. *Strategic Management Journal, 18*(S1), 15–30.

Menz, M., Kunisch, S., Birkinshaw, J., Collis, D. J., Foss, N. J., Hoskisson, R. E., & Prescott, J. E. (2021). Corporate strategy and the theory of the firm in the digital age. *Journal of Management Studies, 58*(7), 1695–1720.

Müller, F. (2017). 'Knit for You': Wie Adidas mit einem Pop-up-Store die Zukunft einläutet. *Horizont.* Available from: www.horizont.net/marketing/nachrichten/Knit-for-You-Wie-Adidas-mit-einem-Pop-up-Store-die-Zukunft-einlaeutet-156393.

Networking and Information Technology Research and Development Program of the United States Government (NITRD; 2015). *Cyber Physical Systems Vision Statement.* Available from: www.nitrd.gov/nitrdgroups/images/6/6a/Cyber_Physical_Systems_(CPS)_Vision_Statement.pdf.

Newbert, S. L. (2007). Empirical research on the resource-based view of the firm: An assessment and suggestions for future research. *Strategic Management Journal, 28*(2), 121–46.

Panagiotou, G. (2006). The impact of managerial cognitions on the structure-conduct-performance (SCP) paradigm: A strategic group perspective. *Management Decision, 44*(3), 423–41.

Peter, M. K. (Hrsg.) (2017). *KMU-Transformation: Als KMU die Digitale Transformation erfolgreich umsetzen. Forschungsresultate und Praxisleitfaden.* FHNW Hochschule für Wirtschaft, Olten/Schweiz, www.kmu-transformation.ch.

Peter, M. K. (Hrsg.) (2021). *Strategieentwicklung im digitalen Zeitalter: Planung und Umsetzung der Digitalen Transformation.* FHNW Hochschule für Wirtschaft und Strategylab, Olten/Schweiz, www.strategische-transformation.ch.

Peter, M. K. (2023). *Digitaler Masterplan für KMU. So gelingt die digitale Transformation in Ihrem Unternehmen.* Verlag Beobachter Edition & Handelszeitung. Zürich/Schweiz, www.digitaler-masterplan.ch.

Peter, M. K. (2024). *The Digital Transformation Canvas. Develop and Implement Your Digital Strategy.* FT Publishing/Pearson, London/UK, www.the-digital-transformation-canvas.com.

Peter, M. K., Kraft, C., & Lindeque, J. (2020). Strategic action fields of digital transformation: An exploration of the strategic action fields of Swiss SMEs and large enterprises. *Journal of Strategy and Management, 13*(1), 160–80.

Piepponen, A., Ritala, P., Keränen, J., & Maijanen, P. (2022). Digital transformation of the value proposition: A single case study in the media industry. *Journal of Business Research, 150*, 311–25.

Porter, M. E. (1979). How competitive forces shape strategy. *Harvard Business Review*, March-April, 137–45.

Porter, M. E. (1985). *Competitive Advantage.* The Free Press. New York.

Porter, M. E. (1991). Towards a dynamic theory of strategy. *Strategic Management Journal, 12*, 95–117.

Porter, M. E. (1996). What is strategy? *Harvard Business Review*, November–December, 61–78.

Prahalad, C. K., & Hamel, G. (1990). The core competence of the corporation. *Harvard Business Review, 68*(3), 79–91.

Rêgo, B. S., Jayantilal, S., Ferreira, J. J., & Carayannis, E. G. (2021). Digital transformation and strategic management: A systematic review of the literature. *Journal of the Knowledge Economy*, 1–28.

Richard, P. J., Devinney, T. M., Yip, G. S., & Johnson, G. (2009). Measuring organizational performance: Towards methodological best practice. *Journal of Management*, *35*(3), 718–804.

Short, J. C., Ketchen Jr, D. J., Palmer, T. B., & Hult, G. T. M. (2007). Firm, strategic group, and industry influences on performance. *Strategic Management Journal*, *28*(2), 147–67.

Sony, M., & Naik, S. (2020). Industry 4.0 integration with socio-technical systems theory: A systematic review and proposed theoretical model. *Technology in Society*, *61*, 101248.

Szalkowski, G. A., & Johansen, C. (2023). Defining and measuring the effects of digital technologies on social sustainability: A systematic literature review. *Sustainable Development*, early view online.

Taylor, S. A., Hunter, G. L., Zadeh, A. H., Delpechitre, D., & Lim, J. H. (2020). Value propositions in a digitally transformed world. *Industrial Marketing Management*, *87*, 256–63.

Teece, D. J., Pisano, G., & Shuen, A. (1997). Dynamic capabilities and strategic management. *Strategic Management Journal*, *18*(7), 509–33.

Treacy, M., & Wiersema, F. (1995). *The Discipline of Market Leaders*. Reading, MA: Persus Books.

Verhoef, P. C., Broekhuizen, T., Bart, Y., Bhattacharya, A., Dong, J. Q., Fabian, N., & Haenlein, M. (2021). Digital transformation: A multidisciplinary reflection and research agenda. *Journal of Business Research*, *122*, 889–901.

Vial, G. (2019). Understanding digital transformation: A review and a research Agenda. *Journal of Strategic Information Systems*, *28*, 118–44.

Volberda, H. W., Khanagha, S., Baden-Fuller, C., Mihalache, O. R., & Birkinshaw, J. (2021). Strategizing in a digital world: Overcoming cognitive barriers, reconfiguring routines and introducing new organizational forms. *Long Range Planning*, *54*(5), 102110.

von Kutzschenbach, M., & Daub, C. H. (2020). Digital transformation for sustainability: A necessary technical and mental revolution. In Dornberger, R. (eds) *New Trends in Business Information Systems and Technology*. Studies in Systems, Decision and Control, vol 294. Cham: Springer.

Warner, K. S., & Wäger, M. (2019). Building dynamic capabilities for digital transformation: An ongoing process of strategic renewal. *Long Range Planning*, *52*(3), 326–49.

Wernerfelt, B. (1984). A resource-based view of the firm. *Strategic Management Journal*, *5*(2), 171–80.

Wiener, A. (2017). Inside Adidas' robot-powered, on-demand sneaker factory. *Wired*. Last accessed: 8 March 2024 from www.wired.com/story/inside-speedfactory-adidas-robot-powered-sneaker-factory.

3

DIGITAL TRANSFORMATION IN CONTEXT

INNOVATION AND SUSTAINABILITY

Learning Goals

By the end of this chapter, you should...

- Be able to explain the importance of innovation as the shared enabling activity for economic value creation and the realisation of a more sustainable future.
- Be able to explain the inherent tensions in the pursuit of societal, economic, and natural environmental sustainability.
- Be able to understand how a systems design approach can allow opportunities for digital transformation to contribute to realising the economic and societal sustainability transitions.
- Be able to critically evaluate the opportunities and risks associated with a sustainable digital transformation of firms, the economy, and society.

The Transition to Digital Photography

The transition from traditional analogue to digital photography is one of the most visible digital transformations of business and society in the last 30 years. The technological disruption of the photography industry and the resulting impact on the two dominant firms in the industry, Eastman Kodak (Kodak) in the US and Fujifilm (Fuji) in Japan, has been the subject matter of numerous academic papers and teaching cases. In most studies the focus is on the strategic responses of the incumbent firms to the digital technology innovation (Ho & Chen, 2018; Lucas & Goh, 2009), a rivalry that continues till this day. Most recently, for example, in March 2024 Fuji filed a patent infringement lawsuit against Kodak related to lithographic printing plate products (Fujifilm, 2024).

Fujifilm's strategic response is argued to have been better than that of Kodak, because Fujifilm was better able to respond to the change in technology more effectively. Kodak is argued to have fallen victim to the innovator's dilemma (Christensen, 1997) by not being able to overcome core rigidities in its business model to transition in time to the new digital technology. It could be argued that Kodak sought to align the traditional analogue film processing core competence and the innovative digital photography technologies, in contrast to Fujifilm that diversified. Fujifilm is argued to have responded more effectively in terms of balancing the exploitation of its established business and exploring the potential of digital photography technologies (Ho & Chen, 2018). This type of response is also referred to as organisational ambidexterity (O'Reilly & Tushman, 2011).

The case of digital innovation at Kodak is even more striking, given that the firm invented the digital camera in 1975, invented the first 'megapixel sensor capturing 1.4 million pixels to produce a high-quality 5 x 7 print', and began commercialisation of first professional and then consumer digital photography products in the 1990s. However, by this time new entrants in all aspects of digital photography posed a significant competitive threat to the firm. From a sustainability perspective, the emergence of digital photography in which Kodak played a significant role is an under-explored facet of the story.

Analogue photography requires significant equipment and chemicals for both manufacturing and processing film, and the transition to digital photography would at first take suggest a clear contribution to a more sustainable photography industry. The complexity of the potential for digital technologies is perfectly captured in the transition from analogue photography and film to digital technologies. While the move to digital images reduces the need for chemicals in the manufacturing and processing of film, as well as less unwanted image prints, green chemicals today would alleviate some of the associated negative impacts on the environment (Urth, 2024). At the same time, the manufacturing processes of the technologies in digital cameras and home printers used for printing photos are produced using potentially unsustainable processes and require rare minerals that must be mined. The analogue to digital photography transition is a perfect example of the dilemmas and contradictions in all sustainability transitions (Meadows et al., 1972), which have come to be known as wicked problems (Rittel & Webber, 1973).

Acknowledgement

The authors would like to thank Prof. Dr Michael von Kutzschenbach for the invaluable conversations that identified and helped shape this opening case study.

3.0 INTRODUCTION

Chapter 2 provided a detailed account of the complementary theories of how firms can think strategically about digitally transform to create value, with a focus on economic value creation and competitive advantage. This chapter puts the foundational strategic thinking from Chapter 2 into perspective, by focusing on the relationship between the digital and sustainable transformations of firms. The strategic and sustainable digital transformation of firms have a common emphasis on the potential for innovation to realise a digital and sustainable transformation of society, the economy, and firms. While the integration of digital technologies and the digital transformation of existing processes and activities for economic value creation have the potential for realising efficiency and effectiveness gains, it is in the innovation of how value is created that the potential for digital transformation to enable a transition to a fundamentally more sustainable future is seen. This chapter provides an introduction to this framing of strategic digital transformation.

3.1 INNOVATION AND VALUE CREATION

Innovation is implicit to the theories of strategic value creation in Chapter 2; this can be seen most clearly in the work of Michael Porter in relation to market conditions (Furman et al., 2002) and the need for firm adaptation in the dynamic capabilities literature (Salvato & Vassolo, 2018), where a central thesis is that competitive forces need to be allowed to exert their influences to actively incentivise innovation. Furman et al. (2002) show how the national innovation system and institutions governing national markets can establish the necessary conditions for enabling and encouraging innovation by firms. At the level of the firm and its employees, Salvato & Vassolo (2018) highlight how important interpersonal relationships and interpersonal communication are for realising the innovative potential of a firm and developing firm level dynamic capabilities, given the national institutional environment. In line with resource-based thinking, it is the social complexity of employee communication and relationship-building needed for an effective dynamic capability in a firm, that results in innovations that can lead to competitive advantage in the marketplace. It is employee communication and relationship-building within and across the boundaries of the firm enhance a firm's ability to sense/identify the need for change and then actually change/adapt, that increase the willingness of employees to contribute to and accept new ways of working and creating value, that are more aligned with the (changing) external environment of the firm.

Box 3.1: Full Oslo Manual Definitions of Innovation

The high-level definitions of the four main types of innovation according to the Oslo Manual are provided below, but the full document provides much more detail and is very accessible (OECD, 2005).

Product Innovation

'A product innovation is the introduction of a good or service that is new or significantly improved with respect to its characteristics or intended uses. This includes significant improvements in technical specifications, components and materials, incorporated software, user friendliness or other functional characteristics' (OECD, 2005, 51).

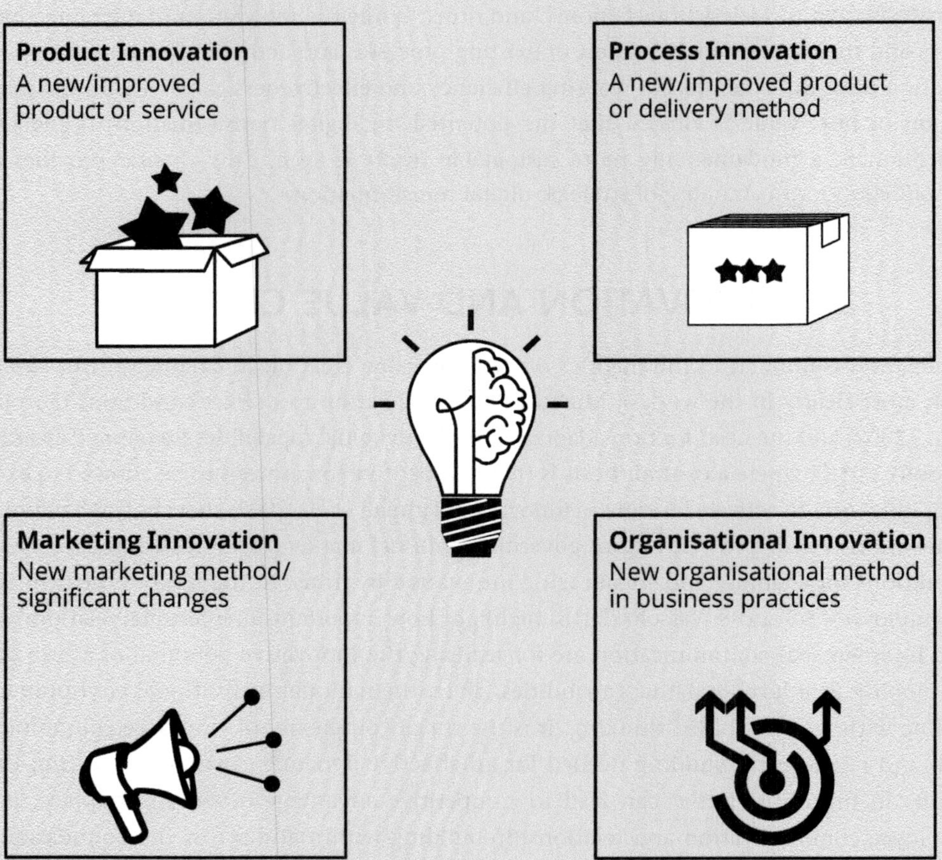

Figure 3.1 The four main types of innovation

Source: own illustration following OECD (2005)

Process Innovation

'A process innovation is the implementation of a new or significantly improved production or delivery method. This includes significant changes in techniques, equipment and/or software' (OECD, 2005, 51).

Marketing Innovation

'A marketing innovation is the implementation of a new marketing method involving significant changes in product design or packaging, product placement, product promotion or pricing' (OECD, 2005, 49).

Organisational Innovation

'An organizational innovation is the implementation of a new organizational method in the firm's business practices, workplace organization or external relations' (OECD, 2005, 51).

Innovation can then be understood as an adaptation response to perceived opportunities or risks in a dynamic external environment. According to the Oslo Manual (OECD, 2005), there are four firm level innovations that can be observed/measured (as per Box 3.1):

1 Product innovations, this includes products/goods or services;
2 Process innovations;
3 Marketing innovation; and
4 Organisational innovations.

O'Reilly and Tushman (2011) explain that the ability to innovatively respond to external change, enabled by a firms' dynamic capability (capabilities), can be understood as an exploration for new opportunities for value creation, that is often if not almost always in tension with the need to full exploit existing competitive advantages of a firm, by increasing efficiency and effectiveness in established processes. The reason for this tension is that the innovations resulting from exploratory (sensing) behaviour inevitably not only represent a threat to competitors but also established value creation strategies (exploitation) of the exploring firm. Firms that are able to effectively manage the tension between exploration and exploitation are described as ambidextrous organisations (O'Reilly & Tushman, 2011, pp. 13–15, Table 2) and the authors argue that there are five conditions that facilitate organisational ambidexterity:

1 There is a clearly articulated strategic intent that justifies ambidexterity in a firm.
2 A shared strategic vision and set of firm values that promote a common identity, but enable different cultures of value creation to co-exist in a firm.
3 A senior management team that explicitly owns the ambidextrous strategy, seen in common responsibility, rewards, and shared and consistent communication.

4 Separate business units with aligned architectures and targeted integration.
5 A leadership style that is able to facilitate the ambidexterity of the firm through effective conflict resolution and resource allocation to exploitative and exploratory activities.

Digital transformation of firms is then the integration of digital technologies into business organisations to enable more efficient and effective value creation (exploitation), as well as the transformation of the way value is created through digitally enabled innovation opportunities for new value creation (exploration). In Chapter 1 it was argued that a cyber-physical systems perspective should be adopted to understand the co-evolution of innovative technologies and society. In this chapter this systems thinking about the innovative potential of digital technologies is extended to reflect on the potential for the coevolution of the digital and sustainability transitions, specifically focusing on the potential of firms to contribute to a more sustainable future through their digital transformation in response to a changing society and economy.

3.2 SYSTEM DYNAMICS OF TECHNOLOGY AND SUSTAINABILITY TRANSITION MANAGEMENT

In the digital age firms should be understood as bounded open socio-technical systems (Wolstenholme, 2003), that take renewable and non-renewable resources inputs from the natural environment, as-well-as other resources, while combining (digital) technologies and employees to develop and maintain processes to transform these resources into outputs, products, and services that offer value to customers outside the firm, while producing waste outputs. It is through the impact of digital technologies and digital transformation on how firms create value that digital transformation can contribute to natural environmental, societal, and economic sustainability.

Systems dynamics approaches have long been advocated for, not only to understanding firms as business organisations, but also for understanding sustainability transitions (Marshall & Brown, 2003). Taking a system dynamics approach to understanding how digital transformation can contribute to sustainability is aligned with an understanding of digital transformation as the transformation of the socio-technical systems, within and external to the firm, that underpin economic and social activities in the digital age (Sony & Naik, 2020; Pappas et al., 2023). It is also clear that both these transformation processes are related to firm innovation and strategic value creation (Lan & Zhou, 2024). It is the shared potential for and dependency on firm level innovation, by both the digital and sustainability transitions, that is seen as the enabler of their alignment and even mutually reinforcing co-evolution (George et al., 2021; Lan & Zhou, 2024; Lu et al., 2023). This emphasis on firm innovation is at the same time also highly aligned with the competitive strategy literature and its emphasis on innovation as a critical source of competitive advantage.

Famously from a sustainability perspective, system dynamics (see Box 3.2) were applied to communicate socio-ecological system collapse at a global scale in *The Limits to Growth* by

Meadows et al. (1972). Their work is of particular interest when considering the potential of digital transformation to contribute to sustainability, as it was the first work to show that a technologically driven solution to an environmental problem, while solving the focal problem, can be expected to lead unintended negative outcomes that will require new efforts to solve their impact on the natural environment and society. Complex phenomena that require action, where any intended solution is likely to create new problems that demand attention due to the unintended effects of feedback loops, have come to be known as 'wicked problems' (Rittel & Webber, 1973). Digital transformation and sustainability represent two such complex contemporary global transformation processes that require and are creating dramatic societal change and are likely to be 'wicked' in nature.

Box 3.2: Elements of a System Dynamics Analysis

Elsawah et al. (2017) explains that systems dynamics was developed by Forrester (1961) and his colleagues at the Massachusetts Institute of Technology (MIT) and later extended to apply to large socio-economic systems. System dynamics analysis allows complex models to be developed to allow (1) predictive modelling, (2) development of holistic frameworks to understand feedback mechanisms, and/or (3) to facilitate stakeholder engagement through participatory modelling.

Elsawah et al. (2017) provide a succinct summary of five common diagrammatic system representation techniques for taking a system dynamics approach to integrating socio-ecological systems. For the purpose of this textbook, but also any business/managerial context, the goal of any attempt to model a complex socio-technical/socio-ecological system is to capture the complexity and uncertainties in a given system, while making the system accessible enough to allow decision-making. In this context system dynamics 'provides a set of conceptual and quantitative methods that can be used to represent, explore and simulate the complex feedback and non-linear interactions among system elements, management actions, and performance measures' Elsawah et al. (2017, p. 128). In the context of strategic digital transformation, these perspectives can be summarised as follow (see also Figure 3.2).

Managerial Decision-Making Perspective

- Dynamic Behaviour
- Problem(s)
- Action(s)
- Feedback Loops (Positive / Negative)

Information Systems / Knowledge Management Perspective (Digital Resources)

- Information / Knowledge Stocks
- Information / Knowledge Flows
- Information / Knowledge Flow Rates

(Continued)

Physical/Ecological Perspective (Renewable and Non-Renewable Natural Resources)

- Resource Stocks
- Resource Flows
- Resource Flow Rates

Figure 3.2 System dynamics in socio-economic systems

Source: own illustration following Elsawah et al., 2017

3.3 DIGITAL SUSTAINABILITY

The sustainability transition of society and business has over multiple decades seen a complex societal change take place, with every increasing emphasis being placed on creating natural environmental, societal, and economic value (Loorbach & Wijsman, 2013; Porter & Kramer,

2011). The Brundtland definition of sustainability (WCED, 1987) remains the foundational and institutionally legitimised definition of sustainable development, emphasising intergenerational responsibilities (see Box 3.3). A more practical and accessible framing of the Brundtland definition is found in the triple bottom line (TBL) framework (Marshall & Brown, 2003, see also Figure 3.3 and 3.4), which frames sustainability in terms of economic/profit (e.g., SDG 01 No Poverty; SDG 02 Zero Hunger; SDG 08 Decent Work and Economic Growth), social/people (e.g., SDG 04 Quality Education; SDG 05 Gender Equality) and the natural environment (SDG 12 Responsible Consumption and Production; SDG 13 Climate Action) (also see Box 3.6 for an explanation of these UN Sustainable Development Goals (SDG)). It should not be overlooked that the Brundtland definition of sustainability (WCED, 1987) clearly recognises the importance of technology and social organisation in achieving sustainable development. Digital technologies and the digital transformation of society and the economy represent such a significant transition in the way that the economy and society is organised that it may well offer an opportunity to shift the limits on the ability of the natural environment to meet present and future human needs. Digital technologies are in fact already positively impacting the world's poorest and allow more sustainable economic development.

Box 3.3: Brundtland Definition of Sustainability

'Sustainable development is development that meets the needs of the present without compromising the ability of future generations to meet their own needs. It contains within it two key concepts:

- the concept of "needs", in particular the essential needs of the world's poor, to which overriding priority should be given; and
- the idea of limitations imposed by the state of technology and social organization on the environment's ability to meet present and future needs.'

World Commission on Environment and Development (WCED, 1987, p. 37)

The sustainability transition of society and business has over multiple decades seen a complex societal change take place, with every increasing emphasis being placed on the creation of natural environmental, societal, and economic value by firms (Loorbach & Wijsman, 2013; Porter & Kramer, 2011). George et al. (2021, p.1000) have coined the term digital sustainability to refer to 'organizational activities that seek to advance sustainable development goals through creative deployment of technologies that create, use, transmit, or source electronic data'. This focus on the contribution of digital technologies to sustainable innovation (Lu et al., 2023) aligns with the work of Porter and Kramer (2006) on shared value creation, by emphasising the contribution of digital technologies and the digital transformation of firms to 'improvements or transformations in products, services, technologies and organizational processes, which not only aid companies in maintaining competitive advantage to sustain their business [economic performance] but also significantly improve their social and environmental performance (Cillo et al., 2019)' (Lu et al., 2023, n.p.). This framing is also in alignment with the Oslo Manual (OECD, 2005) definitions for the four main innovation types. From a more strategic perspective it also reflects the need to clearly articulated strategic intent that justifies ambidexterity in a firm seeking to balance exploitation and exploration during an organisational transformation process (O'Reilly & Tushman, 2011).

Box 3.4: Environmental Sustainability and Planetary Boundaries

The planetary boundaries framework (Richardson et al., 2023; Rockström et al., 2009) is based on the science of earth systems and the recognition that we today live in the Anthropocene, which recognises humans as the primary drivers of changes to earth systems. Earth systems are the fundamental systems that support life on earth and the planetary boundaries framework identifies nine boundaries that represent safe operating thresholds for human activity on earth, which if consistently crossed could lead to dramatic and unfavourable changes for humans in terms of the conditions on earth. The planetary boundaries include (Rockström et al., 2009, p. 7):

- 'the global biogeochemical cycles of nitrogen, phosphorus, carbon, and water; the major physical circulation systems of the planet (the climate, stratosphere, ocean systems);
- biophysical features of Earth that contribute to the underlying resilience of its self-regulatory capacity (marine and terrestrial biodiversity, land systems); and
- two critical features associated with anthropogenic global change (aerosol loading and chemical pollution).'

Taking this approach emphasises the impact of humans on the natural systems of earth and can at first glance seem to be entirely focused on natural environment sustainability; this however would not sufficiently recognise how central these earth systems are to economic and social activities of humans. It is because of this interconnectedness that many advocate for strong sustainability arguments. It is the breaching of six of the identified planetary boundaries that also underlies arguments of urgency for action on sustainability (Richardson et al., 2023). It is the potential for digital transformation to change how society consumes, and the value created in the economy and thereby reducing the pressure on the planetary boundaries that is driving the interest in digital sustainability, not least because digital transformation has already changed many processes of value creation that previously relied heavily on natural resource extraction and processing.

It is also clear that changes in the physical environment are an integral part of sustainable development (WCED, 1987, see also Box 3.5) and here the effects of digital transformation have the potential to reverse past impacts on the natural environment and contribute to economic and societal development that remains within the planetary boundaries of the earth (see Box 3.4). The planetary boundaries approach argues that the earth systems (land, water, living things, and atmosphere) have a maximum carrying capacity and that these limits are the boundaries for human development. The contribution of digital transformation to limiting the impact of firms on fundamental earth systems and thereby contribute to operating within the limits/boundaries of the carrying capacity of the earth is arguably the most foundational contribution that digital technologies and transformation can make to a more sustainable world. Sustainable development is, however, not only concerned with the natural environment, but also fundamentally concerned with social and economic development.

Box 3.5: Sustainability – An Emerging Success Factor for Digital Transformation

Corporate social responsibility (CSR) describes organisations' social responsibility in terms of sustainable business practices. Organisations have a responsibility for the impact of their activities on society and the environment (Peter, 2024).

The concept of sustainability can be traced back to the principle of sustainable forestry - Hans Carl von Carlowitz first wrote about the sustainable use of forests in 1713 – that is, a resource should only be used to the extent that it is able to regenerate (Schmithüsen, 2013). Sustainability means fulfilling our current need for resources without compromising the possible needs of future generations. Three criteria are equally important to determine sustainability: is it economically efficient, socially just and ecologically viable? In order to preserve global resources for the future, all decisions should balance these three criteria for sustainability.

Overall, more sustainable business practices lead to greater resilience at all levels of the business. This also has advantages for the organisation. Those who use less plastic are less exposed to oil price fluctuations. Those who pay fair wages stabilise the organisation's workforce. Fairness towards employees and customers increases the organisation's credibility and makes it more attractive as an employer. Sustainability also means that customer needs are taken seriously; for example, by offering barrier-free websites or analogue alternatives for older people without access to a computer.

There are three principles of sustainability, often referred to as the '3Rs', namely 'reduce, reuse, and recycle':

- Reduce: the best way to act in a sustainable manner is to reduce the amount an organisation (or consumer) consumes. This means using fewer resources, using less energy, producing less waste, travelling less, using less workspace, using less production space, and so on.
- Reuse: if something is used, there should be a plan for its reuse. It should be discussed before, for example, computers, mobile phones, production machines, or shop fittings are purchased.

(Continued)

- Recycle: materials or products that are no longer needed can be recycled into new materials and products. This will reduce the consumption of new raw materials, reduce the amount of waste, and slow down global warming.

The '3Rs' are also at the core of the circular economy. In this economic system, products and materials should be shared and used for as long as possible (reused) so that less must be produced (reduce). This also reduces the number of materials to be recycled (recycle).

In order to implement such measures, every organisation should develop a sustainability/CSR strategy in which concrete goals are formulated that are both suitable and feasible for the industry and the organisation itself. Sustainability can thus become a fourth success metric for digital transformation.

The definition of digital sustainability and the associated understanding of the needed innovation to realise more sustainable ways of doing business are clearly aligned with the widely adopted triple bottom line (Elkington, 1997) framework and the Brundtland definition of sustainability (WCED, 1987). As can be seen in Box 3.6, the potential contribution of digital technologies and digital transformation to realising a more sustainable world are available across all socio-economic contexts and promise to contribute to realising more sustainable outcomes for individuals, organisations, and society.

Box 3.6: Key Idea

United Nations Sustainable Development Goals (SDG)

The United Nations (UN) 2030 Agenda for Sustainable Development (United Nations, 2024) developed 17 Sustainable Development Goals (SDG), with a total of 169 targets, focused on people and peace (social sustainability), the planet (sustainability of the natural environment), and prosperity (economic sustainability), realised through partnership.

The UN SDGs have become a key reference framework for global efforts to collectively realise a more sustainable future; the digital transformation of business or the support that business can provide to the digital transformation of government and society is critical for most if not all of the 17 SDGs. This potential for a positive contribution from business to the SDGs, however, reflects the 'wicked problem' (Rittel & Webber, 1973) nature of grand challenges, e.g., sustainability transitions, in that business through its pursuit of sustainability through digital transformation inevitably creates new sustainability challenges. At the same time business and managers are seen to have the potential to make valuable contributions to solving grand challenges, like the sustainability transition, through co-creation of solutions with stakeholders in a 'wicked problem' (Sharma et al., 2022). Table 3.1 illustrates how the SDGs can be organised into the TBL and provides examples of digital transformation supporting the realisation of all 17 SDGs.

Table 3.1 UN Sustainable Development Goals

TBL	UN SDGs	Description (UN, 2024)	Examples of Interaction between Digital Transformation and UN Sustainable Development Goals	Sources
Social Sustainability	Goal 2	End hunger, achieve food security and improved nutrition and promote sustainable agriculture	Digital technologies have the potential to improve food distribution by government in India	Kumar et al. (2021)
	Goal 3	Ensure healthy lives and promote well-being for all at all ages	Digital technologies can empower patients, realise operational efficiencies in healthcare organisations, change work practices, and enable healthcare professionals' communication.	Kraus et al. (2021)
	Goal 4	Ensure inclusive and equitable quality education and promote lifelong learning opportunities for all	Participation in education can be supported through e-government policies in Egypt.	ElMassah & Mohieldin (2020)
	Goal 5	Achieve gender equality and empower all women and girls	E-government policies reduce gender inequalities by providing clearer evidence in Egypt.	ElMassah & Mohieldin (2020)
	Goal 6	Ensure availability and sustainable management of water and sanitation for all	Kenya's SDGs localisation, e-government and big data contribute to providing 'clean water and sanitation at the local level'.	ElMassah & Mohieldin (2020, 6)
	Goal 10	Reduce inequality within and among countries	Digital technologies and the digital transformation of societies socio-technical systems is urgently needed. Microfinance could play an important role in this regard.	Subramaniam & Masron (2024)
	Goal 11	Make cities and human settlements inclusive, safe, resilient and sustainable	The Philippines is seeking to develop sustainable and inclusive cities by focusing on (basic) infrastructure.	ElMassah & Mohieldin (2020)
	Goal 16	Promote peaceful and inclusive societies for sustainable development, provide access to justice for all and build effective, accountable and inclusive institutions at all levels	'e-governance policies in improving individual participation shows a high potential to engage with citizens at a local level, reduce negative impacts of political and economic crises' in Egypt	ElMassah & Mohieldin (2020, 6)

(Continued)

Table 3.1 (Continued)

TBL	UN SDGs	Description (UN, 2024)	Examples of Interaction between Digital Transformation and UN Sustainable Development Goals	Sources
	Goal 17	Strengthen the means of implementation and revitalise the global partnership for sustainable development	E-government policies 'build trust in and engagement with local government and civil societies institutions' in Egypt	ElMassah & Mohieldin (2020, 6)
Environmental Sustainability	Goal 7	Ensure access to affordable, reliable, sustainable and modern energy for all	Colombian electric utility AES Colombia has developed a digital platform using industry 4.0 technologies to provide affordable, reliable, sustainable and energy from a hydropower project.	Giraldo et al. (2021)
	Goal 13	Take urgent action to combat climate change and its impacts	Digitalisation has the potential to indirectly reduce greenhouse gas (GHG) emissions, while also directly impacting GHG through energy needs for data centers.	Liu et al. (2019)
	Goal 14	Conserve and sustainably use the oceans, seas and marine resources for sustainable development	A variety of monitoring digital technologies offer the potential to improve the management of the oceans, seas and marine resources, as well as inland waterways.	Liu et al. (2019)
	Goal 15	Protect, restore and promote sustainable use of terrestrial ecosystems, sustainably manage forests, combat desertification, and halt and reverse land degradation and halt biodiversity loss	The potential for digital transformation to enable a circular economy has significant potential for positively impacting land and resource use. There is however a critical need to engage in e-waste management, which is inevitable with digital technologies	Liu et al. (2019)
Economic Sustainability	Goal 1	End poverty in all its forms everywhere	Telephone and mobile penetration of sub-Saharan Africa (SSA) reduces poverty, while internet and broadband penetration drives poverty in SSA	Dzator et al. (2023)
	Goal 8	Promote sustained, inclusive and sustainable economic growth, full and productive employment and decent work for all	The digital economy development, digital infrastructure, industry and integration, and technology progress improve factor productivity in China	Zhang et al. (2021)

TBL	UN SDGs	Description (UN, 2024)	Examples of Interaction between Digital Transformation and UN Sustainable Development Goals	Sources
	Goal 9	Build resilient infrastructure, promote inclusive and sustainable industrialisation and foster innovation	Telephone and mobile penetration of sub-Saharan Africa (SSA) reduces poverty, while internet and broadband penetration drives poverty in SSA	Dzator et al. (2023)
	Goal 12	Ensure sustainable consumption and production patterns	The role of digital technologies in enabling the circular economy, including the participation of firms through the implementation of circular principles.	Vaezinejad et al. (2024)

Source: Dzator et al. (2023); ElMassah & Mohieldin (2020); Giraldo et al. (2021); Kraus et al. (2021); Kumar et al. (2021); Liu et al. (2019); Subramaniam & Masron (2024); UN (2024); Vaezinejad et al. (2024); Zhang et al. (2021)

The TBL provides a widely adopted and very accessible framework for business to systematically assess their potential for contributing to a more sustainable future, despite the critiques of the TBL (see Box 3.7) (Isil & Hernke, 2017). The TBL is also very well aligned with global political initiatives, such as the United Nations Sustainable Development Goals (SDG, United Nations, 2024) (see Box 3.6), as well as firm level approaches such as the shared value creation framework, which argues that firms can contribute to sustainability by undertaking their core value creating activities in such a manner that they realise both economic, social, and environmental goals (Porter & Kramer, 2011). It is the ability of the triple bottom line framework to be applied at all levels of analysis and its explicit focus on sustainable development that has led to its adoption in this text, in preference to the more recently developed and disseminated ESG approach, which focuses on environmental, social, and governance factors in assessing sustainability of firms in particular. Any consideration of how the digital transformation of firms, economies, and society contributes to sustainability, needs to understand these impacts not only at the firm level, but also systemically in terms of socio-technical and earth systems and their associated planetary boundaries (George et al., 2021) (see Box 3.4).

Box 3.7: Major Critiques of the Triple Bottom Line Approach to Sustainability

A common critique of the triple bottom line (TBL) is that it is based on an unrealistic assumption of the possibility for win-win outcomes for firm-level sustainability and has not sufficiently acknowledge the tensions that arise between the pursuit of economic, social and environmental sustainability (Isil & Hernke, 2017). The firm level approach to the pursuit of sustainability is also often critiqued for not sufficiently acknowledging the need for systemic change to achieve sustainability (Isil & Hernke, 2017). The strongest

(Continued)

critiques of the triple bottom line are made by those actors that believe that incremental change is not sufficient (weak sustainability) and only systemic change that leads to a break with current approaches to how value is created (strong sustainability) can lead to the needed sustainability outcomes.

- From a strong sustainability perspective, the 'unequivocal link between economic activity and planetary environmental degradation conclusively demonstrates the untenability of win–win' logic, which is only tenable if weak sustainability is assumed.
- From an ecological perspective the emphasis should be on systems at the planetary scale, and not on systems at the organisational level, if sustainability is to be achieved. There is an assumption that human economic activity needs to be understood as existing within the Earth's biosphere and is dependent on operating within the carrying limits of that biosphere; the planetary boundaries.

Source: Isil & Hernke (2017, p. 1234)

3.4 DIGITAL SUSTAINABILITY AND SYSTEM DYNAMICS: IDENTIFYING OPPORTUNITIES FOR IMPACT

There is clearly great interest in understanding the relationship between the digital transformation and the sustainability transition of the economy and society (Lan & Zhou, 2024; Li, 2022; Lu et al., 2023), as the potential of digital technologies to change the way value is created and consumed is seen as a significant opportunity for more sustainable development. Although this potential is only beginning to receive attention in relation to sustainability (George et al., 2021). Drawing on systems design, the triple bottom line and UN SDGs, Figure 3.3 provides a visual representation of the opportunities for a sustainable digital transformation. The digital transformation of business and society is argued to contribute to a more sustainable future by enabling firms to not only improve how the sustainability of how they currently create value (Porter & Kramer, 2011), but also potentially enable a transition to a fundamentally more sustainable way of creating value (Loorbach & Wijsman, 2013).

Sustainable Strategic Digital Transformation

From a system design logic, the opportunities for strategic digital transformation to contribute to sustainability lie in the impact of digital technologies and the transformation process on stocks and effects on flow rates between stocks, within and across the triple bottom line domains.

United Nations Sustainable Development Goals (SDG)

SDG 01: No Poverty
SDG 02: Zero Hunger
SDG 03: Good Health and Well-Being
SDG 04: Quality Education
SDG 05: Gender Equality
SDG 06: Clean Water and Sanitation

SDG 07: Affordable and Clean Energy
SDG 08: Decent Work and Economic Growth
SDG 09: Industry, Innovation, & Infrastructure
SDG 10: Reduce Inequality
SDG 11: Sustainable Cities and Communities
SDG 12: Responsible Consumption & Production
SDG 13: Climate Action
SDG 14: Life Below Water
SDG 15: Life on Land
SDG 16: Place, Justice and Strong Institutions
SDG 17: Partnership for the Goals

Sources: NOAA (2024); UN (2024)

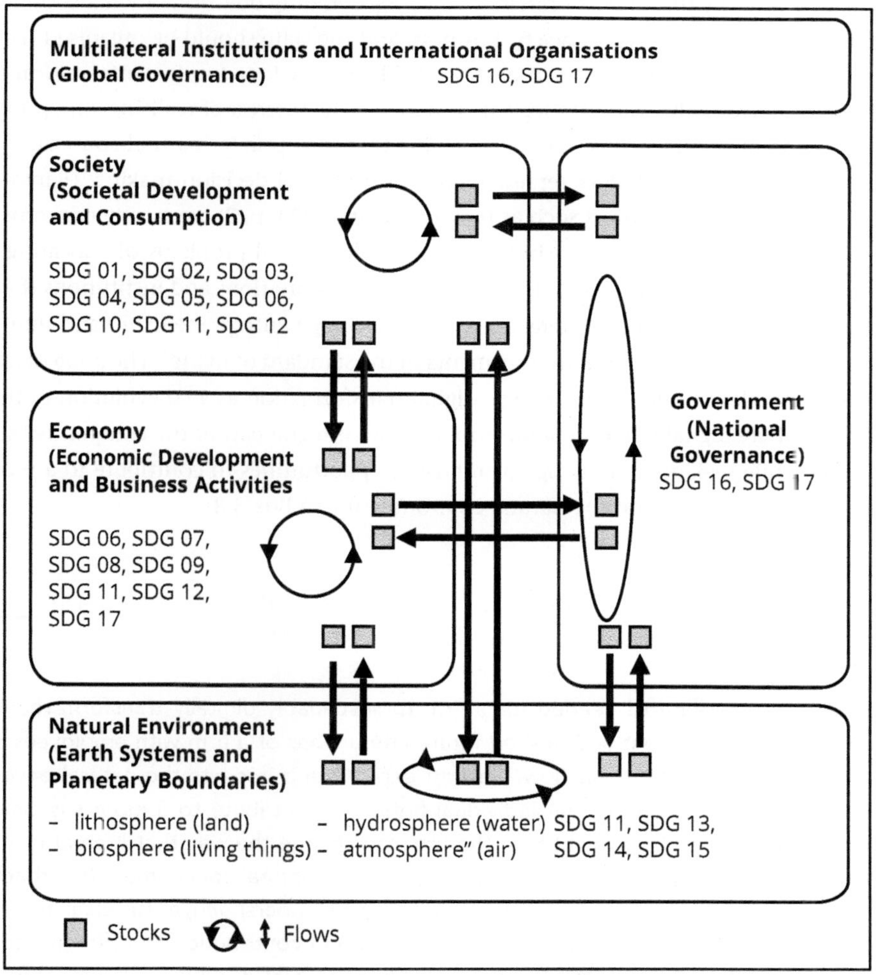

Figure 3.3 A system dynamics representation of the opportunities for sustainable strategic digital transformation

Source: own illustration following NOAA (2024); UN (2024)

The digital transformation of a firm is most likely to contribute to a transition to a more sustainable development of the economy and society if the firm does not only seek to realise internal efficiencies and effectiveness with digital technologies but rather seeks to take a lead in transforming the socio-technical systems within which it is embedded as well. Reflecting the ambidexterity literature, achieving a more transformative sustainable digital transformation of firms and society will require explicit strategic intent to align the digital and sustainability transitions (Loorbach & Wijsman, 2013). From a system design perspective this requires individual firms and their wider socio-technical systems to understand the socio-ecological systems that interact with the socio-technical systems creating economic value (see Figures 3.3 and 3.4). Once the systems are understood and their interactions mapped, it is possible for a firm to purposefully digitally transform to change the stocks and flows in the respective systems that are impacted by the firm's economic value creation activities.

This thinking is reflected in broader discussions on the potential need for a new paradigm for thinking about the strategic management of the firm (Bansal et al., 2024; Foss & Klein, 2024). Fundamentally this discussion reflects the long-standing question of what should be the primary foundation of how civil society, business, and the state should be organised (Lehrer & Delaunay, 2009), with authors like Bansal et al. (2024) arguing for a fundamental reform of how traditional strategic analysis and strategising is done, in the interest of realising 'an opportunity to pursue a complementary direction of modelling that incorporates natural constraints into a multi-level and multi-stakeholder representation of firm-level decision making' (Bansal et al., 2024, p. 28). Meanwhile, authors such as Foss and Klein (2024, p. 2) are raising concerns about the impact of such a fundamental shift away from 'the critical problems of allocating scarce resources to high-valued ends, building and sustaining organisations and institutions that coordinate tasks, jobs, and complex interactions, and encourage entrepreneurship and innovation that drives economic growth and improvements in the standard of living'. The approach in this textbook is to seek to understand strategic digital transformation as a co-evolution of business and society, where digital transformation should be an integral part of the competitive strategy of the firm, while seeking and taking advantage of opportunities to contribute to a more sustainable future for society and the natural environment (see Box 3.8).

Box 3.8: Firm Specific Assessment of the Potential for a Sustainable Digital Transformation

Knowing the specific foci needed for a firm to sustainably digitally transform requires understanding the current and desired future interactions of a firm with employees and customers in civil society and how the firm exploits and impacts the natural environment. At its core is a thesis that individual firms can contribute to a more sustainable future by actively thinking about how the firm can change the way that it creates value to have a positive impact on society, the economy and natural environment (Loorbach & Wijsman, 2013; Porter & Kramer, 2011). From a systems perspective it is clear that this approach requires an assessment of the firm's use and contribution to different stocks and also how the firm changes the rate of use of or contribution to (flows) different stocks across the three dimensions of the TBL (see Figure 3.4). A first high-level attempt at formulating the questions that need to be asked by managers and employees of a firm seeking to pursue a sustainable digital transformation is presented below.

Mini-Challenge

If you pick a specific firm, could you reformulate these questions to be tailored to the sustainable digital transformation of that firm?

Generic Questions

Opportunities for Digital Transformation to Contribute to a Sustainable Natural Environment (Planet dimension)

1 Focus on digital transformation that reduces the need to exploit non-renewable stocks of natural resources in the earth systems in economic value creation activities
2 Focus on digital transformation that increases the potential to exploit renewable stocks of natural resources in the earth systems in economic value creation activities
3 Focus on digital transformation that reduces the rate at which non-renewable stocks of natural resources in the earth systems are exploited in economic value creation activities
4 Focus on digital transformation that increases the rate at which renewable stocks of natural resources in the earth systems are exploited in economic value creation activities
5 Focus on digital transformation that either reduces or avoids economic value creation activities that result in undesirable/harmful stocks in the earth systems (e.g., pollution)
6 Focus on digital transformation that reduces the rate at which unavoidable undesirable/harmful stocks in the earth systems (e.g., pollution) are created

Opportunities for Digital Transformation to Contribute to a Sustainable Economy (Profit dimension)

1 Focus on digital transformation that contributes to desirable stocks of sustainability enabling capital for economic value creation activities
2 Focus on digital transformation that increases the rate at which desirable stocks of sustainability enabling capital for economic value creation activities is accumulated
3 Focus on digital transformation that either decreases the rate at which or it avoids undesirable stocks of unsustainable capital for economic value creation activities is accumulated
4 Focus on digital transformation that enables business processes that increase the sustainability of the use of capital stocks

Opportunities for Digital Transformation to Contribute to a Sustainable Society (People dimension)

1 Focus on digital transformation that contributes to desirable social stocks delivered by economic value creation activities

(Continued)

2 Focus on digital transformation that reduces undesirable social stocks delivered by economic value creation activities
3 Focus on digital transformation that increases the rates of increases in desirable social stocks delivered by economic value creation activities
4 Focus on digital transformation that decreases the rates of increases in undesirable social stocks delivered by economic value creation activities

Figure 3.4 Sustainability contributions of digital transformation (triple bottom line (TBL) framework)

Source: own illustration following Loorbach & Wijsman (2013); Marshall & Brown (2003); and Porter & Kramer (2011)

3.5 CONCLUSION

The chapter builds on strategic theories from Chapter 2, focusing on the relationship between digital and sustainable transformations. It argues that innovation in value creation is crucial for achieving a sustainable future through digital transformation.

Innovation is central to strategic value creation. The chapter discussed various theories, including Michael Porter's work on market conditions and dynamic capabilities literature. It emphasises the importance of interpersonal relationships and communication within firms for fostering innovation. The Oslo Manual's definitions of innovation types (product, process, marketing, and organisational) are also presented, guiding conversations on how digital innovation can support those innovation archetypes.

Firms are viewed as socio-technical systems that interact with natural resources and society. Digital transformation can contribute to sustainability by changing how firms create value, and the systems dynamics approaches help understand these complex interactions and the potential for digital transformation to support sustainability transitions.

The concept of digital sustainability, which involves using digital technologies to advance sustainable development goals, aligns with the triple bottom line framework (TBL), emphasising economic (profit), social (planet), and environmental (planet) metrics for organisational success, linking to the Brundtland (WCED, 1987) definition of sustainability and the United Nations Sustainable Development Goals (SDGs).

To conclude, this chapter explores how digital transformation can contribute to a more sustainable future. It emphasises the need for firms to align their digital and sustainability strategies and understand their interactions with socio-ecological systems. The potential for strategic digital transformation to reduce the exploitation of non-renewable resources and increase the use of renewable resources, supporting sustainable transformation from both an environmental and societal perspective, is discussed.

Case Studies

Take your assigned or self-selected focal case study from week 1 (Chapter 1) or one of the cases provided with this text to complete the following tasks and answer the questions posed below.

Students should complete the following tasks:

1 Describe the types of innovation that can be observed in the case study (see Box 3.1).
2 Describe how the innovation in the focal firm of the case study enables economic value creation and/or the realisation of a more sustainable future for the firm (profit dimension), society (people dimension), and the natural environment (planet dimension) (see Chapter 3.3).
3 Describe the primary flows and stocks in the internal systems of the firm and the external systems the firm is embedded. How do these systems interact?
4 Discuss the degree to which the case study shows evidence of the active management of inherent tensions in the pursuit of societal (people dimension), economic (profit dimension), and natural environmental (planet dimension) sustainability (see Chapter 3.3).
5 Explain the degree to which a systems design approach can be observed in the case study and if this is effectively leveraged to allow opportunities for digital transformation to contribute to the economical and societal sustainability transitions to be realised.
6 Discuss the opportunities and risks associated with a sustainable digital transformation of the economy and society in the case study.

You will find the collection of case studies for strategic digital transformation in the Appendix and additional cases online at www.strategic-digital-transformation.com

Exercises

Discuss the following questions in your class, in your group, or assignment:

1. How did digital photography impact and contribute to economic value creation and/or the realisation of a more sustainable future for the firm (profit dimension), society (people dimension) and the natural environment (planet dimension) (see also Box 3.8 in light of the opening case 'The Transition to Digital Photography')?
2. How should managers enable innovation projects to effectively achieve digital and sustainability goals?
3. How should managers respond to the inherent tensions in the pursuit of societal, economic, and natural environmental sustainability when undertaking the digital transformation of a firm?
4. Forming two small groups (2–4 students in each group), assign a pro and contra position to each group and debate the degree to which sustainability is important and critical for society and businesses (group 1), or overrated and not that important (group 2).
5. Critically evaluate the opportunities and risks associated with a sustainable digital transformation of the economy and society.
6. Discuss the degree to which it is possible for individual firms that are pursuing digital transformation, and seeking to do so in a sustainable manner, to contribute to realising global sustainability goals associated with the United Nations Sustainable Development Goals (SDG) (see Box 3.6).

Further Reading List

- Furman, J. L., Porter, M. E., & Stern, S. (2002). The determinants of national innovative capacity. *Research Policy, 31*(6), 899–933.
- O'Reilly III, C. A., & Tushman, M. L. (2011). Organizational ambidexterity in action: How managers explore and exploit. *California Management Review, 53*(4), 5–22.
- Salvato, C., & Vassolo, R. (2018). The sources of dynamism in dynamic capabilities. *Strategic Management Journal*, 39(6), 1728–52.

References

Bansal, P., Durand, R., Kreutzer, M., Kunisch, S., & McGahan, A. M. (2025). Time to renew our strategy paradigm: Environmental crises have revealed cracks in strategy's foundations. *Journal of Management Studies, 62*(2), 965–85.

Christensen, C. (1997). *The Innovator's Dilemma: When New Technologies Cause Great Firms to Fail.* Harvard Business School Press.

Cillo, V., Petruzzelli, A. M., Ardito, L., & Del Giudice, M. (2019). Understanding sustainable innovation: A systematic literature review. *Corporate Social Responsibility and Environmental Management, 26*(5), 1012–25.

Dzator, J., Acheampong, A. O., Appiah-Otoo, I., & Dzator, M. (2023). Leveraging digital technology for development: Does ICT contribute to poverty reduction? *Telecommunications Policy*, *47*(4), 102524.

Elkington J. (1997). *Cannibals with Forks: Triple Bottom Line of 21st Century Business.* Capstone: Oxford.

ElMassah, S., & Mohieldin, M. (2020). Digital transformation and localizing the sustainable development goals (SDGs). *Ecological Economics*, *169*, 106490.

Elsawah, S., Pierce, S. A., Hamilton, S. H., Van Delden, H., Haase, D., Elmahdi, A., & Jakeman, A. J. (2017). An overview of the system dynamics process for integrated modelling of socio-ecological systems: Lessons on good modelling practice from five case studies. *Environmental Modelling & Software*, *93*, 127–45.

Forrester, J. (1961). *Industrial Dynamics.* Productivity Press, Portland.

Forrester, J. (1969). *Urban Dynamics.* MIT Press, Cambridge.

Foss, N. J. and Klein, P. G. (2025), Do we need a 'new strategy paradigm'? No. *Journal of Management Studies*, *62*(2), 986–1003.

Fujifilm (2024) Fujifilm Files Patent Infringement Lawsuit Against Eastman Kodak Company. Accessed on 8 May 2024 from www.fujifilm.com/us/en/news/graphic-arts-and-printing/fujifilm-files-patent-infringement-lawsuit-against-eastman-kodak-co.

Furman, J. L., Porter, M. E., & Stern, S. (2002). The determinants of national innovative capacity. *Research Policy*, *31*(6), 899–933.

George, G., Merrill, R. K., & Schillebeeckx, S. J. (2021). Digital sustainability and entrepreneurship: How digital innovations are helping tackle climate change and sustainable development. *Entrepreneurship Theory and Practice*, *45*(5), 999–1027.

Giraldo, S., la Rotta, D., Nieto-Londoño, C., Vásquez, R. E., & Escudero-Atehortúa, A. (2021). Digital transformation of energy companies: A colombian case study. *Energies*, *14*(9), 2523.

Ho, J. C., & Chen, H. (2018). Managing the disruptive and sustaining the disrupted: The case of Kodak and Fujifilm in the face of digital disruption. *Review of Policy Research*, *35*(3), 352–71.

Isil, O., & Hernke, M. T. (2017). The triple bottom line: A critical review from a transdisciplinary perspective. *Business Strategy and the Environment*, *26*(8), 1235–51.

Kraus, S., Schiavone, F., Pluzhnikova, A., & Invernizzi, A. C. (2021). Digital transformation in healthcare: Analyzing the current state-of-research. *Journal of Business Research*, *123*, 557–67.

Kumar, A., Paul, M., & Upadhyay, P. (2021). From physical food security to digital food security. Delivering value through blockchain. *Scandinavian Journal of Information Systems*, *33*(2), Article 5.

Lan, L. & Zhou, Z. (2024). Complementary or substitutive effects? The duality of digitalization and ESG on firm's innovation. *Technology in Society*, 102567.

Lehrer, M., & Delaunay, C. (2009). Multinational enterprises and the promotion of civil society: The challenge for 21st century capitalism. *California Management Review*, *51*(4), 126–47.

Li, L. (2022). Digital transformation and sustainable performance: The moderating role of market turbulence. *Industrial Marketing Management*, *104*, 28–37.

Liu, R., Gailhofer, P., Gensch, C.-O., Köhler, A., & Wolff, F. (2019). Impacts of the digital transformation on the environment and sustainability. Issue Paper under Task 3 from the 'Service contract on future EU environment policy'. Öko-Institut e.V., Berlin, 20/12/2019.

Loorbach, D., & Wijsman, K. (2013). Business transition management: exploring a new role for business in sustainability transitions. *Journal of Cleaner Production*, 45, April, 20–8.

Lu, H. T., Li, X., & Yuen, K. F. (2023). Digital transformation as an enabler of sustainability innovation and performance–Information processing and innovation ambidexterity perspectives. *Technological Forecasting and Social Change, 196*, 122860.

Lucas Jr, H. C., & Goh, J. M. (2009). Disruptive technology: How Kodak missed the digital photography revolution. *The Journal of Strategic Information Systems, 18*(1), 46–55.

Marshall, S.R., & Brown, D. (2003). Corporate environmental reporting: what's in a metric?. *Business Strategy and the Environment*, *12*(2), 87-106.

Meadows, D., Meadows, D., & Randers, J., 1972. *The Limits to Growth*. Universe Books, New York.

National Oceanic and Atmospheric Administration (NOAA, 2024) *Information and Activities for Earth Science Students and Teachers.* NOAA Earth System Research Laboratories (ESRL). Accessed 7 May 2024 from https://gml.noaa.gov/outreach/info_activities.

O'Reilly III, C. A., & Tushman, M. L. (2011). Organizational ambidexterity in action: How managers explore and exploit. *California Management Review, 53*(4), 5–22.

OECD (2005). *Oslo Manual: Guidelines for Collecting and Interpreting Innovation Data, 3rd Edition*, The Measurement of Scientific and Technological Activities, OECD Publishing, Paris, www.oecd.org/en/publications/oslo-manual_9789264013100-en.html.

Pappas, I. O., Mikalef, P., Dwivedi, Y. K., Jaccheri, L., Krogstie, J., 2023. Responsible digital transformation for a sustainable society. *Information Systems Frontiers*, *25*(3), 945–53.

Peter, M.K. (2024). *The Digital Transformation Canvas. Develop and implement Your Digital Strategy*. FT Publishing/Pearson, London/UK, www.the-digital-transformation-canvas.com.

Porter, M. E., & Kramer, M. R. (2011). Creating Shared Value. *Harvard Business Review, 1*(2), 62–77.

Richardson, K., Steffen, W., Lucht, W., Bendtsen, J., Cornell, S. E., Donges, J. F., ... & Rockström, J. (2023). Earth beyond six of nine planetary boundaries. *Science Advances, 9*(37), eadh2458.

Rittel, H. W., & Webber, M. M. (1973). Dilemmas in a general theory of planning. *Policy Sciences*, *4*(2), 155–69.

Rockström, J., Steffen, W., Noone, K., Persson, Å., Chapin, F. S., Lambin, E., Lenton, T. M., Scheffer, M., Folke, C., Schellnhuber, H. J., Nykvist, B., de Wit, C. A., Hughes, T., van der Leeuw, S., Rodhe, H., Sörlin, S., Snyder, P. K., Costanza, R., Svedin, U., ... Foley, J. (2009). Planetary boundaries: Exploring the safe operating space for humanity. *Ecology and Society*, *14*(2), Article 32.

Salvato, C., & Vassolo, R. (2018). The sources of dynamism in dynamic capabilities. *Strategic Management Journal*, *39*(6), 1728–52.

Schmithüsen, F. J. (2013). Three hundred years of applied sustainability in forestry. *Unasylva, 64*(240), 3-11.

Sharma, G., Greco, A., Grewatsch, S., & Bansal, P. (2022). Cocreating forward: How researchers and managers can address problems together. *Academy of Management Learning & Education*, *21*(3), 350–68.

Sony, M., & Naik, S., 2020. Industry 4.0 integration with socio-technical systems theory: A sys-tematic review and proposed theoretical model. *Technology in Society*, *61*, 101248.

Subramaniam, Y., & Masron, T. A. (2024). Digital technologies, poverty and microfinance in developing countries. *Journal of Strategy and Management*, early online view.

Tajvidi, R., & Karami, A. (2021). The effect of social media on firm performance. *Computers in Human Behavior*, *115*, 105174.

United Nations (UN, 2024) Transforming our world: The 2030 Agenda for Sustainable Development. Accessed from https://sdgs.un.org/2030agenda on 29 April 2024.

Urth HQ (2024) Is Analogue or Digital Photography More Environmentally Friendly? Accessed on 8 May 2024 from https://magazine.urth.co/articles/analogue-versus-digital-photography-eco-friendly.

Vaezinejad, S., Kouhizadeh, M., Schniederjans, D., & Sarkis, J. (2024). *Digital Technologies and the Circular Economy: A Theoretical Perspective*. Available at SSRN 4748938.

Wolstenholme, E.F. (2003). Towards the definition and use of a core set of archetypal structures in system dynamics. *System Dynamics Review*, *19*(1), 7–26.

World Commission on Environment and Development (WCED, 1987) *Our Common Future*, Oxford and New York: Oxford University Press.

Zhang W, Zhao S, Wan X, & Yao Y (2021) Study on the effect of digital economy on high-quality economic development in China. *PLOS ONE*, *16*(9), e0257365.

4
STRATEGIC ACTION FIELD OF CUSTOMER CENTRICITY

Learning Goals

By the end of this chapter, you should...

- Be able to explain the importance of customer centricity for firms in the digital age.
- Be able to explain how digital technologies are uniquely suited to realising customer centricity.
- Be able to critically evaluate both the opportunities and challenges of customer-centric strategies for firms in the digital age.
- Be able to critically evaluate the suitability of a customer-centric value creation strategy for firms in the digital age.
- Be able to critically evaluate how well a firm is leveraging digital technologies to realise a customer-centric value creation strategy.
- Be able to develop a digital technology enabled customer-centric value creation strategy for firms in the digital age.

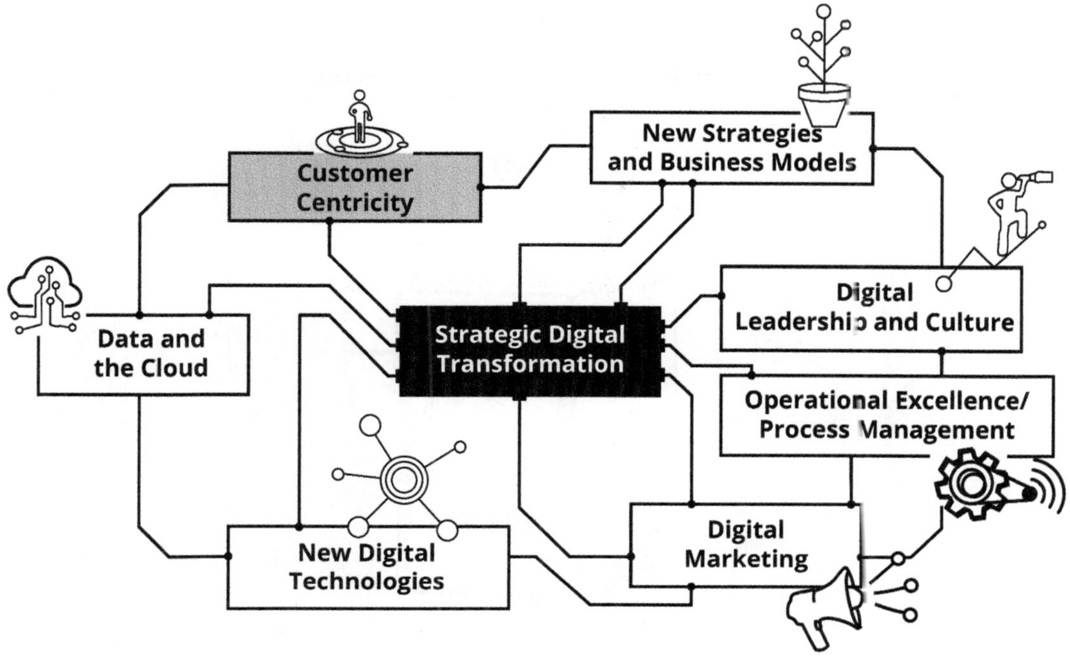

Figure 4.1 Customer centricity is the first Strategic Action Field of Digital Transformation

Source: Peter et al. (2020); Peter (2017, 2021, 2023, 2024)

General Electric's Co-Creation Strategy for the Opal™ Nugget Ice Maker

The General Electric (GE) Appliances crowdsourcing open innovation strategy for the Opal Nugget Ice Maker shows how even large firms that face no resource constraints can use open innovation through co-creation strategies as a way to identify new products in a customer-centric manner (Ivanov, 2019). This integration of customers into the design processes represents a unique approach to customer centricity as it ensures that the preferences and jobs to be done of customers are designed into the product from the very start of product development and the associated value proposition. GE Appliances for example leveraged its FirstBuild™ (2024) co-creation community to design 'a residential ice maker that would appeal to nugget ice enthusiasts' (General Electric, 2015) and in 2016 made it available to purchase via the crowdfunding platform Indiegogo (2024). Natarajan Venkatakrishnan, director of FirstBuild™, explained that at the time consumer surveys showed a strong preference for nugget ice over crescent ice and that First Build™ had 'developed Opal to offer an affordable nugget ice maker for home use and we are using Indiegogo as a selling platform to gauge market acceptance of the product'. This active scanning of the market and relationship building with key customers allows firms to anticipate and respond to customer needs before competitors.

(Continued)

Figure 4.2 Co-creation of the Opal Nugget Ice Maker

Source: own illustration following General Electric (2015, 2024)

GE's FirstBuild™ started with a first micro-factory on the University of Louisville campus and an online forum (General Electric, 2015), today GE Appliances (2018) leverages FirstBuild™ as 'a global co-creation community backed by GE Appliances, a Haier company, [which] has already engaged thousands of makers in person and online to invent a new world of appliances'. By 2018 FirstBuild™ had centres of excellence in Hyderabad, India, Louisville, Kentucky, and Shanghai, China (GE Appliances, 2018).

Source: GE Appliances (2018), General Electric (2024)

4.0 INTRODUCTION

Digital technologies and the digital transformation of firms have created new opportunities for engaging and understanding customers. Firms that are able to leverage these opportunities to build relationships with their customers will be able to effectively realise a customer-centric approach to creating value. Adopting a customer-centric approach, that leverages digital technologies, tools, and the digital transformation of business and society, allows improvements in customer experiences and the potential for tailored products and services (Peter, 2023, 2024).

Strategically, customer centricity has been shown to be a key strategic action field in digital transformation of firms, speaking directly to Treacy and Wiersema's (1995) generic strategy of customer intimacy. Customer centricity is often discussed in relation to a broader customer orientation, reflecting the relationship between a customer intimacy strategy focused on long-term personalised relationship building with focal customers to allow specialised solutions for niche customer segments and the arguably broader niche differentiation strategy of Porter (1985), that focuses on brand-based customer relationship building for larger customer segments. The discussion of customer centricity below understands that it is possible to be customer-centric for both individualised relationship-based and broader brand-based customer segment strategies, but that digital technologies – in light of a holistic, strategic digital transformation – need to be applied differently for these alternative approaches to be realised successfully.

4.1 CUSTOMER CENTRICITY

Peter et al. (2020) show that customer centricity is one of the seven strategic action fields of the digital transformation of firms. Peter (2024, p. 63) and Peter et al. (2020) argue that customer centricity is 'reflected in an organisation's ability to meet the needs and expectations of its customers by responding to them as precisely as possible'. Fader and Winer (2012, p. 9) go even further in seeking to explain customer centricity as a strategy that seeks to 'fundamentally align a company's products and services with the wants and needs of its most valuable customers'.

Table 4.1 compares how such a customer-centric approach differs from a product centric approach and how there is a shift from a focus on what and how the firm is producing to understanding how the firm can serve its customers by meeting their needs and wants. The more customer-centric the firm, the more the internal activities are organised to respond to the customer, ideally within the development of a long-term customer relationship, which can be either highly personalised or more general in nature depending on the product and market segmentation. Table 4.1 makes clear that for those firms that are not already actively developing a customer-centric approach, there will be a need for substantial transformation in the philosophy, business orientation, organisational structure, organisational focus, performance metrics, how sales take place, and the nature of the value of customer data (Shah et al., 2006). It is the transformational nature of integrating digital technologies into firms that opens the potential for firms to simultaneously also realise a more customer-centric approach. Critically digital transformation of a firm results in far greater potential for generating and using customer data needed for a more customer-centric strategy.

Customer centricity has, however, also increasingly been subject to critique as a leading logic for seeking competitive advantage (Gummesson, 2008a,b). (Gummesson (2008b) critiques customer centricity by questioning its practicality and effectiveness as a universal marketing strategy. Gummesson argues that while customer orientation has been a popular concept for decades, it is often not fully implemented due to its inherent challenges. One major issue is the unrealistic expectation that a single stakeholder, the customer, can be the sole focus of a company's efforts. Instead, Gummesson proposes 'balanced centricity', which considers the needs of multiple stakeholders, including employees, shareholders, and suppliers. Additionally, Gummesson highlights the complexity of customer needs and the difficulty in consistently delivering value.

Table 4.1 Product vs customer-centric approaches

Dimension	Product-Centric Approach	Customer-Centric Approach
Philosophy	• Sell products; we'll sell to whoever will buy	• Start with the customer ('we serve the customer')
Business Orientation	• Transaction-oriented	• Relationship-oriented
Product Positioning	• Highlight product features and advantages	• Highlight product's benefits in terms of meeting individual customer needs
Organisational Structure	• Product profit centres • Product managers • Product sales team	• Customer segment centres • Customer relationship managers • Customer segment sales team
Organisational Focus	• Internally focused • New product development • New account development • Market share growth • Customer relations are issues for the marketing department	• Externally focused • Customer relationship development, • Profitability through customer loyalty • Employees are customer advocates
Performance Metrics	• Number of new products • Profitability per product • Market share by product / sub-brands	• Share of wallet of customers • Customer satisfaction • Customer lifetime value • Customer equity
Management Criteria	• Portfolio of products	• Portfolio of customers
Selling Approach	• How many customers can we sell this product to?	• How many products can we sell this customer?
Customer Knowledge	• Customer data are a control mechanism	• Customer knowledge is a valuable asset

Source: adapted from Table 1 in Shah et al. (2006)

Therefore, at a fundamental level if all firms were to adopt and implement a customer-centric approach, then it cannot be expected that customer centricity would lead to a competitive advantage, it would become necessary simply to maintain parity with competitors. It is also unclear how completely a customer-centric approach has truly been implemented by firms and if all customers want such a close relationship with the firms offering them products and services. Customer centricity as a concept has also been critiqued for not sufficiently addressing the complexities of the relationships between price, quality, and value, as perceived by customers. Indeed, the subjective perception of price, quality, and value are subject to the influences of customers' individual personalities, lifestyles, and group membership for business-to-consumer (B2C) customers. Business-to-business (B2B) customers will equally be influenced by the unique conditions under which a firm is doing business. At the same time managers may be concerned that committing to realising customer centricity will bring additional costs with limited gains. Managers also face challenges in developing performance indicators for managing the implementation of a customer-centric approach to serving customers. Finally, the emphasis that customer centricity places on long-term relationships with (key) customers for firm success requires the implementation of customer relationship management systems (CRM), but the effectiveness of CRM systems is very reliant on the capturing and analysis of customer data, so that it can be used for making decisions and implementing activities (Gummesson, 2008b). The critical role of customer data is increasingly subject to regulatory control to protect customers and protect their privacy, which may constrain the ability of firms to collect customer data depending on the legal jurisdiction they are operating in.

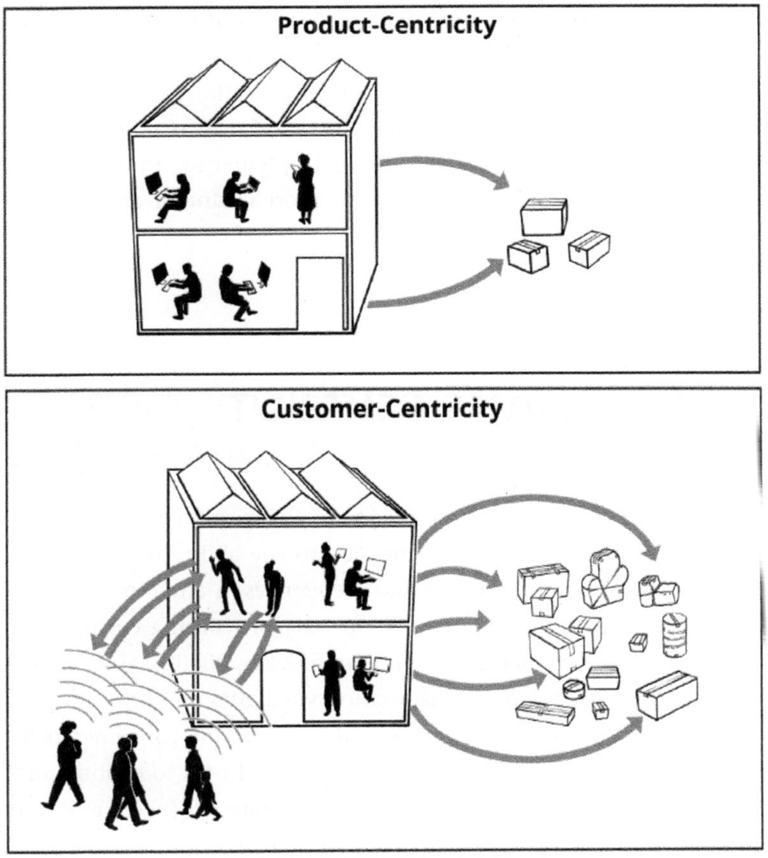

Figure 4.3 Product vs customer centricity

Source: own illustration

4.2 CUSTOMER CENTRICITY AND DIFFERENT CUSTOMER TYPES

The appropriateness of a customer-centric firm strategy can be explored by considering the conditions under which customer centricity would lead to a competitive advantage in B2C and B2B markets for different products and/or services in terms of their price, quality, and value propositions and value realisation (Gummesson, 2008b). For the firm considering a customer-centric approach the fundamental consideration is whether it is possible to realise a long-term relational approach to serving customers. A spontaneous response may be that this is only possible with customers that are purchasing expensive products and/or services or large volumes of less expensive products over time, with this most likely being the case in B2B markets When thinking of B2C markets, the luxury consumer goods industry may initially appear to reflect a customer-centric approach, but closer inspection suggests that a product-based approach is driving the value proposition and realisation in the market. Instead, the large volume retail sector, with firms like Tesco and Sainsbury in the UK with their loyalty schemes, arguably reflect a more customer-centric approach. It has long been argued that these retail firms through their data on consumer purchasing patterns over time better understand the needs, wants, and preferences of customers than the customers themselves do, allowing customer loyalty to be realised (Rowley, 2007). It is thus advisable to be careful in making assumptions about the degree to which customer centricity is being implemented in a given firm or sector, which is not to exclude the potential for taking a more customer-centric approach, given the digital transformation of a firm.

4.3 CUSTOMER CENTRICITY, DIGITAL TECHNOLOGIES, AND THE DATA ECONOMY

Customer centricity has grown in prominence in parallel with the increasing digital transformation of business, society and government, due to the ability of digital technologies to facilitate the capturing of customer needs and preferences in a manner that was previously prohibitively complex and expensive. The complexity of realising customer centricity is a recognised barrier to its full implementation (Gummesson, 2008b). Digital technologies are highly scalable, allowing small group collaboration via digital platforms for innovation projects (Ivanov, 2019), while also allowing large datasets about consumer behaviour to be created (Sestino et al., 2025). The ability of digital technologies to capture and understand data about customers' unobservable needs and wants, behaviour (needs and wants that have been acted on), and preferences has fundamentally changed the barriers to realising customer centricity for many firms. At the same time digital technologies are enabling the needs and wants of customers to be addressed, by offering products and services that more closely reflect customer preferences (see Box 4.1).

Box 4.1: Artificial Intelligence and Customer Centricity

The combination of artificial intelligence (AI) technology and the collection of as much data about customer wants, needs, and preferences as possible is allowing customer centricity to be realised in the retail industry. The application of AI to these large datasets allows retail firms to 'customize their offerings, create personalized shopping experiences, and make the purchase process simpler and more convenient' (Latinovic and Chatterjee, 2019, n.p.). Three key opportunities for improving the competitive advantage of retail firms that emerge as a result are as follows:

1 AI allows firms to better identify the customers that they should cultivate.
2 AI enables firms to develop individualised product recommendations.
3 AI supports the development of a more seamless shopping experience.

Source: Latinovic & Chatterjee (2019)

Digital technologies and the digital transformation of business, society, and government are at the heart of the growing data economy, which is 'a global ecosystem where data is gathered, organized, and exchanged to create economic value' (Sestino et al., 2025, p. 1). This emerging and increasingly important change in economic value creation is featured by risks, opportunities, and challenges, that need to be understood and responded to (see Box 4.2). The increasingly digitalised normalcy and associated data generation from the adoption of digital technologies has significant potential to advance the ability of firms to realise customer-centric approaches to doing business. The hyper-connectivity of the digital age, the ability of digital technologies and devices to capture and store data, and the emergence of increasingly sophisticated analytical techniques for exploiting large datasets are fundamental characteristics of the digital age (Sestino et al., 2025). Especially the Internet of Things (IoT), Big Data, Big Data Analytics, artificial intelligence (AI), and cloud solutions are seen as key to enabling digital technologies for the data economy.

Box 4.2: The Central Role of Information Systems in Tesco's Customer Loyalty

Tesco, a major UK-based retailer, has for decades operated a customer loyalty scheme, the Tesco Clubcard, where customers are awarded points for scanning the membership card when making purchases and thereby allowing customer purchases to be associated with specific customers over time. While customers are offered rewards for staying loyal, the Tesco Clubcard, when understood from a relational and knowledge perspective, is central to developing the marketing competences and performance of Tesco. Indeed Rowley (2007, p. 366) clearly articulates a customer-centric approach when arguing that loyalty schemes allow firms to shift to focusing on how 'business in partnership with, and with the consent of their customers, [can] be loyal to their customers, by continually

(Continued)

enhancing the value that they offer to those customers'. While most marketing research on customer loyalty schemes focuses on the types of loyalty realised, behavioural or attitudinal, and the design of rewards for participation by customers, the greatest value is to be found in the exploitation of the resulting data and the integration of the insights from this analysis into the customer relationship management (CRM) strategy of a firm. The resulting benefits are dependent on information systems (digital technologies) at Tesco that allow customer insights to be exploited in business development, promotions, recruitment, expanding into new services, channel migration strategies (e.g., store to online), and relationship building.

Source: Rowley (2007)

Gulati and Oldroyd (2005) argue that firms that wish to adopt a firm level customer-centric approach should follow a four-phase process (see Figure 4.4), with the phases building on each other and following in order. The first phase of communal collaboration develops a shared central repository of all customer data, organised by customer, drawn from touchpoints from across the firm. Digital information and communication technologies (ICT) and infrastructure are essential for making this coordinated gathering (communicating and storing), standardising, and organising of customer data possible. In practice this means cross organisation / functional contributions to the communal customer data pool, typically under the control of a neutral entity like the IT function, which understands both technical and business needs. This phase is made challenging by the volume of granular customer data being pooled, the time required, and significant investments in ICT infrastructure required (Gulati and Oldroyd, 2005). This initial foundation is essential for realising the next phase.

A second phase of serial coordination develops the necessary capabilities to gather and organise standardised customer data over time and enable the analysis of the data by specific functions of the firm). Data analytics and how diverse analytical activities are organised and coordinated across the firm becomes a key focus of this phase. Critically, the pooling of firm wide customer data enables more holistic analysis that has the potential to contribute to more effective decision-making across the firm, but developing the optimal (serial) organisation of the analysis to support decision-making is challenging (Gulati and Oldroyd, 2005). This phase of the process may require a reorganisation of how the firm operates, and staff development to fully realise the potential of the new data resource, reflecting the human–machine relationships at the heart of information systems.

The third phase of (3) symbiotic coordination is fundamental to seeking to understand past behaviours for making decisions to seek to realise predictive analytics (Gulati and Oldroyd, 2005). Building on the historical analysis of customer data, predictive analytics experiments with (a) developing models to predict customer behaviour, and (b) to experiment with interventions to influence customer behaviour (i.e., A/B testing). The complexity of managing this approach to understanding customer needs, wants, and preferences often leads to a reorganisation of the firm or new organisational units for coordinating the cross-functional collaboration needed.

In the final fourth phase of integral coordination, firms focus on 'bringing a now-sophisticated understanding of their customers into the present, incorporating that understanding into all of their day-to-day operations' (Gulati and Oldroyd, 2005, pp. 99–100). In this phase, firms can respond to the needs, wants, and preferences of customers on an individual basis, reflecting a customer-centric logic. Employees are enabled by the digital technologies that facilitate their timely and effective access to the needed data for making decisions.

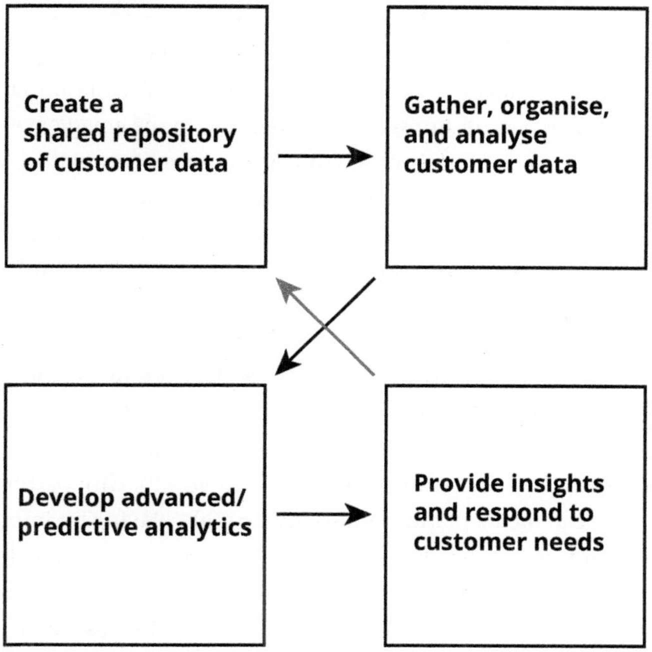

Figure 4.4 Data-driven customer centricity

Source: own illustration following Gulati & Oldroyd (2005)

There are, however, concerns about data security, privacy concerns, and implications for society as a result of such increasing data intensity in firms, business (eco-)systems, society, and government. The storage of personal and sensitive data requires secure storage that is able to ensure that the confidentiality of the data and protect it from cyber-attacks (Sestino et al., 2025). Firms that are seeking to develop insights on customer data need to ensure that access to the data is well managed and that unauthorised access by staff and external cyber-criminals is prevented. Firms also need to ensure that they comply with the appropriate national and regional legal frameworks for collecting, sharing, and exploiting consumers data; see, for example, Article 8 of the European Union (EU) Charter of Fundamental Rights, for a digital society, and the EU General Data Protection Regulation (GDPR). Firms need to understand how their participation in the data economy, when seeking to realise customer centricity, may impact the lives of their customers and infringe on individuals' rights to privacy and autonomy.

4.4 CUSTOMER CENTRICITY AND THE CUSTOMER JOURNEY

Digital technologies have expanded the channels through which customers can interact with a firm, while enabling greater understanding of a customer's interaction with the firm across different analogue and digital channels, thereby contributing to a growing pressure to shift first to multi-channel and increasingly to omni-channel strategies (Verhoef et al., 2015) (see Table 4.2). The relevance of these changes to the delivery of customer centricity along the customer journey is not only for B2C retail and marketing, but also for B2C sales and marketing (Habel et al., 2020; Hayes & Kelliher, 2022). Meanwhile, the initial introduction of online and then mobile (especially apps) channels resulted in the emergence of multi-channel strategies, typically with an emphasis on channels as alternatives, with customers moving between channels for specific activities along the customer journey.

Omni-channel strategies add a further degree of complexity to realising a customer-centric approach to creating value, as the lines between the channels become increasingly blurred, with channels becoming interchangeably and seamlessly available to customers at all stages of the customer journey (Verhoef et al., 2015). Clearly enabling this kind of seamless engagement with customers requires firms to develop new data resources, most likely at least a shared data pool. The simultaneous increase in emphasis on firm embeddedness in value creating ecosystems also means that not all phases and activities of the customer journey will have touchpoints owned by a focal firm or brand (see Table 4.2), with partners, the customer, or third parties like social media platforms also increasingly playing an important role in the customer journey. Capturing this behaviour of customers creates new challenges in terms of data gathering (see Box 4.3).

Customer centricity is fundamentally concerned with the customer journey and the associated customer experience of that journey, for both B2C (Lemon & Verhoef, 2016) and B2B firms (Habel et al., 2020), as it is along the customer journey that firms are able to co-create value with their customers. The growing complexity of the customer journey and increasing loss of control that firms have over the customer experience along the customer journey creates new challenges for firms that require multi-functional responses. Digital technologies and the digital transformation of firms represent critical opportunities for developing the necessary resources and capabilities for firms to effectively and efficiently respond to these trends with a customer-centric approach. Customer centricity then is the design and management of the customer experience along the customer journey, including sensory (sense), affective (feel), cognitive (think), physical (behavioural), and social-identity (relational) customer experiences (Lemon & Verhoef, 2016). Digital technologies and channels should be integrated into the customer journey to positively affect the customer experience and increase customer loyalty and satisfaction. This however can only be fully realised if a firm is willing to proceed with moving through Gulati and Oldroyd's (2005) four phases for developing a data-centric approach to realising customer centricity.

Table 4.2 Model of customer journey and experience in the digital age

Previous Experience (t – 1)	**Current Customer Experience (current time period, t)**				**Future Experience (t + 1)**
		Prepurchase Stage	**Purchase Stage**	**Post-purchase Stage**	
	Customer Behaviours	Need recognition	Choice	Consumption	
		Consideration	Purchase intention	Usage	
		Search	Ordering	Engagement	
		Preferences	Payment	Service Requests	
Pre purchase Stage	**Channel Strategy (Omni- / Multi-channel)**	Internet of Things			Pre purchase Stage
		Mobile Internet / Applications			
Purchase Stage		World Wide Web (Internet)			Purchase Stage
		Telephone			
		Mail / Catalogue			
Post-purchase Stage		Text / Print			Post-purchase Stage
		Store			
	Control of Touch points	Firm / Brand owned			
		Partner owned			
		Customer owned			
		Social / External			

Source: adapted from Figure 1 in Lemon & Verhoef (2016)

Box 4.3: Customer Personas

Customer personas are 'a semi-fictional representation of [an] ideal customer based on market research and real data about [...] existing customers' (Kusinitz, 2014). They allow a focus on specific customer segment in terms of the needs, wants, and preferences of the typical customer or other customer group represented by the persona (Lemon & Verhoef, 2016). The value of customer personas lies in their ability to enable firms' employees to empathise with and understand the lives of customers and understand the customer journey from the perspective of the customer (Lemon & Verhoef 2016). Because many different types of customers might purchase a firms' products and/or services, it often makes sense to develop a number of personas.

(Continued)

Figure 4.5 Illustrative example of a persona description

Source: Peter (2023, 2024)

4.4.1 Omni-Channel Customer Centricity Along the Customer Journey

The customer journey can be divided into phases of prepurchase activities and touchpoints with the firm, the activities, and touchpoints associated with the purchase phase, and finally the post-purchase phase activities and touchpoints (see Table 4.2 following Lemon & Verhoef, 2016). With customers approaching the customer journey with previous experiences and each completion of the customer journey contributing to the experiences that influence the next purchasing process, the management of these touchpoints (omni-channel management) becomes crucial: 'Omni-channel management [can then be defined] as the synergistic management of numerous available channels and customer touchpoints, in such a way that the customer experience across channels and the performance over channels is optimized' (Verhoef et al., 2015, p. 176). Digital technologies also create new opportunities for engaging customers (see Box 4.4).

4.4.2 Prepurchase Phase of Customer Journey

In the prepurchase phase a customer will become aware of a need or want and this awareness will lead to the consideration of products and services that could address that need or want. This process of considering alternatives will lead to a preference for a specific product or service that is preferred and then the customer will search for offers in the marketplace for that product or service. As a result, a potential customer establishes a preference for which a purchase intention emerges. These activities are likely to take place over a mix of analogue and digital channels, often simultaneously in an omni-channel approach.

Box 4.4: Open Innovation and Co-Creation with Customers

Digital technologies enable firms to undertake a far more open approach to product and/or service innovation processes, enabling customers and other stakeholders to be integrated into open innovation processes or even co-creation processes. By opening up a dialogue with customers the firm can far better understand their needs, wants, and preferences, allowing more effective and efficient product development processes. As was seen in the opening case study to the chapter, this can even develop to a stage where expert customers or stakeholders are integrated into the development process, leading to the co-creation of products and/or services that meet customers' needs, wants, and preferences more effectively. Critical to these processes is an open dialogue and mutual respect.

Source: Peter (2023, 2024)

4.4.3 Purchase Phase of Customer journey

The purchase phase starts with a customer choosing a specific product or service and then they may or may not develop an intention to purchase that chosen offering. Once the purchase intention is established the customer goes through the ordering and payment process (see Box 4.5).

Box 4.5: Social Media and Online Monitoring of / Listening to Customer Engagement

Social media has become an extremely important source of insights about products and services for customers in the prepurchase phase of the customer journey. The information is however very often the reviews/comments on products and/or services by customers that have just purchased and used them for the first time.

Firms can either monitor social media platforms inhouse or purchase data from firms specialised in monitoring social media; typically, this will seek to provide a sense of the ratio of positive, neutral, and negative sentiment in posts over time for a given firm, its

(Continued)

products, and/or services. There are also a range of social media sites that could be monitored, and it would be important for a firm to understand where its stakeholders are active on social media; each of the social media platforms has its own unique characteristics that could allow unique insights for a firm that undertakes social media monitoring/listening. In this sense it is very similar to the analysis commonly done with the Net Promotor Score (see Box 4.6).

Social media data is however much richer than just the sentiment analysis and the comments about the products and/or services could provide valuable insights about how a firm might improve the customer experience, its products and/or services.

Source: Schweidel & Moe (2014)

4.4.4 Post-purchase phase of customer journey

In the post-purchase phase customers consume the services or use the products they purchased and as a result may engage with the firm or other communities that they are members of to communicate their satisfaction with the experience of the products or services (see Box 4.6). If needed, customers may activate a service request to address deficiencies with the product or service.

Box 4.6: Net Promoter Score

The Net Promoter Score (NPS) is a type of customer survey that almost every person that has completed a purchase online could be expected to have experienced. The aim of the NPS is to establish the satisfaction and loyalty of a customer to a firm/brand after a purchase and the request to complete the survey is commonly received via email channel. It typically has one rating question, commonly using a 10-point Likert scale (0 = not at all likely / 10 = extremely likely to recommend), the question is formulated as follows:

- 'How likely is it that you will recommend us or company X to others (your friends and family)?'

This question is often followed by an open question, to gain deeper insights:

- 'What is it that you like about our products or services?'

Customers/respondents are categorised into one of three categories depending on their responses:

0–6 points detractors: These customers can be expected to stop purchasing from the firm and to advise friends and family to do the same. There is a risk that they will write bad reviews. It is likely that they had a bad customer experience and gaining deeper insights into why they are dissatisfied could help improve the customer experience, products and/or services.

7-8 points indifferent customers: This group of customers can be expected to be satisfied by their experience of the purchasing process, products, and/or services. They will not necessarily recommend the firm and its products and services to friends and family. Typically, they receive less attention from the firm compared to the detractors and promoters.

9–10 points promoters: These customers are likely to have had an excellent customer experienced and are highly likely to recommend the firm, its products, and services to friends, family, and colleagues.

The NPS is calculated by subtracting the percentage of detractors from the percentage of promoters. The NPS has received criticism because of its simplicity and the risk that it could be biased by cultural influences on the likelihood for respondents to give higher ratings to the first question.

Source: Peter (2023, 2024)

What is a good NPS score?

-100 0 30 70 100

Needs improvement	Satisfied	Good	Excellent
-100 to 0	1 to 30	31 to 70	71 to 100

Figure 4.6 Net promotor score levels driven by promotors and detractors

Source: Peter (2023, 2024)

4.5 ENABLERS AND CHALLENGES FOR CUSTOMER CENTRICITY ORGANISATIONS

Despite the growing number of firms committing to a customer-centric approach to creating value, these firms struggle to transform successfully (Hemel & Rademakers, 2016). The transition to a customer-centric organisation is enabled by organisational agility. Agile approaches accept risk and adopt a learning approach. This need not be quick but does require flexibility and a timely responsiveness. Ensuring that the firm does not lose touch with customers is also key; this requires direct and two-way communication with customers, as well as employees from across the organisation interacting with customers. Firms should also develop incentive systems that are aligned with the customer experience and make customers the shared responsibility of all functions in the firm. To ensure that the customer is truly understood, firms should integrate customers into value creation processes and actively monitor customer trends and developments. In terms of employees and how the firm is organised, firms should breakdown pyramid structures and develop an organisational culture focused on serving the customer. This means that employees should be hired to fit with this culture and their approach to doing business.

This culture and type of employee will respond positively to being empowered to respond to customers, within clear boundaries.

Dalsace et al. (2025) explored the gap between the concept of customer centricity and its practical application in leadership practices. They identified three organisational traps (product focalisation, rigid organisational boundaries, and a 'fixed-pie' mindset) that hinder customer centricity. The authors propose using digital technology and leadership behaviours to overcome these traps. Digital tools provide constant customer insights, while leadership fosters a customer-centric culture.

As a result, the main barriers to building a customer-centric firm, beyond the technical challenges of developing the necessary information systems (see above), are cultural values such as fear and judgment, where employees are punished for occasional/inevitable mistakes, rather than to drive a positive leadership approach and organisational values that drive customer centricity. Overwhelming customers can also negatively impact the realisation of value for the firm and customers; it is better to have a focused range of offerings that meaningfully address the needs and wants of customers (Hemel & Rademakers, 2016). Avoid measuring performance in the short run only, as a customer-centric strategy is a long-term strategy.

4.6 CUSTOMER CENTRICITY AND COMPETITIVE ADVANTAGE

Customer centricity is seen as a source of sustained competitive advantage. That will lead to improved firm performance, by creating value for customers in the long term by serving them well and allowing the firm to capture value through improved financial performance (Hemel & Rademakers, 2016). The need to operate the firm in entirely new ways requires a transformation of the firm and how it is organised and operates, reflecting the dynamic capabilities and resource-based views of the firm. As was made clear in discussing the four phases of becoming a data-centric firm (see above), initial phases are not that demanding, but to fully realise the customer-centric logic requires a fundamental transformation enabled by digital technologies. The result is an entirely new method of operating and decision-making that places the customer experience at the centre of the way in which value is created. It is possible to argue that customer centricity is the full realisation of Treacy and Wiersema's (1993) customer intimacy strategic discipline for competing. From a positional strategic approach customer centricity can be understood as choosing the most profitable customer segments to serve by understanding their needs, wants, and preferences. This may require the development of new products and/or services (i.e., value propositions) or developing existing offerings (Hemel & Rademakers, 2016).

4.7 CUSTOMER CENTRICITY AND SUSTAINABILITY

Digitally enabled customer centricity offers a unique opportunity to contribute to realising a more sustainable future, by allowing firms to effectively respond to customer consumption behaviour more effectively. Sheth et al. (2011) describe a customer-centric approach to thinking about consumption of goods and services and how this affects economic, environmental, and social sustainability, offering a unique opportunity for firms to realise more sustainable consumption. They point out that the act of consuming is affected by and effects the consumptive behaviour of customers, due to the importance of individual and collective customer attitudes, values, and expectations in relation to consuming a specific product. A customer-centric approach enabled by digital technologies gives firms the opportunity to offer customers the possibility to consume a product differently. Importantly this includes not only offering the same product in a more sustainable manner by digitising elements or even all of the product, but also offering innovative products that are more tailored to the attitudes, values, and expectations of customers with respect to sustainability concerns. Digital technologies can, importantly, enable the effective communication of the resulting product-market fit with customers' preferences.

4.8 CONCLUSION

Customer centricity enabled by digital technologies offers firms a very attractive opportunity to more effectively build relationships with their customers. In addition, customer centricity and co-creation are two methods to drive digital innovation.

The chapter highlights the shift from product-centric to customer-centric strategies, stressing the need for firms to understand and meet customer needs and expectations in the fourth/fifth industrial revolutions. It discusses the role of digital transformation in facilitating this shift, enabling firms to gather and analyse customer data more effectively. The dependence of the customer-centric approach on customer data for building those relationships is, however, increasingly associated with significant privacy and security concerns that firms need to address. The trend is, however, clearly for an ever-greater digital transformation of the customer journey and, as this increasingly becomes an omni-channel journey, the opportunities and necessity of a customer-centric approach increase.

Enablers and challenges of implementing customer-centric strategies include organisational agility, employee empowerment, and the need for a customer-focused culture. In summary, the first strategic action field of customer centricity is a source for potential competitive advantage, also noting the privacy and security concerns associated with the increased use of customer data in strategic and operational systems and processes.

Case Studies

Students can complete the following tasks either based on the focal case study, or work on the recommended case study for this chapter (*Switzerland Tourism – cross-media campaign 'The ride of a lifetime'*) and answer the questions below.

1 How well does the marketing strategy of Switzerland Tourism reflect a customer-centric approach?
2 Develop a customer persona (see Box 4.3) based on a summarised persona description of a typical segment which would/might visit Switzerland.

3 Develop the customer journey (see Chapter 4.4) for the campaign until a tourist visits Switzerland: what steps will the tourist take and what channels will be used to obtain information and communicate with businesses (e.g., travel agency, airport, train)?
4 How is the digitally enabled customer journey reflected in the multi-channel marketing campaign (see also Chapter 4.4.1)?
5 Evaluate the choice to integrate world-famous personalities Roger Federer and Trevor Noah into the campaign: in your opinion does this speak to a customer-centric mindset at Switzerland Tourism?
6 How do you think digitally enabled customer centricity could be further enhanced in the customer experience of tourists that become aware of Switzerland as a destination after watching the campaign?

Additional cases with student questions for the strategic digital action field of *Customer Centricity* are covered in:

- Adelbodner mineral water – the digital roadmap of a SME (available online).
- Autodesk Asia-Pacific – customer lifecycle management and marketing automation (available online).
- Action fields of digital transformation at Synchrony Financial (USA) (available online).

You will find the collection of case studies for strategic digital transformation in the Appendix and additional cases online at www.strategic-digital-transformation.com

Exercises

Discuss the following questions in your class, group, or assignment:

1 Review the opening case (General Electric's Opal Nugget Ice Maker) in light of a product vs customer-centric approach (see Table 4.1): how would General Electric's approach be different under each strategy?
2 Select a small or medium-sized firm of your choice (it is recommended that it has a narrow product focus for this exercise) and analyse the potential of the firm to leverage digital technologies to implement a more customer-centric approach to value creation.
3 Forming two small groups (2–4 students in each group), assign a pro and contra position to each group and debate the degree to which product vs customer-centric approaches (see Table 4.1) are more successful.
4 Analyse and discuss how data needs to be managed (see Figure 4.4) in order for a firm to benefit from data for customer-centric strategies (select a concrete industry/business to discuss your points).
5 Based on above industry/business in exercise 4, elaborate the implications and risks towards data security, privacy concerns, and implications for society.

6 For the selected industry/business in exercise 4, map the customer journey and align it to customer touchpoints to identify all channels that should be managed (omni channel management).

7 Explain why customer centricity and competitive advantages for firms are linked. Provide at least three concrete examples.

Further Reading List

- Boston Consulting Group (2022). Delivering Government Services Like a Digital Native, www.bcg.com/publications/2022/delivering-customer-centric-digital-government-services.
- Boston Consulting Group (2023). Building Customer Experience for the Future www.bcg.com/publications/2023/building-customer-experience-for-the-future.
- Gummesson, E. (2008). Customer centricity: reality or a wild goose chase? *European Business Review*, 20(4), 315–30.
- Latinovic, Z., & Chatterjee, S. C. (2019). Customer centricity in the digital age *Sloan Management Review*, 60(4), 0_1–0_2.
- Läubli, D., & Sänger, F. (2024). Building the future: Focusing on digitalization and sustainability, www.mckinsey.com/industries/retail/our-insights/building-the-future-focusing-on-digitalization-and-sustainability.
- Sankur, A., Duncan, E., Cilento, G., & Fuchs, S. (2024). True customer-centricity: An operating model for competitive advantage, www.mckinsey.com/industries/industrials-and-electronics/our-insights/true-customer-centricity-an-operating-model-for-competitive-advantage.

References

Dalsace, F., Bonnet, D., & Lange, K. (2025). Customer centricity: Digital and leadership to the rescue. *Business Horizons*, in press.

Fader, P. S., & Winer, R. S. (2012). Introduction to the special issue on the emergence and impact of user-generated content. *Marketing Science*, *31*(3), 369–71.

FirstBuildTM. (2024) Home Page. Last accessed 26 July 2024 from https://firstbuild com/.

GE Appliances. (2018). FirstBuild™ by GE Appliances Expands Innovation Model Overseas. Last accessed 26 July 2024 from https://pressroom.geappliances.com/news/firstbuildTM-by-ge-appliances-expands-innovation-model-overseas.

General Electric. (2015) First Nugget Ice Maker for Home Use Launches. Last accessed 26 July 2024 from www.ge.com/news/press-releases/first-nugget-ice-maker-home-use-launches.

General Electric. (2024). GE Profile™ Opal™ Nugget Ice Maker + Side Tank and Bluetooth. Last accessed 26 July 2024 from www.geappliances.com/appliance/GE-Profile-Opal-Nugget-Ice-Maker-Side-Tank-and-Bluetooth-OPAL01GEPKT.

Gulati, R., & Oldroyd, J. B. (2005). The quest for customer focus. *Harvard Business Review*, *83*(4), 92–101.

Gummesson, E. (2008a). Extending the service-dominant logic: From customer centricity to balanced centricity. *Journal of the Academy of Marketing Science, 36*, 15–17.

Gummesson, E. (2008b). Customer centricity: Reality or a wild goose chase? *European Business Review, 20*(4), 315–30.

Habel, J., Kassemeier, R., Alavi, S., Haaf, P., Schmitz, C., & Wieseke, J. (2020). When do customers perceive customer centricity? The role of a firm's and salespeople's customer orientation. *Journal of Personal Selling & Sales Management, 40*(1), 25–42.

Hayes, Ó., & Kelliher, F. (2022). The emergence of B2B omni-channel marketing in the digital era: a systematic literature review. *Journal of Business & Industrial Marketing, 37*(11), 2156–68.

Hemel, C. V. D., & Rademakers, M. F. (2016). Building customer-centric organizations: Shaping factors and barriers. *Journal of Creating Value, 2*(2), 211–30.

Indiegogo. (2024) Home Page. Last accessed on 26 July 2024 from www.indiegogo.com.

Ivanov, I.I. (2019). Chasing the crowd: Digital transformations and the digital driven system design paradigm. In: Shishkov, B. (eds), *Business Modeling and Software Design*. BMSD 2019. Lecture Notes in Business Information Processing, vol. *356*, 64-80. Cham: Springer.

Kusinitz, Sam (2014). 'The Definition of a Buyer Persona [in Under 100 Words],' Hubspot, (8 March), [available at http://blog.hubspot.com/marketing/buyer-persona-definition-under-100-sr].

Latinovic, Z., & Chatterjee, S. C. (2019). Customer centricity in the digital age. *Sloan Management Review, 60*(4), 0_1–0_2.

Lemon, K. N., & Verhoef, P. C. (2016). Understanding customer experience throughout the customer journey. *Journal of Marketing, 80*(6), 69–96.

Peter, M. K. (Hrsg.) (2017). *KMU-Transformation: Als KMU die Digitale Transformation erfolgreich umsetzen. Forschungsresultate und Praxisleitfaden.* FHNW Hochschule für Wirtschaft, Olten/Schweiz, www.kmu-transformation.ch.

Peter, M. K. (Hrsg.) (2021). *Strategieentwicklung im digitalen Zeitalter: Planung und Umsetzung der Digitalen Transformation.* FHNW Hochschule für Wirtschaft und Strategylab, Olten/Schweiz, www.strategische-transformation.ch.

Peter, M. K. (2023). *Digitaler Masterplan für KMU. So gelingt die digitale Transformation in Ihrem Unternehmen.* Verlag Beobachter Edition & Handelszeitung. Zürich/Schweiz, www.digitaler-masterplan.ch.

Peter, M. K. (2024). *The Digital Transformation Canvas. Develop and Implement Your Digital Strategy.* FT Publishing/Pearson, London/UK, www.the-digital-transformation-canvas.com.

Peter, M. K., Kraft, C., & Lindeque, J. (2020). Strategic action fields of digital transformation: An exploration of the strategic action fields of Swiss SMEs and large enterprises. *Journal of Strategy and Management, 13*(1), 160–80.

Porter, M.E. (1985). *Competitive Advantage. Creating and sustaining superior performance.* New York, NY: The Free Press.

Rowley, J. (2007). Reconceptualising the strategic role of loyalty schemes. *Journal of Consumer Marketing, 24*(6), 366–74.

Schweidel, D. A., & Moe, W. W. (2014). Listening in on social media: A joint model of sentiment and venue format choice. *Journal of Marketing Research, 51*(4), 387–402.

Sestino, A., Kahlawi, A., & De Mauro, A. (2025). Decoding the data economy: A literature review of its impact on business, society and digital transformation. *European Journal of Innovation Management, 28*(2), 298–323.

Shah, D., Rust, R. T., Parasuraman, A., Staelin, R., & Day, G. S. (2006). The path to customer centricity. *Journal of Service Research*, *9*(2), 113–24.

Sheth, J. N., Sethia, N. K., & Srinivas, S. (2011). Mindful consumption: A customer-centric approach to sustainability. *Journal of the Academy of Marketing Science*, *39*, 21–39.

Treacy, M., & Wiersema, F. (1995). *The Discipline of Market Leaders*. Reading, MA: Persus Books.

Verhoef, P. C., Kannan, P. K., & Inman, J. J. (2015). From multi-channel retailing to omni-channel retailing: Introduction to the special issue on multi-channel retailing. *Journal of Retailing*, *91*(2), 174–81.

5
STRATEGIC ACTION FIELD OF NEW DIGITAL TECHNOLOGIES

Learning Goals

By the end of this chapter, you should…

- Be able to identify the main types of digital technologies.
- Be able to explain why technologies are adopted and accepted by firms and employees.
- Be able to explain how different digital technologies create value in terms of underlying value drivers.
- Be able to explain how digital technologies contribute to the competitive advantage of firms.
- Be able to explain how digital technologies support greater sustainability.
- Evaluate the opportunities and risks associated with the adoption and use of digital technologies.

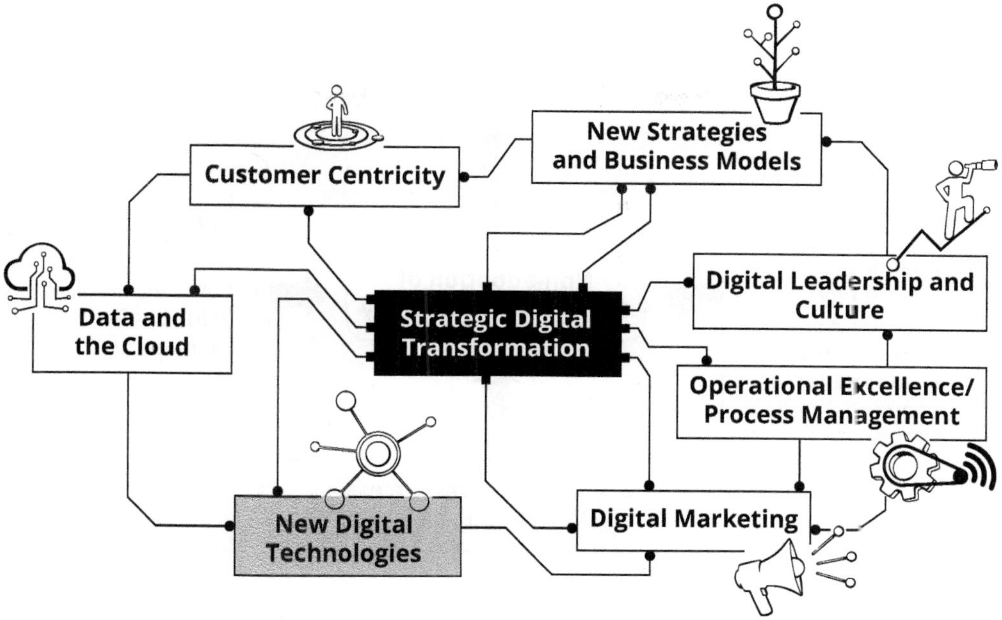

Figure 5.1 New digital technologies is the second Strategic Action Field of Digital Transformation

Source: Peter et al. (2020); Peter (2017, 2021, 2023, 2024)

The Surprising Case of Blockchain Technology Non-Adoption in Supply Chains

Blockchain technology has received significant attention over the last decade, most notably as the enabling technology for digital currencies like Bitcoin. Blockchain technology adds sets of new records (transactions/activities) to the blockchain in interconnected blocks, with each block including a timestamp, transaction data, and the cryptographic hash of the preceding block, making retroactive modification of the blocks impossible (Rajasekaran et al., 2022). There are in fact a number of different approaches to blockchain technology, which differ in the degree to which they are centralised or decentralised and their degree of privacy.

Blockchain technology is argued to have significant potential for business applications where a transparent, immutable, and irreversible record of transactions/activities (Rajasekaran et al., 2022) is of importance. From an industry perspective, these characteristics are of particular interest for businesses in finance, banking, insurance, but also logistics and transportation, as well as in business functions like supply chain management, by enhancing transparency, traceability, efficiency, and information security (Moosavi et al., 2021). A recent study by Hubenova et al. (2024), however, found that supply chain managers were not yet entirely convinced that it was the right time to adopt blockchain technology for governing the global value chains in which they were participating (see Figure 5.2).

(Continued)

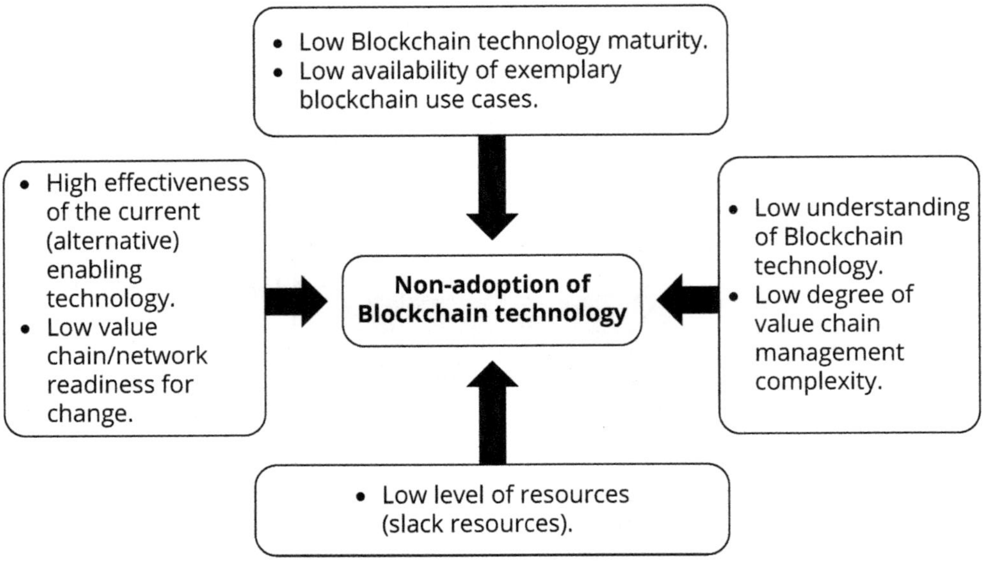

Figure 5.2 Simplified model of blockchain adoption barriers

Source: Own illustration following Hubenova et al. (2024)

Reflecting the technology adoption models and theories addressed in this chapter, the findings of their research revealed that the non-adoption of blockchain technology was affected by technology factors, internal and external factors that influenced the perceived usefulness and ease of use of the technology. As a novel technology the managers had concerns about the maturity of blockchain technology and the lack of exemplary use cases also affected this concern. Within the broader external context of the supply chain, managers, existing technology was perceived as very efficient and effective, making it even more challenging to transition to blockchain technology. Managers also did not experience a great degree of challenge with the current implemented solution, which would advocate for adopting a novel technology, especially when it was not well understood and required external partners to adopt the novel technology. Finally, the lack of internal financial and knowledge resources needed to invest in blockchain technology further created barriers for adopting the technology. As a result, for the supply chain managers in the study it was difficult to identify sufficient usefulness and ease of use after adoption to make a case for integrating the technology into the governance of their global value chains.

Source: adapted from Hubenova et al. (2024)

5.0 INTRODUCTION

Computer, information, communication, sensing, and controlling technologies are actively being integrated into firms in response to the digital transformation of the economy and society. Many of these technologies are novel and require managers to make a decision about the adoption and use of technologies that can vary significantly in terms of the understanding of decision-makers about the technologies available to their firms (see Box 5.1). This chapter opens with an introduction to widely adopted models for explaining firm level and employee level technology adoption and acceptance decisions. Next a selection of important contemporary digital technologies is presented and discussed. The chapter concludes with assessments of the impact of new technologies on firm competitive performance and sustainability, before assessing the increased cybersecurity risks from the integration of digital technologies and the associated digital transformation of value creation by firms and in the economy and society more broadly. In addition, the two important themes of AI as part of the fifth industrial revolution, and cybersecurity as a success factor to operate in the digital age, will be covered.

Box 5.1: Definition of New Digital Technologies

Digital technologies include computing, information, communication, connectivity, sensing, and controlling technologies central to the digital transformation of firms, the economy, and society in the digital age. A digital technology is considered new when it conforms to the OECD Oslo Manual definition of an innovation (OECD, 2025); that is when the technology allows product, process, marketing, and/or organisational innovations (see Chapter 3). This means that an existing technology may be new in a novel domain of application, even if already applied in other domains or it may be an entirely novel invention that is driving innovation for the first time. Blockchain technology was a new invention when it was first proposed and then developed to allow the innovation of distributed cryptocurrencies. Later, when the blockchain was separated from the cryptocurrencies, and increasingly the focus moved to its potential in other domains of application the technology was new in the spirit of the Oslo Manual as it allowed different forms of innovation across multiple domains, e.g., smart contracts and record-keeping.

5.1 TECHNOLOGY ADOPTION DECISIONS

Table 5.1 organises four widely adopted theories and models of technology diffusion (Moore & Benbasat, 1991; Rogers, 1983; Tornatzky & Fleischer, 1990), adoption (Davis, 1989), and acceptance (Venkatesh et al., 2003):

- Technology Diffusion Model (TDM);
- Technology, Organisation and Environment Model (TOE);
- Technology Adoption Model (TAM); and
- Unified Theory of Acceptance and Use of Technology (UTAUT).

It is important to remember that in all these models, the perceptions of technology users, managers and technology adoption decision-makers plays a critical role in the diffusion and acceptance of novel technologies (see Table 5.1 for an overview of the most important technology models).

Table 5.1 Comparison of Selected Theories and Models of Technology Adoption

Model	Technology Atributes	External Environmental Influences	Organisational Influences	Employee Attributes / Influences
Technology Diffusion Model (TDM) [1]	• Relative Advantage • Trialability • Results Demonstrability • Visibility • Ease of Use	• Compatibility within Ecosystem	• Compatibility with internal processes	• Image • Voluntariness of Use
Technology, Organisation and Environment Model (TOE Model) [2]	• Relative Advantage • Compatibility • Complexity	• Competitive Advantage • Partner Support	• Org. Competency • Org. Complexity • Org. Readiness • Org Compatibility • Leadership Support	
Technology Adoption Model (TAM / TAM2 / TAM3) [3]	• Perceived Usefulness • Perceived Ease of Use			• Subjective Norm • Voluntariness of Use • Experience • Gender
Unified Theory of Acceptance and Use of Technology (UTAUT) [4]	• Performance Expectations • Effort Expectations	• Facilitating Conditions	• Facilitating Conditions	• Social Influence • Voluntariness of Use • Experience • Gender • Age

Sources: 1) Moore & Benbasat (1991), Rogers (1983); 2) Chatterjee et al. (2021), Gangwar et al. (2015), Tornatzky & Fleischer (1990); 3) Chatterjee et al. (2021), Gangwar et al. (2015), Davis (1989); Venkatesh et al. (2003); 4) Venkatesh et al. (2003)

5.1.1 Technology Diffusion Model (TDM)

The technology diffusion model (Moore & Benbasat, 1991) emphasises the perceived characteristics of using a technology innovation, seeking to explain the adoption and diffusion of novel technologies. It is important to remember the subjective perceptions are relevant and dependent on the circumstances and experiences of the technology adoption decision-maker. Extending the work of Rogers (1983), Moore and Benbasat (1991) defined eight attributes of technology innovations as:

1. Relative Advantage: 'the degree to which an innovation is perceived as being better than its precursor';
2. Compatibility: 'the degree to which an innovation is perceived as being consistent with the existing values, needs, and past experiences of potential adopters';
3. Trialability: 'the degree to which an innovation may be experimented with before adoption';
4. Result Demonstrability: 'the degree to which the more advantages of an innovation can be demonstrated and are observable';
5. Visibility: 'the degree to which the adoption and acceptance of an innovation by others can be observed';
6. Ease of Use: 'the degree to which an innovation is perceived as easy or difficult to use';
7. Image: 'the degree to which use of an innovation is perceived to enhance one's image or status in one's social system'; and
8. Voluntariness of Use: 'the degree to which use of the innovation is perceived as being voluntary, or of free will'.

A technology will diffuse (be adopted and accepted) more quickly the greater the perceived relative advantage, the greater the trialability, the greater the results from use of a technology can be demonstrated and the technology's adoption by others is visible. The greater the perceived ease of use, effects on image and perceived voluntariness of the use of a technology, the quicker a technology will diffuse.

5.1.2 Technology, Organisation, and Environment Model (TOE)

The technology, organisation, and environment (TOE) framework is a widespread approach for explaining digital technology adoption by organisations like firms (Chatterjee et al., 2021; Gangwar et al., 2015). The approach provides a holistic approach that is free of industry or firm-size effects on the technology adoption decision. The TOE framework has in fact been critiqued for being too general and unclear. Thus, while it is a very useful framework for categorising and organising using the factors that determine technology adoption, it needs to be integrated with another model to operationalise its categorisation of the effects on technology adoption / acceptance (Gangwar et al., 2015).

- Technology: The attributes of the technology being considered for adoption;
- Organisation: Internal facilitating conditions for the adoption of a technology; and
- Environment: External facilitating conditions for the adoption of a technology.

The technology attributes are often conceptualised using the perceived usefulness (PU) and perceived ease of use (PEOU) factors from the technology acceptance model (Chatterjee et al., 2021; Davis, 1989). Fundamentally, for the organisation these factors are related to the complexity of the technology, its compatibility with the processes of the firm and the relative advantage the technology offers the firm compared to previous or alternative technology options (see Table 5.1).

Internal organisational facilitating conditions influence the PU and PEOU and include factors like organisational competences, organisational complexity, organisational readiness, and organisational compatibility (Chatterjee et al., 2021, p. 4).

- Organisational Competences: 'employees' skill, knowledge, capabilities, and other relevant traits essential for effective performance in an employment position';
- Organisational Complexity: 'the level of inconvenience and constraints towards understanding and using a system';
- Organisational Readiness: 'the accessibility of the required organizational resources for adoption'; and
- Organisational Compatibility: 'the level to which an innovation is considered to be consistent with the potential users' existing values, previous experiences and requirements'.

External environmental facilitating conditions include factors like the competitive advantage gained from the adoption of a technology and the degree of partner support for a technology, which also affect the PU and PEOU of a technology being considered for adoption (Chatterjee et al., 2021, pp. 4–5):

- Competitive Advantage: 'the level at which a technological factor seems to provide a better benefit for organizations';
- Partner Support: The network of partner organisations that are needed to integrate a novel digital technology into the socio-technical systems within which collaborating firms are embedded. Partners are sources of collaboration, financing, and knowledge.

5.1.3 Technology Acceptance Model (TAM)

The technology acceptance model (TAM) explains (digital) technology acceptance and usage (Venkatesh et al. 2003). The greater the degree to which a (novel) digital technology is perceived to be useful and the greater the perceived ease of use of the technology, the greater the expected attitudinal and behavioural intentions to use the technology (Davis, 1989). The attitudinal and behavioural intensions are at the same time subject to the subjective norms of a technology adoption decision-maker (Venkatesh et al., 2003):

- Perceived Usefulness: 'the degree to which a person believes that using a particular system would enhance his or her job performance' (Davis, 1989, p. 320);
- Perceived Ease of Use: 'the degree to which a person believes that using a particular system would be free of effort' (Davis, 1989, p. 320); and
- Subjective Norm: 'the person's perception that most people who are important to him thin he should or should not perform the [behaviour] in question' (Fishbein & Ajzen, 1975, p. 302).

It should be noted that the TAM and TOE models are often integrated (Chatterjee et al., 2021; Gangwar et al., 2015). The organisational and external environment concepts of the TOE model (see Figure 5.3), then serve as predictors of the ease of use (PEOU) and perceived usefulness (PU) of the technology.

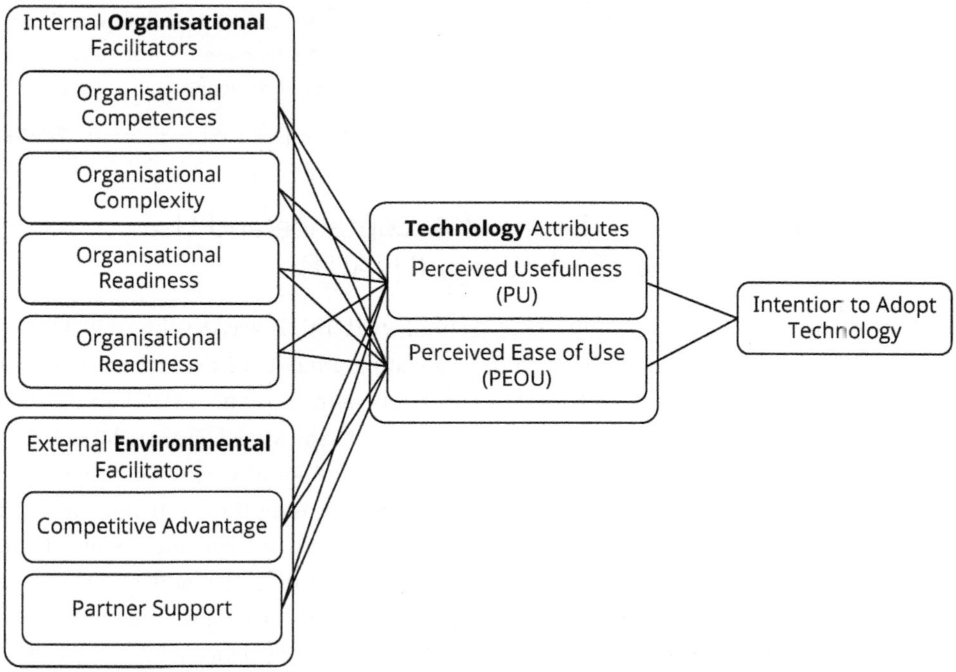

Figure 5.3 Integrated TOE-TAM technology adoption model

Source: adapted from Chatterjee et al. (2021)

Box 5.2: Technology Adoption Under Conditions of Uncertainty

A common assumption of the technology diffusion model, technology organisation and environment model, the technology acceptance model, and unified theory of acceptance and use of technology is that, while subjective, it is possible to assess the merits of adopting a novel technology. It has, however, also been shown that, under conditions of high levels of uncertainty about the assessment of the merits for the adoption of a new technology, managers will take a comparative approach to make technology adoption decisions. These processes lead to conformity in technology adoption decisions across business organisations and/or employees, which is referred to as an isomorphic state. There are three institutional mechanisms that lead to isomorphic outcomes: mimetic, normative, and coercive isomorphic pressures, but there is also a competitive (economic) mechanism that can lead to isomorphic positions for technology adoption and use. Managers may decide to copy the technology adoption decisions that they observe others making (mimetic isomorphism), managers can make technology adoption decisions based on professional legitimised norms (normative isomorphism) or be coerced into adopting a technology by an authoritative entity that for example has the power to regulate an industry (coercive isomorphism). In free markets competitive outcomes can lead to a technology being adopted by all competing firms, if it is believed that the technology is the underlying driver of the competitive advantage of a high performing firm (competitive isomorphism). Ambrozio et al. (2025) showed that these different mechanisms may act at different times along a technology assessment and adoption decision-making timeline and be leveraged by advocates for a given technology, such as consulting firms and technology producers.

Source: Based on Ambrozio et al. (2025)

5.1.4 Unified Theory of Acceptance and Use of Technology (UTAUT)

The Unified Theory of Acceptance and Use of Technology (UTAUT) was developed in an extensive empirical study by Venkatesh et al. (2003), validating a model of technology acceptance that integrated the Motivational Model (MM), Theory of Planned Behavior (TPB), Decomposed Theory of Planned Behavior (DTPB), Technology Acceptance Model (TAM), Model of PC Utilisation (MPCU), Innovation Diffusion Theory (IDT), and Social Cognitive Theory (SCT). The paper systematically reviewed previous empirical studies using these different theoretical models and then synthesised the direct determinants of technology acceptance, while identifying any moderating effects (Venkatesh et al., 2003). The final result was a model that explained technology acceptance by individuals that included four main determinants and four moderating effects. Technology acceptance is more likely if there are high performance expectations, low effort expectations, the technology is perceived positively in the decision-makers' reference groups (social influence), and the needed facilitating conditions are present.

- Performance Expectations: 'the degree to which an individual believes that using the system will help him or her to attain gains in job performance';

- Effort Expectations: 'the degree of ease associated with the use of the system';
- Social Influence: 'the degree to which an individual perceives that important others believe he or she should use the new system'; and
- Facilitating Conditions: 'defined as the degree to which an individual believes that an organizational and technical infrastructure exists to support use of the system'.

There is clear evidence that the four direct effects of performance expectations, effort expectations, social influence, and facilitating conditions are affected by the gender, age, experience, and perceived voluntariness of use of a technology when a technology is being assessed by a potential user (Venkatesh et al., 2003). Uncertainty also plays an important role, see Box 5.2.

5.2 DIGITAL TECHNOLOGIES

Going deeper into the major specific digital technologies allows a deeper engagement with those technologies as listed in Table 5.2, as each technology should be discussed in terms of its informational, computing, communication, networking, controlling, and sensing capabilities. Furthermore, each technology should be linked to managerial and/or operational work. Finally, the degree to which human–technology networks and the degree to which the technology is assisting humans or vice versa, can be assessed and critically evaluated (see Box 5.7).

5.2.1 Blockchain Technology

Blockchain technology is based on distributed ledger technology (DLT), which enables information to be recorded and stored by multiple networked entities to create a transparent, immutable, and irreversible record of transactions/activities (Rajasekaran et al., 2022). The blockchain is a set of interconnected blocks of information, with each block holding a time-stamp, transaction data, and the cryptographic hash of the preceding block, which makes the retroactive modification of the blocks impossible. While blockchain technology is generally associated strongly with cryptocurrencies, e.g., Bitcoin, the blockchain also enables other capabilities, not least smart contracts. Additionally, there are multiple approaches to implementing blockchain technology, that are distinguished by the degree to which the information in the blockchain is public centralised or decentralised, whether they are permissioned (private) or permissionless (public) and the consensus mechanism used.

Permissionless blockchains depend on anonymity for ensuring confidentiality, as they can be accessed by anyone at any time and the transaction blocks are publicly visible. There are three types of permissioned blockchains: private, consortium, and hybrid networks. Fully private blockchains are considered the most secure, as only entities with permission are able to access the network and transact and see transaction information. Consortium blockchains are semi-decentralised and allow managers of the blockchain to decide which aspects of the blockchain to make public or keep private. Hybrid blockchains allow for transactions to be verified privately and publicly (Rajasekaran et al., 2022). Different consensus mechanisms are typically used, with non-permissioned (public) blockchains widely adopting Proof-of-Work,

Proof-of-Stake, and Delegated Proof-of-Stake (see also Figure 5.6), while private networks tend to adopt practical Byzantine Fault Tolerance (pBFT), Istanbul BFT, and federated BFT consensus mechanisms (Bains, 2022).

Table 5.2 Exemplary Digital Technologies

Digital Technology	Digital Technology Attributes					
	Information	**Communication**	**Networking**	**Computation**	**Sensing**	**Controlling**
Blockchain	YES	–	YES	YES	–	–
Cloud Computing	YES	(YES)	(YES)	YES	–	(YES)
Artificial Intelligence	YES	YES	–	YES	(YES)	YES
Fixed Industrial Robotics	–	(YES)	–	–	YES	YES
Mobile Drones and Robots	(YES)	(YES)	–	–	YES	YES
Social Media	YES	YES	YES	YES	–	–
Digital Platforms / Ecosystems	YES	YES	YES	YES	–	–
Virtual Reality / Augmented Reality / XR / MR	YES	YES	YES	YES	YES	–
Internet of Things (Consumer)	YES	YES	YES	YES	YES	YES
Industrial Internet of Things	YES	YES	YES	YES	YES	YES

Source: own synthesis based on the available literature

5.2.2 Cloud Computing

In the ideal case, but in practice not entirely realised, 'clouds are pools of endless computing resources with unlimited performance that provide endless amounts of resources at any time and automatically scale the performance of the system up and down as needed' (Egwutuoha et al., 2013, p. 8). As a result, cloud solutions are very attractive to firms as the migration of data storage and running of applications into the cloud promises benefits such as flexibility and lower investment, operating and maintenance costs, as well as improved organisational resilience, while significantly improving (re)scalability through on demand consumption of services. The most well-known cloud solution provider is Amazon Web Services, which provides storage (Amazon S3), CPU capacity (Amazon EC2), or databases (SimpleDB) as services that can be consumed on a pay-as-you-go basis.

Firms that transition their IT into the cloud must decide on whether they wish to adopt private, public, community, or hybrid cloud solutions. Private clouds are hosted on the servers of a company and the services provided are only used by the members of that organisation or its partners, which increases security. Public clouds provide 'computing, computer resources (e.g., CPU, storage, bandwidth, databases, load balancers) [...] to the public' via a cloud service provider, reducing security and control for users (Egwutuoha et al., 2013). Community clouds serve a specific group of users that share common goals or missions; they have greater security and cost savings than public clouds, but less security than private clouds. Hybrid clouds are a combination of private, public, and community clouds and dependent on interoperability and the management of complexity from the required coordination.

Cloud solutions are offered in four architectures, Hardware as a Service (HaaS), Platform as a Service (PaaS), Infrastructures as a Service (IaaS), and Software as a Service (SaaS) (Egwutuoha et al., 2013, pp. 9–10):

- Hardware as a Service (HaaS) cloud provider basically rent out bare-bone hardware, like computers, data servers, firewalls, load-balancer, and routers, which has to be installed, configured, and maintained by the cloud user via the internet.
- Infrastructure as a Service (IaaS) is similar to HaaS, but virtual machines are rented out instead of real hardware. IaaS cloud users have to install, configure, and maintain the virtual machines they rent and are free to choose the operating system and software stack they install.
- Platform as a Service (PaaS) provides the cloud user with a fully configured and managed computing platform, ready to run custom software developed by the user.
- Software as a Service (SaaS) is the highest abstraction level in the cloud and offers cloud users ready-to-use online applications that are already deployed in the cloud, hidden from the user, and managed by the SaaS provider. The user does not need to do or understand anything about the setup, apart from how to use them.

Could solutions raise significant concerns for managers about trust in the service providers, the security of data in the cloud, service guarantees, the location of data and data protection regulations, cybersecurity, and risk of lock-in with a provider (Egwutuoha et al., 2013).

5.2.3 Artificial Intelligence

Artificial intelligence (AI) can be thought of as computer-based learning and reasoning systems (Sarker, 2021; van Harmelen & ten Teije, 2019; Witschel et al., 2022) that tries to mimic human behavior (Turing, 1950). AI therefore refers to the simulation of human intelligence in machines ('digital computers' according to Alan Turing (1950)) that are programmed to think and learn like humans (see Box 5.3). AI encompasses a broad range of technologies and techniques that enable computers to perform tasks that typically require human intelligence, such as reasoning, learning, problem-solving, perception, and language understanding. AI systems can be classified into narrow AI (designed for specific tasks like voice recognition or image classification) and general AI (designed to perform any intellectual task that a human can do). There are essentially two levels of AI in terms of their levels of complexity and learning capabilities, namely machine learning (ML) and deep learning (DL) (see Figure 5.4). See Box 5.4 and 5.5 for a critical perspective.

Machine learning (ML), as a subset of AI, focuses on the development of algorithms and statistical models that enable computers to learn from and make predictions or decisions based on data. Unlike traditional programming, where explicit instructions are provided, ML algorithms identify patterns and relationships in data to build models. Deep learning (DL) is a subset of ML that uses neural networks with many layers (hence 'deep') to model and understand complex patterns in data. These neural networks, inspired by the structure and function of the human brain, consist of interconnected nodes (neurons) that process input data through multiple layers. Each layer extracts higher-level features from the raw input, enabling the network to learn intricate patterns and representations. Deep learning can complete tasks involving unstructured data, such as image and speech recognition and natural language processing. It requires large amounts of data and computational power for training but can achieve remarkable accuracy and performance in various applications. Within DL, one application is generative AI (GenAI) (such as Claude AI (Antropic), ChatGPT (OpenAI), Google Gemini, Microsoft Copilot, Midjourney), which leverages deep learning techniques to create models capable of generating new data.

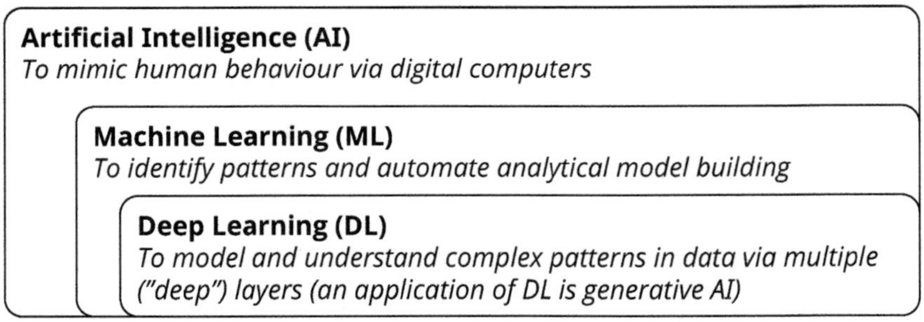

Figure 5.4 Simplified AI terminology

Source: own illustration following Sarker (2021, p. 420); Turing (1950); and Wietschel et al. (2022)

Box 5.3: Alan Turing and the Dawn of AI

In his seminal paper 'Computing Machinery and Intelligence' from 1950, Alan Turing explores the question 'Can machines think?' He proposes replacing this question with a more practical one: 'Can machines play the imitation game?' This game involves an interrogator who must distinguish between a human and a machine based solely on their responses to questions. If the machine's responses are indistinguishable from the human's, it can be said to 'think.' Turing discusses the capabilities and limitations of digital computers, which he defines as discrete-state machines capable of performing any operation a human computer can. He emphasises the universality of digital computers, meaning they can mimic any other human 'machine' given sufficient storage and speed.

Important quotes from Turing's (1950) paper:

- 'The idea behind digital computers may be explained by saying that these machines are intended to carry out any operations which could be done by a human computer.'
- 'The reader must accept it as a fact that digital computers (...) can in fact mimic the actions of a human computer very closely.'
- 'Sometimes such a machine is described as having free will.'
- 'The original question, "Can machines think?" I believe to be too meaningless to deserve discussion. Nevertheless I believe that at the end of the century (...) one will be able to speak of machines thinking without expecting to be contradicted.'
- 'We may hope that machines will eventually compete with men in all purely intellectual fields (...) and then teach it to understand and speak English'.

Source: Turing (1950)

Box 5.4: The Future of AI and its Impact on Humanity

Grace et al. (2024) presented the findings of a large-scale survey conducted among 2,778 AI researchers, focusing on their predictions regarding the future of AI. The survey revealed that there is at least a 50% chance of AI systems achieving significant milestones by 2028, such as autonomously creating a payment processing site, composing songs indistinguishable from those by popular musicians, and fine-tuning large language models. Researchers estimate a 10% chance of AI outperforming humans in all tasks by 2027 and a 50% chance by 2047. However, the full automation of all human occupations is expected to reach a 10% probability by 2037 and 50% by 2116.

The survey highlights substantial uncertainty about the long-term impacts of AI, with 68% of respondents believing that good outcomes are more likely than bad ones. Nonetheless, 48% of these optimists still consider a 5% chance of extremely bad outcomes, such as human extinction. Additionally, 51% of respondents give at least a 10% chance to AI leading to catastrophic outcomes.

The survey also identifies several AI-related scenarios that warrant substantial or extreme concern, including the spread of false information, authoritarian population control, and increased inequality. There is a lack of consensus on whether faster or slower AI progress would be better for humanity, but there is broad agreement on the need to prioritise research aimed at minimising potential risks from AI systems.

Box 5.5: The European Union's AI Act

The European Union's AI Act (European Union, 2025) aims to regulate artificial intelligence (AI) to ensure safety, transparency, and human oversight. The Act classifies AI systems into four risk categories: unacceptable, high, limited, and minimal risk.

1. Unacceptable Risk: AI systems that pose significant threats, such as social scoring by governments or manipulative techniques that exploit vulnerabilities, are prohibited.
2. High Risk: These systems, which include critical infrastructure, education, employment, and law enforcement applications, are subject to stringent requirements. Providers must ensure robust risk management, data governance, transparency, human oversight, and cybersecurity measures. They must also conduct conformity assessments before placing these systems on the market.
3. Limited Risk: AI systems with limited risk, such as chatbots and deepfakes, must meet transparency obligations. Users should be informed that they are interacting with AI.
4. Minimal Risk: Most AI applications, like spam filters and AI-enabled video games, fall under this category and are largely unregulated.

The Act places the majority of obligations on providers (developers) of high-risk AI systems, including those outside the EU if their systems are used within the EU. Users (deployers) of high-risk AI systems also have responsibilities, though less extensive than those of providers. Additionally, the Act addresses general-purpose AI (GPAI) models, requiring providers to offer technical documentation, usage instructions, and summaries of training data. Providers of GPAI models that present systemic risks must conduct evaluations, adversarial testing, and report serious incidents.

The AI Act entered into force on 1 August 2024 and will be fully applicable two years later (in August 2026), with some exceptions, such as the rules for high-risk AI systems that have an extended transition period until August 2027.

5.2.4 Robotics (Fixed and Mobile)

Robotics and robots have been critical to many industrial automation processes and are an integral element of Industry 4.0, introducing new topics like collaborative robotics (cobots), autonomous robots and human–robot interactions. Traditionally robots have been physical and fixed in position, but increasingly physical robots are becoming mobile and autonomous (e.g., drones) (Grau et al., 2020; Tóth et al., 2022). Robots in the traditional sense are automated devices that perform activities normally done by humans, relying on sensing and controlling technologies to engage with their environment and collaborate with humans. In addition, robots are able to take any physical form their designers deem appropriate. This decision is significantly determined by the degree to which the robot is intended to complete general or very specific tasks, but also the degree to which the task needs to be completed in the physical world or in cyberspace.

Recent advances in artificial intelligence have enabled the emergence of AI robots that 'are semi-autonomous, insensate entities that exhibit behaviours of living beings and possess the abilities of learning and decision-making to facilitate human activity' (Tóth et al., 2022, p. 898). AI Robots can have a physical form, when machines are complemented with artificial intelligence, or take a virtual form when there is no need to interact with the physical environment, these virtual robots are, however, also endowed with intelligence, are able to learn and have the capability of taking autonomous action, as for example with agents. Both physical and virtual robots can do tasks previously completed by humans, by combining automation, learning, and decision-making capabilities, but a key distinction from humans is that robots do not experience emotions.

Box 5.6: Technology Radar

A technology radar (see Figure 5.5) is a tool that a firm can use to support the identification of relevant digital technologies, as well as structuring the observation and evaluation of those tools in practice. As a monitoring tool it supports the leadership team in a firm with the strategic technology development off the business. A technology radar provides information about technology trends within the environment of the firm and thereby provides critical information for the planning of research and development activities by the firm. Technology radar does not only support the identification and development of new technologies but also allows the identification of technologies that are no longer attractive given broader market and technology trends, thus potentially needing to be replaced. Critically a technology radar allows the leadership team of a firm to compare technology trends to the actual technology portfolio of the business, thereby allowing any needed change initiatives to be identified and subsequently implemented (Peter, 2023, 2024).

The Following Steps are Necessary to Create a Technology Radar:

- Identify relevant technology or application areas.
- Collect information about relevant technology and application areas.
- Evaluate these technologies and applications.
- Visualise and communicate the results in the radar.

For Example, the Following Questions can be Answered:

- When will a technology be ready for the market?
- How relevant is a technology to a specific business unit?
- What is the maturity of a technology?
- How likely is it that a technology will make an existing product or service obsolete?
- What is the barrier to adoption of a technology directly into production?

(Continued)

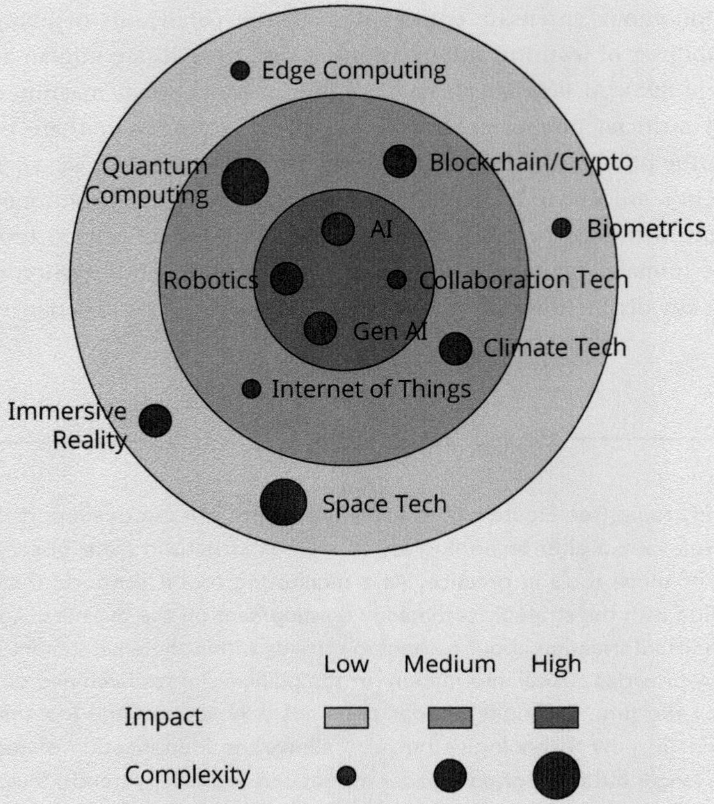

Figure 5.5 Example of a technology radar

Note: The digital technology radar is a visual representation of digital technologies with its two dimensions of Impact (from low to high) and Complexity (from low to high). The radar was developed from the viewpoint of a typical, small or medium-sized commercial organisation (which doesn't necessarily have the resources of a large enterprise). The categorisation is based on a medium-term (3–5 years) perspective, aligning with the planning horizon of most strategy roadmaps.

Source: Wingenter & Peter (2025)

5.2.5 Social Media

Social media is a Web 2.0 enabled set of internet- and mobile-enabled applications that allow users to build communities, interact, and communicate, with the purpose of sharing, exchanging, and consuming user-generated content (Kapoor et al., 2018; Ngai et al., 2015). Social media is enabled by digital platforms and the users of social media include not only individuals, but also organisations. The popularity of social media with individual users, but also its adoption by organisations, is explained by a range of theories, but they can be divided into explanations that focus on individual human users and mass communication theories. These foci reflect the nature of social media, where individuals join social media platforms, forming social networks, which allow one-to-one and one-to-many communication on social media platforms at a very low cost.

Social media has developed into a significant enabler of business activity, especially for building reputation, enabling transactions, developing customer relationships and building brands. These activities typically take place on dominant social media platforms, such as LinkedIn, X (formerly Twitter), Facebook, TikTok, WeChat, Instagram, Pinterest, and YouTube. An important aspect of social media is the large amounts of data that the user-generated content creation and consumption provides social media companies about their users (Kapoor et al., 2018), which is a highly valuable resource for advertising services on the platforms. Indeed, advertising revenues on social media platforms are now well understood as one of a number of streams of value being created on social media platforms and being distributed to content creators on the platforms. The reach of popular creators is very attractive for brands and advertisers, but firms can also use the social media platforms to undertake reputation building and for communicating with stakeholders. The user generated reviews of company products and services can also be of critical importance to firms.

5.2.6 Digital Platforms and Ecosystems

Social media is arguably a special case of a broader category of digital platforms and ecosystems, which are arguably the organisational form most strongly associated with the digital age (Gawer, 2022). Digital platforms and the associated ecosystems are enabled by a socio-technical system of pervasive connectivity and data generation, enabled by computers and mobile devices, the internet, connectivity technologies, increasingly sensor technologies; and the community of (human) users which engage as additional actors on the platform, or in the ecosystem (examples are Airbnb in the Western world (or Tujia in China) and Uber (or DiDi respectively)). The ability to process the resulting ongoing generation of data is additionally dependent on progress in computing, cloud services, and, as seen most recently, advances in artificial intelligence. The development of digital platforms and their ecosystems relies on connectivity; re-programmable functionality and re-purposable digital devices; and data generation, capture, and analysis. The resulting distributed socio-technical systems allow an unprecedented capacity for identifying, monitoring, and/or controlling agents or assets in a given ecosystem (this might be illustrated by the ability of employers to monitor the work of employees working from home, and by monitoring how they use their devices). Despite the diversity of contexts within which digital platforms and their ecosystems are deployed, they have some common characteristics in terms of how they create value, including 'the generation of economies of scale and scope and network effects, leading to winner-take-all monopolistic positions' (Gawer, 2022, p. 112) for dominant platforms. These sources of value are realised in the provision of matching services and low search costs, enabling market expansion and facilitation of innovation. While technologies enable these characteristics to emerge, it is important to remember that these socio-technical systems are also reliant on and taking advantage of human behaviour to create value.

5.2.7 Extended, Virtual, Augmented, and Mixed Reality

Extended reality (XR) is an umbrella term which covers all real and virtual combined digital environments and interactions generated by computer technology. It includes virtual reality (VR), augmented reality (AR), and mixed reality (MR).

XR/VR technology has a long history, conceptualised in the 1960s, first commercialised in the 1980s, and in the last 20 years realised in products like the Oculus Rift and Sony PlayStation VR (Cipresso et al., 2018). In addition to XR/VR, there has more recently been extensive interest in augmented reality (AR). Virtual reality systems seek to immerse a user in a modelled digital world and allow the user to interact with that world in real time, enabled by computing, display, and multiple sensory technologies. These VR systems are distinguished by their degree of immersion, with common applications being in gaming, training, design, education and learning, learning of procedures, and psychological treatments. Augmented reality (AR) systems are a 'newer technological system in which virtual objects are added to the real world in real-time during the user's experience' (Cipresso et al., 2018, p. 4). These AR systems combine real world and virtual objects in real time and in an interactive manner, with the real world and virtual objects interacting. Applications of VR systems include architecture, maintenance, entertainment, education, medicine, and psychological treatments. Finally, mixed reality (MR) blends elements of both AR and VR, where physical and digital objects co-exist and interact in real time.

5.2.8 (Industrial) Internet of Things

The Internet of Things (IoT) refers to a computing concept that describes the ever-increasing connectivity of common devices to the internet (e.g., as a component of cyber-physical systems, see Chapter 1). The idea is 'to deploy billions or even trillions of smart objects capable of sensing the surrounding environment, transmit and process acquired data, and then feedback to the environment' (Sisinni et al., 2018, p. 4724). The aim is to improve the connection between the physical and digital worlds in an integrated cyber-physical system, for instance, via a Wireless Sensor Network (WSN see Box 5.7), allowing the exchange of information and enabling digital systems to sense via and control devices in the physical world. Initially the focus was on the everyday lives of people and the use of ordinary devices in the normal conduct of their lives, but the IOT concept developed to also include the industrial Internet of Things (IIoT), which includes 'the domains of machine-to-machine (M2M) and industrial communication technologies with automation applications' (Sisinni et al., 2018, p. 4724). This is argued to have the potential to increase efficiency and sustainability of manufacturing activities. The IOT is thus a consumer and human-centred system that needs to be able to integrate a wide variety of devices flexibly, while the IIOT is an industrial application that is machine-oriented, requiring highly reliable integration of devices and standards, as well as connectivity to ensure mission critical activities are not at risk in terms of timing, reliability, security, and privacy.

Box 5.7: Long Range Wide Area Network (LoRaWAN)

LoRa (Long Range) is a wireless sensor network (WSN) technology that enables low-power, long-range data transmission between sensors and gateways. LoRa gateways are radio modules that serve as a bridge between electronic devices (end nodes) and the Internet of Things (IoT). A LoRa gateway is used to transmit sensor data from an electronic device to the cloud. A Long Range Wide Area Network (LoRaWAN) enables energy-efficient data transmission over long distances. and is specifically designed for the Internet of Things (IoT) and the Industrial Internet of Things (IIoT). With LoRaWAN, it is possible to manage hundreds of sensors in a network and process large amounts of sensor data. The sensors can be operated for up to ten years without charging the batteries. Such a network can be used, for example, to continuously monitor a large area with multiple sensors – for example, the temperature, pollution levels, or humidity in a cold storage facility.

Also see the '*BRUGG Lifting and its industrial Internet of Things (IIoT) asset management solution "PVS"*' case in the case study collection (Appendix).

5.3 METHODS OF DEVELOPING AND TESTING DIGITAL TECHNOLOGY SOLUTIONS

Using various methods, digital technologies can be tested within the organisation or with partners (e.g., start-ups or universities). Following Duggan & Leurs (2018), these are the most common methods in business practice (Peter, 2023, 2024):

- A **proof of concept (POC)** is the technical implementation of an idea (in this case using digital technologies) to demonstrate its feasibility or to check whether the general idea/concept can be implemented in practice. The functionalities developed in a proof of concept are usually limited, so the newly developed product can only be used to a limited extent.
- A **prototype** is a technically developed solution (product or service) with a limited range of functions. However, it is sufficiently developed that it can be used for (limited) testing of a concept. The results from the tests (functional tests, technical tests, market acceptance tests) are used to test and validate the original idea with the aim of finalising the requirements for the pilot.
- A **pilot** is a technical solution that can be tested in a limited circle and with limited use cases. The pilot is usually not made available or marketed externally. Organisations use pilot projects to test technical feasibility and determine the effectiveness of its implementation. Pilot projects are typically of limited scope and duration in terms of progression to a minimum viable product (MVP) or directly to a fully engineered solution.

- A **minimum viable product (MVP)** is a technical product with sufficient (i.e., minimally usable) functions to test a product idea in the market and often with selected customers. It helps to get customer feedback quickly (and often before the actual launch) in order to further develop the solution in later iterations. An MVP corresponds to the basic needs of the customer and can be already advanced enough to achieve market success.

Depending on various factors such as the scope of the solution (components of an innovation/ solution, or to build an entire solution/service/product), the maturity and required market readiness of the innovation (from idea to a final product), and available budgets/funding, the above approaches for digital technology development and testing can be utilised.

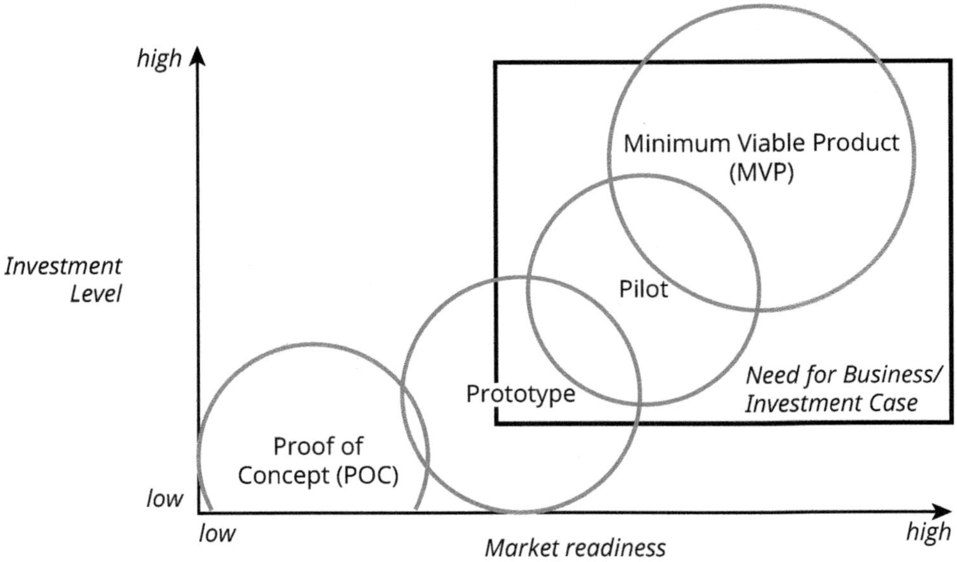

Figure 5.6 Methods of developing and testing digital technology solutions

Source: own Illustration adapted from Duggan & Leurs (2018)

5.4 NEW DIGITAL TECHNOLOGIES AND CYBERSECURITY

Digital technologies are featured by connectivity to the internet, the exchange of information and, increasingly, sensing and controlling the physical environment; additionally consumers and firms are increasingly conducting business online via electronic commerce and more recently mobile commerce. These trends are increasingly associated with ever greater concerns about cybersecurity (Garrett, 2019) to guard against the ongoing emergence and evolution of cyber threats to citizens, consumers, firms, and governments (see Box 5.8). Cyber threats can be divided into technical cybercrimes, attacks that alter the normal functioning of a device (e.g., malware and ransomware) and social cybercrimes, which exploit human errors and use social engineering to gain access to sensitive or private information (e.g., phishing or spam attacks) (Martens et al., 2019). For firms it is critical to assess both organisational and employee cybersecurity readiness to counter cyber threats. While there are cybersecurity risks associated with technologies adopted by firms, it is critical to acknowledge the central role of individual employees in ensuring cybersecurity in the increasing complex socio-technical/cyber-physical systems that underpin value creation in firms today. Employees respond to cyber threats on the basis of their cyber threat awareness and coping awareness for cyber threats, thus any initiative to improve the capability of employees to identify and know how to respond to a cyber threat is going to increase the likelihood that cyber threats can be effectively addressed (Martens et al., 2019). Employees that have awareness of, and confidence they can respond effectively to, a cyberthreat are more likely to develop attitudes towards cyber threats that will lead to, undertaking protective behaviour; importantly these attitudes are affected by subjective norms of employees' social groups (Martens et al., 2019).

Box 5.8: Verizon's Data Breach Investigations Report (DBIR)

The 2024 Data Breach Investigations Report (DBIR) by Verizon provides a comprehensive analysis of the current cyber threat landscape. Some key findings include:

- *Attack vectors*: phishing, exploitation of vulnerabilities, and the use of stolen credentials are the main pathways to breaches. In addition, ransomware and Denial of Service (DoS) attacks continue to be significant threats.
- *Emerging threats*: the report notes the rise of new and innovative attacks, alongside variations of traditional methods. For instance, the exploitation of zero-day vulnerabilities.
- *Key stats:*
    - 68% of breaches involved a non-malicious human element, like a person falling victim to a social engineering attack or making an error.
    - 62% of financially motivated incidents involved ransomware or extortion, with a median loss of $46,000 per breach.
    - 15% of breaches involved a third party or supplier, such as software supply chains, hosting partner infrastructures, or data custodians.
    - 14% of breaches involved the exploitation of vulnerabilities as an initial access step.

To combat these threats, the report emphasises the importance of robust security measures, including regular updates and patches, employee training on phishing and social engineering, and the implementation of multi-factor authentication.

Source Verizon, 2024

5.5 NEW DIGITAL TECHNOLOGIES AND COMPETITIVE ADVANTAGE

Studies of the impact of digital technologies on firm performance to date have a tendency to focus on the relationship between digital technology adoption and innovation activities, including service innovations, and product innovations (Blichfeldt & Faullant, 2021). Interestingly, the degree to which there is evidence for a relationship between the adoption of digital technologies and increases in innovation is mixed, with some authors finding evidence (Blichfeldt & Faullant, 2021,) and others finding no direct effect (Usai et al., 2021). Usai et al. (2021), for example, argue that while they found that digital technologies increased efficiency, the source of competitive advantage for firms in their study remained the firm's unique knowledge that was not dependent on the underlying technology. One reason for this may be the imitability and general-purpose nature of most digital technologies.

5.6 NEW DIGITAL TECHNOLOGIES AND SUSTAINABILITY

It is not possible to assess the impact of individual digital technologies on the sustainability of a firm in isolation (as discussed in the previous section), as the impact of digital technology adoption and the digital transformation of a firm requires a careful assessment of the degree to which the technology impacts the rate of desirable and undesirable flows and drawing on and contributions to desirable and undesirable stocks in the external natural environment and society. As has been pointed out by Bohnsack et al. (2022), this leads to an ambiguous picture of the sustainability of digital technologies, which is more often than not featured by simultaneous intended and realised outcomes that may differ to varying degrees, while also having associated unintended positive and negative consequences.

5.7 CONCLUSION

Chapter 5 focuses on the strategic action field of new digital technologies, exploring their adoption, value creation, competitive advantage, and sustainability. The opening case study on the non-adoption of blockchain technology in supply chains, demonstrates the concerns about its maturity, lack of use cases, and resource constraints.

The successful integration of digital technologies in response to the digital transformation of businesses (and society) can use four key models of technology adoption and acceptance, including the Technology Diffusion Model (TDM), Technology, Organisation, and Environment Model (TOE), Technology Acceptance Model (TAM), and Unified Theory of Acceptance and Use of Technology (UTAUT). These models explain how perceptions of technology users and decision-makers influence the adoption and diffusion of new technologies. In addition, they can be applied to specific digital technologies, such as blockchain, cloud computing, artificial intelligence (AI), robotics, social media, digital platforms, extended reality (XR), and the

Internet of Things (IoT), to understand and remove barriers, and identify future strategic opportunity. Here, a technology radar (see Box 5.6) and the ongoing development and testing of digital technology solutions (see Figure 5.6) provide meaningful tools and method to both evaluate and build new digital technology based products and services.

The chapter concludes by addressing the cybersecurity risks associated with digital technologies and their potential impact on firm performance and sustainability. It emphasises the importance of careful consideration and strategic planning in adopting new technologies to ensure they align with a firm's goals and ecosystem.

Case Studies

Students can complete the following tasks either based on the focal case study, or work on the recommended case study for this chapter (*BRUGG Lifting and its industrial Internet of Things (IIoT) asset management solution 'PVS'*) and answer the questions below.

1. What are the challenges when developing solutions/products based on new technologies (i.e., technologies that an organisation previously did not use)?
2. What are the challenges when introducing a new technology to the market?
3. What are the benefits of a POC (proof of concept) test installation on a customer's site or in the customer's work environment (see Chapter 5.3)?
4. What is the link between new digital technologies and cybersecurity (see Chapter 5.4). Why does cybersecurity need to be considered in light of new digital technology?
5. Why and how can new (digital) technology support the competitiveness of an organisation with existing products and services (see Chapter 5.5)?
6. Why is the definition of a business model important for new technology-based solutions/products?
7. Why do organisations need to balance technology versus go-to-market (sales and marketing) investments?

Additional cases with student questions for the strategic digital action field of *New Digital Technologies* are covered in:

- Adelbodner mineral water – the digital roadmap of a SME (available online).
- IT portfolio management and corporate knowledge – Colloquial enterprise architecture management (available online).
- Action fields of digital transformation at Synchrony Financial (USA) (available online).
- Sulzer – strategic leadership in sustainable, digital tech-enabled value-adding services (available online).
- CRM and sales automation at Transgourmet Switzerland (available online).
- From limited budget to limitless potential: the digital journey of OSHE@UTMKL (available online).
- Valuu: a corporate start-up for digital business model innovation (available in the Appendix).

You will find the collection of case studies for Strategic Digital Transformation in the Appendix and additional cases online at www.strategic-digital-transformation.com.

Exercises

Discuss the following questions in your class, in your group, or assignment:

1. Analyse and discuss the opening case study (The Surprising Case of Blockchain Technology Non-Adoption in Supply Chains) in light of the four technology adoption theories (TDM, TOE, TAM, and UTAUT) as presented in Table 5.1. Why was blockchain adoption so low?
2. What are the success factors for digital technology innovation to create value and a firm's competitive advantage? Identify and describe at least three success factors.
3. Based on a selected industry/business, select a technology (see for instance the digital technologies as presented in Table 5.2), and describe how you could test and develop them with a POC, prototype, pilot, or MVP (see Figure 5.6).
4. How will AI impact businesses in the future? Discuss both opportunities and risks associated with AI based on the selected industry/business in exercise 3.
5. Forming two small groups (2–4 students in each group), assign a pro and contra position to each group and debate whether AI has more positive or negative benefits for society and businesses in the long-run (reference Turing's 1950 statements in Box 5.3).
6. For your selected industry/business in exercise 3, identify and evaluate the most prominent digital technologies on a technology radar (see Box 5.6).
7. Identify and describe the cybersecurity risks impacting organisations? How can cybercriminals attack a firm's IT system, steal or manipulate data, or blackmail the organisation (ask for ransomware)? For each identified risk, describe how the business can protect itself from the threats/risks.

Further Reading List

- Moore, G. C., & Benbasat, I. (1991). Development of an instrument to measure the perceptions of adopting an information technology innovation. *Information Systems Research*, 2(3), 192–222.
- Verizon (2024): 2024 Data Breach Investigations Report (DBIR). *Verizon*, May, www.verizon.com/business/resources/Te3/reports/2024-dbir-data-breach-investigations-report.pdf.
- Wingenter, T., & Peter, M.K. (2025). Digital Technology Radar 2025, Digital-Technology-Radar.net, https://digital-technology-radar.net/ (accessed on 6 March 2025). The following fact sheets are available online:
  - Artificial Intelligence (A)
  - Generative AI (Gen AI)

- Biometrics
- Blockchain and Crypto
- Climate Tech
- Collaboration Tech
- Robotics
- Edge Computing
- Immersive Reality (VR, AR, XR)
- Internet of Things (IoT)
- Quantum Computing
- Space Tech

References

Ambrozio, S., Lindeque, J. P., & Peter, M.K. (2025). Navigating uncertainty: Isomorphic pressures in cloud computing adoption, in: Moussa, M., & McMurray, A. (eds), *Palgrave Handbook of Breakthrough Technologies in Contemporary Organisations* (pp. 221–234). Singapore: Springer Nature.

Bains, P. (2022). *Blockchain Consensus Mechanisms: A Primer for Supervisors.* International Monetary Fund, January 2022.

Blichfeldt, H., & Faullant, R. (2021). Performance effects of digital technology adoption and product & service innovation: A process-industry perspective. *Technovation, 105*, 102275.

Bohnsack, R., Bidmon, C. M., & Pinkse, J. (2022). Sustainability in the digital age: Intended and unintended consequences of digital technologies for sustainable development. *Business Strategy and the Environment, 31*(2), 599–602.

Chatterjee, S., Rana, N. P., Dwivedi, Y. K., & Baabdullah, A. M. (2021). Understanding AI adoption in manufacturing and production firms using an integrated TAM–TOE model. *Technological Forecasting and Social Change, 170*, 120880.

Cipresso, P., Giglioli, I. A. C., Raya, M. A., & Riva, G. (2018). The past, present, and future of virtual and augmented reality research: a network and cluster analysis of the literature. *Frontiers in Psychology, 9*, 309500.

Davis, F. D. (1989). Perceived usefulness, perceived ease of use, and user acceptance of information technology. *MIS Quarterly*, 319–40.

Davis, F. D., & Venkatesh, V. (1996). A critical assessment of potential measurement biases in the technology acceptance model: three experiments. *International Journal of Human-Computer Studies, 45*(1), 19–45.

Duggan, K. and Leurs, B. (2018): 'Proof of Concept, Prototype, Pilot, MVP – What's in a Name? Four Methods for Testing and Developing Solutions', Nesta, London/UK, www.nesta.org.uk/blog/proof-of-concept-prototype-pilot-mvp-whats-in-a-name/.

Egwutuoha, I. P., Schragl, D., & Calvo, R. (2013). A brief review of cloud computing, challenges and potential solutions. *Parallel & Cloud Computing, 2*(1), 7–14.

European Union (2025): AI Act, https://digital-strategy.ec.europa.eu/en/policies/regulatory-framework-ai, last update 18 February 2025.

Fishbein, M. & Ajzen, I. (1975). *Belief, Attitude, Intention and Behavior: An Introduction to Theory and Research.* Reading, MA: Addison-Wesley.

Gangwar, H., Date, H., & Ramaswamy, R. (2015). Understanding determinants of cloud computing adoption using an integrated TAM–TOE model. *Journal of Enterprise Information Management, 28*(1), 107–30.

Gangwar, H., Date, H., & Raoot, A. D. (2014). Review on IT adoption: Insights from recent technologies. *Journal of Enterprise Information Management, 27*(4), 488–502.

Garrett, G.A. (2019). Introduction, in Garrett, G.A. (ed.) *Cybersecurity in the Digital Age: Tools, Techniques, & Best Practices* (pp. ix-x). Wolters Kluwer.

Gawer, A. (2022). Digital platforms and ecosystems: Remarks on the dominant organizational forms of the digital age. *Innovation, 24*(1), 110–24.

Grace, K., Stewart, H., Sandkühler, J. F., Thomas, S., Weinstein-Raun, B., & Brauner, J. (2024). Thousands of AI authors on the future of AI. arXiv preprint arXiv:2401.02843.

Grau, A., Indri, M., Bello, L. L., & Sauter, T. (2020). Robots in industry: The past, present, and future of a growing collaboration with humans. *IEEE Industrial Electronics Magazine, 15*(1), 50-61.

Hubenova, T., Lindeque, J. P., & Peter, M. K. (2024). Explaining the non-adoption of blockchain technology in global value chains: a micro-foundational perspective. *Journal of Industrial and Business Economics*, 1–33.

Kapoor, K. K., Tamilmani, K., Rana, N. P., Patil, P., Dwivedi, Y. K., & Nerur, S. (2018). Advances in social media research: Past, present and future. *Information Systems Frontiers, 20*, 531–58.

Martens, M., De Wolf, R., & De Marez, L. (2019). Investigating and comparing the predictors of the intention towards taking security measures against malware, scams and cybercrime in general. *Computers in Human Behavior, 92*, 139–50.

Moore, G. C., & Benbasat, I. (1991). Development of an instrument to measure the perceptions of adopting an information technology innovation. *Information Systems Research, 2*(3), 192–222.

Moosavi, J., Naeni, L. M., Fathollahi-Fard, A. M., & Fiore, U. (2021). Blockchain in supply chain management: A review, bibliometric, and network analysis. *Environmental Science and Pollution Research, 2021*, 1–15.

Ngai, E. W., Tao, S. S., & Moon, K. K. (2015). Social media research: Theories, constructs, and conceptual frameworks. *International Journal of Information Management, 35*(1), 33–44.

OECD (2005). *Oslo Manual: Guidelines for Collecting and Interpreting Innovation Data, 3rd Edition, The Measurement of Scientific and Technological Activities*, OECD Publishing, Paris, www.oecd.org/en/publications/oslo-manual_9789264013100-en.html.

Peter, M. K. (Hrsg.) (2017). *KMU-Transformation: Als KMU die Digitale Transformation erfolgreich umsetzen. Forschungsresultate und Praxisleitfaden.* FHNW Hochschule für Wirtschaft, Olten/Schweiz, www.kmu-transformation.ch.

Peter, M. K. (Hrsg.) (2021). *Strategieentwicklung im digitalen Zeitalter: Planung und Umsetzung der Digitalen Transformation.* FHNW Hochschule für Wirtschaft und Strategylab, Olten/Schweiz, www.strategische-transformation.ch.

Peter, M. K. (2023). *Digitaler Masterplan für KMU. So gelingt die digitale Transformation in Ihrem Unternehmen.* Verlag Beobachter Edition & Handelszeitung. Zürich/Schweiz, www.digitaler-masterplan.ch.

Peter, M. K. (2024). *The Digital Transformation Canvas. Develop and Implement Your Digital Strategy.* FT Publishing/Pearson, London/UK, www.the-digital-transformation-canvas.com.

Peter, M. K., Kraft, C., & Lindeque, J. (2020). Strategic action fields of digital transformation: An exploration of the strategic action fields of Swiss SMEs and large enterprises. *Journal of Strategy and Management, 13*(1), 160–80.

Rajasekaran, A. S., Azees, M., & Al-Turjman, F. (2022). A comprehensive survey on blockchain technology. *Sustainable Energy Technologies and Assessments, 52*(PA), 102039.

Rogers, E. M. (1983). *Diffusion of Innovations.* 3rd ed. The Free Press, New York.

Sisinni, E., Saifullah, A., Han, S., Jennehag, U., & Gidlund, M. (2018). Industrial Internet of Things: Challenges, opportunities, and directions. *IEEE Transactions on Industrial Informatics, 14*(11), 4724–34.

Sarker, I. H. (2021). Deep learning: A comprehensive overview on techniques, taxonomy, applications and research directions. *SN Computer Science, 2*(6), 1–20.

Tornatzky, L.G. & Fleischer, M. (1990). *The Processes of Technological Innovation*. Issues in organization and management series. Lexington, MS: Lexington Books.

Tóth, Z., Caruana, R., Gruber, T., & Loebbecke, C. (2022). The dawn of the AI robots: Towards a new framework of AI robot accountability. *Journal of Business Ethics, 178*(4), 895–916.

Turing, A.M. (1950). Computing machinery and intelligence. *Mind, 49*, 433–60.

Usai, A., Fiano, F., Petruzzelli, A. M., Paoloni, P., Briamonte, M. F., & Orlando, B. (2021). Unveiling the impact of the adoption of digital technologies on firms' innovation performance. *Journal of Business Research, 133*, 327–36.

Van Harmelen, F., & Ten Teije, A. (2019). A boxology of design patterns for hybrid learning and reasoning systems. *Journal of Web Engineering, 18*(1-3), 97-123.

Venkatesh, V., & Bala, H. (2008). Technology acceptance model 3 and a research agenda on interventions. *Decision Sciences, 39*(2), 273–315.

Venkatesh, V., & Davis, F. D. (2000). A theoretical extension of the technology acceptance model: Four longitudinal field studies. *Management Science, 46*, 186–204.

Venkatesh, V., Morris, M. G., Davis, G. B., & Davis, F. D. (2003). User acceptance of information technology: Toward a unified view. *MIS Quarterly, 27*(3), 425–78.

Venkatesh, V., Thong, J. Y., & Xu, X. (2016). Unified theory of acceptance and use of technology: A synthesis and the road ahead. *Journal of the Association for Information Systems, 17*(5), 328–76.

Verizon (2024): 2024 Data Breach Investigations Report (DBIR). Verizon, May, www.verizon.com/business/resources/Te3/reports/2024-dbir-data-breach-investigations-report.pdf.

Wingenter, T., & Peter, M.K. (2025). *Digital Technology Radar* 2025, Digital-Technology-Radar.net, https://digital-technology-radar.net/ (accessed on 6 March 2025).

Witschel, H. F., Pande, C., Martin, A., Laurenzi, E., & Hinkelmann, K. (2020). Visualization of patterns for hybrid learning and reasoning with human involvement. In Dornberger, R. (ed.) *New Trends in Business Information Systems and Technology Studies in Systems, Decision and Control, vol 294* (pp. 193–204). Cham: Springer International Publishing.

Yli-Huumo, J., Ko, D., Choi, S., Park, S., & Smolander, K. (2016). Where is current research on blockchain technology? – a systematic review. *PloS One, 11*(10), e0163477.

6

STRATEGIC ACTION FIELD OF DATA AND THE CLOUD

Learning Goals

By the end of this chapter, you should...

- Be able to describe the differences between data, information, and knowledge, and apply the taxonomy to concrete business situations.
- Be able to explain the advantage of hybrid systems based on human and machine-based knowledge creation.
- Be able to develop a data management plan, which provides organisations with an overview of their data sources, data quality levels, data usage, and connected software and data security measures.
- Be able to understand and assess the infrastructure and service model offerings of Cloud providers.
- Be able to evaluate the strategic and operational benefits of the data economy to improve the competitiveness of a firm (including products and services).
- Be able to articulate the legal requirements to organisations in light of data protection laws.

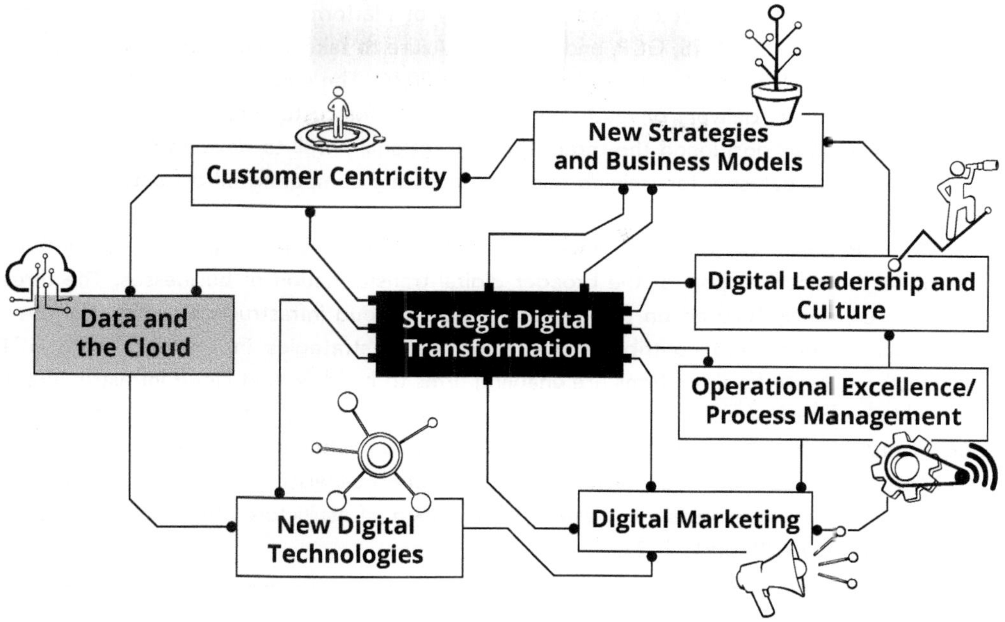

Figure 6.1 Data and the cloud is the third Strategic Action Field of Digital Transformation

Source: Peter et al. (2020); Peter (2017, 2021, 2023, 2024)

Cloud Services

Amazon AWS, Microsoft Azure and Google Cloud

Cloud computing has emerged as an important and widely adopted aspect of digital transformation (Ambrozio et al., 2025; Wright et al., 2023), offering firms 'ubiquitous, convenient, on-demand network access to a shared pool of configurable computing resources (e.g., networks, servers, storage, applications, and services) that can be rapidly provisioned and released with minimal management effort or service provider interaction' (Mell & Grance, 2011). Gartner identified Amazon Web Services (AWS, 2024), Google Cloud Platform (GCP, 2024) and Microsoft Azure (2024) as the leading firms in public strategic cloud platform services (Wright et al., 2023). Gartner's Magic Quadrant analysis showed these three firms to have the strongest ability to execute, and they have the most complete visions for cloud computing services, with distinctive strengths compared to Oracle, IBM, Alibaba Cloud, Huawei Cloud, and Tencent Cloud, which are also included in their study (Wright et al., 2023).

AWS is the oldest of the three leading cloud service providers, founded in 2006, and holds the largest market share, which are between the three, at 32% (Borra, 2024). Microsoft Azure was established in 2010 and has approximately 23% market share, while Google Cloud (GCP) was established in 2008 and has about 10% market share (Borra, 2024). All three firms are global in scale and have been able to leverage their ICT infrastructure, developed for other core businesses, to develop their cloud services businesses. Today the investments the three firms

(Continued)

have made into ICT infrastructure and the delivery of platforms and services built on that infrastructure is allowing AWS, GCP, and Microsoft Azure to take a lead in the emerging generative artificial intelligence (GenAI) market (Robuck, 2024). The emphasis in cloud services on shared infrastructure, delivery of platforms, and services for customers to process data and serve customers has positioned the three firms exceptionally well to develop GenAI services that require large datasets for training and the necessary computing infrastructure to serve customers globally.

AWS, GCP, and Microsoft Azure have played an important role in enabling the transition of firms to the cloud as part of the broader digital transformation of businesses. The three firms have especially focused on the delivery of public cloud infrastructure, which has overtaken private clouds and contributed to hybrid cloud strategies in terms of firms' ICT infrastructures. Now the three firms are enabling firms to build on that cloud infrastructure in the development of proprietary GenAI models, while also having access to the latest open source GenAI. Interestingly, as GenAI models are increasingly becoming available and training data is no longer the primary concern, it is the computing capacity needed for implementing the models that is emerging as a key aspect of the cloud infrastructure offered by AWS, GCP, and Microsoft Azure (Robuck, 2024).

6.0 INTRODUCTION

In Chapter 4 (see Figure 4.4), the concept of data management (in the context of customer centricity) was introduced. The underlying data economy can be defined as 'a global ecosystem where data is gathered, organised, and exchanged to create economic value' (Sestino et al., 2025, p. 1). The digital transformation of the economy (and firms), society and government is creating societies permeated by digital technologies and the primary output of this digital transition is data. The growing availability and access to data, as well as the ability to process this data, not least because of cloud computing services (see the opening case study), has resulted in data being argued to be the 'new black gold' in the digital age, as there is a view that firms have the potential to create significant value from the increasingly ubiquitous data resources (Sestino et al., 2025). At the same time, unprocessed data has long been understood as less valuable than information (processed data), and lastly a significant emphasis has been placed on knowledge (information in context) as the ultimate source of value creation for firms (Alvi & Leidner, 2001; Grant & Phene, 2022). The recent explosion in generative artificial intelligence (GenAI) has put into stark contrast how increasingly the relationships between the collection and processing of data in relation to knowledge are being affected by emerging hybrid systems of human cognition and machine computing power (Witschel et al., 2020). It is not a coincidence that firms with large datasets, access to user-generated content, and access to established cloud computing or data centre infrastructure, like AWS, GCP, and Microsoft Azure or social media platforms like Facebook (Meta) or X (formerly Twitter), have been able to take a lead in bringing new GenAI products and/or services to market most rapidly during 2024.

Indeed, these events put the relationship between data, information, and knowledge and the products and/or services of firms into the limelight. Established products and/or services are critical sources of data, but data, information and knowledge are also critical drivers of new product and/or service innovations. So, while customer centricity (see Chapter 4) is fundamentally reliant on customer information and knowledge about the customer journey, the use of products and consumption of services by customers are critical sources of data for the firm, which is increasingly accessible through the integration of digital technologies. This fundamental shift is of course associated with significant privacy, security, and legal consequences that need to be understood. This chapter seeks to address these complex inter-relationships.

Data, information, and knowledge (see Figure 6.2) are the basic building blocks of information systems as an academic discipline (Zins, 2007) and the practical realisation of the digital transformation of the economy, civil society, and government in the digital age. In Chapter 4 it was argued that realising customer centricity required firms to follow a four-phase process, with each phase building on the preceding phases (Gulati & Oldroyd, 2005). Firms first need to develop the digital information and communication technologies (ICT) and infrastructure which are essential for making the coordinated gathering (communicating and storing), standardising, and organising of customer data needed for a central customer data repository possible. In the second phase, the necessary capabilities to gather and organise standardised customer data over time to enable the analysis of the data by specific functions of the firm are developed. For this, managers and firms need to understand the data available to them (see Box 6.1). In the third phase, this information resource is not only analysed retrospectively for making decisions, but a predictive analytics capability is developed. This arguably can be understood as moving from information to knowledge. In the fourth phase, this knowledge-intensive approach is incorporated into all day-to-day operations (Gulati & Oldroyd, 2005).

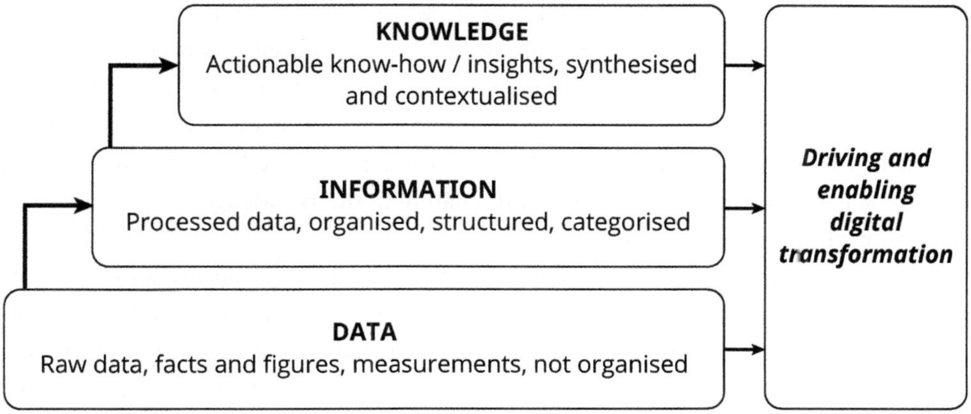

Figure 6.2 Building blocks of information systems and enablers of digital transformation

Source: own illustration following Zins (2007)

Box 6.1: Developing a Data Overview

Regardless of the size of the firm, in the data economy it is essential to understand the data your firm has available and is able to process and what gaps may exist in terms of data that needs to be accessed in addition. As a first step, it can be useful to map the different kinds of data the firm relies on and should actively integrate into decision-making, which might include:

- **Customer data:** demographic data, purchasing history, contact data, etc.
- **Purchasing and supplier data:** raw materials purchases, goods/products delivered, services consumed, input delivery times, service quality, etc.
- **Financial data:** financial performance indicators, cashflow, etc.
- **HR data:** recruitment data, employee development data, etc.
- **Production and distribution:** inventory data, production data, finished goods data, orders and delivers data, etc.
- **Technical data:** Equipment rental costs, storage costs, ITC maintenance costs, cybersecurity monitoring, etc.
- **Geodata:** transportation data, branch network data, etc.

Source: Peter (2024)

This understanding of the relationship between data, information, and knowledge is well established and widely accepted (Figure 6.2). It is the hierarchical understanding of data as 'raw numbers and facts, information as processed data, and knowledge as authenticated information, [that is personalised information] varying along some dimension, such as context, usefulness, or interpretability' (Alvi & Leidner, 2001, p. 109). This is, however, not the only understanding of how to think about the relationship between the core information systems building blocks of data, information and knowledge (Alvi & Leidner, 2001; Zins, 2007) and this results in differences in the definitions of these three essential concepts (Zins, 2007). Table 6.1 makes clear how diverse the different types of knowledge present in an organisation can be, but essentially the key interests are the degree to which knowledge is tacit (implicit) or explicit, whether the knowledge is held by individuals or shared by a group (e.g., teams or even the entire organisation), and what the nature of the knowledge is in relation to the activities of a business organisation.

The hierarchical view is, however, increasingly challenged by approaches that emphasise the centrality of prior knowledge in the interpretation of new data and the emergence of information. In this alternative perspective 'knowledge is information possessed in the mind of individuals; it is personalized information' (Alvi & Leidner, 2001, p. 109). This understanding changes the role of knowledge as a framework for processing data to formulate information and there is no data that precedes knowledge, as it is preexisting knowledge that determines the identification and collection of data needed to create information (Alvi & Leidner, 2001). Indeed, tacit knowledge when articulated, verbalised, and structured becomes information, while information becomes knowledge when it is internalised by the mind of an individual (a knower). It is exactly this cycle that more recently has been central to the emergence of generative artificial intelligence (GenAI), which is emerging as a non-human knower. Put differently, today firms have access to both human (cognition) and machine-based (computing) processing of data and information to create knowledge (Witschel et al., 2020).

Table 6.1 Knowledge taxonomy

Knowledge Types			Definitions	
Expression / Manifestation	Tacit	Description	Knowledge is based on actions, experience, and participation within specific organisational contexts that has not been made explicit; could be both individual and/or social	
		Cognitive	Mental models of how specific aspects of business function	
		Technical	Know-how applicable to specific tasks in organisation	
	Explicit		Articulated generalised knowledge that has been captured in an information system, which may be local or organisation wide (e.g., about an important customer of a firm)	
Organisation	Individual (not shared)		Knowledge that has been created by an individual and is carried by an individual employee	Could be both tacit and/or explicit
	Social (shared)		Knowledge that is created and inherent to the collective actions of a social group, e.g., a team	
Nature	Declarative		Know-about a specific topic/activity	
	Procedural		Know-how a specific activity/task needs to be undertaken	
	Causal		Know-why specific causal relationships exist and their effects	
	Conditional		Know-when specific conditions will affect an outcome	
	Relational		Know-with knowledge relates to how causal systems interact	
	Pragmatic		Useful knowledge for an organisation, including best practices, business frameworks, project experiences, technical information, market information, etc.	

Source: adapted from Table 2 in Alvi & Leidner (2001)

Box 6.2: Evaluating Data Quality

Both operational and legal requirements of firms mean that in the data economy it is essential that firms ensure that the data they collect and store is of a high quality. Indeed, in a data-driven decision-making environment and legal environment that requires timely data disclosure, a firm that does not ensure it has high-quality data is at serious risk. While challenging to realise simultaneously, here are some of the qualities that high-quality data has:

- **Completeness:** a record must include all the required details
- **Unambiguity:** the interpretation of the data must be clear and easy
- **Correctness:** the data must accurately reflect reality
- **Timeliness:** all data must be up-to-date
- **Accuracy:** the data needs to reflect reality at the correct level of accuracy
- **Redundancy Free:** duplication in the dataset should be avoided
- **Relevance:** the data collected and stored must be relevant to the activities of the firm
- **Uniformity:** the data should adhere to a uniform structure
- **Reliability:** the original data sources should be traceable
- **Comprehensibility:** the data should be structured and labelled in such a manner that the recipients (users) of the data are able to interpret it.

Source: Peter (2024)

Box 6.3: Importance of Data Management Plans

The quality of the data a firm collects and stores can be supported through the development of a data management plan (see Figure 6.3). Such a data management plan includes an overview of the sources of data, the intended data quality goals, current data usage, future data usage goals, the applied data management systems, and data security measures.

In turn, this data will then be stored in data management systems (software), such as:

- ***Enterprise Resource Planning (ERP) software***: the ERP software stores, or logistical/technical information related to a product (e.g., EAN code, brand, price, size, etc.). The ERP can be used to manage all of a firm's operational processes in real time with models that are function specific allowing task specific access to the data. As a result, all employees have access to standardised, reliable, and useable high-quality data to allow them to complete their work.
- ***Customer Relationship Management (CRM) software***: typically used by the go-to-market team, the CRM software allows the firm to manage all data collected and stored related to the customer journey. It is the CRM system that enables a multichannel customer experience along the customer journey. The CRM system is used for both current and prospective customers and supports customer experience delivery and retention. This data will be typically linked to product information.

- ***Product Information Management (PIM) software***: The PIM is a centralised information resource for product and marketing teams, that provides access to product details. It provides complete, reliable, and up-to-date information about products.

Source: Peter (2024)

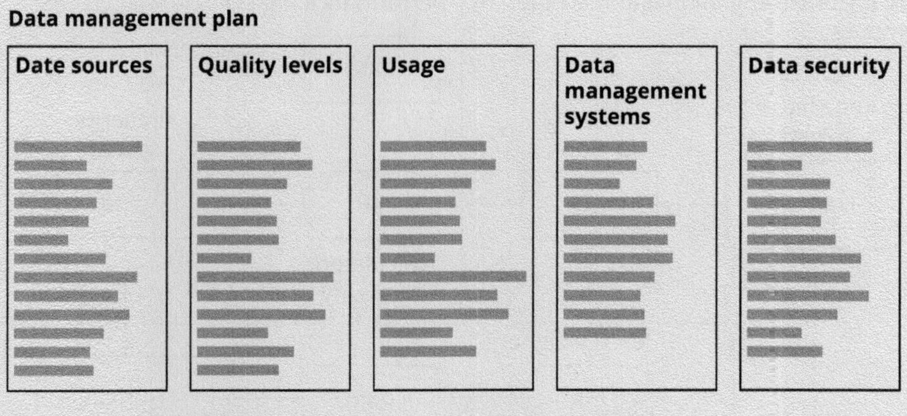

Figure 6.3 The data management plan for digital transformation

Source: Peter (2023, 2024)

6.1 HYBRID SYSTEMS OF HUMAN AND MACHINE-BASED KNOWLEDGE CREATION

Artificial intelligence (AI) is today most commonly associated with machine learning (ML) approaches that require very large data sets (Big Data) to train models that then are able to be applied in different application domains. Common examples include recommender systems (e.g., movie recommendations on streaming platforms) or most recently GenAI (e.g., ChatGPT). Such approaches to AI are referred to as sub-symbolic approaches and are an alternative to the original symbolic AI systems that sought to represent expert knowledge in the development of AI systems (van Harmelen & ten Teije, 2019). Machine learning (sub-symbolic) learning systems emphasise inference, which requires computing power and large data sets, while the symbolic knowledge-based reasoning systems require access to expert knowledge and the ability to formally represent this. Increasingly, however, these alternative AI techniques are recognised as complementary approaches that can mutually reinforce the effectiveness of learning and reasoning systems (van Harmelen & ten Teije, 2019). Critically, Witschel et al. (2020) go further and point out the importance of integrating human knowledge into hybrid systems that analyse large datasets and generate knowledge representations as a result of that analysis. Human knowledge is critical in shaping initial knowledge representations that might precede machine learning, as well as in providing input to guide training (i.e., adaptation of weights in models) and to correct potential errors in machine learning outcomes (i.e., correcting attributes of a model). These hybrid systems are then composed of systems of humans (Human), machine learning systems (ML), knowledge representation (KR), data (data), and human interpretable symbols (sym). See Figure 6.4 for a representation of such a hybrid system.

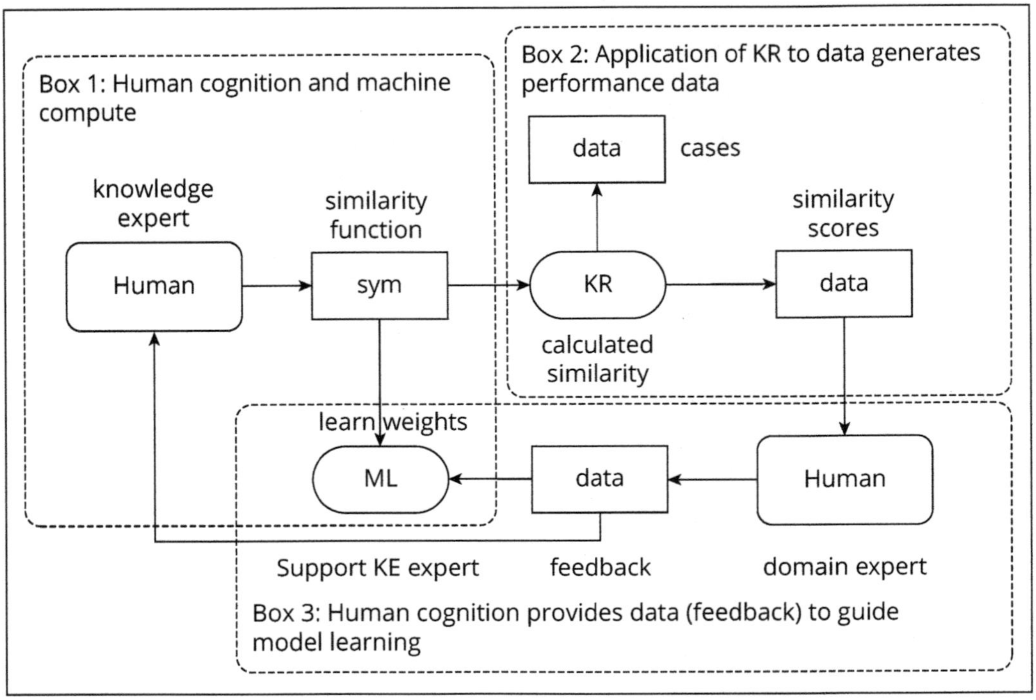

Figure 6.4 Exemplary hybrid human–machine system: similarity metric engineering example

Source: adapted from Figure 6 in Witschel et al. (2020)

Without getting too deeply into the details of the example illustrated in Figure 6.4, there is an opportunity to reflect on how both human knowledge (Human) and machine learning (ML) can lead to symbolic representations (sym) of knowledge, derived from human cognition and machine computation respectively (see dashed Box 6.1 in Figure 6.4). Applying the knowledge-base (symbolic) technique to a dataset (case) produces new data (see Box 6.2), which can then be interpreted by a human domain expert (see Box 6.3), allowing feedback to be provided to guide a machine learning (ML) technique to learn model weights. Data and knowledge will play a central role in the growing application of different types of AI in firms, with employees and their expertise contributing critical insights for applying models in firm specific applications. A key enabling trend for the application of AI in firms is the adoption of cloud computing services (CCS).

6.2 CLOUD COMPUTING SERVICES

Cloud computing services have been defined by the US Department of Commerce National Institute of Standards and Technology (NIST) as 'a model for enabling ubiquitous, convenient, on-demand network access to a shared pool of configurable computing resources (e.g., networks, servers, storage, applications, and services) that can be rapidly provisioned and released with minimal management effort or service provider interaction'. (Mell & Grance, 2011) (see Box 6.4). The European Union (EU) has reported that about 77% of large firms, 59% of medium-sized firms, and 41% of small firms in the EU have purchased cloud computing services in 2023.

Box 6.4: NIST Description of Cloud Infrastructure

'A cloud infrastructure is the collection of hardware and software that enables the five essential characteristics of cloud computing [: on-demand self-service; broad network access; resource pooling; rapid elasticity; measured service]. The cloud infrastructure can be viewed as containing both a physical layer and an abstraction layer. The physical layer consists of the hardware resources that are necessary to support the cloud services being provided, and typically includes server, storage and network components. The abstraction layer consists of the software deployed across the physical layer, which manifests the essential cloud characteristics. Conceptually the abstraction layer sits above the physical layer.'

Source: Mell & Grance (2011, p. 2)

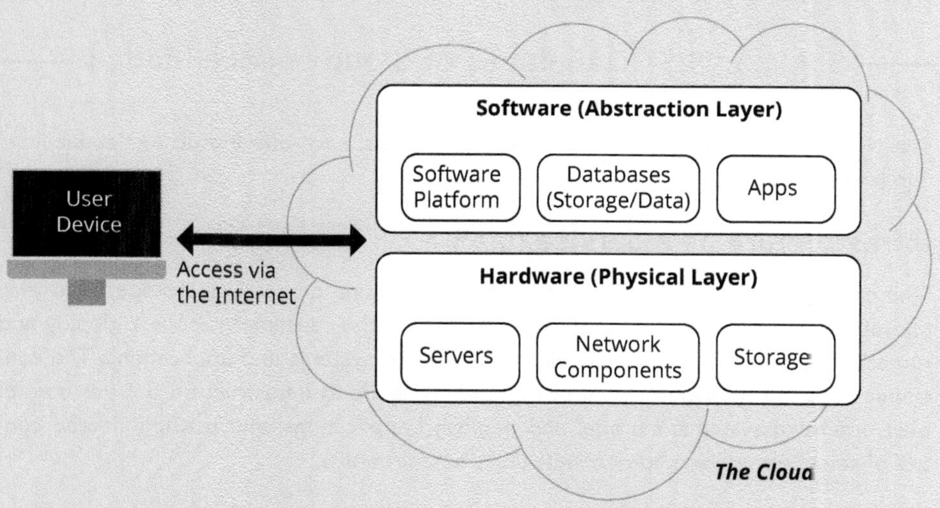

Figure 6.5 Overview of cloud infrastructure

Source: Own illustration following Mell & Grance (2011)

The types of services that EU firms use the cloud for are in descending order of prevalence in 2023, email (82.7%), storage of files (68.0%), office software (66.3%), security software applications (61.0%), financial or accounting software applications (51.6%), hosting enterprise database(s) (43%), platform(s) for application development, testing or deployment (26.1%), ERP software applications (25.9%), computing power for enterprise's own software (25.4%), and CRM software applications (25.0%). The leading EU countries for enterprise Cloud Service Provider (CSP) adoption in 2023 are Finland (78.3%), Sweden (71.6%), Norway (71.3%), Denmark (69.5%), Malta (66.7%), Ireland (63.1%), Italy (61.4%), and the Netherlands (61.2%).

Cloud computing represents a clear shift of from inhouse, firm specific provision of IT infrastructure and management of access to this infrastructure over the internet (Garrison et al., 2015) (see Figure 6.6). Initial expectations had been that firms would have a preference for building inhouse private clouds, owning and managing the IT infrastructure and the management of the access to the private cloud of the firm. But the primary growth has been seen in the adoption of public cloud computing services, representing a strategic shift that has accepted a greater reliance on external suppliers of infrastructure, software and services, but often with hybrid cloud solutions that include both private and public implementations of CSP (Garrison et al., 2015). Community clouds have also been implemented, with the intension for the shared resource to be used exclusively by group of organisations with shared interests and concerns (Mell & Grance, 2011), representing an intermediary implementation between the private and public clouds. Cloud computing 'offers dynamic and scalable resources using internet-based services like Software as a Service (SaaS), Infrastructure as a Service (IaaS) and Platform as a Service (PaaS)' (Garrison et al., 2015, p. 377) (see Box 6.5).

Box 6.5: NIST Definitions of Cloud Service Models

The NIST defines three primary cloud service models, each offering distinct capabilities and levels of control.

Infrastructure as a Service (IaaS)

'The capability provided to the consumer is to provision processing, storage, networks, and other fundamental computing resources where the consumer is able to deploy and run arbitrary software, which can include operating systems and applications. The consumer does not manage or control the underlying cloud infrastructure but has control over operating systems, storage, and deployed applications; and possibly limited control of select networking components (e.g., host firewalls).'

Platform as a Service (PaaS)

'The capability provided to the consumer is to deploy onto the cloud infrastructure consumer-created or acquired applications created using programming languages, libraries, services, and tools supported by the provider. [This capability does not necessarily preclude the use of compatible programming languages, libraries, services, and tools from other sources.] The consumer does not manage or control the underlying cloud infrastructure including network, servers, operating systems, or storage, but has control over the deployed applications and possibly configuration settings for the application-hosting environment.'

Software as a Service (SaaS)

'The capability provided to the consumer is to use the provider's applications running on a cloud infrastructure. The applications are accessible from various client devices through either a thin client interface, such as a web browser (e.g., web-based email) or a program interface. The consumer does not manage or control the underlying cloud infrastructure including network, servers, operating systems, storage, or even individual application capabilities, with the possible exception of limited user-specific application configuration settings.'

Source: Mell & Grance (2011, pp. 2–3)

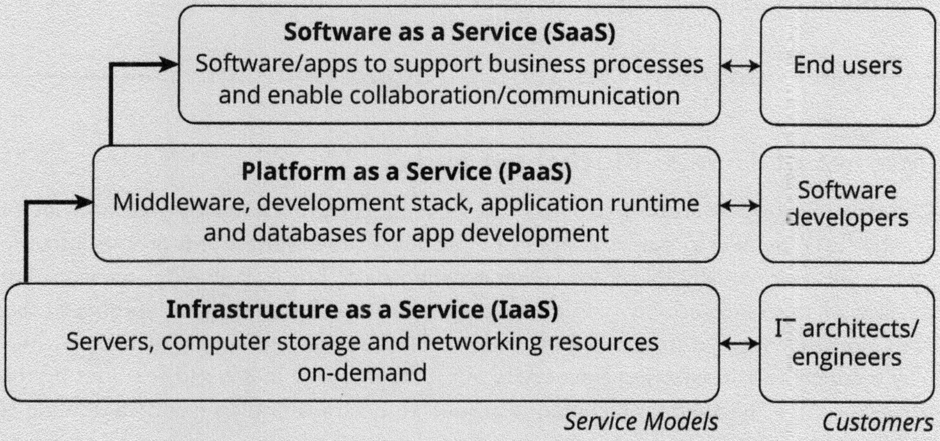

Figure 6.6 Cloud service models

Source: own illustration following Mell & Grance (2011)

6.3 PRODUCTS AND SERVICES IN THE DATA ECONOMY

The role of products and services in the data economy is complex, due to its multifaceted nature. Possibly the easiest place to begin is with entirely analogue products, an example may be artisanal art pieces sold in a local market, and services such as a gardening service that only uses analogue tools. As will become apparent very quickly, such examples are extremely rare in the digital age, and to imagine these examples is to immediately start to make connections as to how digital technologies are today integrated in the customer journey for both examples in the vast majority of cases. At the very moment that the artist posts an offer to purchase their art on a platform like Etsy (2024) or the gardening service creates a website that can be found via a search engine online, data is created about the product/service and the online phases of the subsequent customer journeys. For every digital channel, e.g., social media, that is subsequently added to the customer journey more data is generated.

It is now well understood that this data that is collected by the platform businesses (e.g., Etsy in this example) and the internet search engines then, in a next step, itself is commoditised in its own right and is sold either as a product or service (Sestino et al., 2025). This data about customer behaviour and preferences has significant potential value to a diverse range of organizations. The customer journey is most easily captured in data for digital channels (e.g., the internet / World Wide Web, social media, in-application purchases, etc.). Physical (analogue) customer journeys are challenging to collect data about, which is why firms first started customer loyalty schemes, allowing customers to volunteer their data in return for benefits. Payment systems are a critical aspect of capturing customer behaviour and in combination with customer loyalty schemes can in aggregate provide deep insights about customers and result in very big datasets over time.

Box 6.6: Evolution of Cloud Computing

Internet of Things, Blockchain and AI

Cloud computing is argued to have been changed significantly by the Internet of Things (IoT), as ever greater numbers of products (devices) are integrated into the global network, initially these are communicating data, but it is already foreseen that devices will also increasingly gain computing capacities. Ensuring data integrity in this scenario is not without its challenges, and some argue that blockchain technology may play a critical role in ensuring traceability and data integrity in a world featured by the IoT. Finally, the third digital technology argued to be transforming cloud computing is AI. As explained in this chapter, the access to every larger and longitudinal datasets over cloud platforms is emerging as a critical enabler of the development of AI techniques and their commercialisation, this includes developing algorithms to control IoT devices (e.g., in-home energy usage), but also new products (e.g., GenAI applications like ChatGPT).

Source: draws on Gill et al. (2019)

The Internet of Things (IoT) represents in a first instance the integration of digital sensing, storage and communication technologies into physical products, so that they can become integrated into the emerging national, regional and even potentially global digital network of data transfer and communication (Sestino et al., 2025). Indeed, IoT in combination with cloud computing, blockchain technology, big data and AI is emerging as a driver of change (see Box 6.6). Edge (of the network) computing represents the addition of computing capabilities to products (Gill et al., 2019), potentially transforming the data into information on the device before the need for communication. The IoT and edge computing are expected to contribute to an exponential expansion of the data available about device usage by customers/consumers. It represents the transformation of devises into local data collection and communication devices, offering potentially even greater insights into product usage and consumer preferences. These trends are at the heart of privacy and cybersecurity concerns and the associated legal and regulatory responses.

6.4 BUSINESS ECOSYSTEMS AND THE DATA ECONOMY

It should be clear that the data economy is enabled by digital technologies and an ecosystem of different actors that implement these technologies in such a manner that data can be collected, stored, and processed to generate insights (knowledge). These ecosystems include government and regulatory bodies at national level, but also regional levels, e.g., the EU. Sestino et al. (2025) explains that the EU Data Strategy 2020 (European Commission, 2022) incentivises the creation of European data spaces so that more data can become available in the economy and society, while allowing individuals and firms to remain in control of their data.

6.4.1 Data Protection and Legal Aspects of the Data Economy

While the data economy has the potential to very positively affect society and customers may benefit from better products and/or services and an improved overall customer journey by contributing the data to the data economy, there are clear privacy concerns associated with the sharing their personal data. There is a clear and urgent need to develop the data economy in such a manner that data is used in a responsible and ethical manner (Sestino et al., 2025). The EU has responded to these concerns with the General Data Protection Regulation (GDPR, 2016), which seeks to ensure privacy and security of personal data, as well as govern the collection, processing, and sharing of data. The broader EU Single Digital Market seeks to enable the development of the data economy, while protecting individuals and firms and have been referred to as a minimalist approach that allows individuals and organisations to retain ownership of their data. It should be noted that other jurisdictions, like the United States of America (USA) (see Box 6.6), have different approaches to the data market and the protection of privacy in relation to personal data (Sestino et al., 2025). It is as a result essential for firms operating across national or regional jurisdictions to be familiar with data protection and security laws and regulations.

Box 6.7: Examples of Data Protection Laws Around the World

- Data Protection Act (UK)
- Data Security Law / Personal Information Protection Law (China)
- Digital Personal Data Protection Act (India)
- Federal Personal Information Protection and Electronic Documents Act (Canada)
- General Data Protection Regulation (GDPR) (EU)
- Privacy Act (Australia)
- Various State and Federal Laws (US)

Source: Peter (2024)

The legal frameworks intended to ensure data protection require firms to develop strong data governance, requiring a clear understanding of where data is located, how it is used and protected. Data governance requires the development of processes, role specification, the development of guidelines, standards, and indicators to ensure data is correctly collected, stored, and used (Peter, 2024). Ensuring high data quality, see Box 6.2, is an integral part of good data governance. Managing who has access to data and ensuring personal data is treated correctly are two measures that can most directly contribute to ensuring data protection obligations are met in firms (Peter, 2024). The treatment of data is affected by its type and the intended use case, with personal data commonly requiring most care in its collection and use.

6.4.2 Data Security and the Data Economy

Data security is a key concern in efforts to create a data economy. It is essential that there is trust in the security of data provided and collected if the data economy is to function effectively. The goals of data security include ensuring only authorised employees have access to confidential data, that that employees should be able to access the data they are authorised to view at all times, that the authenticity and trustworthiness of data is guaranteed, and finally that the data has a high degrees of integrity, and that the data is protected from manipulation (Peter, 2024). There are a number of practical steps firms can take to develop secure data (see Box 6.7 and 6.8).

Box 6.8: General Data Protection Regulation (GDPR) Framework

Most countries have data protection laws that define the minimum requirements for how organisations have to protect data, most importantly, their customer data. According to the UN (UNCTAD, 2023), 137 out of 194 countries have already introduced legislation to protect data and privacy. In the EU, the General Data Protection Regulation (GDPR) framework introduced in 2016 covers eight important principles for data protection. Organisations therefore need to provide the following:

1. Data inventory: an inventory that provides an overview of where and how personal data is stored (see Box 6.3).
2. Principles: an overview of the principles of how personal data is being used.
3. Standards: the definition of standards and processes of how employees utilise personal data.
4. Data subject rights: definition of the processes of how natural persons' requests will be handled (e.g., the right of data access, or the right to be forgotten).
5. Data processing records: similar to the data inventory, but with a focus on the processes that utilise personal data.
6. Personal data breaches: definition of the process of how to inform stakeholders (and authorities) if data breaches occurred.
7. Data protection officer: nomination of an officer in charge of GDPR compliance.
8. Data protection impact assessment: creation of an impact assessment to identify risks and define mitigation strategies.

Source: Peter (2024)

Data security is also related to 'the measures and protocols put in place to protect sensitive and confidential data collected, stored and shared by organizations from cyber-attacks that are becoming more complex and raising complicated security problems' (Sestino et al., 2025, p. 9). An additional and increasingly contentious aspect of data protection and security is the sharing of data held by firms in relation to crimes, it should be noted that governments do not have an automatic right to personal data of customers and are required to provide a legal reason(s) for a data request, but these laws do vary across countries and firms must act in accordance with the jurisdictions where they operate. Firms are in the strongest position with regard to such requests if they ensure they have secure and high-quality data, allowing them to respond to legal requests as required in a specific jurisdiction (Peter, 2024).

6.5 DATA, INFORMATION, AND KNOWLEDGE AND COMPETITIVE ADVANTAGE

This chapter has emphasised two themes that are relevant to a to the strategy literature on competitive advantage. Firstly, how data is transformed into information, emphasising the role of knowledge, and the importance of focusing on the relationship between products and services and data creation and capture. This discussion draws directly on the discussions of competitive strategy in Chapter 2. The central focus of this chapter on the relationship between digital technology adoption in relation to products and/or services and the resulting data creation and capture speaks directly to the arguments that increasingly technology adoption decisions (integration into products and service delivery) are integral to competitive strategising (Bharadwaj et al., 2013) in the data driven economy. Indeed, digital technologies across actors in the different business ecosystems in which firms and their customers are embedded are creating ever greater potential for value creation (Bharadwaj et al., 2013) from capturing, collating, and processing data (Sestino et al., 2025).

From the perspective of the firm then data, information, and knowledge can be understood as key resources that firms need to either gain ownership and/or control over, reflecting the resource-based view of the firm (Barney, 1991; Wernerfelt, 1984). The question is whether data alone is sufficient to achieve a sustained competitive advantage, especially when acquired from third party providers. More likely firms will need to draw on their internal knowledge resources to process the data into proprietary information that is more likely to meet the criteria of the resource-based view for leading to a competitive advantage. One way to think about this is that collectively the knowledge needed for effectively processing the data is going to be embedded in the capabilities needed to orchestrate these resources effectively for creating and capturing value, what have been referred to as core competences of the firm (Prahalad & Hamel, 1990). It is the strength of the core competences of a firm that will allow resource orchestration of existing and new knowledge and digital technologies to create (new) value in relation to the potential for digital technologies to create data. These ideas reflect the knowledge-based view of the firm, an extension of the resource-based and capabilities perspective on competitive advantage, that through its influence on management processes, 'the sourcing of knowledge and its application to the production of goods and services provided the basis for coordination, strategic decision-making and organizational design' (Grant & Phene, 2022, p. 5).

The creation and capture of data, possibly also its processing into information, clearly reflects the open system perspective (Menz et al., 2021; Sony & Naik, 2020) and the need for the firm to co-evolve with its context (Short et al., 2007) in the data economy and ongoing digital transformation of both firms and the economy and civil society. The ecosystems that firms choose to embed themselves in will be critical determinants of the potential for firms to participate in the data economy. But this chapter has also emphasised the central and evolving role of products and/or services the firm offers in the creation and capture of data. This makes clear that firms at the same time need to think carefully about their market positioning strategies (Panagiotou, 2006; Porter, 1979). The legitimacy of different digital technologies and their potential for data collection and transmission could vary dramatically depending on the generic strategies of a firm.

These perspectives thus arguably converge in the generic strategies typologies of Porter (1985) and Treacy and Wiersema (1995), with the respective typologies articulating clear and distinct value propositions to customers of firms that require different resource and capability configurations to be realised, including technology resources embedded in products or the service delivery process. From a positional generic strategy perspective (Porter, 1979), it is illustrative to consider the highly differentiated product offering of Tesla (2024) cars, highly associated with digital technologies and data collection, transmission, and analysis to improve understanding of the performance of the different capabilities of the vehicles and which, by transfer of software updates subsequently improve the driving experience. While Apple (2024), a firm that clearly has a highly differentiated market positioning strategy for digital devices, that through the servitisation of the product value proposition (e.g., iPhone Apps) – despite or possibly because of the significant potential for data driven value creation – has focused on providing customers as much control as possible over their data and privacy.

The product leadership value discipline of Treacy and Wiersema (1995), which focuses on a value proposition around product and service innovation to become the firm that is defining the state of the art in a particular product category, highlights a different set of considerations in relation to products and/or services. The Austrian children's digital camera Hoppstar (2024) has brought a differentiated product offering to market that clearly is built around digital technologies, but in response to parental concerns around the digitalisation of children's lives, data security has meant design choices like no additional games, only limited picture filters, and SD Card and wire only data transfer for pictures. This contrasts strongly with the product leadership in the electric vehicle market by Tesla. Product leadership in the digital age could be data driven or not; the strategic choice for firms pursuing product or service leadership is to understand how digital technologies should contribute to product and/or service innovation, given their customer segments and their preferences in relation to the data economy.

6.6 DATA, THE CLOUD, AND SUSTAINABILITY

The relationship between digital transformation and the sustainability transition of business, society, and government is complex, but these contemporary transitions are increasingly understood as highly interconnected. The central role of ICT in enabling the digital transformation and the ever-greater demand for ICT equipment in realising the digital transformation is seen as having a variety of negative impacts from a sustainability perspective, including e-waste and increased energy demand, with an impact on the withdrawal of natural resources stocks to produce the energy, while contributing to negative stocks like CO2 emissions. Cloud computing is equally dependent on ICT infrastructure and energy consumption, but is arguably a more efficient use of the ICT infrastructure than proprietary infrastructure. At the same time, cloud infrastructure, not least because of the need to build infrastructure that supports the developments in AI solutions, is expanding significantly, creating greater pressures on the resources needed to produce the equipment for the needed infrastructure and creating greater demand for energy. At the same time cloud solutions reduce energy use by firms making use of the cloud services, with associated positive impacts on CO2 emissions (Kumar & Vidhyalakshmi, 2012). This complexity and the associated tensions are unlikely to dissipate soon as the data economy grows and products and services are increasingly embedded and profit from data generation, processing, and leveraging for value creation.

6.7 CONCLUSION

This chapter has explored how digital technologies are fundamentally intertwined with the emergence of the data economy, with significant impacts on how we need to think about the integration of data and digital technologies into products and services. Cloud services providers such as Amazon AWS, Microsoft Azure, and Google Cloud, dominate the market due to their extensive infrastructure and capabilities. These services enable firms to access scalable computing resources, facilitating the adoption of generative artificial intelligence (GenAI) and other advanced technologies. Cloud computing services are defined and categorised into Infrastructure as a Service (IaaS), Platform as a Service (PaaS), and Software as a Service (SaaS). The chapter outlines the benefits of cloud adoption, such as cost savings, scalability, and enhanced data processing capabilities. It also addresses the challenges, including data security, privacy concerns, and the need for robust data governance.

Data, when processed into information and knowledge, becomes a valuable asset for firms. The integration of human cognition and machine learning in hybrid systems showcase the synergy between human expertise and AI in knowledge creation. The inherent potential of digital technologies for producing more data is changing the way value is created and will increasingly affect the competitive strategies of firms.

Case Studies

Students can complete the following tasks either based on the focal case study, or work on the recommended case study for this chapter (*BRUGG Lifting and its ™industrial Internet of Things (IIoT) asset management solution 'PVS'*) and answer the questions below.

1 What is the value of data in an organisation; and how important are customer, product, and usage/transaction data (and why)?
2 What data can BRUGG collect with its sensors? Provide an overview of data categories with examples for each category (see also Box 6.1).

3 Should this data be stored and made available via an IaaS, PaaS, or SaaS Cloud solution (see Box 6.5)? Describe the reasons for your choice.
4 How can BRUGG use this data for process improvements, including automation/digitalisation, efficiency increase, and cost reduction?
5 How can BRUGG use this data strategically to build, for instance, new service offerings, strategic partnerships with other organisations (e.g., an ecosystem or digital platform) or expand into new industries (see also Chapter 6.5)?
6 How can BRUGG protect this data from unauthorised access or use from an organisational and technological point of view?
7 What skills are required for BRUGG or any other organisation to use data operationally (for e.g., automation) and strategically (e.g., to build new services)?

Alternatively, students can work on the supplementary case study (available online) for this chapter (*CRM and sales automation at Transgourmet Switzerland*) and answer the questions below.

1 What is the value of data in an organisation; and how important is customer data (and why)?
2 What is a possible CRM (customer relationship management) software vision and project scope for a small business (like for example, a bikeshop)?
3 Which internal teams (human resources) have the potential and the ability to plan and implement a CRM project?
4 What skills are required to implement a CRM project?
5 How can/should senior management support a CRM project?
6 Into which other IT systems/platforms will a CRM integrate with, and why?
7 What processes can be automated via a CRM platform?
8 How can an organisation protect its data from unauthorised access or use?
9 How and why could a mobile version of the CRM system support your employees?

Additional cases with student questions for the strategic digital action field of *Data and the Cloud* are covered in:

- Adelbodner mineral water – the digital roadmap of a SME (available online).
- Action fields of digital transformation at Synchrony Financial (USA) (available online).

You will find a collection of case studies for Strategic Digital Transformation in the Appendix and additional cases online at www.strategic-digital-transformation.com

Exercises

Discuss the following questions in your class, in your group or assignment:

1 Review the features (product offering) and prices of Cloud services such as Amazon AWS, Microsoft Azure, and Google Cloud (see opening case) using online information and prepare an overview regarding their capabilities and advantages.

2 Based on a selected industry/business, identify various types of data, information and knowledge which the organisation likely currently has in operation (for each level, define at least three types) (see Figure 6.2).
3 Review Table 6.1 (Knowledge Taxonomy) and define/describe for the selected organisation in exercise 2 what tacit and explicit knowledge is available to managers and employees.
4 For your selected organisation in exercise 2, create a data management plan (see Figure 6.3) that provides an overview of available data for strategic and operational use. Make assumptions, if required.
5 Forming two small groups (2–4 students in each group), assign a pro and contra position to each group and debate to which degree humans (e.g., employees and managers) are still required (and why), or not required any more (and why), to build AI-driven knowledge management systems (see also Figure 6.4).
6 Based on the organisation from exercise 2, explain for what processes / use cases they would use Infrastructure as a Service (IaaS), Platform as a Service (PaaS), and Software as a Service (SaaS) cloud service models.
7 Finally, explain how the organisation selected in exercise 2 can fulfil the General Data Protection Regulation (GDPR) framework (as described in Box 6.7). How can the organisation fulfil the legal requirements; what policies, resources, systems, and processes are required?

Further Reading List

- European Commission (2022). European Data Strategy, https://commission.europa.eu/strategy-and-policy/priorities-2019-2024/europe-fit-digital-age/european-data-strategy_en.
- Hogan, M., Liu, F., Sokol, A., & Tong, J. (2011). NIST Cloud Computing Standards Roadmap. NIST Special Publication, 35(6), 11, https://csrc.nist.rip/library/NIST%20SP%20500-291%20Cloud%20Computing%20Standards%20Roadmap,%202011-07-05.pdf.
- Sestino, A., Kahlawi, A., & De Mauro, A. (2025). Decoding the data economy: A literature review of its impact on business, society and digital transformation. *European Journal of Innovation Management*, 28(2), 298–323.
- UNCTAD (2023). Data Protection and Privacy Legislation Worldwide. United Nations Conference on Trade and Development, Geneva, Switzerland, https://unctad.org/page/data-protection-and-privacy-legislation-worldwide.

References

Alvi, M., & Leidner, D. E. (2001). Knowledge management and knowledge management systems: Conceptual foundations and research issues. *MIS Review Quarterly, 25*(1), 107–146.
Amazon Web Services (2024). Home Page. Last accessed from https://aws.amazon.com on 6 August 2024.
Ambrozio, S., Lindeque, J. P., & Peter, M. K. (2025). Navigating uncertainty: Isomorphic pressures in cloud computing adoption. In: M. Moussa & A. McMurray (eds), *The Palgrave Handbook of Breakthrough Technologies in Contemporary Organisations*. Palgrave Macmillan, Singapore. https://doi.org/10.1007/978-981-96-2516-1_18.

Apple (2024). Control is yours. Last accessed from www.apple.com/privacy/control on 12 August 2024.

Barney, J. (1991). Firm resources and sustained competitive advantage. *Journal of Management*, *17*(1), 99-120.

Bharadwaj, A., El Sawy, O. A., Pavlou, P. A., & Venkatraman, N. V. (2013). Digital business strategy: toward a next generation of insights. *MIS Quarterly*, *37*(2),471-482.

Borra, P. (2024). An overview of cloud computing and leading cloud service providers, *International Journal of Computer Engineering and Technology* (*IJCET*), *15*(3), 122–33.

Etsy (2024) Etsy Home Page. Last accessed from www.etsy.com on 12 August 2024.

European Commission (2022). European data strategy, https://commission.europa.eu/strategy-and-policy/priorities-2019-2024/europe-fit-digital-age/european-data-strategy_en.

Garrison, G., Wakefield, R. L., & Kim, S. (2015). The effects of IT capabilities and delivery model on cloud computing success and firm performance for cloud supported processes and operations. *International Journal of Information Management*, *35*(4), 377-393.

General Data Protection Regulation (GDPR) (2016). Regulation (EU) 2016/679 of the European Parliament and of the Council of 27 April 2016 on the protection of natural persons with regard to the processing of personal data and on the free movement of such data. Available from https://eur-lex.europa.eu/eli/reg/2016/679/oj.

Gill, S. S., Tuli, S., Xu, M., Singh, I., Singh, K. V., Lindsay, D., ... & Garraghan, P. (2019). Transformative effects of IoT, blockchain and artificial intelligence on cloud computing: Evolution, vision, trends and open challenges. *Internet of Things*, *8*, 100118.

Google Cloud (2024). Last accessed from https://cloud.google.com/ on 6 August 2024.

Grant, R., & Phene, A. (2022). The knowledge based view and global strategy: Past impact and future potential. *Global Strategy Journal*, *12*(1), 3–30.

Gulati, R., & Oldroyd, J. B. (2005). The quest for customer focus. *Harvard Business Review*, *83*(4), 92–101.

Hoppstar (2024). What Is Important to Us. Last accessed from www.hoppstar.com/en/was-uns-wichtig-ist on 12 August 2024.

Kumar, V., & Vidhyalakshmi, P. (2012). Cloud computing for business sustainability. *Asia-Pacific Journal of Management Research and Innovation*, *8*(4), 461–74.

Mell, P. & Grance, T. (2011). The NIST Definition of Cloud Computing. *Last accessed* from https://nvlpubs.nist.gov/nistpubs/legacy/sp/nistspecialpublication800-145.pdf on 9 September 2025.

Menz, M., Kunisch, S., Birkinshaw, J., Collis, D. J., Foss, N. J., Hoskisson, R. E., & Prescott, J. E. (2021). Corporate strategy and the theory of the firm in the digital age. *Journal of Management Studies*, *58*(7), 1695-1720.

Microsoft Azure (2024). Home Page. Last accessed from https://azure.microsoft.com on 6 August 2024.

Panagiotou, G. (2006). The impact of managerial cognitions on the structure-conduct-performance (SCP) paradigm: A strategic group perspective. *Management Decision*, *44*(3), 423–41.

Peter, M. K. (Hrsg.) (2017). *KMU-Transformation: Als KMU die Digitale Transformation erfolgreich umsetzen*. Forschungsresultate und Praxisleitfaden. FHNW Hochschule für Wirtschaft, Olten/Schweiz, www.kmu-transformation.ch.

Peter, M. K. (Hrsg.) (2021). *Strategieentwicklung im digitalen Zeitalter: Planung und Umsetzung der Digitalen Transformation*. FHNW Hochschule für Wirtschaft und Strategylab, Olten/Schweiz, www.strategische-transformation.ch.

Peter, M. K. (2023). *Digitaler Masterplan für KMU. So gelingt die digitale Transformation in Ihrem Unternehmen.* Verlag Beobachter Edition & Handelszeitung. Zürich/Schweiz, www.digitaler-masterplan.ch.

Peter, M. K. (2024). *The Digital Transformation Canvas. Develop and Implement Your Digital Strategy.* FT Publishing/Pearson, London/UK, www.the-digital-transformation-canvas.com.

Peter, M. K., Kraft, C., & Lindeque, J. (2020). Strategic action fields of digital transformation: An exploration of the strategic action fields of Swiss SMEs and large enterprises. *Journal of Strategy and Management, 13*(1), 160–80.

Porter, M. E. (1979). The structure within industries and companies' performance. *The Review of Economics and Statistics*, 214-227.

Porter, M.E. (1985). *Competitive advantage. Creating and Sustaining Superior Performance.* New York: The Free Press.

Prahalad, C.K. & Hamel, G. (1990). Strategic Analysis. The Core Competence of the Corporation. *Harvard Business Review*, May-June, 79-91.

Robuck, M. (2024). Analysis: Google, Amazon, Microsoft fight for AI dominance. Last accessed from www.mobileworldlive.com/google/analysis-google-amazon-microsoft-fight-for-ai-dominance on 10 August 2024.

Sestino, A., Kahlawi, A., & De Mauro, A. (2025). Decoding the data economy: A literature review of its impact on business, society and digital transformation. *European Journal of Innovation Management, 28*(2), 298–323.

Short, J. C., Ketchen Jr, D. J., Palmer, T. B., & Hult, G. T. M. (2007). Firm, strategic group, and industry influences on performance. *Strategic Management Journal, 28*(2), 147-167.

Sony, M., & Naik, S. (2020). Industry 4.0 integration with socio-technical systems theory: a systematic review and proposed theoretical model. *Technology in Society 61*, 101248.

Tesla (2024). Home Page. Last accessed from www.tesla.com/ on 12 August 2024.

Treacy, M., & Wiersema, F. (1995). *The Discipline of Market Leaders.* Reading, MA: Persus Books.

UNCTAD (2023). Data Protection and Privacy Legislation Worldwide. United Nations Conference on Trade and Development, Geneva, Switzerland, https://unctad.org/page/data-protection-and-privacy-legislation-worldwid.

van Harmelen, F., & ten Teije, A. (2019). A boxology of design patterns for hybrid learning and reasoning systems. *Journal of Web Engineering, 18*(1-3), 97–123.

Wernerfelt, B. (1984). A resource-based view of the firm. *Strategic Management Journal, 5*(2), 171-180.

Witschel, H. F., Pande, C., Martin, A., Laurenzi, E., & Hinkelmann, K. (2020). Visualization of patterns for hybrid learning and reasoning with human involvement. In Dornberger, R. (ed.) *New Trends in Business Information Systems and Technology Studies in Systems, Decision and Control, vol 294* (pp. 193–204). Cham: Springer International Publishing.

Wright, D., Smith, D., Ji, K., Borrega, M. A., Galimberti, A., & Bauman, S. (2023). Magic Quadrant for Strategic Cloud Platform Services. Last accessed from www gartner.com/doc/reprints?id=1-2FTDYPQN&ct=231204&st=sb on 6 August 2024.

Zins, C. (2007). Conceptual approaches for defining data, information, and knowledge. *Journal of the American Society for Information Science and Technology, 58*(4), 479–93.

7

STRATEGIC ACTION FIELD OF NEW STRATEGIES AND BUSINESS MODELS

Learning Goals

By the end of this chapter, you should...

- Be able to identify and articulate a value proposition in the digital age for a specific organisation.
- Be able to elaborate the difference on sustaining innovations versus disruptive innovations.
- Be able to critically evaluate a firm's business strategy in light of the three generic digital strategies of the digitally enhanced business, digitally expanded business and new digital business.
- Be able to analyse and evaluate a firm regarding their competitive strategy, business models and tactics in the digital age.
- Be able to describe different business models and evaluate them for enabling a specific organisation to compete in the fourth/fifth industrial revolutions.
- Be able to articulate how digital value chains, driven by data and technology, are providing insights for future digital innovation and value capture.

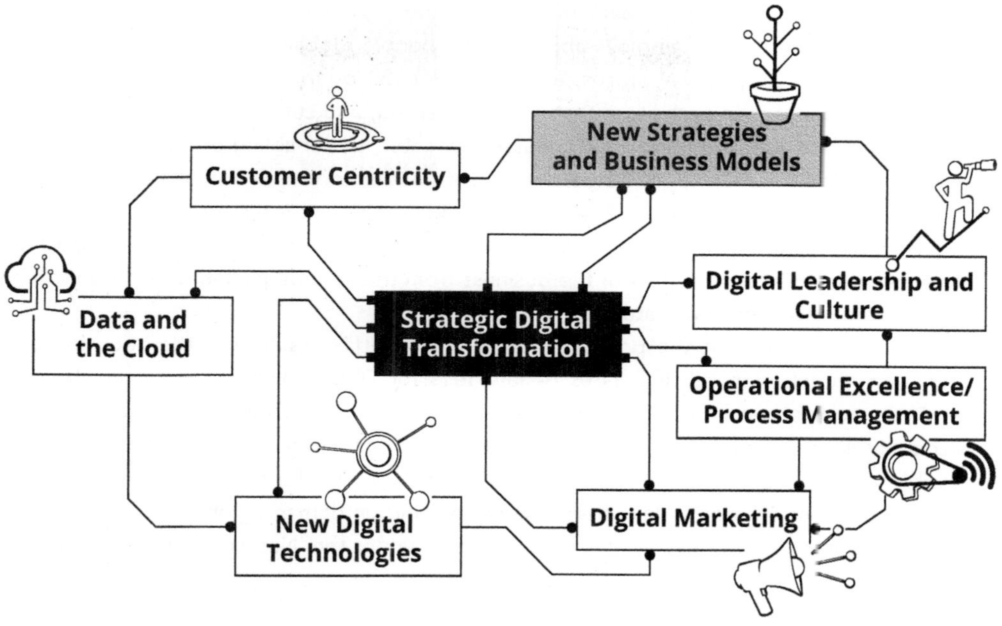

Figure 7.1 New strategies and business models are the fourth Strategic Act on Field of Digital Transformation

Source: Peter (2017, 2021, 2023, 2024); Peter et al. (2020)

The Evolving Netflix Value Proposition

In an interview on The Diary of a CEO podcast (Bartlett & Randolf, 2024), hosted by entrepreneur Steven Bartlett, Marc Randolf recounted the origins and evolution of the video streaming service Netflix (2024), co-founded with Reed Hastings in August 1997. Initially the idea for a mail order video rental was disregarded because of the form factor of the analogue VHS (Video Home System) tape cassette, which was considered too bulky, heavy, and expensive for the value proposition to work. The development of DVD (digital versatile disc) technology, which did not have the same challenges as VHS tapes, allowed next day delivery of a full movie on a DVD to the home of a customer using the US Postal Service for the cost of a stamp. Initially the physical DVDs were mailed to customers, later, with the emergence of streaming online, Netflix was able to also digitise the delivery of the movies and dramatically increase the accessibility and convenience of renting movies. At the time as launching there were, however, fewer than 250,000 DVD players sold in the United States of America (USA) and this was a significant bet by Netflix. Later, high-speed internet connections would allow the full digitalisation of the on-demand video service and the development of a digital platform business model.

The changing digital technologies allowed Netflix to develop a value proposition of variety and convenience for the $8 billion US video rental market at the time of its founding, by actively seeking to offer customers a solution that addressed the practices in the market that customers disliked, exemplified by the dominant incumbent Blockbuster Video rental service. Marc Randolf explains that the initial innovation was a single store concept with full video

(Continued)

inventory that could be accessed over the internet and movies delivered by post, relying on 12–15 people. Today Netflix employs about 13,000 people globally. In contrast, Blockbuster had about 9,000 local physical stores, employing 60,000 people in total at its peak, with limited stocks of videos in each store that could be rented, and customers had to drive to the store to select and rent the films on VHS cassettes. Later, the enabling of an online store by digital technologies made the movie catalogue even easier to search and allowed movies to be listed in multiple categories, which was not possible in the physical stores, thereby offering convenience to customers during the search process. The collection and analysis of customer preferences was an integral aspect of the business from the very beginning, including through rapid testing of ideas for new features.

This focus on improving the product–market fit at Netflix resulted in the adoption of a subscription model, with no due dates or late fees for DVDs, allowing customers to have three DVDs available at home and the next DVD on their 'want to watch list' sent to them immediately after returning a film. This business model innovation made Netflix films more accessible than those of Blockbuster, and this advantage was further accelerated with the advent of streaming. Netflix today offers video streaming on demand globally and has diversified, including into the production of in-house content under the 'Netflix Original' content.

Source: Based on Barlett & Randolf (2024), an interview on 'The Diary of a CEO' podcast

7.0 INTRODUCTION

Digital technology driven innovation is at the very heart of the emergence of new strategies and business models, as well as innovation within established strategies and business models. The opening case study makes clear that these opportunities are often most clearly discernible in new ventures, which do not have legacy strategies and established business models that also need to be accommodated. The challenges associated with transformation of existing businesses / business units in multi-business firms have become known as the innovator's dilemma (Christensen, 2015). Traditionally, these innovation and transformation processes have been discussed in terms of corporate and competitive strategies, but increasingly the concepts of corporate business models, business models of the individual business units, and corporate and business unit business model innovation/transformation are being used to capture technology driven change processes. In all of these transformation processes, senior management teams are argued to play a critical role, most importantly in the enabling of ambidextrous strategies that allow the exploitation of existing business models, as well as the exploration of the opportunities enabled by digital technologies and the digital transformation of firms. This chapter discusses these trends and the new strategies and business models that are emerging as a result, with an emphasis on the differences between multi-business and single business firms.

7.1 DIGITAL TRANSFORMATION AND THE INNOVATOR'S DILEMMA

The digital transformation of firms is fundamentally driven by the adoption of digital technologies and the associated opportunities for new ways of creating value (e.g., taking advantage of the data economy). As the digital transformation of businesses, the economy and society progress, it is notable how divergent the degree of transformation and success with the digital transformation of firms can be, also for previously successful incumbents. Clayton Christensen (1997) coined the term 'innovator's dilemma' to explain why the emergence of new technologies can lead previously very successful incumbent firms to fail in the face of needing to transform the way they create value. Responding to the opportunities and challenges posed by digital technology adoption and its use by competitors can require firms to consider the businesses they are involved in (corporate strategy / business models) as well as how these technologies could be incorporated to enhance the competitiveness of a firm (competitive strategy). Christensen (1997) distinguished between sustaining technology innovations, that enable a firm to execute existing value creating strategies more effectively, and disruptive technologies, that reduce the performance of a firm by enabling value propositions that had not previously been possible. Assessing and responding to such technological changes is the responsibility of senior management teams (see Chapter 9 for more on leadership and digital culture transformation, especially the management of the resulting tensions in a firm that has a profitable established business and also recognises the need to integrate digital technologies and more broadly digitally transform how it creates value). It is generally accepted that, more often than not, new entrants are in a stronger position to take advantage of the opportunities created by disruptive technologies (Wang et al., 2022) (see Box 7.1).

Box 7.1: The Innovator's Dilemma

Established companies tend to focus on *sustaining innovations*, which are incremental improvements to their existing products. This focus is driven by the need to meet the demands of their current customers and maintain profitability. However, this approach can make them vulnerable to disruptive innovations, which they may initially overlook or dismiss as insignificant.

On the other side, *disruptive innovations* often start as lower-quality, cheaper alternatives that initially appeal to a niche market. However, over time, they improve and eventually capture the mainstream market, displacing established products.

The *innovator's dilemma* arises because investing in disruptive innovations often requires a shift in resources and attention away from the core business, which can be risky and unpopular with stakeholders. Additionally, the potential market for disruptive innovations may seem small and uncertain compared to the established market. This highlights the difficulty of balancing the need to innovate with the need to sustain existing business operations. Companies that successfully navigate this dilemma are those that can recognise the potential of disruptive innovations early and are willing to take calculated risks to invest in them.

Source: Christensen (1997)

The core idea of the innovator's dilemma is that it is not technological competences that explains the inability of firms to respond to emergent disruptive technologies, but rather firms' failure to effectively respond to technological change due to the inability of senior managers to effectively perceive technology changes and decide how to respond (Christensen, 1997; Henderson, 2006; Wang et al., 2022). Additionally, internal political dynamics among senior managers around serving profitable markets and customers may prevent the adoption of disruptive technologies (Henderson, 2006; Wang et al., 2022). An alternative explanation is that deeply embedded and complex organisational competences make it difficult for a firm to change the way it creates value for customers (Henderson, 2006). This explanation argues that even if senior managers correctly perceive and understand the need to respond to a disruptive technology and there is no political resistance to responding, they may hesitate or even choose not to seek to respond, because the firm is ill-equipped to build the necessary resources and capabilities demanded for adopting the new technology (Henderson, 2006). O'Reilly and Tushman (2008) locate this in the ability of senior managers to manage the tension between exploiting existing capabilities and exploring opportunities presented by a new technology.

The authors argue that dynamic capabilities by enabling organisational ambidexterity are the key to enabling an organisation to overcome the innovator's dilemma. Where dynamic capabilities are 'the ability of senior managers to seize opportunities through the orchestration and integration of both new and existing assets to overcome inertia and path dependencies' (O'Reilly and Tushman, 2008, p. 187). Dynamic capabilities enable ambidexterity when they support the 'firm's ability to exploit existing assets and positions in a profit producing way and simultaneously to explore new technologies and markets; to configure and reconfigure organizational resources to capture existing as well as new opportunities' (O'Reilly and Tushman, 2008, p. 189). The senior management team have a critical role in making this possible and the likelihood of a successful response to the imperative to digitally transform increases when the senior management team is able to do the following (O'Reilly and Tushman, 2008, pp. 197–199):

1. Communicate 'a compelling strategic intent that justifies the importance of both exploitation and exploration';
2. Articulate 'a common vision and values that provide for a common identity';
3. Establish a 'clear consensus among the senior team about [the ambidextrous] strategy, relentless communication of this strategy, and a common-fate incentive system' for the senior management team;
4. Establish temporal, organisational and/or physical 'separate [but] aligned organisational architectures (business models, competencies, incentives, metrics, and cultures) for explor[ative] and exploit[ative] subunits and [implement] targeted integration' of the resulting business units; and
5. Finally, the senior management team is able to tolerate 'the contradictions of multiple alignments and is able to resolve the tensions that ensue'.

Such orchestration of resources and decisions about what the business portfolio of a firm should be are at the heart of corporate strategy and the emerging concept of corporate business models. The adoption of digital technologies however takes place in the business or business units and is expressed in the impact on competitive strategies and business models.

7.2 DIGITAL TRANSFORMATION, CORPORATE STRATEGY AND CORPORATE BUSINESS MODELS

The corporate strategy of a firm specifies the businesses a firm currently serves and intends to be participate in in the future and the degree to which the resulting strategic business units should be related (i.e., the degree of diversification), so that the firm can achieve a competitive advantage. Corporate strategies are argued to have the potential to lead to corporate advantage built on strategic choices about the optimal combination of resources and capabilities for achieving a competitive advantage, the desirable approach to exercising control within the larger organisation given the businesses it is involved in, while seeking optimal coordination of resources and capabilities for the entire organisation (Caldart & Ricart, 2004; Collis & Montgomery, 1998).

Business model thinking (see Figure 7.2) shifts the focus from competitive advantage to value creation. The corporate business model is 'the corporate top managers' perceived logic of how value is created by the corporation, especially regarding the value-creating links between the corporation's portfolio of businesses', allowing 'for the concise examination of the main aspects of interlinkedness and value creation logics between a firm's businesses over time' (Aspara et al., 2013, p. 460). In larger multi-business organisation, corporate strategy is a critical aspect of the value creation by a firm in a distinctly different way to single business firms (Bowman & Helfat, 2001) (see Box 7.2), but single business firms also undertake corporate strategising when for example shifting to entirely new business activities.

Box 7.2: Corporate Strategising and Corporate Business Model Development at Nokia

Nokia is an example of a firm that has become famous for its radical divestment strategy during the 1990s that transformed it from a diversified multi-business firm into a multinational enterprise active in two highly related businesses. This strategy contributed to Nokia becoming synonymous with mobile telecommunications during the 1990s, especially with respect to its mobile phone devices, but Nokia failed to maintain its competitive advantage with the shift to smartphones in the early 2000s. Nokia was active in six major businesses, including (1) rubber products, (2) communications and power cables, (3) information systems, (4) consumer electronics, (5) mobile phones, and (6) tele-networks, as well as a large number of less important businesses. This diversification was increasingly perceived as lacking legitimacy in the early 1990s; the need for a new corporate business model was recognised by Nokia's senior management team, but establishing the required consensus was challenging due to micro-politics amongst senior managers. The senior management team assessed all businesses for profitability and Nokia's competitiveness, as well as the legitimacy of the business in terms of corporate reputation, national status, and

(Continued)

employment attractiveness. At the same time the businesses were assessed for shared complementary products and customers as well as whether businesses possessed attributes that had led to previous lack of competitiveness, excluding firms that had these attributes. By 1996 over 90% of Nokia's sales were from the mobile phones and tele-network business units, which showed clear value creating links between the two business units. Despite this radical corporate business model transformation, Nokia had by the early 2000s lost its commanding position in the mobile phone markets globally. In 2024 Nokia is primarily active in highly related fixed and IP networks, mobile networks, cloud and network services, and some other businesses (Nokia, 2024a), with a large number of licensed products based on intellectual property from the late 1990s (Nokia, 2024b).

Source: Adapted from Aspara et al. (2013)

The concept of corporate strategy is still important and should ideally be understood as the driver, pacer, and framer of a firms overall (co-)evolution with its external environment (Caldart & Ricart, 2004). This is true for the digital transformation of firms and their embeddedness in the external socio-technical systems that provide inputs and receive the outputs (goods and services) of the internal transformation processes of the firm (see Box 7.2). Corporate strategy in the digital age is tasked with seeking to adapt the resources and capabilities bundles of the firm, the design of the organisational coordination mechanism and control systems, as well as the breadth of the scope of the portfolio of businesses a firm participates in, as a response to the digital transformation of society and the economy. Corporate management does this by developing a representation of the fitness of a firm in the evolving external socio-technical systems the firm is embedded in (to drive the needed co-evolution), then deciding on a desirable positioning of the firm and the related degree of incremental, radical or recombination change needed (the pace of the needed co-evolution), and finally, deciding on the ideal organisation of the firm, the architecture of coordination mechanism and control systems, to manage the resulting resources and capabilities bundles and portfolio of businesses (to frame the co-evolution) (Caldart & Ricart, 2004). The framing of the co-evolution of the firm with the ecosystems it is embedded in is the foundation for the development of corporate managers corporate business model at any one point in time. The need for a shift in corporate and business managerial cognition to accurately represent the changing external competitive environment is often one of the most critical barriers to effectively respond to the digital transformation of the economy and society (see Chapter 9 on digital leadership and culture). It is important to remember that corporate business model transformation is as much about senior managerial cognition related to changing external conditions as it is about perceiving and understanding the inter-organisational linkages of the existing strategic business units of a firm, the so called inter-organisational cognition of senior managers (Aspara et al., 2013).

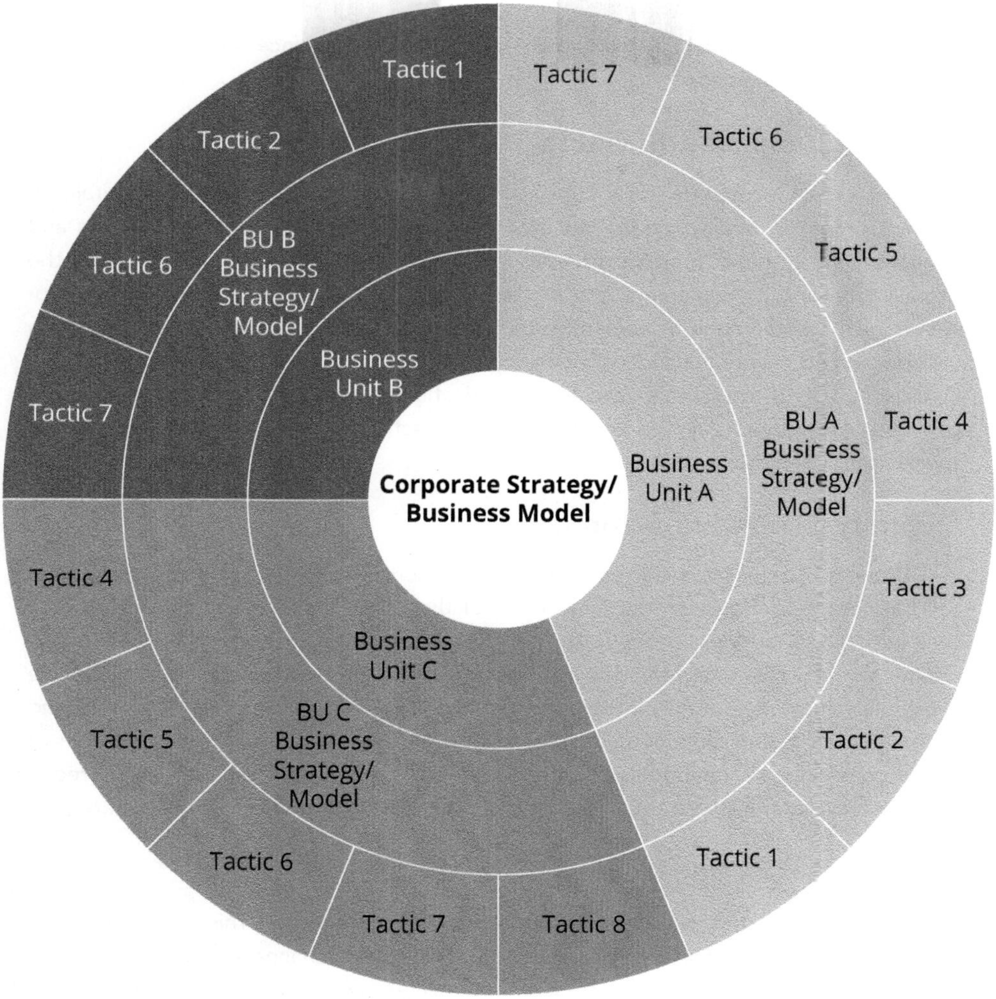

Figure 7.2 Corporate strategy, competitive strategies, and business model thinking

Source: adapted from Aspara et al. (2013); Caldart & Ricart (2004); and Casadesus-Masanell & Ricart (2010)

Box 7.3: Three Generic Digital Strategies

The three generic digital strategies are aligned to the three digital maturity levels of organisations as introduced in Chapter 1 (Figure 1.6). The three generic digital strategies are usually implemented sequentially. By starting with the 'Digitally Enhanced Business' (digital enablement), analogue tasks are digitised, and on the other hand, digital competencies are developed that enable the later step to the 'Digitally Expanded Business' (digital optimisation/digitalisation). In order to be able to build a 'New Digital

(Continued)

Business' (strategic digital transformation), appropriate experience with the two preceding stages is recommended.

Digitally Enhanced Business

With the aim of increasing efficiency, this involves simplifying and digitising/digitalising existing processes and functions, but also offering customers enhanced products and services. Typical areas of application are the digitalisation of interaction between the organisation and its customers, the digital transformation of core or production processes or the automation of human resources (HR) processes. Agile practices are often introduced and new digital skills are developed in this phase as a basis for further steps. Without going through this step for organisational learning and experimentation, phases 2 and 3 can hardly be implemented successfully. The focus often is on *revised functional strategies.*

Digitally Expanded Business

This often far-reaching transformation of organisations involves the digital expansion of the business model or even the reinvention of the existing business. The development of a new digital business model, driven by, e.g., new value creation chains/processes, creates the basis for differentiation and new growth in the existing market. An example is a retailer that offers a fully integrated customer experience across all its physical and digital channels. The alignment of traditional organisational silos, the introduction of appropriate governance models and the addition of new talent are important prerequisites for a successful transformation. The focus often is on a *revised business strategy.*

New Digital Business

This diversification step is about creating new sources of revenue. This can be achieved by tapping into new geographical markets via digital sales channels, forward and backward integration via digital value creation systems (ecosystems) or the development of new business areas. The latter can be established, for example, through the acquisition of start-ups or organically through independent development. The focus often is on a *revised corporate strategy.*

Source: Adapted from Kaltenrieder, Peter, & Reinhardt (2024)

7.3 DIGITAL TRANSFORMATION, COMPETITIVE STRATEGIES AND BUSINESS MODELS

Casadesus-Masanell and Ricart (2010) argue that for the full potential of advances in ICT, digital transformation, and social responsibility to be realised it is important to establish clear distinctions between strategy, business model, and tactics conceptually (see Box 7.3, 7.4 and Figure 7.2). Business unit business models are focused on the logics of value creation and capture, as concretely realised in daily managerial practice; such business models have been described as the realised strategy of a firm (Casadesus-Masanell & Ricart, 2010). The 'business unit-level business model [is] the business unit managers' perceived logic of how the unit in question functions and creates value, in connection with both its market environment, and within the corporation' in relation to other business unit's business models (Aspara et al., 2013, p. 460). At the same time the business model can be expected to be aligned with a higher-level competitive strategy, in terms of the orchestration resources and capabilities, as well as market positioning, with the aim to achieve a competitive advantage. The business model of a business (unit) is then a reflection of a business' realised competitive strategy (Casadesus-Masanell & Ricart, 2010), which is the high-level conceptualisation of how competitive advantage will be realised (see Chapter 2). This reflects Porter's (1996) view that competitive strategy is concerned with selecting between alternative activity systems to fit a preferred market positioning from which to compete, while the specific activity set adopted can be understood as the business model of the firm. It is important to remember that this activity system will more likely than not span the boundaries of the focal firm (Zott & Amit, 2010). To round out the alignment with Casadesus-Masanell and Ricart (2010), the specific manner in which the activities are executed can be understood as the tactics of the firm (see Box 7.4). The perspective on competitive strategies, business models, and activities also allows the resource-based and capabilities-based views (Barney, 1991, 2001; Porter, 1996) of competitive advantage to be related to the above arguments, as it is the resources and capabilities of the firm and those of external partners that enable the activity bundles of a specific business model to be realised in practice.

Box 7.4: Competitive Strategy, Business Models, and Tactics

Understanding the interplay between competitive strategy, business models, and tactics is crucial for firms aiming to achieve a competitive advantage.

Competitive Strategy

Competitive strategy is 'the choice of business model through which the firm will compete in the marketplace' (Casadesus-Masanell & Ricart, 2010, p. 196). The choice of business model is determined by classic strategic analyses of the competitive environment (positional strategy) and the resource and capability endowments of the firm (resource-based and capabilities view), to identify opportunities for realising a competitive advantage. A firm may decide to directly compete with incumbents based on the planned execution of a business model or compete indirectly by offering a new value proposition, that leverages digital technologies to innovate the business model. A classic example of this is how Virgin Air decided to compete directly with British Airways on the most profitable routes only, while Ryanair and EasyJet decided to compete by bringing a new value proposition to the European air travel market, not least by leveraging digital technologies for booking flights and famously using underserved regional airports.

(Continued)

Business Models

A business model is 'the logic of the firm, the way it operates and how it creates value for its stakeholders' (Casadesus-Masanell & Ricart, 2010, p. 196) (see Figure 7.3. and Box 7.5). Business model thinking was popularised in the business model canvas of Osterwalder and Pigneur (2010) that focused decision-making on nine elements, including (1) customer segments, (2) value propositions design, (3) communication, sales, and distribution channels for delivering value, (4) customer relationship management, and (5) the resulting revenue streams, but also a specification of (6) the key resources and (7) activities, that collectively could be considered as the capabilities of a firm, as well as (8) the key partnerships needed to access external essential resources and activities, resulting in (9) the cost structure of a firm.

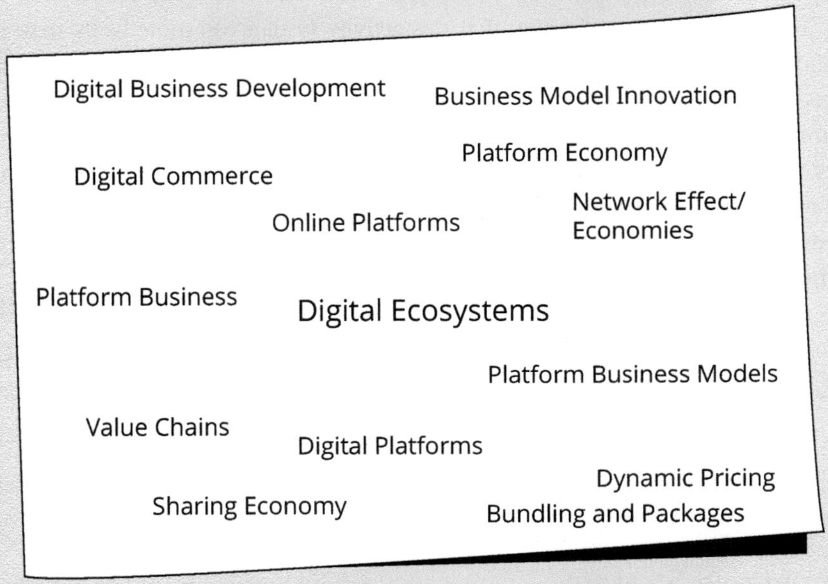

Figure 7.3 New business models and concepts in the digital age

Source: Peter (2023, 2024)

Tactics

Tactics (the how-to) are 'the residual choices open to a firm by virtue of the business model it chooses to employ' (Casadesus-Masanell & Ricart, 2010, p. 196). The tactics a firm selects focus attention on the how of delivering the nine elements of a business model to compete, i.e., create and capture value. Two firms with the same business model through their tactics could deliver it in meaningfully different ways; at the same time the business model selected constrains the tactics available to a firm for making such decisions.

7.4 DIGITAL TRANSFORMATION AND BUSINESS (UNIT) MODEL INNOVATION

As the socio-technical systems within which firms are embedded are changing at increasing rates due to structural changes, driven by digital transformation and other macro-trends like globalisation and pressures for more socially responsible business, the firms that have grown most quickly are those that have been able to take advantage of these changes to innovate their business models (Casadesus-Masanell & Ricart, 2010). Business models (see Box 7.5), if understood as the activity systems though which firms commercialise new ideas and technologies, will require firms to innovate their business models for the digital age (Chesbrough, 2010). As was noted in the early sections of this chapter, balancing the exploitation of existing business models and allowing the needed business model innovation for successfully bringing new value propositions to market can be very challenging for firms and their senior managers (Christensen, 1997; Henderson, 2006; Peter, 2019; Wang et al., 2022).

Box 7.5: Overview of Business Models for the Digital Age

- **Auction model**: the market determines the price of the product or service (examples: Auction.com, eBay, Sotheby's).
- **Bundle/package prices:** the bundle/package price covers the individual prices of several products or services as a package deal (example: holiday package consisting of flights, rental car, and accommodation).
- **Cross-selling**: a company sells offers from other product categories to the customer (example: a grocery shop that also offers bicycles and clothes, such as Aldi).
- **Crowdfunding**: a new product is crowd financed through donations and loans, often by offering an equivalent value in the form of the discounted product (examples: Indiegogo, Kickstarter).
- **Crowdsourcing**: a product or service is created with the help of the crowd (examples: apps or traffic jam reports on the radio).
- **Direct sales**: organisations that traditionally sell through retailers also offer products or services directly, for example through an e-shop (example: Levi's Jeans).
- **Dynamic prices:** in these models, prices change over time, triggered by competition or strategic considerations, with the aim of maximising profit or strengthening customer loyalty (dynamic prices are for instance used on Booking.com).
- **E-commerce**: this model refers to the sale and trade of goods on the internet. Well-known examples include Alibaba, Amazon, eBay, and Zalando, whose business model is (mostly) exclusively digital and does not maintain physical stores.
- **Ecosystem model/digital ecosystem**: the aim of this model is to lock customers into an ecosystem long-term by means of a lock-in process to a service or a certain technology. For example, anyone who uses a mobile phone from Apple is locked into their ecosystem.

(Continued)

- **Franchising**: the company (the franchisor) offers its products or services via a network of partners (the franchisees) (examples: Hilton Hotels, McDonald's, Pizza Hut).
- **Free model**: products and services are offered free of charge. However, the company retains the right to analyse/use customers' data for advertising or personalised offers (examples are Facebook, Google, and Instagram).
- **Freemium model**: in this frequently used new business model, the consumer is provided with a product or service free of charge. However, only basic functions are offered in the free version. For premium features, such as own branding or an extension of the services, a price must be paid.
- **Guaranteed maximum price (GMP)**: the organisation sets a maximum price for a product/service, which however is billed on a per item or hourly basis. Once the maximum price point of the contract is reached, the customers will not pay more for the product/service, even though they might keep using the product/service.
- **Licensing**: the licence gives you the right to use a company's product or service in another market or as a component in a new product for a fee (e.g., the production of backpacks under the Swiss brand 'Wenger' in the USA).
- **On-demand model**: this business model is based on the motto 'time is money'. Here, immediate access to a service or product is provided or, alternatively, premium access that saves time (examples are Amazon Prime, Fiverr, Uber, or Upwork).
- **Open source**: the product (often software) can be used free of charge and the organisation earns money from the associated services (example: LibreOffice).
- **Pay-per-use model**: the customer pays per use case or for individual use (examples: co-working meeting rooms, car rental, construction machinery rental at an hourly rate).
- **Platforms/platform economy**: on digital platforms, several market players link up either technically or in terms of go-to-market. One of the best-known digital platforms is Amazon, but there are also providers in the travel industry that bundle offers from different organisations, such as Airbnb or Booking.com for hotel rooms and holiday flats. This business model, which is also described as peer-to-peer (from-user-to-user), is considered particularly lucrative for organisations.
- **Sharing economy**: the term 'sharing economy' refers to the systematic lending of objects and the mutual provision of spaces, especially by private individuals and interest groups. The focus is on shared consumption or shared use.
- **Subscription model**: products and services can usually also be offered as subscriptions. This creates a new service that is billed periodically. The aim is to retain customers over the long term. In contrast to a one-time purchase, the customer continuously benefits from service improvements and extensions (typical examples are Disney+ or Netflix).

Source: Peter (2024)

The activity systems allowed by different business models at the same time can lead to very different value creation and capture outcomes and firm strategic competitive advantage for the same value proposition and its underlying idea or underlying technologies. The critical insight here is that the economic value of general-purpose digital technologies remain latent until the technology is commercialised via a business model (Chesbrough, 2010; Gambardella, & McGahan, 2010; Teece, 2010). The required business model innovation is rarely entirely clear from the start of an innovation process and is typically discovered via experimentation with alternative possibilities, that then effectuate new insights through action; this approach is most commonly associated with new ventures in Silicon Valley, as described in Eric Ries' (2011) 'The Lean Startup'. Fundamentally, business model innovation required for commercialising the potential of digital technologies needs experimentation and action to stimulate feedback (new information) about the ideal business model for creating value (Ries, 2011; Teece, 2010); this mechanism was central to the evolving business model of Netflix in the opening case study to this chapter. This thinking can be applied along the entire value chain of incumbent firms (see Box 7.6), or in new ventures, and requires rapid experimentation to identify value creating innovations.

Box 7.6: Digital Technologies and Value Chain-Based Business Model Innovation

Digital technologies and digital transformation more broadly need not always be disruptive in nature, although this is typically the focus adopted (Christensen, 1997; Henderson, 2006); for many firms a careful analysis of the value chains created by their business models can identify opportunities for digital technologies to be adopted and integrated as sustaining innovations of the activities of a specific business model. The aim is to identify opportunities for optimising activities along the value chain to increase their effectiveness or improve efficiency of activities at each stage of the value chain.

Value chain analysis is implicit in the widely adopted Business Model Canvas of Osterwalder and Pigneur (2010). If read from left to right, the canvas encourages managers to consider external partners that enable access to essential external resources and activities (inputs) for the firm's internal value creation/transformation processes (see Chapter 8 on operational excellence); the internal resources and activities enable value creation, which allow specific value propositions to be made to selected customer segments using the most effective communication, sales, and distribution channels for delivering the value proposition. What is missing is the after sales services and customer relationship management necessary for long-term value creation. The digital transformation of existing value chain activities represents business model innovation seeking to sustain the existing business model of a firm. In the digital age, this value chain transformation is highly related to the data creation and analysis potential of the digital technologies being adopted. This is true for coordination of external partners, managing internal operations, and delivering greater value to customers.

When digital technologies are used to improve the efficiency and/or effectiveness of activities along this value chain for a given business model, the aim is to improve value creation and capture, which will become visible in the revenue streams of the firm and the associated cost structure of the firm (see Figure 7.4). The more compelling the

(Continued)

value proposition enabled by the digital transformation of the value chain, the greater the willingness-to-pay on the part of customers in terms of absolute price and frequency of purchase that can be expected. The greater the degree to which digital technologies can improve the effectiveness of the functioning of the value chain, especially in terms of supply chain management and operations, the more likely the firm will have a favourable cost structure. These two aspects of the business model and value chain digital transformation will drive the economic performance of the firm, which is determined by the margin per unit of product or service and the volume of product or service units sold. With the margin per unit determined by the willingness-to-pay in terms of a per unit price and the cost per unit sold. Digital transformation of the value chain at the most fundamental level should be seeking to reduce the cost per unit and increase the willingness-to-pay in terms of price and frequency of purchase. At the same time, the analysis of the digital value chain (with all connected actors/stakeholders of the value chain) (Figure 7.4), will help to identify future digital opportunities through an engagement of the technology and data layers that will help to identify opportunities for digital innovation and value capture.

Source: adapted from Chesbrough (2010) and Peter (2024)

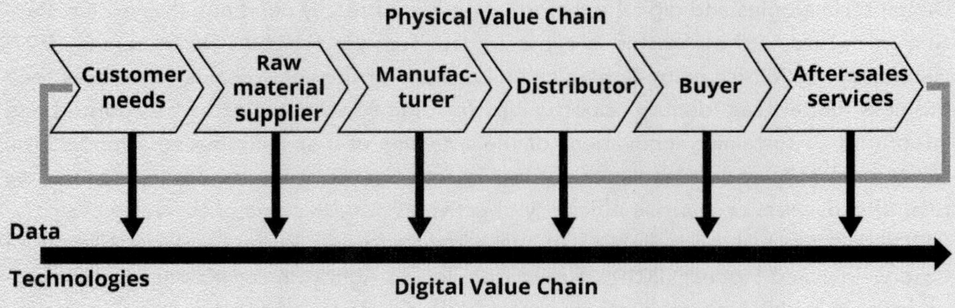

Figure 7.4 The physical and digital value chain

Source: Peter (2024) following Rayport & Sviokla (1996)

7.5 WEB 2.0 AND THE PLATFORM ECONOMY: NEW COMPETITIVE STRATEGIES AND BUSINESS MODELS

Web 2.0 business models 'leverage customer-self-service and algorithmic data management to reach out to the entire web, to the edges and not just the centre, to the long tail and not just the head' (O'Reilly, 2007). Fundamentally these business models create value by leveraging the networks and collective intelligence of users on the web and related user-generated content, with prime examples including Google Search, eBay, and Amazon. Other examples of Web 2.0 businesses are YouTube, LinkedIn, Facebook and social media, and blogging and vlogging sites. All of these business models rely on networks and user-generated content/data. Indeed, much of the value creation and capture by firms in the Web 2.0 space is related to the meta data describing user activity online. Today Web 2.0 is commonly referred to as the platform economy, which incorporates a range of different types of platform-based business models associated with emerging phenomena, like the sharing economy (i.e., Google Drive, Dropbox, etc.), the collaborative economy (i.e., Slack, Miro, Asana, etc.), the gig economy (i.e., Uber, Deliveroo, DoorDash, etc.), the on-demand economy (i.e., ZipCar, Flinkster, etc.), etc. (Derave et al., 2021). While most of the examples here are business-to-consumer (B2C) or consumer to consumer (B2C or P2P (peer to peer)) platforms, they also include business to business (B2B) platforms (Derave et al., 2021; Täuscher & Laudien, 2018). But platforms can also be one-sided, be used for product and/or services, and implemented as web-based and/or mobile app-based platforms. As can be seen from the examples above digital platforms can be used to facilitate digital and offline products and services locally, regionally, or even globally (Täuscher & Laudien, 2018). According to the authors, firms developing a digital platform business model need to consider the type of revenue stream (commissions, subscriptions, advertising, etc.), the pricing mechanism (fixed or dynamic), how pricing can be discriminated (based on features, location, volume, etc.), and who is paying (seller, buyer, third parties, etc.).

7.6 NEW STRATEGIES, BUSINESS MODELS AND COMPETITIVE ADVANTAGE

Firms within the same industry can have very different corporate strategies and the evidence for a dominant corporate strategy for superior returns is mixed (Caldart & Ricart, 2004; Collis & Montgomery, 1998). Bowman and Helfat (2001) argued that when single business firms are excluded from samples the effects of corporate strategies on firm performance are clear. Critics argue that the limited evidence for corporate strategies driving value creation is the result of corporate decision-makers focusing on individual elements of the corporate strategy and not understanding that resources and capabilities, the design of an organisation (coordination mechanism, control systems, and degree of central control), and the breadth of the scope of the portfolio of businesses to participate in as a system, need to be considered as a whole.

At the same time the competitive advantage of a given business model is likely to be sustained, as once a business model is implemented it is largely transparent and subject to a high likelihood of copying, with successful business models becoming best practice adopted by competitors (Teece, 2010); thus, business model innovation needs to be combined with strategic analysis. A business model is likely to be associated with sustained competitive advantage when the firm has ownership over unique (valuable), rare, difficult to imitate, and non-substitutable resources and capabilities. A business model is also likely to lead to competitive advantage when it enables a firm to pursue a market positioning strategy that is attractive to customers compared to competitors. A competitive strategy analysis will reveal the degree to which a business model is likely to enable a unique value proposition that is attractive to customers (i.e., will increase their willingness-to-pay). A further goal of a strategic analysis is to identify any potential 'isolating' mechanisms that will insulate a firm from competition, what has been referred to as a firm's 'moat'. Isolating mechanisms may include internal resources and processes that are difficult to observe, but essential for implementing the business model, reflecting the resource-based view (Barney, 1991).

7.7 NEW STRATEGIES, BUSINESS MODELS, AND SUSTAINABILITY

Sustainable business models have been defined as business models that integrate sustainability concerns into companies, so that they become a source of competitive advantage, creating not only economic, but also social and environmental value. Business model innovations that reduce the negative impact of a firm on the natural environment and society are argued to also be (more) sustainable. Digital technologies have been argued to support the realisation of more sustainable business models by increasing efficiency in value chains and optimise resource consumption (Broccardo et al., 2023), primarily as they can be scaled and replicated across different regions and industries. This scalability ensures that sustainability efforts have a broader impact and can be implemented more efficiently, driving long-term value creation and resilience.

7.8 CONCLUSION

Digital business model innovation is essential to ensure that the latent potential of new digital technologies for value creation is fully realised. Digital transformation of firms requires the careful introduction of new business models without undermining incumbent business models in multi-business firms, while new entrants can leverage new business models to successfully compete against incumbents.

Through analysis, exploration, and debate, the strategic action fields of *Customer Centricity* (Chapter 4), *New Digital Technologies* (Chapter 5), and *Data and the Cloud* (Chapter 6) will very often lead to strategic opportunities and innovations for increased competitiveness in the digital age, as summarised in this chapter on *New Strategies and Business Models*. Figure 7.5 visualises the simplified sequential flow from the identification of customer expectations/requirements, a renewed understanding of the opportunities from new digital technology, and a deep understanding of organisational data towards a new digital strategy. The following chapters (Chapters 8–10) will define how to implement the new digital strategy across operational excellence/processes, new leadership and culture, and digital marketing.

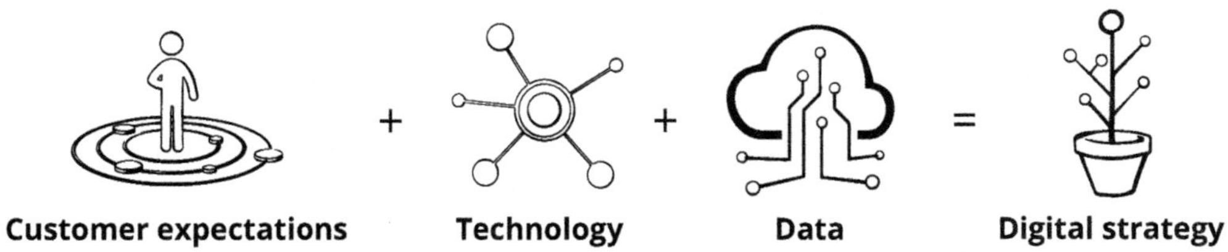

Figure 7.5 Strategic action fields 1–3 leading to the digital strategy

Source: Peter (2023, 2024)

This chapter explores how digital technology-driven innovation is central to the development of such new strategies and business models, as well as the transformation of existing ones. A key challenge is elaborated based on the concept of the innovator's dilemma, where established firms struggle to adopt disruptive technologies due to their focus on sustaining innovations. It emphasises the role of senior management in navigating this dilemma by balancing the exploitation of existing capabilities with the exploration of new opportunities. Dynamic capabilities and organisational ambidexterity are highlighted as key enablers for overcoming the innovator's dilemma. The three generic digital strategies, leading to stronger competitiveness and new business models, are the digitally enhanced business, the digitally expanded business, and new digital business.

For digital transformation, competitive strategies and business models can be defined at the business unit level, emphasising the need for clear distinctions between strategy, business model, and tactics (see Box 7.4). The chapter discusses various business models for the digital age, such as e-commerce, subscription models, and platform-based models, and how these models can drive value creation and capture (see Box 7.5). Finally, the chapter addresses the role of digital transformation in business model innovation, highlighting the importance of the digital value chain (see Box 7.6), experimentation and feedback in discovering the ideal business model for new technologies.

Case Studies

Students can complete the following tasks either based on the focal case study, or work on the recommended case study for this chapter (*Valuu: a corporate start-up for digital business model innovation*) and answer the questions below.

1. Document and analyse an industry's (use the mortgage industry for the Valuu case) digital value chain and identify data and technology components as per Chapter 7 (Box 7.6).
2. Evaluate if the organisation currently covers all digital value chain components (with a focus on data and technology): which digital opportunities did the organisation capture successfully, and what are the future opportunities (make assumptions, if required)?
3. From a board member's perspective, what are the success factors for a digital business model innovation (a digital ecosystem as part of platform economies like Valuu, see Chapter 7, Box 7.5)?
4. From the perspective of the project team (the business model innovation project team), what are the success factors for digital strategy innovation? Refer to Chapter 11 for the success factors of digital transformation implementation).
5. What skills are required in a project team to drive a successful digital business initiative?
6. What 'lessons learned' would you consider for your own digital start-up/business venture?

Additional cases with student questions for the strategic digital action field of *New Strategies and Business Models* are covered in:

- Adelbodner mineral water – the digital roadmap of a SME (available online).
- Blackroll – from Product Innovation to International Expansion via E-Commerce (available online).
- BRUGG Lifting and its industrial Internet of Things (IIoT) asset management solution 'PVS' (available in the Appendix).
- Digital transformation of the city of Lucerne (available in the Appendix).
- Sulzer – strategic leadership in sustainable, digital tech-enabled value-adding services (available online).
- Action fields of digital transformation at Synchrony Financial (USA) (available online).

You will find a collection of case studies for Strategic Digital Transformation in the Appendix and additional cases online at www.strategic-digital-transformation.com

Exercises

Discuss the following questions in your class, in your group or assignment:

1. Based on a selected industry/business which is active in the digital space (i.e., provides a digital product or service), identify their value proposition (also see the opening case 'Evolving Netflix Value Proposition').
2. Based on your selected firm from exercise 1, identify how the innovator's dilemma (see Box 7.1.) could impact their strategy/business, and explain the difference on sustaining innovations versus disruptive innovations based on their current situation.
3. Review the case study firm's business strategy (from exercise 1) in light of the three generic digital strategies (see Box 7.3) of digitally enhanced business, digitally expanded business, and new digital business. Identify at least three concrete suggestions how they could improve their strategy under each generic digital strategy.
4. Analyse the firm from exercise 1 regarding their competitive strategy, business model and tactics (see Box 7.4): in what areas could the firm improve on each level to foster digital transformation?
5. Forming two small groups (2–4 students in each group), each group should select a business model from Box 7.5 and discuss the pros and cons. In a debate, convince the other group that your business model is the more successful choice/option to compete in the digital age.
6. Analyse the digital value chain (with a focus on data and technology) based on the organisation from exercise 1 and identify how the firm could capture future value and develop digital innovations (see Box 7.6).

Further Reading List

- Aspara, J., Lamberg, J. A., Laukia, A., & Tikkanen, H. (2013). Corporate business model transformation and inter-organizational cognition: The case of Nokia. *Long Range Planning, 46*(6), 459–74.
- Christensen, C. M. (1997). *The Innovator's Dilemma: When New Technologies Cause Great Firms to Fail.* Boston: Harvard Business Review Press.
- Osterwalder, A.. & Pigneur, Y. (2010). *Business Model Generation: A Handbook for Visionaries, Game Changers, and Challengers.* New Jersey: Wiley.
- Rayport, J. F., & Sviokla, J.J. (1996). Exploiting the virtual value chain. *McKinsey Quarterly*, 1, 20–36.

References

Aspara, J., Lamberg, J. A., Laukia, A., & Tikkanen, H. (2013). Corporate business model transformation and inter-organizational cognition: The case of Nokia. *Long Range Planning, 46*(6), 459–74.

Barney, J. (1991). Firm resources and sustained competitive advantage. *Journal of Management, 17*(1), 99-120.

Barney, J. B. (2001). Resource-based theories of competitive advantage: A ten-year retrospective on the resource-based view. *Journal of Management, 27*(6), 643-650.

Bartlett, S. (Host), & Randolf, M. (Guest). (August 2024). *Former Netflix CEO: 'Hard Work Does Not Matter!' A $278 Billion Company Wasn't Built on Hard Work!* [Video podcast episode]. In *The Diary of a CEO*. YouTube. https://youtu.be/HSVbD7RhOHU?si=T2cGKbTTUhRV_3Oj.

Bartlett, S. (Host). (2019–present). *The Diary of a CEO* [Video podcast]. YouTube. www.YouTube.com/c/thediaryofaceo.

Bowman, E. H., & Helfat, C. E. (2001). Does corporate strategy matter? *Strategic Management Journal, 22*(1), 1–23.

Broccardo, L., Zicari, A., Jabeen, F., & Bhatti, Z. A. (2023). How digitalization supports a sustainable business model: A literature review. *Technological Forecasting and Social Change, 187*, 122146.

Caldart, A. A., & Ricart, J. E. (2004). Corporate strategy revisited: A view from complexity theory. *European Management Review, 1*(1), 96–104.

Casadesus-Masanell, R., & Ricart, J. E. (2010). From strategy to business models and onto tactics. *Long Range Planning, 43*(2–3), 195–215.

Chesbrough, H. (2010). Business model innovation: Opportunities and barriers. *Long Range Planning, 43*(2–3), 354–63.

Christensen, C. M. (1997). *The Innovator's Dilemma: When New Technologies Cause Great Firms to Fail.* Boston: Harvard Business Review Press.

Christensen, C. M. (2015). *The Innovator's Dilemma: When New Technologies Cause Great Firms to Fail.* Boston: Harvard Business Review Press.

Collis, D. J., & Montgomery, C. A. (1998). Creating corporate advantage. *Harvard Business Review, 76*(3), 71–83.

Derave, T., Prince Sales, T., Gailly, F., & Poels, G. (2021, June). *Comparing digital platform types in the platform economy.* In *International Conference on Advanced Information*

Systems Engineering. CAiSE 2021. Lecture Notes in Computer Science(), vol 12751 (pp. 417–31). Cham: Springer International Publishing.

Gambardella, A., & McGahan, A. M. (2010). Business-model innovation: General purpose technologies and their implications for industry structure. *Long Range Planning, 43*(2–3), 262–71.

Henderson, R. (2006). The innovator's dilemma as a problem of organizational competence. *Journal of Product Innovation Management, 23*(1), 5–11.

Kaltenrieder, B., Peter, K. P., & Reinhardt, K. (2024). *Digitale Wettbewerbsvorteile in der Praxis: Wie Sie erfolgreich digitale Strategien planen, umsetzen und verankern.* Stuttgart, DE: Schäffer-Poeschel.

Kraft, C., Lindeque, J. P., & Peter, M. K. (2022). The digital transformation of Swiss small and medium-sized enterprises: insights from digital tool adoption. *Journal of Strategy and Management, 15*(3), 468–94.

Netflix. (2024). *Netflix Home Page.* www.netflix.com.

Nokia (2024a) *Q3 2024* Financial results, 17 October 2024. Last accessed from www.nokia.com/system/files/2024-10/nokia_slides_2024_q3.pdf on 2 November 2024.

Nokia (2024b) Nokia licensed products: Support information for Nokia licensed products. Last accessed from www.nokia.com/support/licensed-products/ on 2 November 2024.

O'Reilly, T. (2007). What is Web 2.0: Design patterns and business models for the next generation of software. *Communications & Strategies, 65*, 17–37.

O'Reilly III, C. A., & Tushman, M. L. (2008). Ambidexterity as a dynamic capability: Resolving the innovator's dilemma. *Research in Organizational Behavior, 28*, 185–206.

Osterwalder, A., & Pigneur, Y. (2010). *Business Model Generation: A Handbook for Visionaries, Game Changers, and Challengers.* New Jersey: Wiley.

Peter, M. K. (Hrsg.) (2017). *KMU-Transformation: Als KMU die Digitale Transformation erfolgreich umsetzen. Forschungsresultate und Praxisleitfaden.* FHNW Hochschule für Wirtschaft, Olten/Schweiz, www.kmu-transformation.ch.

Peter, M. K. (2019). The evolving approach to strategic corporate foresight at Swiss bank PostFinance in the age of digital transformation, in: D. A. Schreiber & Z. L. Berge (eds), *Futures Thinking and Organizational Policy.* Palgrave Macmillan, New York, pp. 113–32.

Peter, M. K. (Hrsg.) (2021). *Strategieentwicklung im digitalen Zeitalter: Planung und Umsetzung der Digitalen Transformation.* FHNW Hochschule für Wirtschaft und Strategylab, Olten/Schweiz, www.strategische-transformation.ch.

Peter, M. K. (2023). *Digitaler Masterplan für KMU. So gelingt die digitale Transformation in Ihrem Unternehmen.* Verlag Beobachter Edition & Handelszeitung. Zürich/Schweiz, www.digitaler-masterplan.ch.

Peter, M.K. (2024). *The Digital Transformation Canvas. Develop and Implement Your Digital Strategy.* FT Publishing/Pearson, London/UK, www.the-digital-transformation-canvas.com.

Peter, M. K., Kraft, C., & Lindeque, J. (2020). Strategic action fields of digital transformation: An exploration of the strategic action fields of Swiss SMEs and large enterprises. *Journal of Strategy and Management, 13*(1), 160–80.

Porter, M. E. (1996). What is strategy? *Harvard Business Review, 74*(6), 37–55.

Rayport, J. F., & Sviokla, J. J. (1996). Exploiting the virtual value chain. *McKinsey Quarterly, 1*, 20–36.

Ries, E. (2011). *The Lean Startup: How Today's Entrepreneurs Use Continuous Innovation to Create Radically Successful Businesses.* New York, Crown Currency.

Täuscher, K., & Laudien, S. M. (2018). Understanding platform business models: A mixed methods study of marketplaces. *European Management Journal*, *36*(3), 319–29.

Teece, D. J. (2010). Business models, business strategy and innovation. *Long Range Planning*, *43*(2–3), 172–94.

Wang, C., Fang, Y., & Zhang, C. (2022). Mechanisms and countermeasures of 'The Innovator's Dilemma' in business model. *Journal of Innovation & Knowledge*, *7*(2), 100169.

Zott, C., & Amit, R. (2010). Business model design: An activity system perspective. *Long Range Planning*, *43*(2–3), 216–26.

8

STRATEGIC ACTION FIELD OF OPERATIONAL EXCELLENCE / PROCESS MANAGEMENT

Learning Goals

By the end of this chapter, you should...

- Be able to understand and describe how digital technology supports operational excellence / process management.
- Be able to analyse a firm's operational framework from a process-based view of firm operations across management, core, and support processes.
- Be able to critically analyse the current use and future opportunities of digital technology in both manufacturing and services firms (Industry 4.0).
- Be able to analyse a firm's business process management framework for business process creation, monitoring, and improvement.
- Be able to describe the differences between Total Quality Management (TQM) and Six Sigma, and use them to identify operational excellence potential for a specific business.
- Be able to describe the process/management standards of the International Organization for Standardization (ISO).
- Be able to analyse and describe the link between operational excellence and sustainability as part of Industry 5.0 advancements.
- Be able to identify strategic AI opportunities for operational excellence and building competitive advantages.

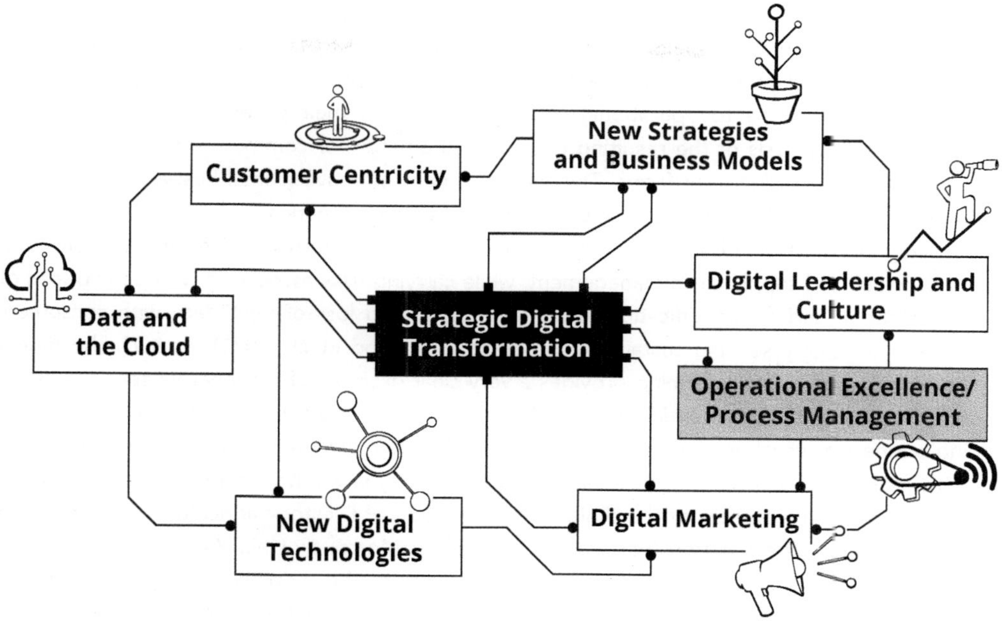

Figure 8.1 Operational excellence and process management is the fifth Strategic Action Field of Digital Transformation

Source: Peter et al. (2020); Peter (2017, 2021, 2023, 2024)

Agriculture 4.0 and Precision Livestock Farming

The integration of digital technologies into the agriculture sector has more broadly become known as Agriculture 4.0 (in line with the 'fourth industrial revolution') and contributed to the emergence of precision livestock farming (PLF; Morrone et al., 2022). While the contributions of digital technologies offer great opportunities for a new agricultural revolution more broadly, the impact on livestock farming is of particular interest (Eastwood et al., 2021; Morrone et al., 2022), as it provides an example of how these technologies are impacting biological systems and life forms that humans may relate to more directly. Agriculture 4.0 and PLF are also clearly integral to realising a more sustainable future, from both an environmental and social perspective in particular.

Agriculture 4.0 and PLF are featured by the active integration of sensing and controlling technologies, as well as the now widely accepted and integrated information and communication technologies (ICT), thereby leading to a data intensive approach to farming. This data enables process optimisation along the entire lifecycle of livestock farming and supply chain management, by employing the Internet of Things (IoT; integrating sensing and controlling technologies), Big Data (capturing and analysis), and communication technologies like 5G and LoRaWAN (see Figure 8.2 and also Box 5.7 in Chapter 5). PLF offers the prospect of an individualised animal management leading to more effective responsiveness to animal needs, while also enabling automation of farm processes and thereby leading to greater efficiencies (Eastwood et al., 2021; Morrone et al., 2022).

In PLF, digital technologies more specifically can be applied to animal identification, tracking, illness detection, feeding, drinking monitoring, animal behaviour, and animal performance

(Continued)

(Morrone et al., 2022; Williams et al., 2019). In dairy, goat, and sheep farming automation contributes to automatic/autonomous milking. In pig farming, stress monitoring is a particular concern that digital monitoring technologies can address (Morrone et al., 2022). The digital technologies contribute to operational excellence, through their potential for uninterrupted monitoring and analysis of the resulting data and automation of common repetitive processes (e.g., feeding and milking) on farms. This leads to more effective animal husbandry and more efficient processes in both industrial and sustainable farming scenarios.

The digital transformation of livestock agriculture or PLF promises a more effective and efficient livestock and supply chain management, while carrying risks associated with perceptions of industrialisation and commodification, leading an associated loss of legitimacy with consumers that are increasingly seeking sustainable products (Eastwood et al., 2021). As such the digital transformation of livestock farming provides a very clear example of the inherent tensions in the process, as well as the potential for digital technologies to contribute to the acceleration of doing business as usual or opening up opportunities for alternative more sustainable futures.

The case of PLF is potentially most interesting for the way in which it contributes to operational excellence in both extremes of the digital transformation of livestock agriculture, industrialised and sustainable value creation (Eastwood et al., 2021; Morrone et al., 2022). Digital transformation can in commoditised industrial farming support the original conceptualisation of operational excellence as the pursuit of value creation strategies emphasising absolute low prices compared to competitors consistently over time. At the same time, in more sustainable approaches Agriculture 4.0 can enable the necessary traceability needed for credible claims of sustainable farming practices and contribute to the management of costs over time for a best-in-class pricing strategy.

Source: Eastwood et al. (2021); Morrone et al. (2022)

Figure 8.2 An Application of LoRaWAN (Long Range Wide Area Network) in Agriculture 4.0 with sensors monitoring and protecting a sheep herd

Source: Peter (2023, 2024)

8.0 INTRODUCTION

The digital transformation of business processes relates to the operational delivery of products/goods and services allowing firms to realise operational excellence in the digital age (Peter, 2024; Peter et al., 2020), such operational excellence has been identified as one of the value disciplines of highly successful firms by Treacy and Wiersema (1995). This chapter adopts a process management perspective on realising operational excellence as part of the strategic digital transformation of firms. Operations scholarship and operations management is widely accepted as being all about processes (Holweg et al., 2018). A process-based understanding of firm operations views all firm operations as composed of processes, which need to be designed, their performance measured, and their performance improved. The digital transformation of firms' operations promises significant opportunities for improved process (re)design and performance measurement, arguably most clearly articulated in the concept of Industry 4.0 and Services 4.0. The remainder of this chapter develops these ideas.

8.1 PROCESS-BASED VIEW OF FIRM OPERATIONS

The process-based view of operations management understands all firm operations as composed of processes, which need to be designed, their performance measured, and their performance improved (Holweg et al., 2018). Where '[b]usiness processes can be thought of as a series of interrelated activities, crossing functional boundaries with inputs and outputs' (Armistead & Machin, 1997, p. 886), that are focused on the conversion of inputs into outputs. From an operations management perspective business processes are constituted by the 'people, processes, technology and other resources [needed] to produce goods and services' (Armistead & Machin, 1997, p. 886). Process management is thus critically important for 'improving the efficiency, effectiveness, and flexibility of production, as well as the quality of the final product' and/or service (Prajogo et al., 2018, p. 95). Such process management includes the design, monitoring (measurement), and improvement of the processes sourcing the inputs (resources and capital), transforming (adding value to) them, and distributing the outputs (products and or services) (Holweg et al., 2018) (see Figure 8.4).

The focus on operational processes has the additional benefit of allowing the focus to move beyond the somewhat artificial distinction between manufacturing and services activities and instead allowing attention to be paid to the commonality or differences in the nature of the operational processes for a given business (Holweg et al., 2018). If operational activities are accepted as the central processes of a firm this leads to the categorisation in Box 8.1. Having said this, this chapter will at the same time have elements that focus exclusively on manufacturing or service digital transformations, as these unitary 'extreme' cases may allow a more focused engagement on the integration of digital technologies into the operations (processes) of contemporary firms that have both manufacturing and services processes. Finally, the processes that need to be managed in relation to the management of firm operations are not only internal but also cross the firm boundary and may even be entirely external from the firm (Prajogo et al., 2018) (see Figure 8.4). These can be described as internal, boundary spanning, and external processes respectively and as a result process management needs to consider the entire value chain of a firm.

Box 8.1: Processes in Practice

Understanding the different types of processes within an organisation is essential for effective management and value creation.

Management Processes

Management processes are focused on the process objectives, instructions for action, and activities for measuring success. These may include organisational culture, the firm mission, and vision.

Core Processes

Core processes are the strategically important processes for value creation and are typically cross functional in nature. These processes are transformational processes, that convert inputs into outputs, designed to ensure that intended customer satisfaction and product/service quality goals are achieved.

Support Processes

Support processes include all necessary activities to enable the core processes, but which are not transformational in nature. These processes represent the tangible and intangible infrastructure of a firm.

Source: Peter (2024)

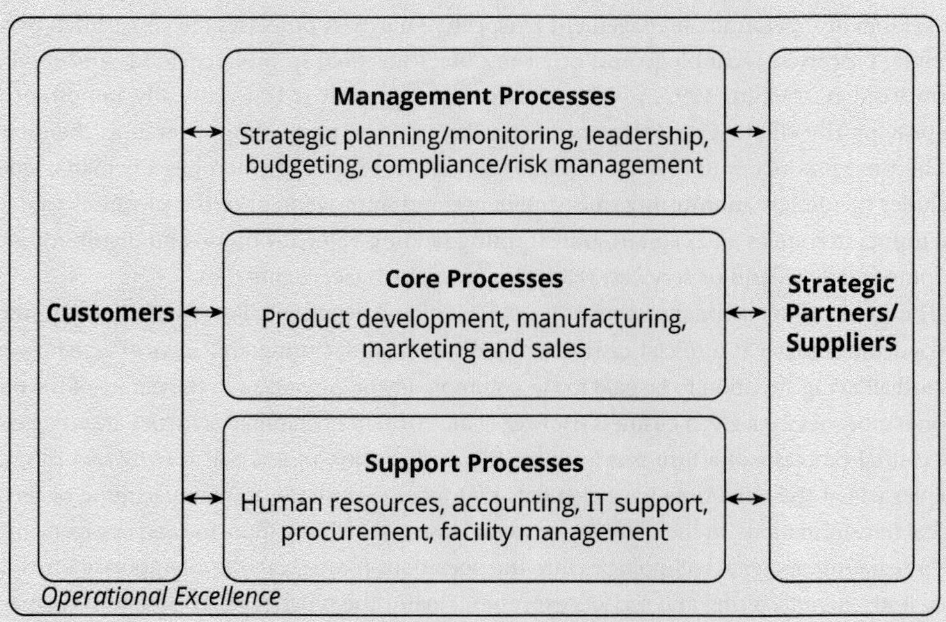

Figure 8.3 Processes in practice (simplified version of Figure 8.4)

Source: own illustration following Peter (2023, 2024)

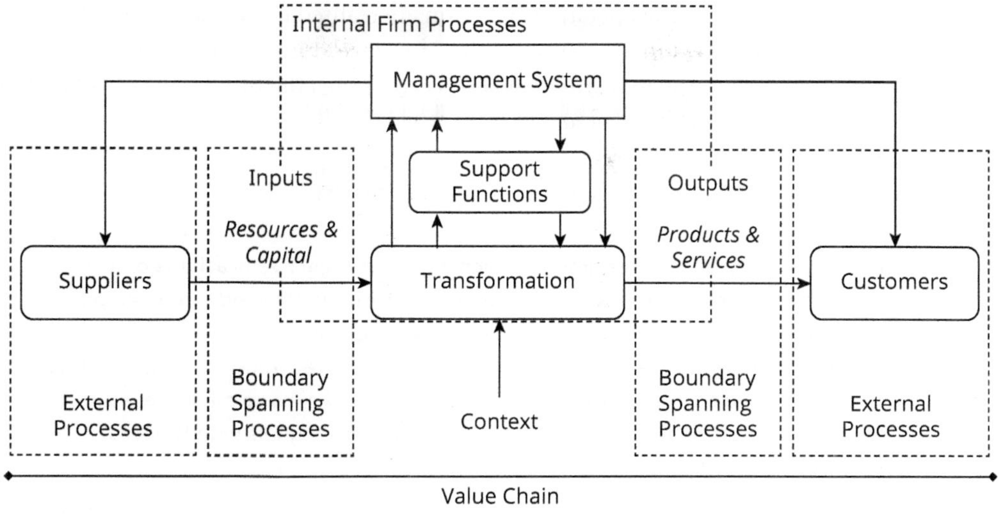

Figure 8.4 Process of operations with a management system

Source: adapted from Armistead & Machin (1997) and Holweg et al. (2018)

The operations of a firm require a range of resources to be able to operate. These inputs take a number of different forms and modes of delivery; some of these inputs are sourced externally (e.g., materials and components), others are internally sourced (e.g., labour), and the relevance of resources can change over time; for example information has emerged as a critical resource in the digital age (Holweg et al., 2018). The firm also relies on generic resources like energy and working capital to run operations and from a production perspective all resources (e.g., inputs) are of equal importance as they are all needed for the operations to function efficiently and effectively. It is the need for resource inputs and the distribution of products and services as outputs that so closely ties the digital transformation of firms to hopes for realising a more sustainable future (see Chapter 3).

The externally sourced and internally available resources are then turned first into work-in-process and later final products and services by the firm's transformation process(es) (Holweg et al., 2018). The firm then passes these final products and services on to its business (B2B) customers or directly to consumers (B2C) as the outputs of its transformation process(es). Within the overall value chain, the firm may be distributing its outputs (products or services) as the inputs into the next value creation step or into the final product and service markets. Arguably the outputs produced are the reason for the firm existing, but that does not mean that all resources are converted into outputs. The degree to which a firm is able to convert inputs into outputs represents the firm's operational efficiency (see Box 8.2). Relatedly the more effectively the firm is able to convert resources into outputs (i.e., the ratio of inputs to outputs) the more productive the operations of the firm.

The management system is the 'control unit' of a firm's operational processes, responsible for the planning, organising, and monitoring of the processes. This includes the design, monitoring, and improvement of all firm processes. Finally, the management function is responsible for ensuring that the operations of a firm are realised in such a manner that they are in alignment with the external context of the firm, including at the regional, national, local levels, but also within the industry or business ecosystems the firm is embedded within and affected by as a result (Holweg et al., 2018).

— Box 8.2: Digital Technologies' Impact on Business Operations —

- **Effectiveness** refers to the degree to which a goal or objective is achieved. It focuses on the *outcome* and whether the desired result is attained. For example, a marketing campaign is effective if it successfully increases sales.
- **Efficiency,** on the other hand, measures how well resources (time, money, effort) are utilised to achieve a goal. It emphasises the *process* and aims to minimise waste. For instance, an efficient marketing campaign achieves its goals with the least amount of resources.

Source: Peter (2024)

8.2 INFORMATION MANAGEMENT, PROCESS MANAGEMENT, AND OPERATIONAL PERFORMANCE

Information management has become a prerequisite for process management and just as firms' processes that need to be managed are increasingly crossing the firm boundary, the information flows that need to be managed are both internal and external in nature (Prajogo et al., 2018). The information management may include the collection of data internally and externally and processing into information and also the management of information flows inside and outside the firm. As was discussed in Chapter 6, implicit and explicit knowledge will play a key role in the processing of data and effectively making use of the available information about the operations of a firm. As will be made clear in the subchapters below addressing Industry 4.0, digital technologies are increasingly central to the creation, capture and processing (analysis) of data and information management. This is also an opportunity to recapitulate that those processes, reflecting the understanding of digital transformation in this text, are fundamentally socio-technical systems (Holweg et al., 2018). Indeed, it is the socio-technical nature of firm processes that enable their digital transformation and it is necessary to understand not only the technical, but also the organisational culture and leadership transformations needed for successful digital transformation of firms (Peter, 2024) (see Chapter 9).

8.3 INDUSTRY 4.0

Industry 4.0, a result of the fourth industrial revolution, most fundamentally draws attention to the integration of information and communication technologies (ICT) and sensing and controlling technologies (SCT) into manufacturing and service delivery processes (Dalenogare et al., 2018). Box 8.3 reminds of the political economy origins of the Industry 4.0 label. This transformation of manufacturing and services production is in particular associated with the creation of cyber-physical systems, the Internet of Things (IoT), and for manufacturing particularly with smart factories / smart manufacturing (Dalenogare et al., 2018; Mariani & Borghi, 2019). Mariani and Borghi (2019) have captured very effectively the fact that the resulting transformation process are impacting not only on the physical and cyber domains, but also the biological domain; this is a different articulation to the social, economic, and environmental categories of a sustainability perspective, which the physical, cyber, and biological domains arguably cut across. By way of illustration, when a farmer attaches a smart tag via an ear tag, subcutaneous insert or collar to an individual animal in livestock farming (e.g., RFID or GPS locating technologies, see Figure 8.2), this makes the biological animal visible in the cyber domain as a 'thing' that can be sensed (e.g., to monitor grazing and drinking activities), located (i.e., the physical location and movement is made digital), and interacted with through controlling technologies (e.g., for milking).

Box 8.3: Industry 4.0 in Historic Perspective

Industry 4.0 was first articulated by the German Government at the 2011 Hannover Trade Fair as an initiative to ensure the long-term competitiveness of the German manufacturing industry, communicating the importance of cyber-physical systems in future manufacturing and logistics, with an emphasising focus on the Internet of Things and the servitisation of manufacturing business models. It should be noted that there were a number of similar contemporaneous articulations of the future for manufacturing in the digital age, including the 2011 US Advanced Manufacturing Partnership (AMP) and later the 2012 Advanced Manufacturing National Program Office (AMNPO), the 2013 French '*La Nouvelle France Industrielle*' and '*Industrie du future*', and the UK 2013 Future of Manufacturing initiatives, as well as the European Commission factories of the future programme. Similar initiatives were later seen in South Korea (2014), China (2015), Japan (2015), Singapore (2016), and Italy (2017), to name a selection. Such national initiatives were also supported by industry initiatives launched by major corporate actors.

Source: adapted from Mariani & Borghi (2019)

This example of the impact of digital technologies on livestock farming may possibly be more controversial example, see opening case, but is essentially the same as the more conventional understandings of how Industry 4.0 in manufacturing, as captured by the smart factory or advanced manufacturing visions, can contribute to operational excellence for both high volume and individualised/customised oriented operations. Indeed, reflecting its origins (Box 8.3), advanced cyber-physical manufacturing systems are the most advanced instances of emerging cyber-physical systems in the digital age, while Services 4.0 remains at the initial stages in its development and understanding of the potential for digital transformation of services delivery (Mariani & Borghi, 2019). Industry 4.0 (see Box 8.4) is fundamentally about seeking to understand the consequences of the ever-increasing integration of the physical and cyber systems, the generation and availability of data, and the immediate and location independent access to data and computing power for its analysis (Zaki, 2019).

Box 8.4: Industry 4.0 Technologies

There are a large number of different technologies, and it can be expected that new technologies will emerge in time that contribute to realising the vision of Industry 4.0. These technologies all serve to increasingly digitalise the value creation (transformation) process in firms and industries, by developing increasingly interconnected cyber-physical systems, to support human decision-making and also enable decentralised or autonomous machine decision-making, with data and information generation and processing as central and essential activities.

- Additive manufacturing (including fast prototyping or 3D impression)
- Artificial intelligence
- Augmented reality
- Big Data
- Big Data Analytics
- Cloud Services (including data storage and computing)
- Computer-Aided Design and Manufacturing (CAD)
- Cybersecurity
- Digital automation with sensors
- Digital Product-Service Systems
- Flexible manufacturing lines (automation with sensors)
- Horizontal and vertical (IT) integration systems for data and information exchange
- Industrial Internet of Things (IioT)
- (Autonomous) Robotics
- Simulations

Source: Capello & Lenzi (2021); Dalenogare et al. (2018); Mariani & Borghi (2019); Zaki (2019)

Overall, there is no single impact of Industry 4.0 on business operations. The impact is determined by the strategic goals and related organisation of equipment and people of a given firm, as well as the broader ecosystems within which the firm is embedded. For some firms, digital transformation and Industry 4.0 will enable more efficient standardisation and greater automation, while other firms will realise greater personalisation and customisation of products and services through the realisation of Industry 4.0 principles using digital technologies (Peter, 2024).

8.3.1 Industry 4.0 and Manufacturing Firms

The nature of manufacturing processes is often distinguished by emphasising the degree of product(ion) variety and the volume of production (Hayes & Wheelwright, 1979; Holweg et al., 2018; Porter et al., 1992), which leads to a five part typology of manufacturing process types (see Figure 8.5): Complex Production (Projects), Jobbing Production, Batch Production, Mass Production, and Continuous Production. Digital technologies can play a role in realising operational excellence for all five types of manufacturing processes, with shifting emphasis on the degree to which effectiveness (quality/variety) and/or efficiency (cost reduction) of the processes is primarily the goal.

Digital transformation, specifically Industry 4.0, offers the opportunity for firms to integrate digital technologies into manufacturing processes to improve them, develop digital services to complement their products (i.e., the servitisation of manufacturing) (Dalenogare et al., 2018) and integrate digital technologies into their products to enable servitisation. Industry 4.0 seeks to realise the potential of digital technology enabled manufacturing processes in terms of automation, flexibility, and customisation of production activities, by creating highly connected cyber-physical systems. This vision is strongly associated with high levels of data generation, analysis, and resulting decision-making, by both humans and machines. The importance of sensors for making the physical environment (i.e., operational process and products) 'visible' to machines and controllers to enable machines to manipulate/engage with the physical world is critically important. The resulting network of sensors and controllers connected to physical manufacturing processes is at the heart of cyber-physical or socio-technical descriptions of Industry 4.0 manufacturing.

Industry 4.0 is most closely associated with manufacturing firms and has the potential to support the competitiveness of firms adopting any one of the archetypal manufacturing processes in Figure 8.5 and described in Box 8.5. Large construction projects are today featured by extensive use of digital technologies to design, plan, implement, and manage the process of project realisation; for example, the precision planning and execution of the extreme tunnelling projects being realised today would not be possible without digital technologies. In the machine tooling industry, both jobbing and batch production is dependent on digital technologies, with firms adopting one or other manufacturing process according to the nature of their specialisation and market niche. Machine tool manufacturers may also include digital sensors in their products to enable monitoring at distance and create the potential to service their customer offerings, the member firms of the Swissmem industry association (www.swissmem.ch) are exemplary firms in this regard. The mass customisation by most sports shoe manufacturers, including Adidas and Nike, is a clear example of how mass production processes can leverage digital technologies to enable greater degrees of customisation to customers, without losing competitiveness, by increasing the variety of products produced. Finally, digital monitoring and controlling technologies contribute to the effective and efficient operation of large-scale chemicals continuous manufacturing processes.

Box 8.5: Manufacturing Processes Typology

The typology of manufacturing processes categorises different production methods based on their characteristics and operational focus.

Complex Production (Projects)

Projects are focused on delivering a single unique product that typically requires large scale inputs. Project work typically relies on general purpose technologies and highly skilled professionals (knowledge / experience carriers) to deliver the desired product within a specific timeframe.

(Continued)

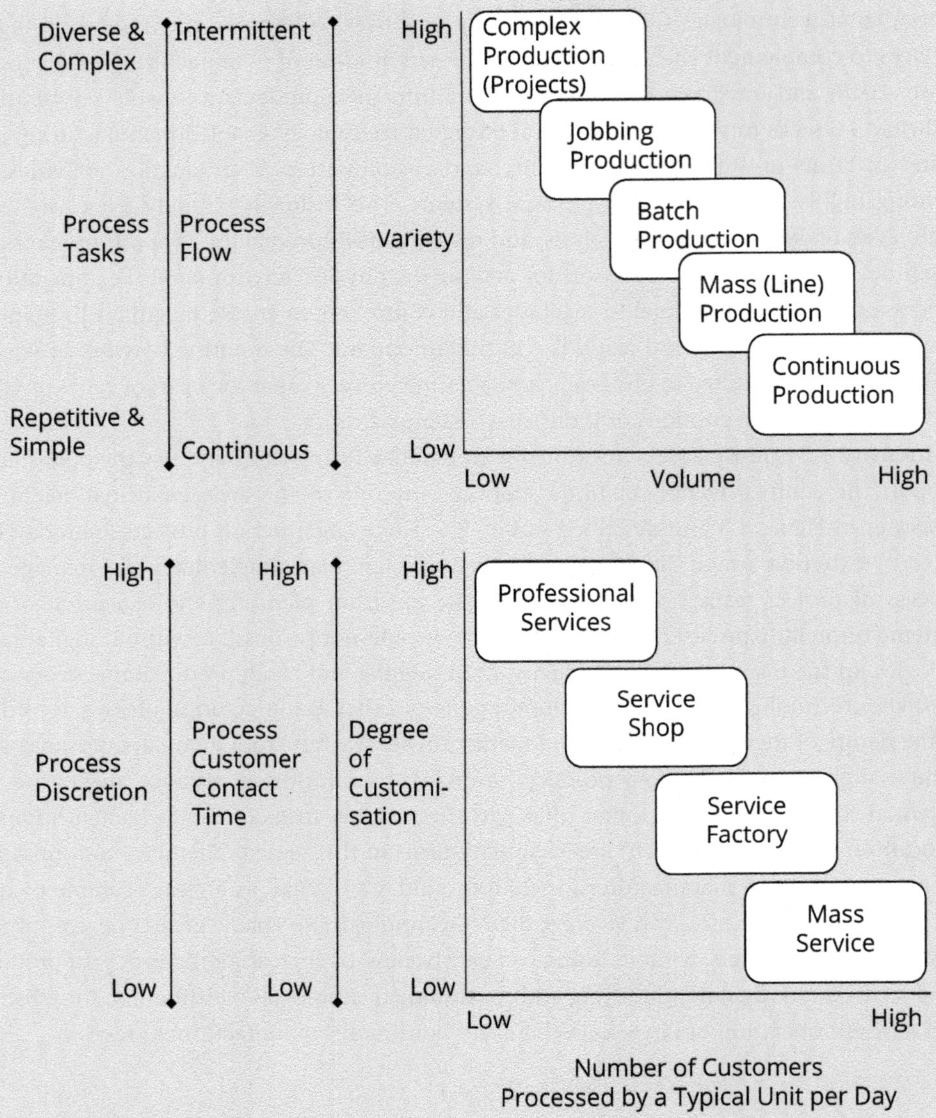

Figure 8.5 Manufacturing and service process categories

Source: adapted from Hayes & Wheelwright (1979); Holweg et al. (2018); Porter et al. (1999); Schmenner (1986); Silvestro et al. (1992)

Jobbing Production

Jobbing production is focused on producing a wide variety of products as efficiently as possible. Equipment with different degrees of specialisation and the organisation of the (complex) flow of materials through the equipment are key aspects of jobbing production. The routing and scheduling of the processing activity makes this production process highly reliant on information about a specific job being processed to ensure efficient and effective production.

Batch Production

Batch flow production is similar to jobbing production, but is featured by a limited variety of products, frequently produced in set quantities, leading to a greater degree of standardisation. Batch production produces established volumes to build inventory and not to customer order, thereby realising the needed economies of scale.

Mass Production

Mass production, also referred to as line flow processes, is most clearly identifiable in assembly line production, with controlled customisation possible and large volumes of production. The process is organised to produce specific products, that typically move through a preset series of activities, reliant on activity specific combinations of labour and equipment.

Continuous Production

Continuous production produces high volumes of standardised/commoditised products in high volumes. These processes are featured by uninterrupted processing by capital intensive equipment. The processes are commonly featured by significant automation and very high volumes of standardised/commoditised products.

Source: Hayes & Wheelwright (1979); Holweg et al. (2018); Porter et al. (1999)

8.3.2 Industry 4.0 and Service Firms

The nature of service delivery processes can be distinguished by emphasising the degree of service customisation (variety) and the volume of production (Holweg et al., 2018; Schmenner, 1986; Silvestro et al., 1992) as per Figure 8.5. The evaluation of the number of customers served per unit per day, the length of the contact time per customer, the degree of customisation, and the amount of discretion in the service delivery process lead to a four-part typology of service process types (see Figure 8.5) and their descriptions in Box 8.6 (Holweg et al., 2018; Schmenner, 1986; Silvestro et al., 1992): Professional Services, Service Shop, Service Factory, and Mass Services. Digital technologies can play a role in realising operational excellence for all four types of service processes, with shifting emphasis on the degree to which effectiveness and/or efficiency of the processes is primarily the goal.

The realisation of Industry 4.0 in service industries and firms has received comparatively little systematic attention, when compared to manufacturing industries and firms (Mariani & Borghi, 2019). The application of Industry 4.0 to service industries and firms is multidimensional, including the development of internal firm service and support functions, but also online/digital service delivery to B2B and B2C customers, as well as the integration of digital services and product offerings (also referred to as smart services), in a manner that reflects the ideas of servitisation (Capello & Lenzi, 2021). Indeed, three dominant forms of servitisation emerge in Industry 4.0 transformations of services industries and firms (see Figure 8.6). These service offerings are differentiated by the degree to which digital technologies are used to provide digital only services (the Digital Services Economy), to provide digital services that enable temporary access to idle capacity in the physical world or in the digital world (the Sharing Economy) and finally, the integration of physical products and services with digital services (Product-Services Economy). At the intersections of these three primary implementations hybrid offerings can be identified. Critically, across all three digital servitisation modes there are different degrees of ownership and/or control of underlying physical products or equipment by customers of the service providers (see Figure 8.6).

Box 8.6: Service Processes Typology

The typology of service processes categorises different service delivery methods based on their characteristics and operational focus.

Professional Services

Professional services are featured by high levels of highly skilled labour (professionals: knowledge/experience carriers), typically requiring general-purpose equipment, to deliver customer specific services featuring significant customisation and higher levels of interaction. The professionals (people) play a central role in service delivery.

Service Shop

Service shops are featured by less intensive labour and interaction with customers, the services are specialised and specific to the customer, but delivered in a manner that allows specialisation in distinct process steps. Both people and equipment play a role in the service delivery.

Service Factory

Service factories deliver high-volume standardised services with little or no customisation and limited interaction with customers. Both people and equipment play a role in the service delivery.

Mass Services

Mass services may have high labour intensity, but limited customisation, short interactions/ customer contact, and limited or no discretion. Equipment/technology may play a greater role in service delivery.

Source: Holweg et al. (2018); Schmenner (1986); Silvestro et al. (1992)

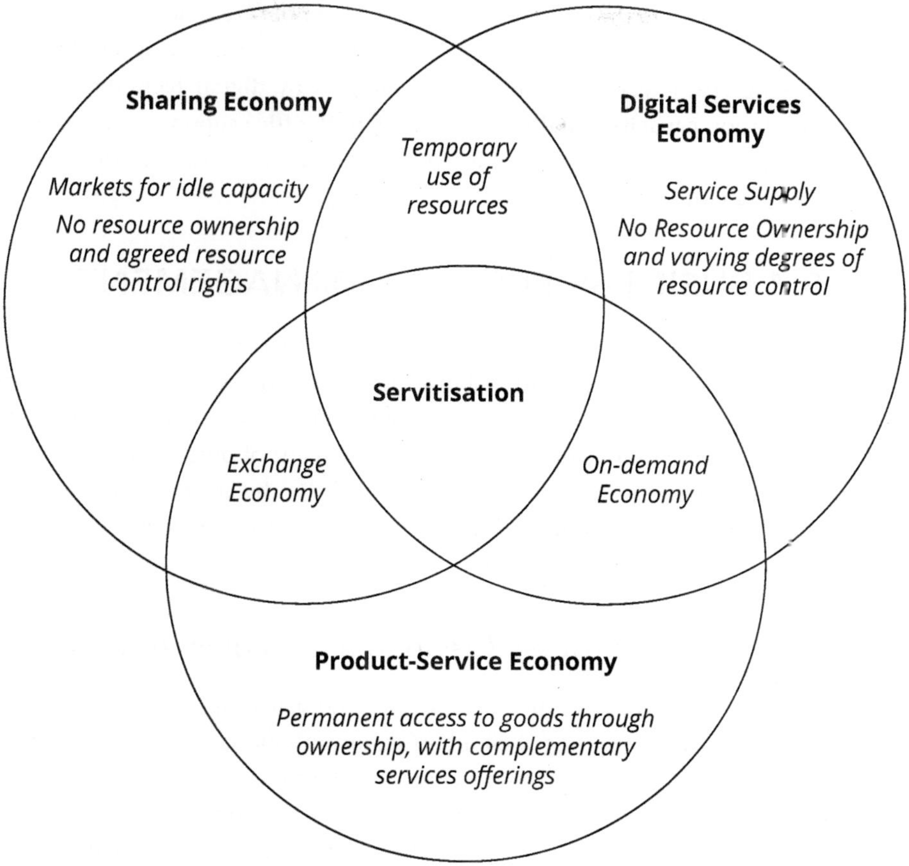

Figure 8.6 Typology of Industry 4.0 servitisation

Source: adapted from Capello & Lenzi (2021)

As in manufacturing operations, digital technologies are increasingly contributing to realising operational excellence in four archetypal service delivery operations. Realising Industry 4.0 in service firms/industries requires different digital technologies to be purposefully employed to realise intended and specific impacts on transformation processes. Digital servitisation (see Figure 8.6) approaches will be suited to each of the different service delivery archetypes (see Figure 8.5, right side) to different degrees. For example, a professional services firm is more likely to be a customer of specialised digital services required to deliver the project specific requirements of a specific customer. Hospitals are an excellent example of an organisation that implements a service shop logic, the customer (patient) moves though the different specialised departments as required by their health condition. From an Industry 4.0 perspective the customer is making use of a mix of equipment and employee expertise in an on-demand fashion, featured by temporary access to equipment and services. The Apple iPhone and its app-based ecosystem for service delivery is an example of a service factory, where limited or mass customisation is made possible, and also simultaneously from the customer perspective is a prime example of a product-service value proposition by Apple. Car sharing firms similarly are service factories in the sharing economy allowing customers temporary access, enabled by digital technologies, to idle vehicle transportation capacity. Finally, much of the back-office support services are today part of the digital services economy enabled by digital technologies and, from an operations perspective, are often mass services.

8.4 BUSINESS PROCESS MANAGEMENT

Armistead and Machin (1997) identified six groups of activities associated with business process management, namely organisational co-ordination; process definition; the organisation and structuring of business processes; ensuring business processes fit an organisational culture; business process improvement; and the measurement of business processes. In this chapter we organise these six categories of activities into (1) the creation and implementation of business processes, (2) the monitoring and maintenance of business processes, and finally, (3) the improvement of business processes.

8.4.1 Business Process Creation and Implementation

The definition of business processes, their organisation and structuring, as well as their organisational co-ordination and ensuring their fit in an organisational culture are part of the process of creating and implementing business processes. Business processes are argued to have an end-to-end nature (Armistead & Machin, 1997), traditionally this has been understood to start with the inputs (resources) that enter across the business boundary, enable the processing of those resources, and then pass the resulting products and/or services as outputs across the business boundary into the external ecosystem within which the firm is embedded. The business operational processes that enable the resource transformation to create value must be defined, then organised and embedded in organisational structures as part of their implementation. Once the operational processes have been implemented, new coordinating processes (managerial work) must be implemented, organised, and embedded in the organisational structures to coordinate the operational transformation activities. This all needs to be done in such a manner that it is aligned with the overall organisational culture, which can be best understood as the social dimension of the larger socio-technical system that is the entire firm.

8.4.2 Business Process Monitoring (Measurement) and Maintenance

The measurement of business processes can best be understood as the managerial and business activity of monitoring and maintenance of processes. This is a critical set of activities, indeed managerial processes in their own right (see Figures 8.3 and 8.4), that typically undertake this monitoring and maintenance work in relation to customer expectations and satisfaction. It is important, however, to be aware that such monitoring and maintenance work is not done only with respect to ensuring the effectiveness of processes related to customers, but that there is simultaneously also a need to ensure necessary efficiency in the processes. This speaks directly to an economic understanding of value creation, where the willingness-to-pay of a customer (price) per unit, less the cost per unit produced reveals the margin per unit. The margin multiplied by the number of units produced (volume) represents the economic value created by the firm's activities. Monitoring and ensuring the maintenance of process efficiency and effectiveness are key managerial activities. An important international standard for the documentation, monitoring, management, and maintenance of process frameworks are the ISO (International Organization for Standardization) standards (ISO, 2025) for process quality management (ISO 9001), environmental management (ISO 14001), and information security management (ISO 27001) (see Box 8.7).

Box 8.7: Process/Management Standards of the International Organization for Standardization (ISO)

- **ISO 9001** is an international standard for *Quality Management Systems (QMS)*. It provides a framework for organisations to ensure they consistently meet customer and regulatory requirements through operational excellence and process management. The standard emphasises a process-oriented approach, focusing on continuous improvement and customer satisfaction. Key principles include a strong customer focus, involvement of top management, a process approach, and continual improvement. ISO 9001:2015, the latest version, incorporates risk-based thinking to identify and address potential issues before they arise.
- **ISO 14001** is the international standard for *Environmental Management Systems (EMS)*. It provides a framework for organisations to manage their environmental responsibilities systematically. The standard helps organisations minimise their environmental footprint, comply with applicable laws, and continually improve their environmental performance. ISO 14001:2015, the current version, emphasises a proactive approach to environmental management, integrating it into the overall business strategy.
- **ISO 27001** is the leading international standard for *Information Security Management Systems (ISMS)*. It provides a systematic approach to managing sensitive company data/information, ensuring its confidentiality, integrity, and availability. The standard outlines requirements for establishing, implementing, maintaining, and continually improving an ISMS. ISO 27001:2022, the latest version, addresses information security, cybersecurity, and privacy protection. By implementing ISO 27001, organisations can reduce the risk of cyber-attacks against their IT infrastructure, protect their data from breaches, comply with legal requirements, and build trust with customers and stakeholders.

Source: ISO (2025)

8.4.3 Business Process Improvement

Finally, the activities associated with improving or renewing existing business processes is a distinct domain that ensures the adaptability of the business organisation (Armistead & Machin, 1997). The improvement of business processes is sometimes referred to as business process re-engineering (BPR). It is important to remember that process improvement can be undertaken in operational processes doing the resource transformation, in the processes supporting the operational processes, but also in direction-setting managerial activities. This is critical from a digital transformation perspective, as there is evidence that process improvement generally (Armistead & Machin, 1997), but also in digital transformation initiatives (Peter et al., 2020), tends to focus on operational and support processes. Practically, business process improvement is most visible in the philosophies of Total Quality Management (TQM) and (Lean) Six Sigma (Armistead & Machin, 1997, p. 886) (see Box 8.8 for more details about TQM and (Lean) Six Sigma, both widely adopted quality management systems focused on improving the quality of products/services and improving operational efficiencies). While TQM has a more decentralised approach, the alternative Six Sigma is an expert-driven approach that tends towards a more centralised quality control, despite using broadly the same tools as TQM (Holweg et al., 2018).

Box 8.8: Total Quality Management and (Lean) Six Sigma

Total Quality Management (TQM) 'refers to the broad set of management and control processes designed to focus an entire organization and all its employees on providing products and services that do the best possible job of satisfying the customer' (Talha, 2004, p. 15). This requires not only ensuring that quality standards are attained (quality assurance), but also that quality is continually improved (quality improvement), which requires ongoing process improvements to be made. TQM is not limited to large firms, where a dedicated management structure can be built to implement TQM as there are more likely to be sufficient financial, employee, and capital resources for its implementation, as the senior (owner-)manager in a small business can also take on this responsibility. Regardless, six steps are arguably essential to realising TQM:

1. The commitment of all employees to quality and customer satisfaction.
2. The commitment of all employees to improving quality and customer satisfaction.
3. The TQM philosophy must be incorporated into all activities of the firm.
4. Prioritise quality and customer satisfaction in such a manner that it is done effectively and efficiently; it does not need to cost more to do.
5. Be open to making significant changes, redesigning processes, to improve quality and customer satisfaction.
6. Do not overlook the significant impact that small advantages across company functions can have on its overall competitive advantage in the marketplace.

(Lean) Six Sigma refers to a data-driven methodology aimed at improving process quality based on the DMAIC (Define, Measure, Analyse, Improve, Control) framework, with Lean

Six Sigma adapting lean principles, focussing primarily on the customer and how customer value can be delivered.

- *Six Sigma* seeks to improve the quality of a process by identifying and removing the causes of defects and minimising variability. It uses statistical tools and techniques to analyse and improve processes. The primary goal is to achieve near-perfect quality, with a defect rate of no more than 3.4 defects per million opportunities.
- *Lean Six Sigma* combines the principles of Lean and Six Sigma to enhance both efficiency and quality. Lean focuses on eliminating waste and improving flow in processes, aiming to deliver maximum value to the customer with minimal resources by streamlining processes and reducing non-value-added activities.

Source: adapted from Montgomery & Woodall (2008) and Talha (2004)

8.5 OPERATIONAL EXCELLENCE AND COMPETITIVE ADVANTAGE

Treacy and Wiersema (1995) in their explanations of operational excellence emphasise that companies that pursue this value creation strategy emphasise low or lowest prices compared to competitors consistently over time. It is important to recall that this aligns clearly with Porter's (1985) pure cost leadership and cost focus generic strategies respectively as discussed in Chapter 2. It is also interesting that Treacy and Wiersema (1995) have a holistic understanding of cost that focuses on total cost across the entire customer journey, that includes price, convenience, cost of product ownership/consumption of a service and reliable hassle-free customer service. The authors emphasised the importance of cooperation and the overall production system, the totality of processes producing products and/or services, both internally and externally, reflecting the need to effectively cooperate with partners and third parties along the value chain. In addition, they also clearly understood the importance of discipline related to product portfolio and the associated processes management, especially the need to avoid product and service proliferation and complexity, and inevitable process inefficiencies that would lead to higher operating costs; this speaks directly to the process-based view of operations management (Holweg et al., 2018; Prajogo et al., 2018).

The criticality of information technology for achieving operational excellence was already emphasised by Treacy and Wiersema (1995), especially for its ability to enable effective monitoring and measuring processes to ensure cost and quality control. AI is a new digital technology, prevalent in the fifth industrial revolution, that is driving the next wav of operational excellence (see Box 8.9).

The developments with Industry 4.0 (and now the fifth industrial revolution), however, put the clear efficiency focus of the original work by Treacy and Wiersema (1995) into stark relief, it could be argued that their ground-breaking work too exclusively focused on an understanding of operational excellence as a pure cost leadership strategy (Porter, 1985), with niche cost focus generic strategies increasingly being enabled with digital technologies, mass customisation represents an example of how technology enables cost advantages for premium market niches. Critically, operationally excellent firms do not seek performance improvements from raising prices, rather '[t]hey work to assure a constant, steady volume of business so as to keep their assets continually working; they find new ways to use their assets; and they replicate their formula in other markets' (Treacy and Wiersema, 1995, p. 60).

Box 8.9: Identification of AI opportunities for Operational Excellence

The Strategic Action Fields (SAF) of *Operational Excellence/Process Management, New Digital Technologies* and *Data and the Cloud* are the basis for the identification of AI opportunities because they provide the foundation for understanding and improving business operations (see Figure 8.7). Process management (SAF number 5 as described in this chapter) involves designing, monitoring, and optimising business processes to enhance efficiency and effectiveness (see Box 8.2). By documenting these processes, organisations can identify areas where AI can be applied to automate tasks, reduce errors, and improve decision-making. However, new digital technology (SAF number 2, Chapter 5) plays a pivotal role in enabling AI opportunities, as advances in computing power, cloud infrastructure, and machine learning algorithms have made it possible to develop and deploy sophisticated AI solutions. Emerging technologies like the Internet of Things (IoT), big data analytics, and edge computing generate vast amounts of data and provide the computational resources needed to process it. It is therefore important to review the current/available IT infrastructure, and highlight any gaps for the successful implementation of AI opportunities. Finally, data (SAF number 3, Chapter 6) is the lifeblood of AI. High-quality, relevant data is essential for training AI models and making accurate predictions. Organisations that manage their data well can leverage it to uncover patterns, trends, and insights that would be difficult to detect manually. This data-driven approach enables businesses to identify specific areas where AI can add value.

Therefore, process management, technology, and data are interdependent action fields (elements) that collectively enable the identification and realisation of AI opportunities, enabling operational excellence through new digital technology.

Source: Peter (2024); Zobair & Peter (2025)

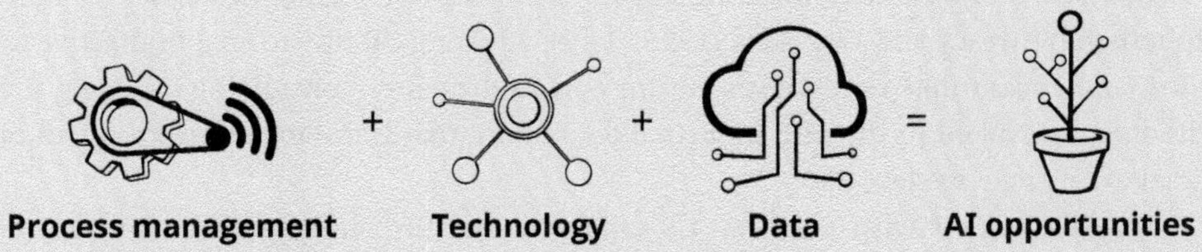

Figure 8.7 Strategic action fields supporting the identification of AI opportunities

Source: own illustration following Peter (2023, 2024)

8.6 OPERATIONAL EXCELLENCE AND SUSTAINABILITY: INDUSTRY 5.0

The European Commission (2021) establishing the concept of Industry 5.0 as an extension of Industry 4.0 that identifies the need to move away from a purely technological understanding of the current transformation of industry (Leng et al., 2022). Industry 5.0 emphasises the need to realise not only competitiveness, but also sustainability goals, emphasising alternative (technology) governance modes for sustainability and resilience, with a human-centric approach to technological transformation processes, while recognising the potential of technology for realising environmental sustainability (European Commission, 2021). To realise this vision, the Industry 5.0 concept emphasises the responsibility of firms for their entire value chains and the need to develop indicators for industrial ecosystems to monitor progress in realising Industry 5.0 (European Commission, 2021). Industry 5.0 is clearly intended to address some of the challenges exposed by Industry 4.0 and the emergence of human-cyber-physical systems that are being developed (Huang et al., 2022). It is also important to note the implicit co-evolution of the Industry 5.0 and Society 5.0 concepts, with Industry 5.0 focusing on the development of 'a human-centric, sustainable, and resilient manufacturing system' and Society 5.0 providing a vision of a future human-centric society guided by scientific and technological innovation that seeks to ensure that 'all citizens can access high quality lives' (Huang et al., 2022, p. 425), by placing human well-being at the centre of manufacturing systems (Leng et al., 2022).

The primary technological enablers of Industry 5.0 are congruous with Industry 4.0 and include the internet of everything (IoE; including sensing and controlling technologies), big data analytics, blockchain, edge computing, artificial intelligence, digital twins, collaborative robots (hard and software-based co-bots) and finally 6G and beyond wireless communication standards (Leng et al., 2022; Maddikunta et al., 2022). Critically, the emphasis in Industry 5.0 is on a human-centric integration of machines and humans into collaborative human-cyber-physical systems of production, where machine and human intelligence is allowed to focus on the tasks that they are uniquely able to complete most effectively. Industry 5.0 is however challenged in addressing the challenges of cybersecurity, privacy, and societal impact (Maddikunta et al., 2022) in the same way that Industry 4.0 is, due to the shared technological foundation for the transformation of industry and society.

Industry 5.0 moves the emphasis on automation and improved coordination of production in human-cyber-physical systems of Industry 4.0 to a focus on resilience at the level of the workforce (self-resilience) and at the human-cyber-physical system level (system resilience) (Leng et al., 2022). This reflects societal (human) and economic sustainability goals within the context of a human-centric society that is knowledge-intensive and data-driven (Leng et al., 2022). It should be noted that environmental sustainability is discussed as explicitly as the societal and economic aspects, which are clearly most visible in the Industry 4.0 and Industry 5.0 transformations with the impacts of production, employment, and how people live. The Industry 5.0 and Society 5.0 transformations, however, offer significant opportunity for minimising the impact of industry and society on the natural environment, most obviously in the enabling of circular principles in production and consumption and thereby reducing the impact on environmental stocks.

8.7 CONCLUSION

The digital transformation of firms has significant opportunities for realising operational excellence in firms of all sizes. It is however important to remember that the digital technologies can be implemented to support very different operational, support, and managerial business processes. It is not the digital technology in itself that determines the nature of the operational excellence goals that will be realised; instead, it is essential to understand the overall value creation strategy of a firm. Carefully consider how the different business processes contribute to realising operational excellence for a given strategy and then implement the digital technologies accordingly.

The chapter promotes the process-based view of firm operations, emphasising the importance of designing, measuring, and improving processes. Digital transformation, particularly through Industry 4.0 and 5.0, integrates information and communication technologies into manufacturing and service delivery, creating cyber-physical systems that enhance operational efficiency and customisation across management, core, and support processes. Total Quality Management (TQM) and (Lean) Six Sigma are well-known tool sets to improve processes, and international standards like ISO 9001, ISO 14001, and ISO 27001 provide a framework in ensuring process quality, environmental management, and information security.

As such, digital transformation may contribute to the maintenance of existing business processes, the creation of new processes or even the re-engineering of existing processes.

Case Studies

Students can complete the following tasks either based on the focal case study, or work on the recommended case study for this chapter (*Valuu: a corporate start-up for digital business model innovation*) and answer the questions below.

1. Which management, core, and support processes would Valuu need to run its business (see Box 8.1)? Please provide an overview (process map) with at least ten processes.
2. What technologies could Valuu use/implement to optimise/streamline its processes towards digitisation (see Box 8.4)? Please link your answer to your process map from question 1.
3. What type of software solution/s could be used in each process (see also Chapter 6, Box 6.3)? Please link your answer to your process map from question 1.
4. Would you recommend to Valuu to document and certify its process and quality management systems according to an ISO standard (see Box 8.7)? Describe the reasons for your decision.
5. Which business process improvement method would you recommend for Valuu (see Box 8.8)? Select one or both and describe how and why it should be used.
6. What strategies can be employed to ensure that all employees are prepared for the adoption of new digital systems and processes?

Alternatively, students can work on the supplementary case study (available online) for this chapter (*From limited budget to limitless potential: the digital journey of OSHE@UTMKL*) and answer the questions below.

1 How can an organisation with limited resources effectively undergo digital transformation and streamline/digitise processes?
2 What role does ISO 45001 certification play in supporting an organisation's health and safety (OH&S) objectives?
3 How can free or open-source tools contribute to the early stages of digital transformation in a cost-conscious environment?
4 What are the potential challenges in scaling up from basic digital systems to more integrated digital platforms?
5 How can organisations measure the success of their digital transformation in terms of employee engagement and safety performance?
6 In what ways can IT tools support both the development of digital skills and the cultural shift towards safety awareness among staff?
7 What strategies can be employed to ensure that all employees are prepared for the adoption of new digital systems and processes?

Additional cases with student questions for the strategic digital action field of *operational excellence / process management* are covered in:

- Adelbodner mineral water – the digital roadmap of a SME (available online).
- IT portfolio management and corporate knowledge – Colloquial enterprise architecture management (available online).
- Action fields of digital transformation at Synchrony Financial (USA) (available online).
- CRM and sales automation at Transgourmet Switzerland (available online).

You will find a collection of case studies for strategic digital transformation in the Appendix and additional cases online at www.strategic-digital-transformation.com.

Exercises

Discuss the following questions in your class, in your group or assignment:

1 How can technology from Industry 4.0/5.0 – in this exercise the Internet of Things (IoT) or Industrial Internet of Things (IIoT) – streamline business processes (see the opening case study on Agriculture 4.0 and precision livestock farming)? Describe at least three possible applications.
2 Based on a selected industry/business, define which processes across management, core, and support processes are central (and/or have the most potential) for digital transformation (see Box 8.1)?
3 Select a business that is manufacturing products and describe the core manufacturing process. In a second step, identify what tasks in the process should be supported by

Industry 4.0 technologies (see Box 8.4) and across the five types of manufacturing processes (see Box 8.5).

4 Select a business in the services industry (which provides services instead of manufacturing products) and identify digital process improvement opportunities in its core process (see Box 8.6 and Figure 8.6).

5 Forming two small groups (2–4 students in each group), each group should pick one digital service operational model (digital services economy, sharing economy or product-services economy as per Figure 8.6), and debate which model is the most successful in the fifth Industrial revolution in light of strategic AI opportunities.

6 Based on the selected firm in exercise 2, describe the success factors for business process management across the three areas of (1) creation and implementation of business processes, (2) the monitoring and maintenance of business processes, and (3) the improvement of business processes (see Chapter 8.4).

7 For your selected firm in exercise 2, explain how Total Quality Management (TQM) and Six Sigma (see Box 8.8) could support business process improvement together with new digital technologies.

8 For your selected firm in exercise 2, identify where AI can be applied in business processes (Chapter 8.5 and Box 8.9) for operational excellence and to build competitive advantages.

Further Reading List

- Armistead, C., & Machin, S. (1997). Implications of business process management for operations management. *International Journal of Operations & Production Management*, 17(9), 886–98.
- EFQM (2025). The EFQM Model (European Foundation for Quality Management). https://efqm.org/the-efqm-model/ (accessed on 8 March 2025).
- ISO (2025): ISO 9000 Family Quality Management (popular standards), www.iso.org/standards/popular/iso-9000-family (accessed on 8 March 2025).
- ISO (2025): ISO 14000 Family Environmental Management (popular standards), www.iso.org/standards/popular/iso-14000-family (accessed on 8 March 2025).
- ISO (2025): ISO/IEC 27000 Family Information Security Management (popular standards), www.iso.org/standard/iso-iec-27000-family (accessed on 8 March 2025).

References

Armistead, C., & Machin, S. (1997). Implications of business process management for operations management. *International Journal of Operations & Production Management, 17*(9), 886–98.

Capello, R., & Lenzi, C. (2021). Industry 4.0 and servitisation: Regional patterns of 4.0 technological transformations in Europe. *Technological Forecasting and Social Change, 173*, 121–164.

Dalenogare, L. S., Benitez, G. B., Ayala, N. F., & Frank, A. G. (2018). The expected contribution of Industry 4.0 technologies for industrial performance. *International Journal of Production Economics*, *204*, 383–94.

Eastwood, C. R., Edwards, J. P., & Turner, J. A. (2021). Anticipating alternative trajectories for responsible Agriculture 4.0 innovation in livestock systems. *Animal*, *15*, 100296.

European Commission (2021). Industry 5.0, a transformative vision for Europe: Governing systemic transformations towards a sustainable industry. Last accessed on 28 August 2024 from https://op.europa.eu/publication-detail/-/publication/38a2fa08-728e-11ec-9136-01aa75ed71a1.

Hayes, R. H., & Wheelwright, S. C. (1979). Link manufacturing process and product life cycles. *Harvard Business Review*, 133–40.

Holweg, M., Davies, J., De Meyer, A., Lawson, B., & Schmenner, R. W. (2018). *Process Theory: The Principles of Operations Management*. Oxford: Oxford University Press.

Huang, S., Wang, B., Li, X., Zheng, P., Mourtzis, D., & Wang, L. (2022). Industry 5.0 and Society 5.0 – comparison, complementation and co-evolution. *Journal of Manufacturing Systems*, *64*, 424–8.

ISO (International Organization for Standardization) (2025). ISO Popular Standards, www.iso.org/popular-standards.html (accessed on 8 March 2025).

Klassen, R. D., & Menor, L. J. (2007). The process management triangle: An empirical investigation of process trade-offs. *Journal of Operations Management*, *25*(5), 1015–34.

Leng, J., Sha, W., Wang, B., Zheng, P., Zhuang, C., Liu, Q., ... & Wang, L. (2022). Industry 5.0: Prospect and retrospect. *Journal of Manufacturing Systems*, *65*, 279–95.

Maddikunta, P. K. R., Pham, Q. V., Prabadevi, B., Deepa, N., Dev, K., Gadekallu, T. R., ... & Liyanage, M. (2022). Industry 5.0: A survey on enabling technologies and potential applications. *Journal of Industrial Information Integration*, *26*, 100257.

Mariani, M., & Borghi, M. (2019). Industry 4.0: A bibliometric review of its managerial intellectual structure and potential evolution in the service industries. *Technological Forecasting and Social Change*, *149*, 119752.

Montgomery, D. C., & Woodall, W. H. (2008). An overview of six sigma. *International Statistical Review/Revue Internationale de Statistique*, 329–46.

Morrone, S., Dimauro, C., Gambella, F., & Cappai, M. G. (2022). Industry 4.0 and precision livestock farming (PLF): An up to date overview across animal productions. *Sensors*, *22*(12), 4319.

Peter, M. K. (Hrsg.) (2017). *KMU-Transformation: Als KMU die Digitale Transformation erfolgreich umsetzen*. Forschungsresultate und Praxisleitfaden. FHNW Hochschule für Wirtschaft, Olten/Schweiz, www.kmu-transformation.ch.

Peter, M. K. (Hrsg.) (2021). *Strategieentwicklung im digitalen Zeitalter: Planung und Umsetzung der Digitalen Transformation*. FHNW Hochschule für Wirtschaft und Strategylab, Olten/Schweiz, www.strategische-transformation.ch.

Peter, M. K. (2023). *Digitaler Masterplan für KMU. So gelingt die digitale Transformation in Ihrem Unternehmen*. Verlag Beobachter Edition & Handelszeitung. Zürich/Schweiz, www.digitaler-masterplan.ch.

Peter, M. K. (2024). *The Digital Transformation Canvas. Develop and Implement Your Digital Strategy*. London: FT Publishing/Pearson, www.the-digital-transformation-canvas.com.

Peter, M. K., Kraft, C., & Lindeque, J. (2020). Strategic action fields of digital transformation: An exploration of the strategic action fields of Swiss SMEs and large enterprises. *Journal of Strategy and Management*, *13*(1), 160–80.

Porter, M.E. (1985). *Competitive advantage. Creating and sustaining superior performance.* New York, NY: The Free Press.

Porter, K., Little, D., Peck, M., & Rollins, R. (1999). Manufacturing classifications: relationships with production control systems. *Integrated Manufacturing Systems, 10*(4), 189–99.

Prajogo, D., Toy, J., Bhattacharya, A., Oke, A., & Cheng, T. C. E. (2018). The relationships between information management, process management and operational performance: Internal and external contexts. *International Journal of Production Economics, 199*, 95–103.

Schmenner, R. W. (1986). How can service businesses survive and prosper? *Sloan Management Review, 27*(3), 21–32.

Silvestro, R., Fitzgerald, L., Johnston, R., & Voss, C. (1992). Towards a classification of service processes. *International Journal of Service Industry Management, 3*(3), 62–75.

Talha, M. (2004). Total quality management (TQM): an overview. *The Bottom Line, 17*(1), 15–19.

Treacy, M., & Wiersema, F. (1995). *The Discipline of Market Leaders*. Reading, MA: Persus Books.

Williams, L. R., Fox, D. R., Bishop-Hurley, G. J., & Swain, D. L. (2019). Use of radio frequency identification (RFID) technology to record grazing beef cattle water point use. *Computers and Electronics in Agriculture, 156*, 193–202.

Zaki, M. (2019). Digital transformation: harnessing digital technologies for the next generation of services. *Journal of Services Marketing, 33*(4), 429–35.

Zobair, K. M., & Peter, M. K. (2025). A meta-analysis of AI-driven digital platforms for optimising real-time value chains in logistics for competitive advantage. *Working Paper*, Olten/Switzerland and Brisbane/Australia.

9

STRATEGIC ACTION FIELD OF DIGITAL LEADERSHIP AND CULTURE

Learning Goals

By the end of this chapter, you should...

- Be able to describe and explain the importance of digital leadership during a digital transformation process.
- Be able to reflect and describe how and why transformational leadership supports digital transformation.
- Be able to describe and explain the importance of digital culture during a digital transformation process.
- Be able to explain why it is important that digital leadership enables the emergence of a digital culture.
- Be able to describe the relationship between social, spatial and technical dimensions during a digital transformation of the way work is done.
- Be able to analyse and describe the changing characteristics of employees in the course of the emergence of new ways of working as a result of digital transformation.

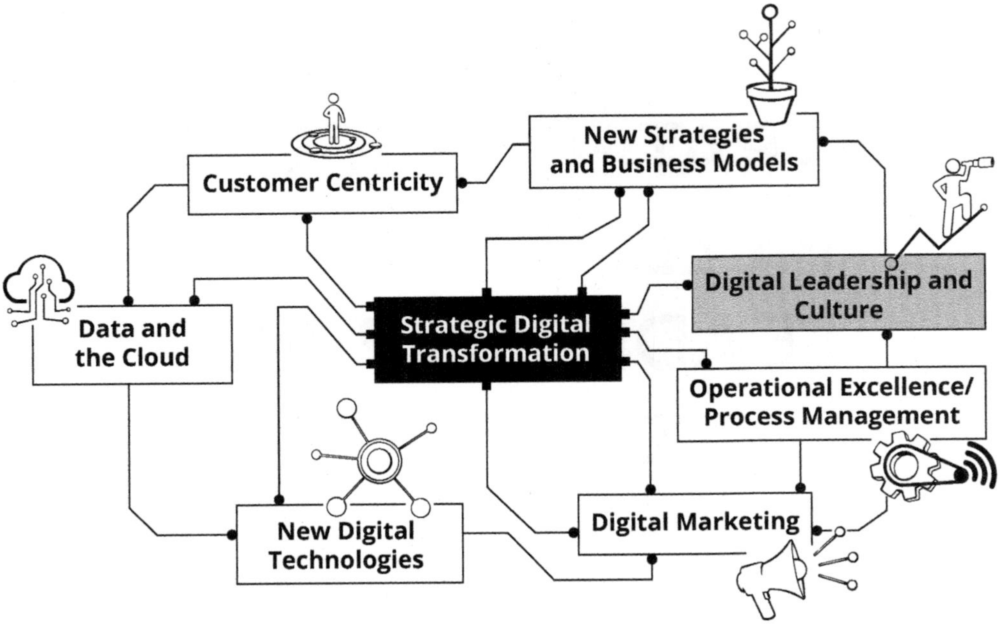

Figure 9.1 Digital leadership and culture is the sixth Strategic Action Field of Digital Transformation

Source: Peter (2017, 2021, 2023, 2024); Peter et al. (2020)

Working-From-Home at Spotify

Spotify Technology S.A. (Spotify), founded in 2006, is a Swedish audio streaming and media services provider with its corporate headquarters in Luxembourg and its operational headquarters in Stockholm, Sweden. Spotify has revolutionised the way people listen to music, by shifting from a transaction-based model of buying and owning audio content to an access-based model that allows users to stream music on demand. Spotify offers a vast library of audio content, including over 100 million songs, 6.5 million podcast titles, and 350,000 audiobooks (Spotify, 2025a). As of 2025, Spotify boasts over 675 million monthly active users, including 263 million paying subscribers, making it the world's most popular audio streaming subscription service. Spotify's platform is available in 184 markets worldwide, covering most of Europe, Africa, the Americas, Asia, and Oceania (Spotify, 2025a). In 2024, Spotify reported a revenue of €15.67 billion, an operating income of €1.365 billion, and a net income of €1.138 billion and has over 7,200 employees (Yahoo Finance, 2025).

In addition to innovating how music is consumed, Spotify has become famous as a great employer – a pioneer for digital leadership and culture – that includes an innovative work culture, comprehensive benefits, commitment to diversity and inclusion, and opportunities for professional growth. The company's unique approach to employee well-being and development makes it an attractive workplace for many. Through its 'Work From Anywhere' programme, employees have the freedom to choose where they work best, whether that's from home, the office, or another location entirely (Spotify, 2025b). This flexibility allows employees to maintain a healthy work-life balance and adapt their work environment to their personal needs and preferences. In 2024, Spotify reached global fame (primarily via social media) with its large billboard that said: 'Our employees aren't children. Spotify will continue working remotely' (Yahoo Finance, 2024) in response to many corporations insisting on, or promoting, a return back to the office, following the Covid-19 pandemic which boosted working-from-home (WFH).

In addition to WFH policies, other components contribute to the unique workplace digital culture (Spotify, 2025b). Spotify promotes learning and development opportunities for staff. Spotify encourages continuous growth and learning through its dedicated team, GreenHouse, which provides various training programmes and resources. Employees are empowered to take ownership of their professional development, ensuring they have the support and guidance needed to thrive in their careers. Spotify has an inclusive and diverse organisational culture, the company is committed to creating a workplace where everyone feels valued and included, regardless of their background or identity. Spotify also provides a comprehensive benefits package to staff. Some of the benefits include global parental leave, which offers six months of fully paid leave for all new parents, and flexible public holidays, allowing employees to swap days off according to their values and beliefs. Additionally, Spotify provides an employee assistance programme called 'All The Feels', which offers resources and support for mental health and self-care. Spotify is also commitment to social responsibility and sustainability. Spotify strives to make a positive impact on the world by integrating efforts to lower emissions into its everyday business operations and advocating for fair competition in the digital marketplace. Finally, Spotify has a collaborative and innovative work culture with its 'process-light' approach, allowing for agility and quick decision-making (Spotify, 2025c). Employees are encouraged to embrace change and think creatively, contributing to a dynamic and engaging work environment. The company's values, such as being innovative, collaborative, sincere, passionate, and playful, are deeply ingrained in its culture and guide employees in their daily work (Rancord Society (2021).

Figure 9.2 Flexible working: promotion of working from home (WFH)

Source: own illustration adapted from Hogg (2024) and King (2024), and as inspired by various social media posts (no credit allocation possible)

9.0 INTRODUCTION

The socio-technical nature of the digital transformation of a firm requires a great deal of employee commitment, know-how, time, and motivation for the process to be successful (Peter, 2019). Digital leadership is essential for preparing, supporting, and helping individuals, teams, and the entire organisation transform the firm and as a result how employees work (Warner & Wäger, 2019). This leadership plays an essential role in enabling effective change management, which supports employees to transition from their current state (before digital transformation) to a desired future state (an organisation capable of achieving competitive advantages in the digital age and delivering profits to its shareholders) (Kotter, 2012). In the medium to longer-term the integration of digital technologies into business processes and broader digital transformation of the firm requires the establishment of a digital culture (Loonam et al., 2018), that is aligned with the new ways of working and employee digital skills required to ensure the full potential of digital technologies and the broader digital transformation of a firm.

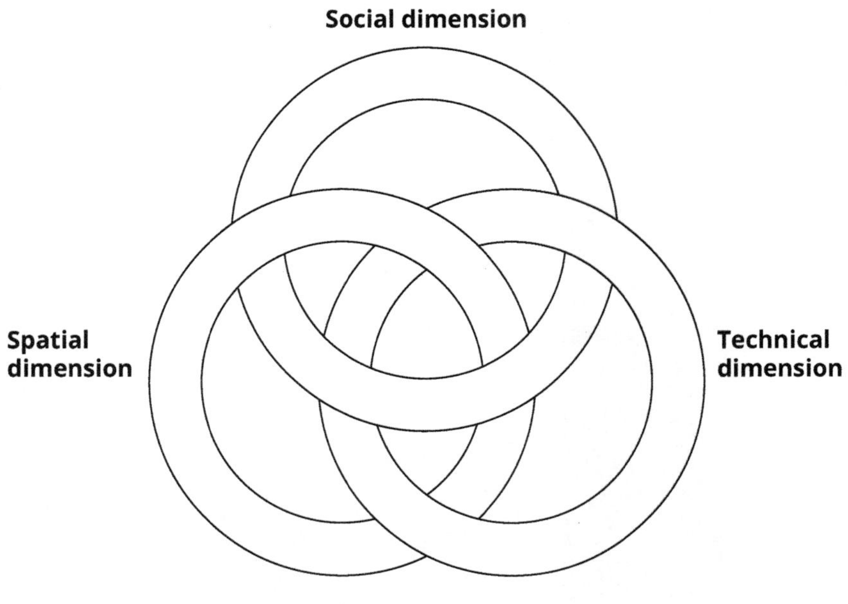

Figure 9.3 New work dimensions

Source: own illustration following Peter (2019) and Krättli & Peter (2021)

This digital leadership and culture perspective focuses attention on the need to integrate technical, social, and spatial aspects of the digital transformation of firms and work in the digital age (Peter et al., 2024a,b; Tigre et al., 2023). This understanding of organisations as socio-technical systems more specifically understands the technical aspects of the digital transformation process to include the organisational (e.g., reporting and decision-making structures) and digital technologies (e.g., information and communication solutions), while the social elements of the system include employee work and the organisational culture, as explained earlier in this text. The spatial dimension emphasises the flexibilisation of where, when, and how work can and is done as firms digitally transform the firm and the work employees do (Peter et al., 2024a,b; Tigre et al., 2023); key concepts to describe this dimension are location (Messenger, 2019) or place (Hackl et al., 2017). This chapter focuses on the socio-spatial dimensions, by addressing the importance of digital leadership, digital culture and the new ways of working that digital technologies enable (Peter, 2024a,b).

9.1 DIGITAL LEADERSHIP

The importance of digital leadership is critical due to the widely accepted belief that broadly speaking both managers and employees of a firm can be expected to prefer avoiding change, because of the disruption and uncertainty it brings (Dent and Goldberg, 1999; Macdonald, 1995; Peter et al., 2024 a,b). At the same time, digital transformation efforts do not only require effort to realise, but also to sustain (Tigre et al., 2023), as the digital transformation of a firm requires both managers and employees to unlearn established beliefs about what is effective and likely to lead to success (Martignoni and Keil, 2021; Warner & Wäger, 2019). It is the sustained unlearning of established beliefs of what works and how work should be done and the willingness to accept the uncertainty and risk associated with digital transformation processes to realise the full potential of digital technologies for the competitive advantage of a firm, that is the focus of digital leadership (Tigre et al., 2023) (see Box 9.1).

Box 9.1: Digital Transformation In Large and Small and Medium-Sized Enterprises

Research by Zoppelletto et al. (2023) reveals that approaches to the organisational setup and nature of the management of digital transformation projects differ in small and medium-sized enterprises (SME) and large enterprises. In large enterprises, a 'digital transformation conductor' (often called '*Chief Digital Officer*') oversees digital transformation, driving a top-down strategy implementation approach, whereas in small businesses, there is a 'digital transformation peer-tutor' approach to digital transformation, characterised by a bottom-up, informal, persuasive, and empathic approach similar to a digital coach or mentor. At the same time, Peter et al. (2024a,b) in their study of the adoption of working from home (WFH) have however found evidence that the owner-manager in SMEs can act as a veto holder in digital workplace transformation processes to e.g., a modern working environment.

Source: Peter et al. (2024a,b); Zoppelletto et al. (2023)

Digital leadership (see Box 9.2) can be defined as a long-term, people focused leadership orientation that emphasises personal ethics and adaptability with the purpose of ensuring the realisation of a digital culture that supports new ways of working enabled by digital technologies integration into business processes (Tigre et al., 2023). It is important to recognise that digital leadership extends core leadership capabilities, including envisioning the future of a digitally transformed firm, establishing strategic goals, showing digital literacy, being adaptable and change oriented, motivating employees, managing teams effectively and internal business communication in response to the digital age and more specifically the digital transformation of firms (Kane et al., 2019; Tigre et al., 2023). Traditional leadership responsibilities like articulating how the change will create value, embodying the ownership of the digital transformation process to lead by example, and finally empowering employees to engage and contribute to the change processes (Kane et al., 2019).

Digital leadership is strongly associated with transformational leadership, which includes decentralisation, the delegation of responsibility and transparency (Tigre et al., 2023; Warner & Wäger, 2019) as important concepts/values. Transformational leadership enables digital transformation processes, as it motivates employees to look 'beyond immediate self-interests through idealised influence (charisma), inspiration, intellectual stimulation, or individualised consideration. It elevates [employees'] level of maturity and ideals as well as concerns for achievement, self-actualization, and the well-being of others, the organization, and society' (Bass, 1999, p. 11). A transformational leadership style is essential in light of the systemic and challenging nature of the impact of advanced digital transformation on a firm and the external ecosystems the firm is embedded in, as society and the economy advance into the digital age. Digital leadership enables the management team to model the open-minded, adaptable, and innovative mindset required for the employees of the firm to successfully contribute to and develop with the broader digital transformation of a firm. The integral transformational leadership style associated with digital leadership further enables the necessary trust-building required for employees to accept uncertainty and risk, while also being highly compatible with high levels of transparency needed, which also supports further trust-building in increasingly dispersed teams across hybrid physical and virtual team collaboration (Tigre et al., 2023).

Box 9.2: E-Leadership Vs Digital Leadership

The origins of digital leadership can be found in e-leadership thinking that emphasised leadership effectiveness in virtual spaces during the initial digitalisation of work and team collaboration, e.g., virtual team effectiveness. Digital leadership incorporates these leadership responsibilities, but as the digital technologies become ubiquitous in business processes, and as a result of the digital transformation of firms and the very nature of how work is done, is changing the focus of leadership as it is increasingly strategic in nature with an emphasis on adaptation and competitive advantage. Digital leadership provides employees an understanding of the changes taking place, allowing shared goal setting and employee motivation during the inherent uncertainties that come with transformation processes. Digital leadership recognises the criticality of experimentations during digital transformation processes and provides the necessary working conditions to enable and encourage this experimentation. This goes beyond an emphasis on effective leadership in virtual spaces and teams.

Source: Tigre et al. (2023)

To implement the change (which can be less or more radical) that is inherent in digital transformation initiatives, organisations implement processes and activities to guide them through significant changes in a systematic and strategic approach, which may look different in large and small or medium-sized firms (see Box 9.1). Digital leadership during the change initiated by digital transformation processes should enable established practices for successful change management (Peter, 2024a,b), which Kotter (2012) suggests include the following:

- Creating a sense of urgency to motivate people to embrace change (help others see the need for change and the importance of acting immediately).
- Building a guiding coalition of influential individuals to lead the change effort (assemble a group with enough power to lead the change effort, and encourage the group to work as a team).
- Developing a clear vision and strategy for the change (clarify how the future will be different from the past, and how everyone in the organisation can make that future a reality).
- Empowering individuals to take action and remove obstacles (everyone in the organisation shall remove obstacles that hinder the change effort).
- Generating short-term wins to build momentum (recognising and rewarding those who make significant contributions to the change effort).
- Sustaining acceleration by maintaining focus and enthusiasm (following initial achievements, the organisation can use increased credibility to change systems, structures, and policies).

So far, this chapter has focused on digital leadership and often on the individual digital leader. His/her individualised understanding of the human dimension of the digital transformation process places significant demands on leadership teams and employees. While it is undoubtedly necessary for clear and purposeful digital leadership in the short term, ideally the associated digital mindsets required for this leadership and ideally developed in employees is most likely to be sustained in the medium and long-term if digital leadership can establish a strong digital culture in the firm. The importance of establishing a digital culture is now well established (Loonam et al., 2018) and discussed further in the next part of the chapter.

9.2 DIGITAL CULTURE

A digital culture cultivates a willingness to take risks and experiment with the integration of digital technologies into business processes, products, and services on a small scale before scaling successful experiments to the whole organisation (Vial, 2019). Balakrishnan and Das (2020) argue that as such successful digital transformation requires changes in human resource management and the development of a strong culture of openness and innovation. They are of the view that 'employees have to be engaged through learning and development initiatives' (Balakrishnan & Das, 2020, p. 539) that require activities around modified/updated organisational structures and processes, to foster a digital culture, and to focus on success factors for successful digital transformation implementation. This culture then becomes manifest in daily practices of agile ways of working that emphasise adaptation and flexibility in the short term to realise the longer-term goal of the digital transformation of the firm and ways of working for employees (see Box 9.3 for an example for more on agile and the project management approach of Scrum).

Box 9.3: Agility and Scrum

Agility is a key capability for effective digital transformation and at the same time, digital technologies are enablers of agility in a firm. Agile organisation allows a firm to effectively respond to changing external conditions. More formally it can be defined as a firm's 'ability to detect opportunities for innovation and seize those competitive market opportunities by assembling requisite assets, knowledge, and relationships with speed and surprise' (Sambamurthy et al., 2003, p. 245).

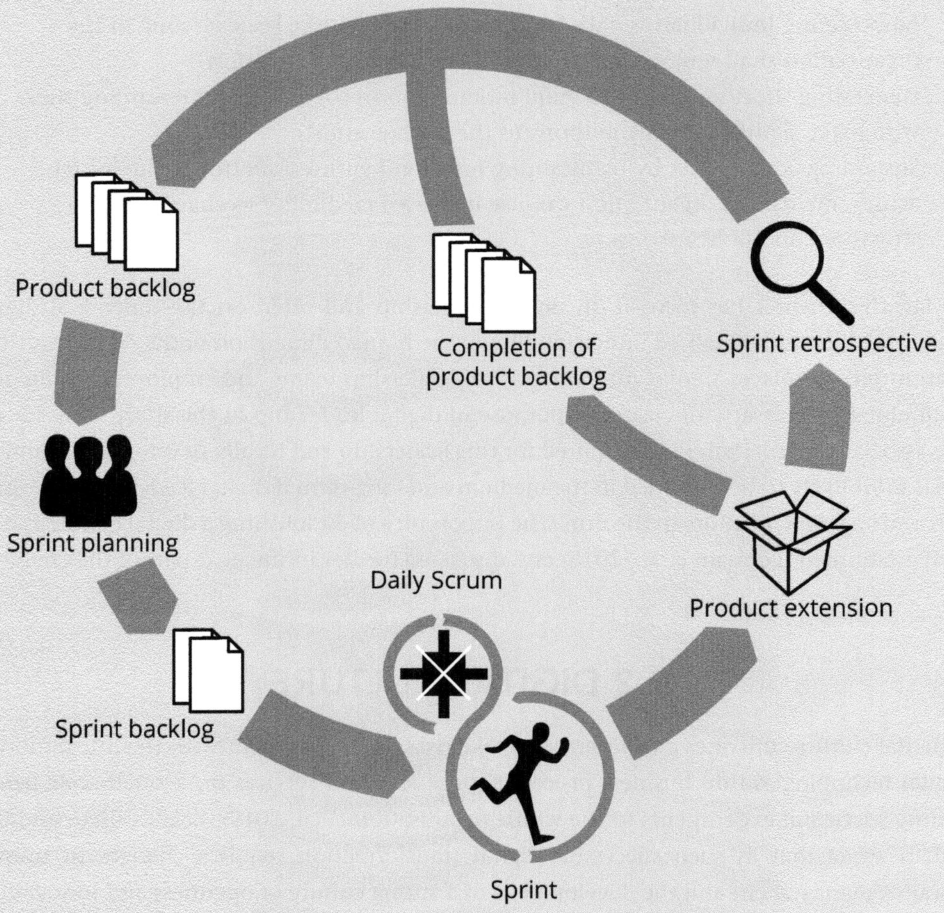

Figure 9.4 Overview of the Scrum method for agile collaboration

Source: Peter (2023, 2024)

Scrum is a technique that firms or teams in firms can adopt to enable agile responses to changing conditions in the external environment, by for example quickly developing and market testing a new product or service (see Figure 9.4 for an illustration of the process). The Scrum technique was developed for software development, but has been adopted for a wide variety of project types that are suited to 'learning through small, incremental and iterative changes while maintaining their ability to adapt long-term plans based on the outcomes of such experiments as well as ongoing changes in their environment' (Jöhnk et al., 2017, in Vial, 2019, p. 127).

The Scrum approach to projects usually involves 5–20 employees that pursue short term goals and tasks in short 'sprints' of typically two weeks that seek to complete tasks and achieve goals. The progress in the project is actively documented/logged and every day the team discusses the progress to seek solutions and prioritise efforts, with an emphasis on finding solutions to challenges/problems.

Given the information technology foundations of digital technologies and the need to learn how best to digitally transform the work done and products and services offered by a firm, the Scrum methodology is highly suited to ensuring agility in digital transformation projects. This approach to executing projects is also highly aligned with a digital culture that emphasises experimentation, technology affinity and customer centricity.

Source: Peter (2024); Vial (2019)

Establishing a digital organisational culture and enabling employees to develop a digital mindset is what distinguishes firms that get stuck at the digitalisation of their existing business model, operating processes and making limited changes to the way that the employees do work from the firms that become digital organisations (Forsythe & Rafoth, 2022). Truly digital organisations must adopt a digital culture and develop a digital mindset in their employees to be able to realise the full potential of advanced digital transformation of business models, business processes, and ways of working. In the most advanced form, the value creation realised by the firm is associated with completely different business models, processes, ways of working, and even value propositions to customers (Forsythe & Rafoth, 2022).

Organisational culture, more specifically for this text the digital culture of a firm, is critical in social processes where the way employees behave is driven by their beliefs, norms, and values (Wilson, 2001) (see Figure 9.5 for the relationship between the various levels of organisational culture). The preceding sections of this chapter have predominantly emphasised the observable behaviours of employees, especially with respect to digital leadership. It is however important to establish a fundamental understanding of what an organisational culture is: Wilson (2001) explains that definitions of organisational culture emphasise its shared nature, learned through group experiences (Schein, 2010). Two examples of formal definitions are:

> 'At the deeper and less visible level, culture refers to values that are shared by the people in a group and that tend to persist over time even when group membership changes. At the more visible level, culture represents the behaviour patterns or style of an organisation that new employees are automatically encouraged to follow by their fellow employees. Each level of culture has a tendency to influence the other.'

> 'The culture of a group can now be defined as a pattern of shared basic assumptions learned by a group as it solved its problems of external adaptation and internal integration, which has worked well enough to be considered valid and, therefore, to be taught to new members as the correct way to perceive, think, and feel in relation to those problems.' (Schein, 2010)

These definitions are extremely helpful as they draw attention to key aspects of establishing a digital culture. Developing a digital culture in a firm requires appropriate social interaction (Wilson, 2001), by employees of all kinds in the firm, to establish shared understandings of the underlying norms and values considered desirable and appropriate within the digital transformation of that specific firm. The development of a digital culture will be challenging, as the encumbent organisational culture in the firm can be expected to be durable and slow to change, which is arguably seen in the ability of digital new ventures to have far more advanced digital cultures compared to incumbent firms. As the organisational culture will shape employee behaviour (Wilson, 2001; see Figure 9.5) it is not surprising that the digital transformation processes often get stuck at the point that established processes of value creation are digitalised (see Box 9.4), as to progress further along the digital transformation process requires the incremental development of a digital culture.

At this point it is useful to recall that the strategies for realising ambidexterity as discussed in Chapter 3. They are not only a response to the tensions related to the differences in resources and capabilities associated with exploitation and exploration initiatives, but that the strategies for enabling ambidexterity are also or even fundamentally also negotiating the tensions between different organisational cultures. An additional point of importance here is that it is far easier to make changes to the visible behaviours and symbols, as well as rules and regulations, to reflect a digital culture, than it is to sustainably change the norms, values, and beliefs of employees to reflect a digital mindset (Wilson, 2001). Change processes for the unobservable dimensions of organisational culture to establish a firm wide digital culture will take significantly more time and effort than for the visible dimensions of organisational culture (Wilson, 2001). Finally, and interestingly, Figure 9.5 shows a slight overlap of observability with norms and values, normally considered unobservable, to capture the concept of espoused values, that are the 'articulated publicly announced principles and values that the group claims to be trying to achieve' (Schein, 2010).

Levels of Organisational Culture

Observable	**Behaviours & Artefacts**	Observable activities of employees, processes, actions and behaviours, as well as the physical environment and symbols that carry meaning for employees. • Organisational structures and informal networks influence the informal and formal relationships that influence how work is done. • Leadership and how leaders think is reflected in decision-making about strategic priorities • Influencing and decision-making, especially how relationships are developed, and influence is exercised • The ways employees do their work in relation to business processes, leadership decision-making, the opportunities for flex bilization and the degree of collaboration in how employees do their work • Symbols are the visual and physical environment of the places where work is done, which can include branding, the office environment, meeting spaces, and dress codes
	Rules & Regulations *Formal Institutions*	Rules and regulations are formalisations of fundamental shared understandings of important expectations for behaviour, enforced by punishment for breach. • Formal organisational structures and formal relationships that influence how work is done. • Formalised processes and systems manifest how a firm is run and includes all the different functional systems and the supporting technology and infrastructure that enables the processes
	Norms & Values *InFormal Institutions*	Informal assumptions about desirable and undesirable behaviour, that are / can be communicated via stories and the use of rituals and routines. • Stories are a critical way for employees to talk and share understandings of what is right and wrong behaviour, what is considered appropriate and inappropriate behaviour. Storying telling allows these values and norms to be communicated and shared understandings to be established • Rituals and routines, which can vary in their frequency, are an important way in which desirable values and normatively acceptable behaviour can be signalled. They signal what is valued by employees and management
Unobservable	**Beliefs** *InFormal Institutions*	Subconscious, taken for granted assumptions, the most difficult to articulate informal foundations of behaviour. • Individual beliefs are socio-cognitive assumptions that are so deeply internalised that they can be difficult for employees or managers to articulate • Importantly the professionalisation of employees / managers in a specific domain or functional role can lead to shared beliefs about how work should be done that are so deeply accepted and held that employees can take them for granted, similarly to beliefs in a more general sense

Figure 9.5 Levels of culture

Source: adapted from Forsythe & Rafoth (2022); Wilson (2001)

Box 9.4: Getting Stuck at the Digitisation of the Established Business

The establishment of a digital culture is essential for enabling the full digital transformation of a firm. It is arguably the development of a digital organisational culture and digital mindset in employees that enables the full digital transformation of a firm. At the same time, it is unlikely that a firm that believes that the digitalisation of business processes, products and services is equivalent to digital transformation will develop a digital culture. In their study of Swiss small and medium-sized enterprises (SMEs), Kraft et al. (2022) further draw attention to the possibility that firms that adopt digital technologies to integrate these unevenly across the different kinds of work that are done in a firm. This raises the possibility that the way that operative employees and managers work can change at different speeds. In the case of Kraft et al. (2022) there is evidence that operative work was far more actively affected than managerial work. This would significantly hinder the potential for a digital culture to be developed across a firm and thereby contribute to the digital transformation process getting stuck at the level of digitalisation of processes and tasks.

Source: Forsythe & Rafoth (2022); Kraft et al. (2022)

Espoused values from a digital transformation perspective are very interesting, as the ability of employees to articulate the norms and values associated with a digital culture could be interpreted as a signal of deeper cultural change in the culture of a firm (Schein, 2010). But Wilson (2001) also cautions that employees may espouse corporate values and still behave differently and interpreting this deviation is going to require contextual evaluation; for the leadership team seeking a digital transformation, the ability to espouse the digital culture even if behaviour is not fully aligned may still be a positive signal. It is also important to note that the professionalisation associated with different functional roles in a larger firm can result in subgroups within a firm; relatedly the accepted norms, values, and beliefs can vary across functional areas (Wilson, 2001). For those seeking to realise a digital transformation of the firm, this points to the need to be aware that different groups in the organisation are likely to find the transition easier and others more challenging, due to these differences in functional subcultures in the firm. Managers responsible for leading the digital transformation of a firm need to engage in self-reflection and seek to initiate reflection in other employees about the norms and values in the firm and seek to collectively develop a shared understanding of the digital culture appropriate for the firm (Schein, 2010) as part of advanced digital transformation processes. Managers can also influence the process through adaptation of symbols used and the physical working environment, as well as leading by example in the adoption of a digital mindset.

9.3 THE CHANGING WORKPLACE

Effective digital leadership and the establishment of a digital culture is required to ensure employees are ready for the new ways of working enabled and even required by the integration of digital technologies into established and new business processes. The digital transformation of business processes either supported or fully automated by digital technologies generate increasing amounts of data and are likely to be highly networked, allowing efficient distribution of that data across time and place with limited cost and effort (Aroles et al., 2021; Peter, 2024). This has led to the coining of the term 'new work' or 'new ways of working', to describe the flexible and self-guided ways of working that emerge as digital transformation progresses (workplace transformation), that are simultaneously increasingly geographically dispersed (places) and making use of diverse channels (spaces) for real-time collaboration enabled by digital technologies (Aroles et al., 2021).

New ways of working (NWW) feature a changed understanding of where (place/location) and when (time) work can and should be done (Aroles et al., 2021), leading to the emergence of concepts like open spaces (see Figure 9.6), desk sharing / hot desking, home office / working from home (WFH), co-working, teleworking, and virtual working / mobile working (Aroles et al., 2021; Peter, 2024). Since Covid-19 and associated move to WFH, many organisations asked their white collar employees 'to come back to the office', which has resulted in conversations (see also the opening case study) regarding culture and brand building, leadership approach, and employer attractiveness (see Table 9.1 for an overview of large organisations and their WFH policies).

Table 9.1 Organisations' WFH and back-to-office strategies (selection)

Company	No. of days in the physical office	Description
AirBnB	No mandate	Airbnb employees have the option to work remotely indefinitely, with the ability to work in 170 countries.
Allianz	3 days	Allianz allows employees to work remotely up to 40% of the time, with flexibility depending on local needs.
Amazon	3–5 days	Amazon currently mandates 3 days in the office, with plans to increase to 5 days by 2025.
Apple	3 days	Apple mandates employees to work in the office on Tuesdays, Thursdays, and a team-chosen day.
Barclays	4–5 days	Barclays expects staff to return to the office full-time or close to it, for 4–5 days.
Dell	5 days	As of March 2025, all hybrid and remote Dell employees who live near a Dell office were called back to work in the office five days a week.

(Continued)

Table 9.1 (Continued)

Company	No. of days in the physical office	Description
eBay	Flexible / role dependent	eBay offers a flexible hybrid work model, where employees can choose to work remotely or in the office.
EY	2 days	EY mandates employees to work in the office at least two days a week under its hybrid work policy.
Google	3 days	Google employees must attend the office at least three days a week.
J.P. Morgan	5 days	Morgan Stanley mandates employees to work in the office.
Microsoft	2–3 days	Microsoft operates a hybrid policy, typically requiring 2–3 days in the office per week.
Spotify	No mandate	Spotify allows employees to work from anywhere, with no mandated office days.
Vodafone	2–3 days	Vodafone adopted a hybrid work model, requiring employees to work in the office 2-3 days a week while continuing to support remote work where possible.

Source: selection from Hubble, 2025

Here it is important to understand that 'new' here 'is always relative, of course, closely associated with technological innovation, in our case digitalization, and integrates spatio-temporal, technological and socio-cultural dimensions of life and organizing' (Aroles et al., 2021, p. 1). Open spaces are associated with large, shared offices that are divided into zones for different types of work and ways of working and stand in contrast to traditional rigid subdivided offices represented by the 'office cubicle' (see Box 9.5).

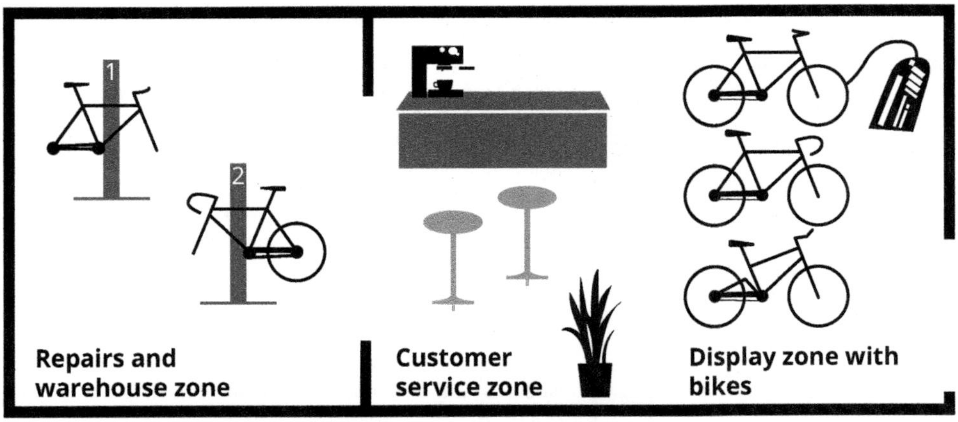

Figure 9.6 Example of a modern, open workplace (Bikeshop) with three zones for products (shop window), customer service (consultation zone) and repairs and warehousing (repair department).

Source: Peter (2023, 2024)

Box 9.5: *Office Space* (1999)

The satirical comedy written and directed by Mike Judge and staring Ron Livingston (as Peter) and Jennifer Aniston (as Joanna) documents the search for meaning by Peter, a worker in a 1990s software company, where he and other employees work in office cubicles completing meaningless tasks in front of generic grey desktop computers for multiple micro-managing corporate bosses, while battling with a non-cooperative printer; the work experience is epitomised with the tagline: 'Work Sucks'. The initial limited success of the film has in time been replaced by the film achieving something of a cult status for its portrait of the relationships between people and technology, shortly before the transition into the early years of the digital age, with the dot com (internet) boom years at the turn of the Millennium.

Source: IMDb (1999)

Figure 9.7 Traditional office workspace (cubicle), a remnant from the third industrial revolution

Source: own illustration inspired by IMDb (1999)

Desk sharing is by now almost ubiquitous and refers to the end of employees having their own desks; instead employees work at the desks that are available at the time, and can flexibly be used as the office infrastructure most suitable to the work (hot desking) they are currently doing (Peter, 2024). Home offices are spaces in the homes of employees dedicated to work, and this may or may not include equipment provided by an employer. Co-working refers to shared infrastructure that individuals share access to and only use when needed. Finally, mobile working is an alternative to home office working, where the work is done independent of a specific location, the employee has no workplace in an office or at home and is instead fully mobile (Peter, 2024). These emerging new ways of working have differing degrees of benefits associated with work–life balance and cost savings, but there are also risks and challenges associated with the mixing of private and work life, as well as IT and data security challenges. New ways of working are then 'closely associated with integrating roughly three dimensions: the spatial, the technological, and the social/cultural' (Aroles et al., 2021, p. 3).

Digital technologies have been central, even essential, for enabling NWW by enabling employee mobility and by changing the nature of work that is done by employees, not least by increasing the information intensity of tasks and work. These changes have brought positive opportunities for employees, such as greater autonomy and flexibility, but also better work–life balance. At the same time, digital technologies also come with 'a series of concerns relating to issues of precarity, surveillance, control, deskilling and, more generally, changed power dynamics', and the blurring of the workplace and private spaces (Aroles et al., 2021, p. 4). This demands that employees develop new skills for managing the resulting challenges associated with being available around the clock and the risks of a self-optimisation/economisation to the point of self-exploitation.

9.4 THE CHANGING EMPLOYEE

Employees are required to developed digital skills in a digitally transformed workplace, but also increasingly expected to be able to complete tasks with greater flexibility and autonomy. At the same time employees are challenged to undertake '[d]igital configuration work, [which] requires human agency, innovation and imagination in making sense of technologies, discourse and practices' (Aroles et al., 2021, p. 4). These changes and demands have also been accelerated by the rapid adoption of digital technologies and the digital transformation of firms as a result of the Covid-19 crisis (Aroles et al., 2021; Peter et al., 2024a,b).

Caputo et al. (2023) have argued that the ideal employee in the digital age can be described as a T-shaped professional (see Figure 9.8), with strong narrow technical competences (deep discipline expertise) and broad cognitive competences (cross-discipline expertise). T-shaped professionals are prepared for the needed skills development associated with a digital transition, including technical competences related to knowledge and skills, methodological competences for problem solving and decision-making, social competences related to cooperation and communication and personal competences related to values, motivation, and attitude. Reflecting on the earlier content of this chapter these competences would ideally be aligned with a digital organisational culture. It is argued that these competences enable employees to approach their work with a critical problem-solving approach, while enabling them to manage themselves and remain adaptable and resilient in an ever-changing work environment (Caputo et al., 2023).

The model of the T-shaped professional proposed by Caputo et al. (2023) (see extended version Figure 9.9), builds on earlier work by Leonard-Barton (1995, p. 75): 'the need for T-shaped skills surfaces anywhere problem solving is required across different deep functional knowledge bases or at the juncture of such deep knowledge with an application area. People possessing these skills can shape their knowledge to fit the problem at hand rather than insist that their problems appear in a recognizable form. Given their wide

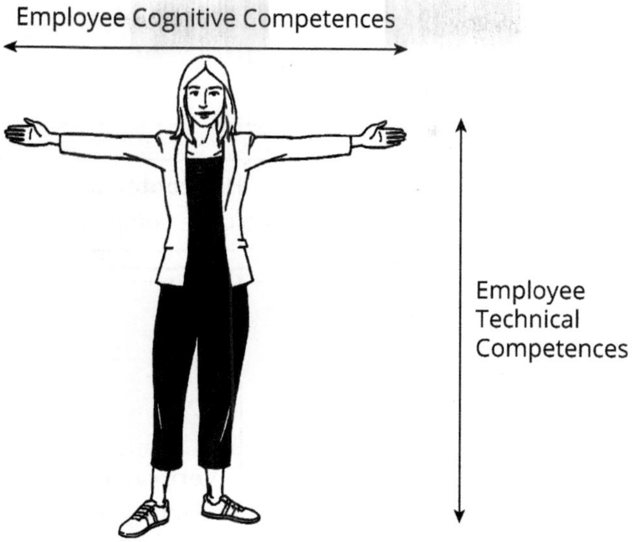

Figure 9.8 T-shaped professionals for the digital age (simplified version of Figure 9.9)

Source: own illustration following Caputo et al. (2023)

experience in applying functional knowledge, they are capable of convergent, synergistic thinking.' Caputo et al. (2023) develop a digital transformation specific conceptualisation of the T-shaped competences profile that integrates Bloom et al.'s (1956) taxonomy of learning to articulate how these professionals are able to master the challenges associated with digital transformation. The strength of this approach is that it visualises the need for deep focused technical competences that can be applied with contextual awareness.

The need for T-shaped professional profiles (see Box 9.6) is not restricted to operative management and employees; leadership/executive teams also need to develop T-shaped profiles (Caputo et al., 2023). This is arguably seen most clearly in the emergence of the Chief Digital Officer (CDO) role in executive management teams (Kunisch, Menz, & Langan, 2022; Wei et al., 2024), even if the role is not as widely present as many may assume. The CDO role is associated with company-wide digital transformation agendas, while symbolising a firm's commitment to digital transformation (Wei et al., 2024). The CDO role contributes to company-wide systems integration through the integration of digital technologies, while providing digital leadership and developing a digital culture in the business (Wei et al., 2024). Reflecting the T-shaped professional model, there is evidence that while CDOs have an organisation-wide integrative perspective on digital transformation, they also tend to adopt roles and undertake activities more actively in functional areas most suitable to rapid digital transformation, such as digital experience, digital marketing, digital innovation, and digital product development (Wei et al., 2024).

Please refer to Chapter 11 (Section 11.5.1) regarding the development of digital competencies and skills for strategic digital transformation.

Box 9.6: Digital Competencies and Skills for the Digital Age

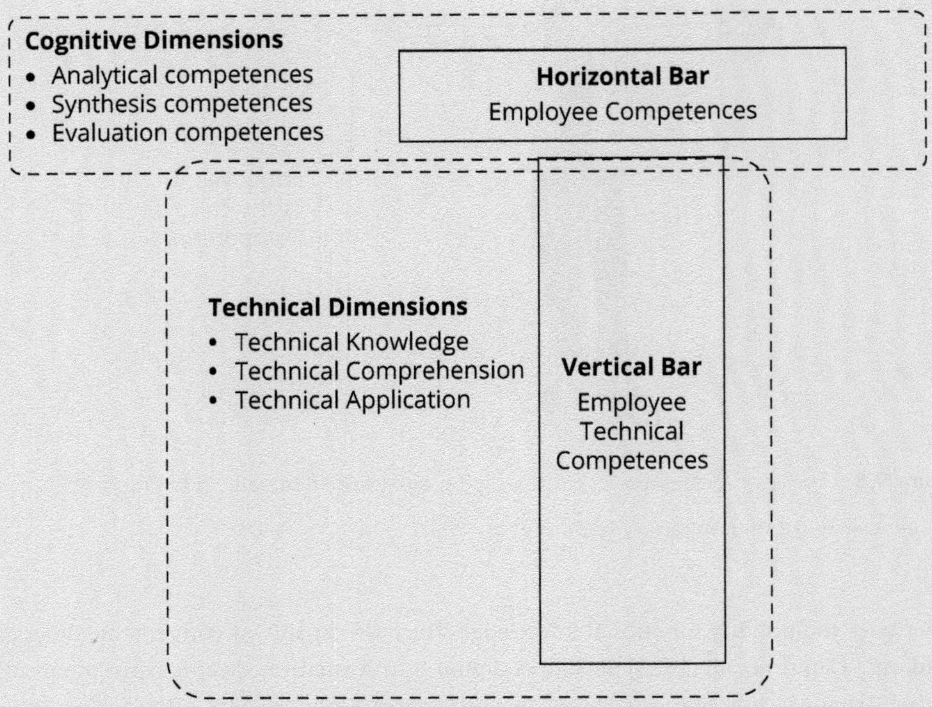

Figure 9.9 T-shaped professionals for the digital age

Knowledge
An actor's ability to replicate the activities needed to use a specific technical tool.

Comprehension
An actor's ability to explain how performed activities / actions contribute to the functioning of a technology and lead to the obtained results.

Application
An 'actors' ability to use knowledge about the functioning and processes of a specific technology in a different well-known scenario or for solving well-known issues for which the technology has not been projected.

Analysis
An 'actors' ability for understanding the functioning of technologies in terms of interactions among its parts and outcome.

Synthesis
The ability of actors to describe and explain how the technology is part of the whole process, how it contributes to the expected results, and how it influences to whole path in which it is part.

Evaluation
An 'actors' ability to evaluate the effective contribution that a technology can provide not only in terms of effectiveness, but also in terms of defin[ing] new protocol[s] and path[s] for solving emerging problems or for achieving new aims.'

Source: adapted from Caputo et al. (2023, p. 5)

9.5 DIGITAL LEADERSHIP AND CULTURE AND COMPETITIVE ADVANTAGE

Wei et al. (2024) in a study of the impact of CDOs on firm performance found clear evidence for a positive impact on the forward-looking performance of firms in their sample, suggesting CDOs contribute to digital transformation related change and create value for the firms that appoint them. In their review article, Khaw et al. (2022) also found support for digital leadership's positive impact on firm performance. Focusing on CDOs, Wei et al. (2024) further suggest that 'the CDO could play a better role when he/she is appointed externally, [and] when he/she is generally responsible for the company-wide digital tasks' (Wei et al., 2024, p. 9). The managerial implications of Wei et al.'s (2024) findings are that CDOs should be understood as boosters of digital transformation; importantly the appointment of a CDO increases the likelihood that the executive team will develop competences associated with a T-shaped profile. The organisation benefits from the integrative effects of the appointment of a CDO and the development of 'a culture of collaboration and continuous improvement, CDOs overcome organizational silos and resistance to change, promoting a more cohesive and responsive operational environment' (Wei et al., 2024, p. 9), which leads to positive performance outcomes (see also Chapter 11).

While the appointment of a CDO is typically a decision associated with large enterprises, Bhatti et al. (2024) provide insights on the impact of the development of a digital culture on the performance of small and medium-sized manufacturing enterprises. The authors argue that the performance effects of a digital strategy are dependent on the presence of a digital culture and this is reflected in their findings. The impact of a digital strategy is found to be mediated by the presence of a digital culture. Another study by Martínez-Caro et al. (2020) of the digital transformation of Saint-Gobain, a large global enterprise manufacturing firm producing products for the building and construction industries, showed a positive impact of digital culture on firm performance. Martínez-Caro et al. (2020) provide evidence that digital culture enables the digitalisation of a business and also organisational learning associated with insights and knowledge from the development of organisational knowledge in the course of the digital transformation of a firm, a separate and complementary process to the integration of digital technologies that then generate data, in the businesses of a large enterprise.

9.6 DIGITAL LEADERSHIP AND CULTURE AND SUSTAINABILITY

Of course, digital leadership and culture can drive environmental sustainability by implementing data analytical capabilities, technologies, and processes which reduce energy consumption, minimise waste, and optimise resource use. In addition, a strong digital culture promotes transparency, ethical practices, and social responsibility.

However, it is very challenging to establish and prove a clear uncontrovertible relationship between the development of digital leadership and culture and the sustainability performance of a firm, although Khaw et al. (2022) suggest that digital leadership and culture may be associated with greater sustainability of the firm itself. At this stage with the limited availability of insights from research, it is challenging to say more on this relationship.

9.7 CONCLUSION

Digital leadership is clearly essential for enabling the digital transformation of a firm, not least by enabling the emergence of a digital culture in a business and developing employees into T-shaped professionals. This enables the firm to create opportunities for new ways of working, that both suite the employees and enable the digitally transformed firm to achieve positive performance effects.

Digital leadership involves preparing, supporting, and helping individuals and teams adapt to new ways of working enabled by digital technologies. It requires a long-term, people-focused approach that emphasises personal ethics, adaptability, and the establishment of a digital culture. Digital leaders must envision the future, set strategic goals, demonstrate digital literacy, and motivate employees while managing teams effectively. At this point, transformational leadership is highlighted as essential for digital transformation, as it motivates employees to look beyond immediate self-interests and embrace change. This leadership style fosters trust, transparency, and collaboration, which are crucial for managing the uncertainties and risks associated with digital transformation. A digital culture encourages risk-taking and experimentation with digital technologies, characterised by openness, innovation, and continuous learning. It supports agile ways of working, such as the Scrum methodology, which enables teams to respond quickly to changing conditions and achieve short-term goals through iterative processes. Additional components of new way of working include remote work, desk sharing, and co-working. These new work arrangements are enabled by digital technologies and offer greater flexibility and autonomy for employees. However, they also present challenges related to work–life balance, cybersecurity, and the blurring of personal and professional boundaries.

Finally, in the centre of the workplace transformation towards a digital culture stand the managers and employees who are expected to develop digital skills and adapt to these new ways of working. The concept of T-shaped professionals, who possess both deep technical expertise and broad cognitive skills, is introduced as ideal for navigating the complexities of digital transformation.

Case Studies

Students can complete the following tasks either based on the focal case study, or work on the recommended case study for this chapter (*Digital transformation of the city of Lucerne*) and answer the questions below.

1 What are the challenges and barriers (including cultural ones) for digital transformation in an organisation; and specifically, in a government organisation?
2 How would you describe the city of Lucerne's effort and progress regarding digital transformation?
3 How could an organisation (such as the city of Lucerne) modify/enrich its technical, social, and spatial dimensions to foster digital transformation (see Chapter 9)? Provide five ideas/recommendations for each dimension.
4 Identify two government stakeholder groups and describe three digital services for each group that might provide value and efficiency gains. What digital skills are required to provide these digital services?
5 Would you recommend Scrum (see Box 9.3) as an agile project and work method to the city of Lucerne? Describe why you would (or would not) recommend Scrum.
6 Overall, what are the digital skills which employees require (refer to Chapter 9.4 and Figure 9.8) for successful digital transformation in an organisation? Define at least eight skills and provide a rationale for your choice.
7 What are your takeaways from this case study regarding digital culture and leadership? What were the key activities at the City of Lucerne that enabled cultural and leadership change?

Additional cases with student questions for the strategic digital action field of *Digital Leadership and Culture* are covered in:

- Adelbodner mineral water – the digital roadmap of a SME (available online).
- Action fields of digital transformation at Synchrony Financial (USA) (available online).
- From limited budget to limitless potential: the digital journey of OSHE@UTMKL (available online).

You will find a collection of case studies for Strategic Digital Transformation in the Appendix and additional cases online at www.strategic-digital-transformation.com.

Exercises

Discuss the following questions in your class, in your group or assignment:

1 Review the three dimensions of new work (social, spatial, and technical dimension) in light of the opening case (Working-from-Home at Spotify): what investments (make assumptions, if required) do you believe does Spotify make in these three dimensions to provide a contemporary working environment (see also Table 9.1)?
2 Discuss how transformational leadership (Chapter 9.1 and Box 9.2) is linked to digital transformation: identify and describe at least three important leadership characteristics which support digital transformation.
3 Based on a selected industry/business, describe how they could embed the Scrum methodology (see Box 9.3) in the way the company develops products or services.

4 For the business selected in exercise 3, develop a culture framework with organisational values, reflecting the dimensions in Figure 9.5. Develop at least three suggestions for each dimension.
5 Forming two small groups (2–4 students in each group), assign a pro and contra position to each group and debate if modern working environments are important (group 1), or if they are overvalued and not that important (group 2) for successfully competing in the digital age.
6 For the business selected in exercise 3, describe the impact on the employees as a result of the fourth/fifth industrial revolutions (see Chapter 9.4 and Figure 9.8). Use the concept of the T-shaped employee and describe the impact on both the strong narrow technical competences (deep discipline expertise) and broad cognitive competences (cross-discipline expertise).

Further Reading List

- Peter, M. K., Wuersch, L., Neher, A., Lindeque, J., & Mändli Lerch, K. (2024). The workplace of the future: the COVID-19 pandemic and working from home in Swiss small businesses, *Journal of Strategy & Management*, 17(4), 707–729.
- WEF (2025): The Future of Jobs Report 2025. World Economic Forum, 7 January, www.weforum.org/publications/the-future-of-jobs-report-2025/.
- WHO (2022): Healthy and Safe Telework: Technical Brief. World Health Organization, 2 February, www.who.int/publications/i/item/9789240040977.
- Zoppelletto, A., Orlandi, L. B., Zardini, A., Rossignoli, C., & Kraus, S. (2023). Organizational roles in the context of digital transformation: A micro-level perspective. *Journal of Business Research*, 157, 113563.

References

Albannai, N. A., Raziq, M. M., Malik, M., Scott-Kennel, J., & Igoe, J. (2024). Unraveling the role of digital leadership in developing digital dynamic capabilities for the digital transformation of firms. *Benchmarking: An International Journal*, early online.

Aroles, J., Cecez-Kecmanovic, D., Dale, K., Kingma, S. F., & Mitev, N. (2021). New ways of working (NWW): Workplace transformation in the digital age. *Information and Organization, 31*(4), 100378.

Balakrishnan, R., & Das, S. (2020). How do firms reorganize to implement digital transformation? *Strategic Change, 29*(5), 531–41.

Bass, B. M. (1999). Two decades of research and development in transformational leadership. *European Journal of Work and Organizational Psychology, 8*(1), 9–32.

Bhatti, S. H., Sumbal, M. S., Ahmed, A., & Golgeci, I. (2024). Digital strategy for firm performance-mediating role of digital platform capabilities and digital culture in manufacturing SMEs. *Technology Analysis & Strategic Management*, 1–15.

Bloom, B. S., Engelhart, M. D., Furst, E. J., Hill, W. H., & Krathwohl, D. R. (1956). *Taxonomy of Educational Objectives: Cognitive Domain.* New York: McKay.

Caputo, F., Cillo, V., Fiano, F., Pironti, M., & Romano, M. (2023). Building T-shaped professionals for mastering digital transformation. *Journal of Business Research*, *154*, 113309.

Dent, E. B., & Goldberg, S. G. (1999). Challenging resistance to change. *The Journal of Applied Behavioral Science*, *35*(1), 25–41.

Forsythe, J., & Rafoth, J. (2022). Being digital: Why addressing culture and creating a digital mindset are critical to successful transformation. *insight*, *25*(1), 25–8.

Hackl, B., Wagner, M., Attmer, L., & Baumann, D. (2017), *New work: Auf dem Weg zur neuen Arbeitswelt: Management-Impulse, Praxisbeispiele, Studien*. Springer, Wiesbaden.

Hofstede, G. (2012). Culture is the collective programming of the mind which distinguishes the members of one group from another. *Journal of Professional Exercise Physiology*, *10*(12), 1.

Hogg, R. (2024). Spotify's HR chief says remote staff aren't 'children' as company reaffirms work-from-anywhere policy. *Yahoo!Finance*, 8 October, https://finance.yahoo.com/news/spotify-hr-chief-says-remote-100021103.html.

Hubble (2025): The official list of every company's back-to-office strategy, 4 February, https://hubblehq.com/blog/famous-companies-workplace-strategies.

IMDb (1999). *Office Space*. Last accessed from www.imdb.com/title/tt0151804 on 24 February 2025.

Jöhnk, J., Röglinger, M., Thimmel, M., Urbach, N. (2017). How to implement agile IT setups: A taxonomy of design options. In *Proceedings of the 25th European Conference on Information Systems (ECIS)*, Guimarães, Portugal, June 5-10, 2017 (pp. 1521–1535). ISBN 978-989-20-7655-3 Research Papers.

Kane, G. C., Phillips, A. N., Copulsky, J., & Andrus, G. (2019). How digital leadership is(n't) different. *MIT Sloan Management Review*, *60*(3), 34–9.

Khaw, T. Y., Teoh, A. P., Khalid, S. N. A., & Letchmunan, S. (2022). The impact of digital leadership on sustainable performance: a systematic literature review. *Journal of Management Development*, *41*(9/10), 514–34.

King, A. (2024). Spotify says its employees aren't children – no return to office mandate as 'work-from-anywhere' plan remains. *Digital Music News*, 8 October, www.digitalmusicnews.com/2024/10/08/spotify-return-to-office-mandate-comments/.

Kotter, J. P. (2012): *Leading Change*. Harvard Business Review Press, Boston/USA.

Kotter, J. P., & Heskett, J. L. (1992). *Corporate Culture and Performance*, Free Press, New York, NY.

Kraft, C., Lindeque, J. P., & Peter, M. K. (2022). The digital transformation of Swiss small and medium-sized enterprises: Insights from digital tool adoption. *Journal of Strategy and Management*, *15*(3), 468–94.

Krättli, N., & Peter, M. K. (2021). Arbeitswelt 4.0 – Das KMU der Zukunft: Führung, Arbeitsplatzgestaltung und Technologieeinsatz im digitalen Zeitalter. *Beobachter Edition & Handelszeitung*, www.kmu-arbeitswelt.ch.

Kunisch, S., Menz, M., & Langan, R. (2022). Chief digital officers: An exploratory analysis of their emergence, nature, and determinants. *Long Range Planning*, *55*(2), 101999.

Leonard-Barton, D. (1995). *Wellsprings of Knowledge: Building and Sustaining the Sources of Innovation*. Cambridge, MA: Harvard Business Press.

Loonam, J., Eaves, S., Kumar, V., & Parry, G. (2018). Towards digital transformation: Lessons learned from traditional organizations. *Strategic Change*, *27*(2), 101–9.

Lyu, J. (2024). How does digital leadership improve organizational sustainability: Theory and evidence. *Journal of Cleaner Production, 434*, 140–8.

Macdonald, S. (1995). Learning to change: an information perspective on learning in the organization. *Organization Science, 6*(5), 557–68.

Martignoni, D., & Keil, T. (2021). It did not work? Unlearn and try again – unlearning success and failure beliefs in changing environments. *Strategic Management Journal, 42*(6), 1057–82.

Martínez-Caro, E., Cegarra-Navarro, J. G., & Alfonso-Ruiz, F. J. (2020). Digital technologies and firm performance: The role of digital organisational culture. *Technological Forecasting and Social Change, 154*, 119962.

Messenger, J. C. (2019), *Telework in the 21st Century: An Evolutionary Perspective.* Edward Elgar, Cheltenham.

Peter, M. K. (Hrsg.) (2017). *KMU-Transformation: Als KMU die Digitale Transformation erfolgreich umsetzen. Forschungsresultate und Praxisleitfaden.* FHNW Hochschule für Wirtschaft, Olten/Schweiz, www.kmu-transformation.ch.

Peter, M. K. (2019). *Arbeitswelt 4.0. Als KMU die Arbeitswelt der Zukunft erfolgreich gestalten. Forschungsresultate und Praxisleitfaden.* Hochschule für Wirtschaft FHNW, Olten/Schweiz.

Peter, M. K. (Hrsg.) (2021). *Strategieentwicklung im digitalen Zeitalter: Planung und Umsetzung der Digitalen Transformation.* FHNW Hochschule für Wirtschaft und Strategylab, Olten/Schweiz, www.strategische-transformation.ch.

Peter, M. K. (2023). *Digitaler Masterplan für KMU. So gelingt die digitale Transformation in Ihrem Unternehmen.* Verlag Beobachter Edition & Handelszeitung. Zürich/Schweiz, www.digitaler-masterplan.ch.

Peter, M. K. (2024). *The Digital Transformation Canvas. Develop and Implement Your Digital Strategy.* FT Publishing/Pearson, London/UK, www.the-digital-transformation-canvas.com.

Peter, M. K., Kraft, C., & Lindeque, J. (2020). Strategic action fields of digital transformation: An exploration of the strategic action fields of Swiss SMEs and large enterprises. *Journal of Strategy and Management, 13*(1), 160–80.

Peter, M. K., Wuersch, L., Neher, A., Lindeque, J. P., & Mändli Lerch, K. (2024a). The workplace of the future: the COVID-19 pandemic and working from home in Swiss small businesses. *Journal of Strategy and Management, 17*(4), 707–29.

Peter, M. K., Wuersch, L., Wong, A., & Neher, A. (2024b). Digital transformation of work: Swiss MSEs working from home behaviour during COVID-19 – pioneers leading the pack. *European Business Review, 36*(2), 249–70.

Rancord Society. (2021). *Spotify's organizational culture & strategic considerations*, www.rancord.org/spotify-organizational-culture-strategic-cultural-characteristics (accessed 17 February 2025).

Sambamurthy, V., Bharadwaj, A., & Grover, V. (2003). Shaping agility through digital options: reconceptualizing the role of information technology in contemporary firms. *MIS Quarterly, 27*(2), 237–63.

Schein, E.H. (2010). *Organisational Culture and Leadership*, 4th ed., Jossey-Bass, San Francisco, CA.

Spotify. (2025a). About Spotify, https://newsroom.spotify.com/company-info/ (accessed 17 February 2025).

Spotify. (2025b). Work isn't somewhere you go, it's something you do, www lifeatspotify.com/being-here/work-from-anywhere (accessed 17 February 2025).

Spotify. (2025c). Here at Spotify, we like to think of ourselves as a band, www.lifeatspotify.com/being-here/the-band-manifesto (accessed 17 February 2025).

Tigre, F. B., Curado, C., & Henriques, P. L. (2023). Digital leadership: A bibliometric analysis. *Journal of Leadership & Organizational Studies*, *30*(1), 40–70.

Van Laar, E., Van Deursen, A. J., Van Dijk, J. A., & De Haan, J. (2017). The relation between 21st-century skills and digital skills: A systematic literature review. *Computers in Human Behavior*, *72*, 577–88.

Vial, G. (2019). Understanding digital transformation: A review and a research Agenda. *Journal of Strategic Information Systems*, *28*, 118–44.

Warner, K. S., & Wäger, M. (2019). Building dynamic capabilities for digital transformation: An ongoing process of strategic renewal. *Long Range Planning*, *52*(3), 326–49.

Wei, Y., Zhu, M., Lam, H. K., Liu, F., Yeung, A. C., Cheng, T. C. E., & Zhou, H (2024). Protagonists in digital transformation: the impact of chief digital officers on firms' financial performance. *Journal of Industrial Information Integration*, *41*, 100678.

Wilson, A. M. (2001). Understanding organisational culture and the implications for corporate marketing. *European Journal of Marketing*, *35*(3/4), 353–67.

Wuersch, L., Neher, A., & Peter, M. K. (2023). Digital internal communication: an interplay of socio-technical elements. *International Journal of Management Reviews*, *25*(3), 614–39.

Wuersch, L., Neher, A., Maley, J. F., & Peter, M. K. (2024). Using a digital internal communication strategy for digital capability development. *International Journal of Strategic Communication*, *18*(3), 167–88.

Yahoo Finance. (2024). Spotify's HR chief says remote staff aren't 'children' as company reaffirms work-from-anywhere policy, https://finance.yahoo.com/news/spotify-hr-chief-says-remote-100021103.html, 8 October.

Yahoo Finance. (2025). Spotify Technology S.A. (SPOT), https://finance.yahoo com/quote/SPOT/profile/ (accessed 17 February 2025).

Zoppelletto, A., Orlandi, L. B., Zardini, A., Rossignoli, C., & Kraus, S. (2023). Organizational roles in the context of digital transformation: A micro-level perspective. *Journal of Business Research*, *157*, 113563.

10
STRATEGIC ACTION FIELD OF DIGITAL MARKETING

Learning Goals

By the end of this chapter, you should...

- Be able to apply the marketing and sales funnel as a basis to manage and analyse customer flows and metrics for lead/revenue generation.
- Be able to describe the challenges and benefits, as well as project steps, of pursuing marketing automation.
- Be able to explain how specific digital technologies contribute to digital marketing strategies over time.
- Be able to critically evaluate a firm's digital marketing strategy across the four areas of technology platforms, digital marketing technology, digital marketing channels and digital marketing competencies.
- Be able to identify the value of content marketing and online communities, and apply the content marketing framework to a business.
- Be able to discuss and define opportunities for Web 3.0 digital marketing technologies.

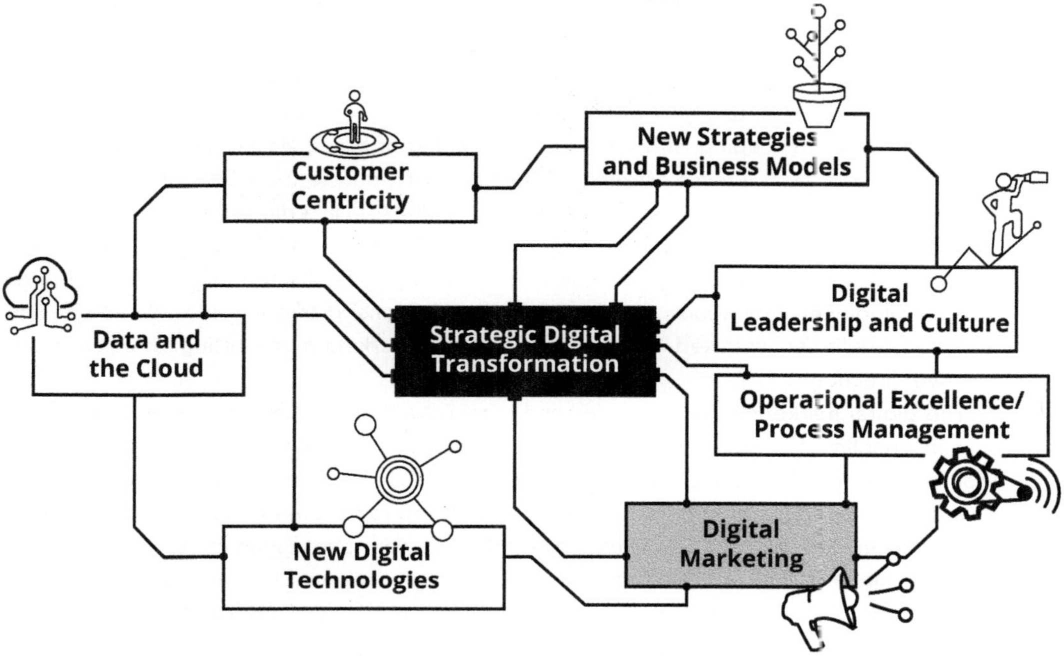

Figure 10.1 Digital marketing is the seventh Strategic Action Field of Digital Transformation

Source: Peter (2017, 2021, 2023, 2024); Peter et al. (2020)

Ryan Reynolds' Multi-Brand Social Media Marketing Strategy on X

Ryan Reynolds (2024) is a part-time actor and business owner who has emerged as one of the most effective digital marketers on social media with an ability to leverage his celebrity status and networks to generate attention for his brands. The digital marketing strategy for the five main profiles established by Reynolds on the social media platform X (formerly Twitter) reflects different combinations of a limited number of main building blocks, namely (1) accessible celebrity, (2) humour, (3) influencer marketing, (4) brand partnering and (5) product placement. Ryan Reynolds X profile identifies his ownership of Aviation American Gin (https://x.com/aviationgin), Mint Mobile (https://x.com/MintMobile), Maximum Effort (https://x.com/maximumeffort), and Wrexham AFC (https://x.com/Wrexham_AFC). His final domain of activity is his acting career and the related promotion of these activities on his personal (https://x.com/VancityReynolds) and Maximum Effort X profiles.

Maximum Effort (2024a) is a social media advertising venture: 'Maximum Effort makes movies, TV series, content, ads, and cocktails for the personal amusement of Hollywood Star Ryan Reynolds. We occasionally release them to the general public.' There is little to no

(Continued)

further information about Maximum Effort on their website or X profile. The Audiovisual Identity Database (2024) describes the firm as 'a film production company and digital marketing agency founded by Ryan Reynolds and former senior vice president of digital marketing at 20th Century Fox and president of digital marketing at Annapurna Pictures, George Dewey'. In keeping with the active leveraging of brand alliances in his social media marketing strategy, the name Maximum Effort is a catchphrase from *Deadpool*, a character now synonymous with Reynolds. Maximum Effort's (2024b) LinkedIn profile shows 118 associated members employed by the firm, mostly in the USA, primarily in Los Angeles and New York, but also in India and Canada. The human resources of the firm are focused on business development, operations, media and communications, marketing and arts and design, and digital skills concentrated on social media, digital marketing, marketing, advertising and creative direction.

The digital marketing competencies and resources of Maximum Effort play a significant role in enabling the social media marketing strategies for Aviation American Gin, Mint Mobile, Maximum Effort and Wrexham AFC. Mint Mobile content primarily focuses on Ryan Reynolds on screen, and adopts a comedic tone to promote the mobile service. The social media content for Aviation Gin uses a product placement strategy in comedic sketches by Reynolds alone or with other celebrities, such as Hugh Jackman. Interestingly the X profile requires acceptance as a follower to gain access to the content, due to age restrictions on drinking alcohol, which has the added benefit of serving as a potential start for a customer funnel (see box below) on X. The social media content for promoting Wrexham AFC, a football club in Wales (UK), is focused on community building; the X profile mostly includes content about the club and its fans and players. Finally, reflecting the work of Kupfer et al. (2018), Reynolds pursues a brand alliance strategy for promoting films he plays in on his personal X profile. The most recent campaign actively involved his friend and co-star Hugh Jackman from the films *Deadpool* and *Wolverine*, with the personal brands and the Marvel Studios characters forming a powerful 'brand alliance' that produced a very powerful social media marketing impact.

Notes: All social media facts and figures for the X profiles were correct at the time of writing this case study in December 2024.

10.0 INTRODUCTION

The first six strategic action fields (SAF) of digital transformation primarily addressed the impact of digital technologies on firms and the socio-technical systems they are embedded in, and how this requires a strategic response from firms. This chapter on digital transformation is the second of two chapters focused on the relationship of firms with their two primary human stakeholders, namely employees (Chapter 9 on digital culture and leadership), and the market/customers (digital marketing in this chapter). Digital marketing focuses on how firms communicate with customers to generate sales in alignment with one or more generic value creation strategy; customer centricity (see Chapter 4), product/service competitive leadership (see Chapter 7), and operational excellence (see Chapter 8). Digital marketing is fundamentally concerned with understanding the opportunities and challenges that digital technologies create for communicating value propositions and capturing value through sales (Meyer & Peter, 2024).

10.1 DIGITAL MARKETING TOOLKIT

Digital marketing is focused on 'grabbing customers' attention, securing patronage, and ultimately, loyalty' (Plangger et al., 2022, p. 1125) of current and potential customers over new channels enabled by digital technologies (Peter, 2024). Digital marketing thus reflects traditional marketing activities, but digital technologies do not only create new channels for engaging customers, but they also create new capabilities, through the inherent data generation capability of digital technologies (see discussion of the data economy in Chapter 6 on customer centricity), thereby ensuring that firms are present at critical customer touchpoints. Digital technologies generate data about customer behaviour along the customer journey in a manner that allows unprecedented insights about customer preferences and behaviour. Digital technologies through the data they generate about customer behaviour over digital and ideally traditional channels enable unprecedented tracking of customers, thereby enabling truly multi- or even omni-channel customer relationship management (Peter, 2024). This is true for both consumers and business customers. Figure 10.3 provides a representation of the complex relationship between technology platforms (e.g., desktop and laptop PCs/mobile devices), the channels that are made possible by those platforms (e.g., websites, email, social media), and the capabilities and activities that digital marketeers must master (e.g., search engine optimisation (SEO) of websites, digital advertising via search engine advertising (SEA), content or affiliate marketing). Critically, it is important to remember that the specific way that a firm will employ the different options made available by digital channels will be determined by the value creating strategy of the firm. A central management tool of digital marketing is the marketing and sales funnel (see Box 10.1). Chapter 10.1 with its four sub-sections (1–4) will be summarised in Figure 10.7 later in the chapter.

Box 10.1: Marketing and Sales Funnel

Marketing and sales funnels are models that represent the customer journey from initial awareness to purchase. They serve different purposes and focus on distinct stages of the buyer's process. While often combined, they can also be utilised separately. The marketing funnel guides potential customers through stages of brand awareness to consideration. Often, the return on marketing investment (ROMI) is measured by the number of generated marketing qualified leads (MQLs). The sales funnel focuses on converting qualified prospects, often referred to as sales qualified leads (SQLs) into customers. The objective of marketing teams is to constantly monitor and improve the funnel, and the conversation rates (CRs) from one step to the other, as even small CR improvements will deliver additional revenue and profit to the organisation (Colicev et al., 2019; Wiraguna & Aulia, 2024.

(Continued)

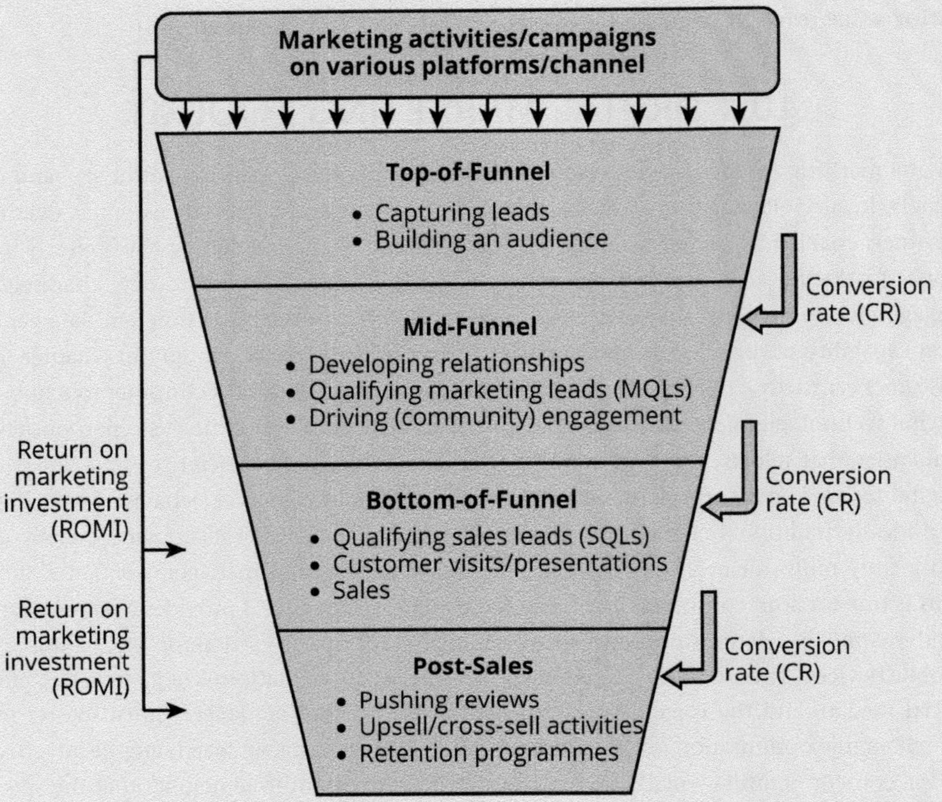

Figure 10.2 Marketing and sales funnel

Source: own illustration following Colicev et al. (2019) and Wiraguna & Aulia (2024)

10.1.1 Technology Platforms

All digital marketing channels are accessed over an information technology hardware platform (e.g., mobile device or personal computer), each with unique characteristics and as a result optimal use cases. In Table 10.1, an emphasis is placed on the degree of mobility of the hardware platform, but other characteristics such as cost, internet connectivity, application availability, screen size, data storage, and data processing capacity are also other relevant attributes. Table 9.1 provides insights about consumer preferences in major EU markets for ICT device attribute-ranked preferences, showing the clear importance of hardware attributes, but with device price consistently being ranked as the first or second most important consideration. Interestingly three of the five devices that were addressed in the survey are mobile devices (laptops, smartphones, and tablets), followed by smart TVs and gaming consoles, reflecting the importance of the television as one of the main stationary consumer electronic devices in European homes for consuming media. The expected lifetime and energy label class are the most important sustainability related attributes EU consumers consider, followed by ease of repair and availability of replacement parts. The device preferences of consumers/customers of firms set technical boundary conditions for the digital channels available to firms for their digital marketing activities.

Table 10.1 European consumer ranking of device attribute importances

Device Attribute	Laptop PC	Smartphone	Tablet	Smart TV	Gaming Console
Price	2	1	1	1	1
Hardware performance / processing speed	1	6	2	–	2
Expected lifetime	3	3	4	3	3
Battery life	5	2	5	–	–
Internet connection quality/speed	4	5	3	6	4
Storage space	–	4	–	–	–
Camera	–	7	–	–	–
Media platform/ apps availability	–	–	–	–	5
Energy label class	–	–	–	5	–
Screen resolution/ quality	6	8	6	2	–
Screen size	8	9	7	4	–
Interoperability	7	11	–	7	–
Customer care	9	13	10	8	8
Ease to repair / replacement parts	10	12	9	10	7
Knowledge about manufacturer/device	11	10	8	9	6
Size/weight	12	14	11	–	–

Source: adaptation of Ipsos (2022, Table 1.2)

Note: ranking with descends in importance from 1 = most important.

10.1.2 Digital Marketing Technology

Important digital marketing technologies, in addition to customer analytics (see Chapter 10.3) are e-commerce and marketing automation (Dalla Vecchia & Peter, 2018; Peter & Dalla Vecchia, 2021).

E-commerce refers to the infrastructure to build and operate a digital marketplace, which allows businesses and consumers to conduct transactions without the need for physical stores. E-commerce encompasses a wide range of activities, including online retail (B2C), business-to-business (B2B) transactions, and consumer-to-consumer (C2C) sales through peer-to-peer platforms (see Chapter 7). The integration of secure payment gateways, efficient logistics, and customer service has further enhanced the user experience, making online shopping an important technology and go-to-market channel for businesses.

Marketing automation involves the use of software and technology to streamline, automate, and measure marketing tasks and workflows. This approach aims to increase operational efficiency and grow revenue faster by automating repetitive tasks such as email marketing, social media posting, and ad campaigns, thus optimising the marketing and sales funnel (see Box 10.1). According to Dalla Vecchia and Peter (2018), marketing automation projects can be structured into ten steps:

1 Define the marketing automation strategy and project goals.
2 Analyse the customer journey to identify automation opportunities.
3 Define the use cases and customer scenarios for automation (process flows).
4 Define customer segmentation and data management frameworks.
5 Identify and define how to analyse customer data for automation (predictive) intelligence.
6 Evaluate content marketing gaps for automation and define the content marketing strategy.
7 Define the channels that shall be connected to the marketing automation platform (channel management).
8 Define the requirements for analytics, reporting and dashboards.
9 Identify the necessary resources and technical infrastructure.

Marketing automation tools help businesses segment their audience, personalise communications, and track customer interactions across multiple channels. The convergence of e-commerce and marketing automation, namely e-commerce automation (Peter et al., 2025), will provide the benefits of automation on e-commerce platforms. By leveraging data analytics, marketing automation provides insights into customer behaviour, enabling marketers to create targeted campaigns that resonate with their audience and optimise conversation rates (CRs) from leads to marketing and sales qualified leads (MQLs/SQLs), to customers and upsell and cross campaigns to increase the customer life-time value (CLV).

10.1.3 Digital Marketing Channels

Digital marketing channels include firms' own websites, social media, emails, search engines, etc. (Peter, 2024; Peter & Dalla Vecchia, 2021). See Figure 10.3 for an overview of the platform, channel, and digital marketing matrix for the Web 1.0 (from the beginning of the Internet until the early 2000s) and Web 2.0 (from about 2005; the beginning of the fourth industrial revolution and still in practice today) eras. Figure 10.4 shows the continuing importance of the channels in Figure 10.3, but also highlights the dominance of seven systemically important

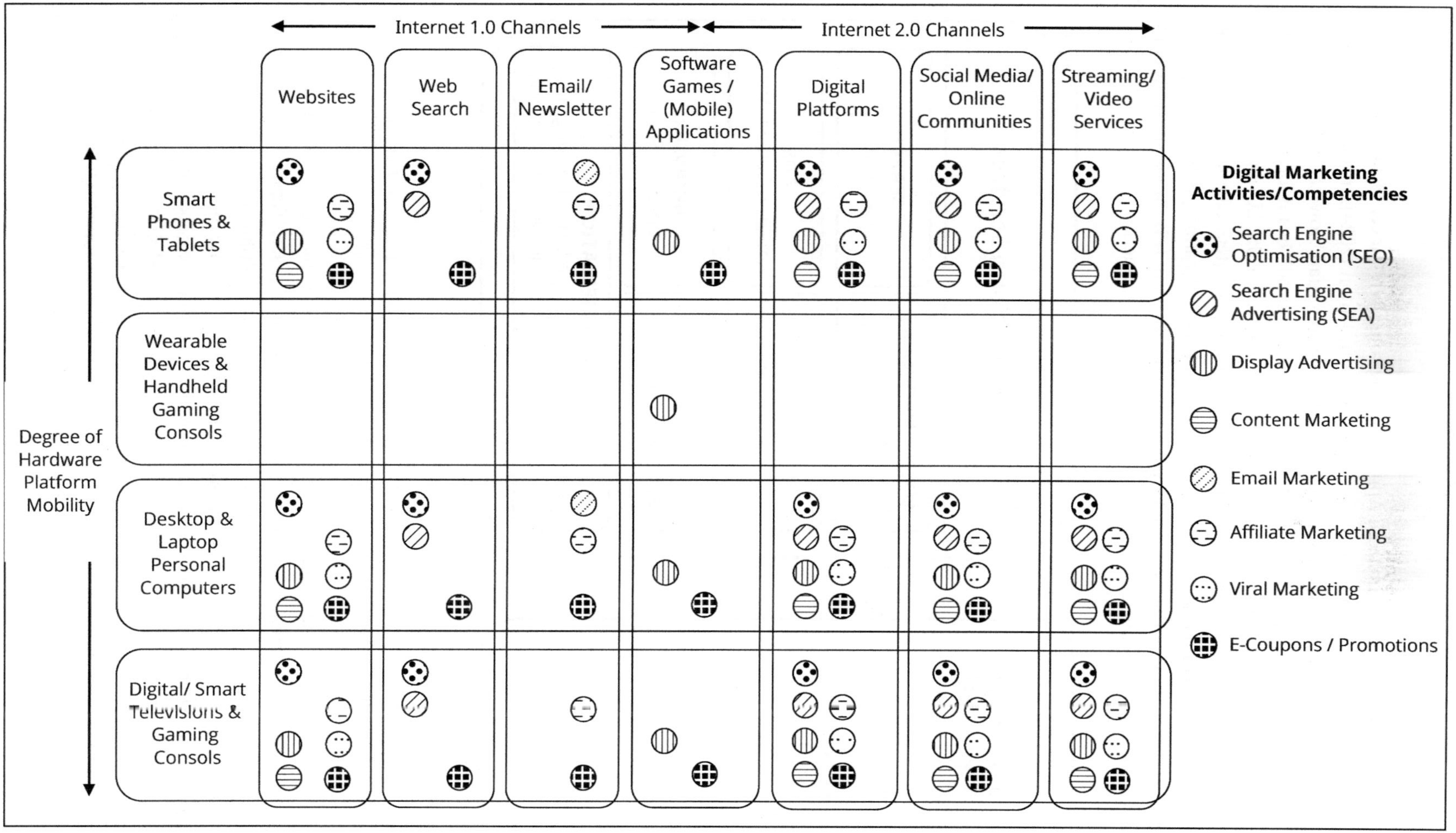

Figure 10.3 Digital marketing platform, channel and competencies matrix for internet (web) 1.0 and 2.0

Source: adapted from Peter (2023, 2024) and Peter & Dalla Vecchia (2021)

gatekeeper firms (Alphabet, Amazon, Apple, Booking.com, ByteDance, Meta, and Microsoft) for accessing digital marketing channels in the European Union (2024). In the EU, company websites can be expected to be accessed over the Chrome and Safari browsers, although outside the EU, Microsoft Internet Explorer or Edge are highly likely to still be important. It is interesting to note that email is not included as a channel related to the EU digital market. The importance of web search, digital advertising, digital platforms (intermediation), mobile application marketplaces (intermediation), social media, and video/streaming services is recognised in the EU designation of digital market gatekeepers (Figure 10.4). It is important to note that search is an important functionality within all these digital channels.

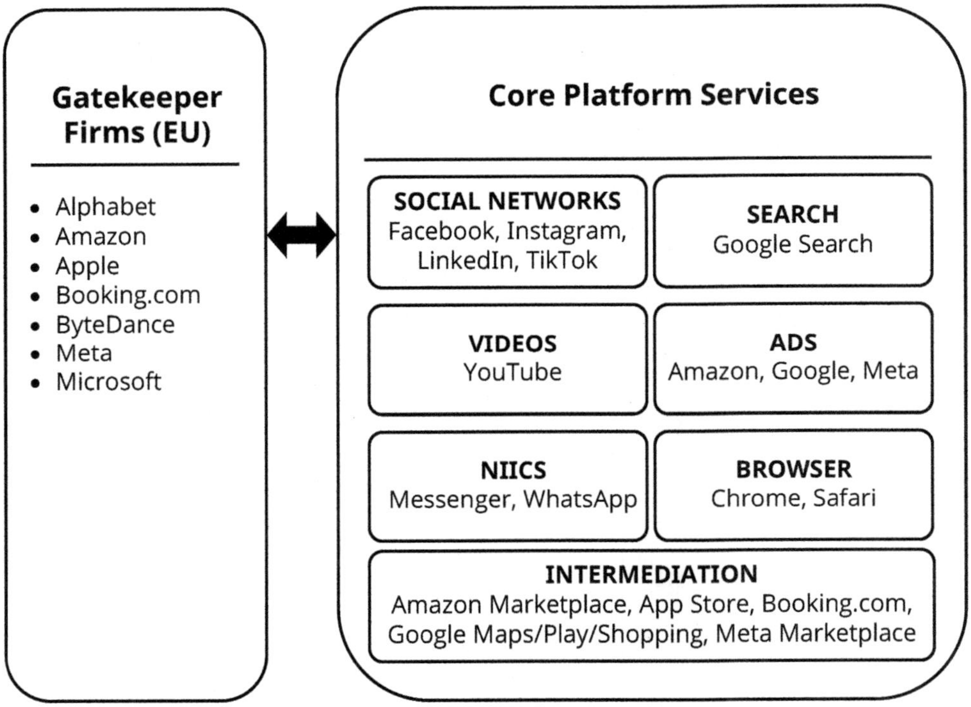

Figure 10.4 Gatekeeper firms and platform services

Note: NIICS stands for 'Number Independent Interpersonal Communications Services'.
Source: own illustration following European Commission (2024)

It is challenging to find usage data for all digital marketing channels across multiple markets. The EU has comprehensive data for enterprise website use (see Figure 10.5), and social media use (see Figure 10.6). The data shows that for both websites and social media, use increases with the size of the firm, with larger firms more likely to use these channels. The most important uses of enterprise websites for all firms is to describe the goods or services they provide. Other relevant digital marketing uses of enterprise websites include ordering or reservations (22% of all firms), tracking orders (10%), chat service for customer service (9%), personalised content for recurrent visitors (8%), and product or service customisation (8%). Enterprises using social media (61% of all EU firms, see Figure 10.5) focus on social networks

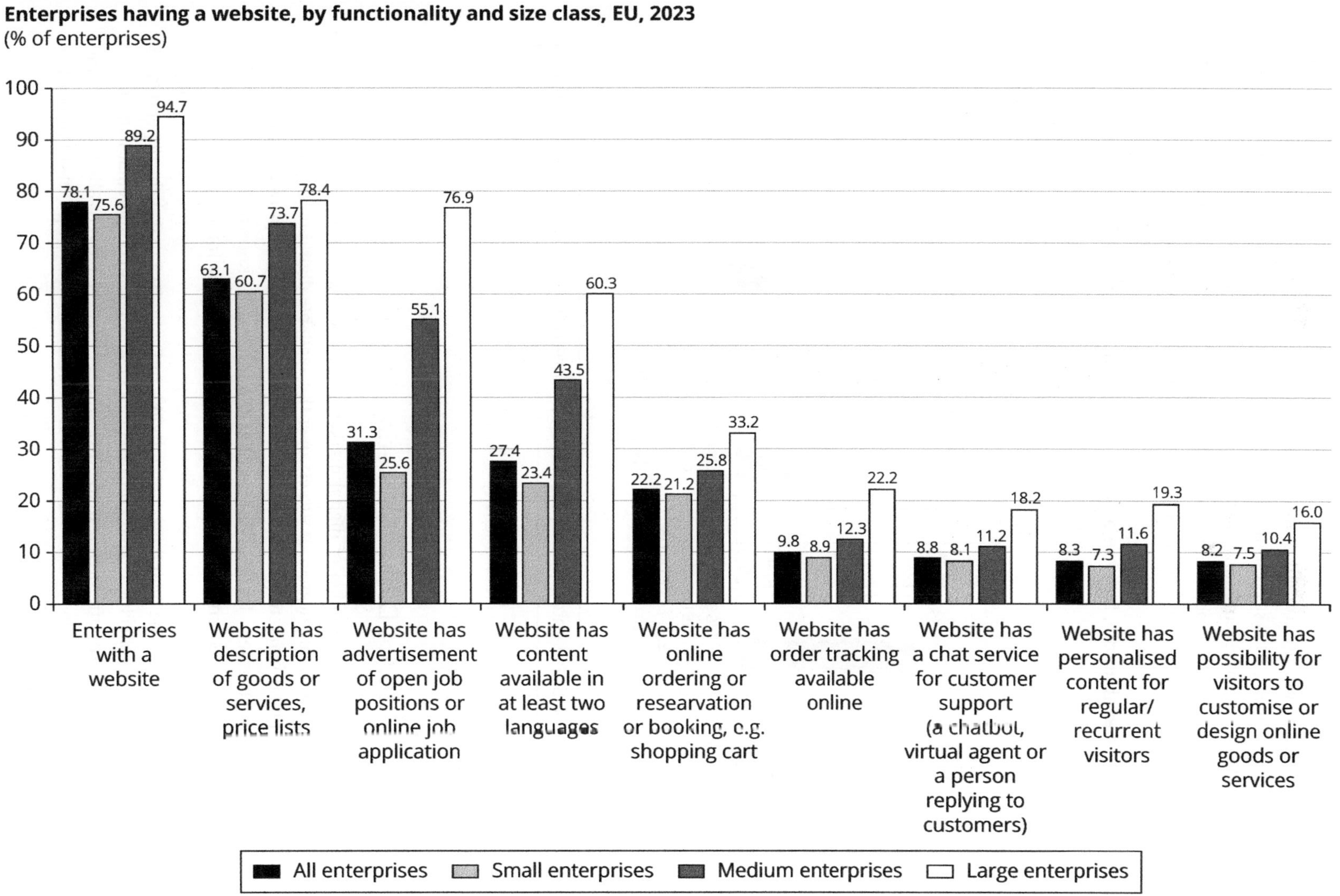

Figure 10.5 EU enterprise digital marketing activity (websites)

Source: Eurostat (2024; isoc_ciweb)

(59%), but only a third use content sharing channels (32%) and only 10% of all EU firms use blogs or microblogging. This suggests that enterprise websites in the EU are predominantly still focused on Web 1.0 implementations, with large firms more likely to have migrated to websites that incorporate Web 2.0 functionality. The most important Web 2.0 channel is likely to be social media networks, although it cannot be definitively confirmed from this data.

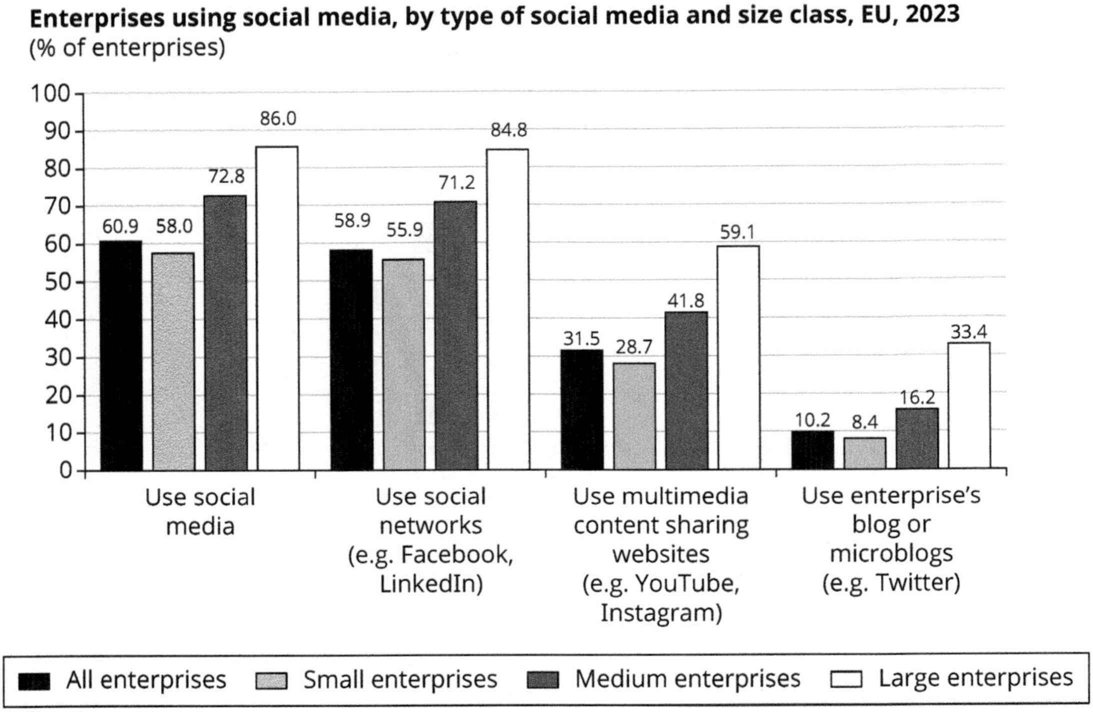

Figure 10.6 EU Enterprise digital marketing activity (social media)

Source: Eurostat (2024; isoc_ciweb)

10.1.4 Digital Marketing Competencies

There is an ever-growing number of digital marketing competencies and activities that can be employed with differing degrees of success over the available digital marketing channels; that is, not all digital marketing competencies can be equally well employed via all of the digital marketing channels. Eight of the most common or well-known digital marketing competencies are included on the right side of Figure 10.3, but it is important to remember that this set of competencies is by no means a comprehensive list of the available digital marketing competencies. The digital marketing toolkit in Figure 10.7 makes the dependences for the development of specific digital competencies clear, digital competencies should be developed to enable a specific digital marketing strategy that is actively aligned with the overall value creation strategy of the firm. Below is an overview of the eight most important digital marketing competencies/activities (as per Figure 10.3):

1 Search engine optimisation (SEO)

Search engine optimisation (SEO) recognises the importance for companies of being findable online and that web search engines / services like Google Search, Bing, Yahoo, Yandex Search, or Baidu, make websites findable in specific ways (sometimes also called organic or natural search). It is a free source of engagement with a company's online presence, including the products it offers. Given the knowledge about how search online functions, SEO seeks to optimise the displayed content and metadata of websites to improve the chances of the site being recognised as relevant in the search process. Techniques for doing so include identifying keywords for specific searches, often identified by specialised tools or services, and then building these keywords into the displayed data and metadata of the website. This approach can be extended by using the identification of keywords for a company product portfolio and then creating content for these keywords, to serve customers with content they are likely to be interested in consuming. SEO is increasingly also focused on the richness of the content and online community building (see Box 10.2 and 10.3). For SEO, the traditional success criteria of for example, keywords, link building, etc. are still relevant, but other criteria such as social media presence/community building, and the richness and value of the content, have most recently become more important criteria. SEO algorithm updates are such changes in SEO criteria, made by search engines, like Google, to their algorithms, which are the complex systems used to retrieve data from their search index and deliver the best possible results for a query. It is important for marketers to understand the most important changes to algorithms to update their SEO strategies and tactics.

2 Search engine advertising (SEA)

Search engine advertising (SEA), sometimes also called paid search, has evolved to be a critical digital marketing tool. SEA relies on paid advertising to customers that insert specific keywords or combinations of keywords into a search query (Peter, 2024). Digital marketers essentially pay for their website to be linked to specific keywords or combinations of keywords. The cost of buying specific keywords is determined by the degree to which they are used in searches and other digital marketers are also seeking to buy those keywords, mostly in the form of an auction (Peter, 2024). In Western digital markets / online activity, the access to SEA is dominated by the near monopoly of Google Search and Google Ads. While more expensive than SEO (organic/natural search), SEA represents an important digital marketing competence. SEO and SEA are often summarised as SEM (search engine marketing).

3 Display advertising

Online display advertising is made possible by an ecosystem of three types of players, guaranteed and non-guaranteed digital channels and the characteristics of the two-sided display ad market (Choi et al., 2020). The two-sided digital display advertising market is facilitated by intermediaries, such as Facebook Ads and Google Ads Display Network. These services provide a market for advertisers seeking digital advertising impressions on a range of digital

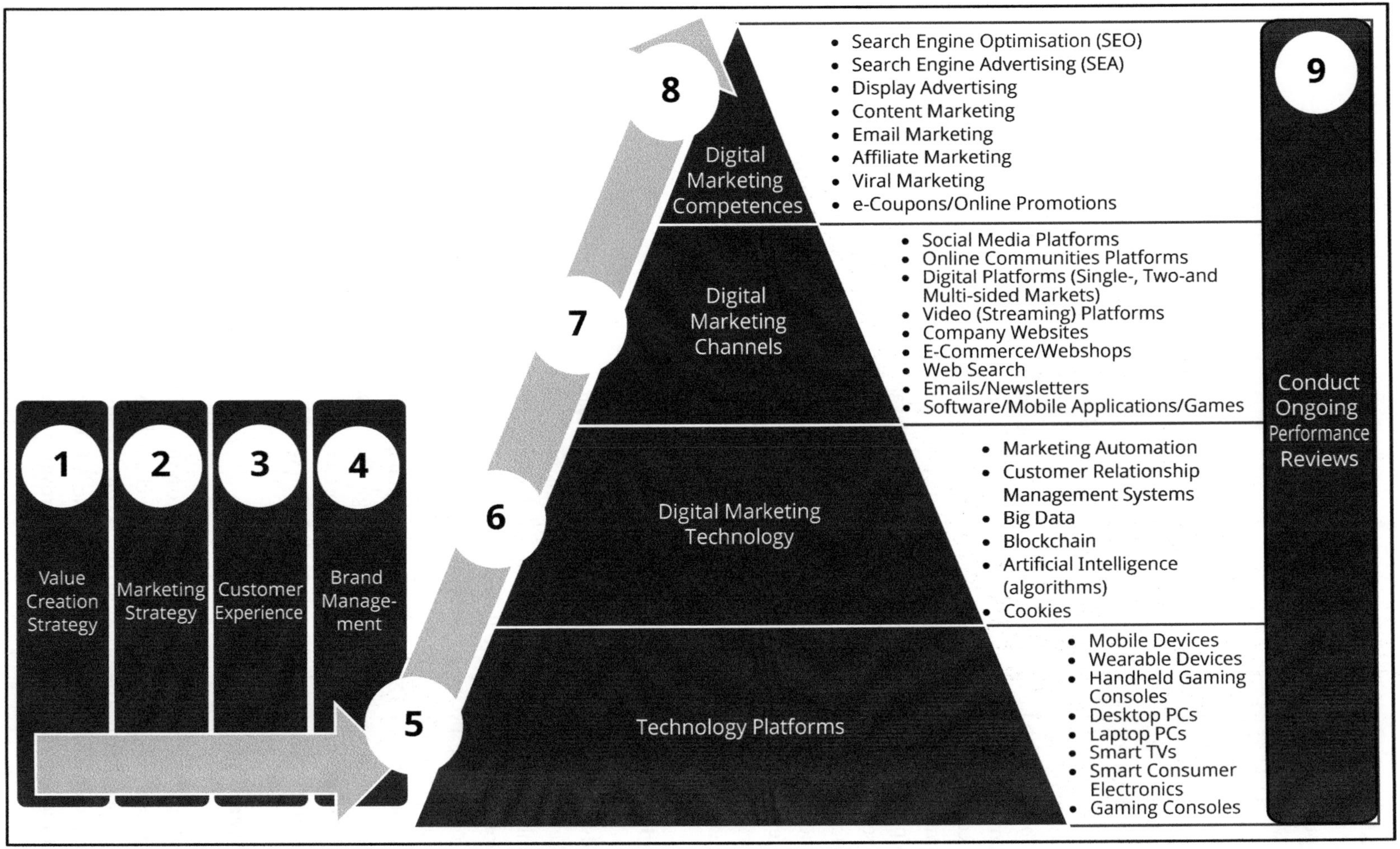

Figure 10.7 The development of a digital marketing strategy requires that a firm first establish a clear (1) value creation strategy and (2) overarching marketing strategy that reflects this strategy. This allows an intended (3) customer experience to be established and purposeful (4) brand management to be executed across all channels. The digital strategy can then be tailored to align with this strategic orientation, in terms of the selection of preferred (5) hardware platforms, the (6) digital technologies that are to be adopted, across (7) selected digital marketing channels. These choices result in a set of (8) digital marketing competences that the firm and its employees need to develop. Finally, the firm should actively (9) conduct performance reviews.

Source: adapted from Peter (2023, 2024) and Peter & Dalla Vecchia (2021)

channels, including websites, social media, video streaming, etc., these represent the advertising publishers. The digital advertising publishers may be owned by the same company as the intermediaries making the market, but they serve a different function, their role is to offer advertisers impressions of digital advertising to users of a website, social media platform, or video streaming platform for a given price. The more demand there is for reaching a specific customer segment the more expensive the cost per impression for the digital advertisement impression. The digital advertising channels are distinguished by guaranteed selling (direct sales), where a specific number of impressions of an advertisement are contractually agreed between advertiser and publisher, specifying when, where, and how an advert will be displayed for a fixed price (the Cost per Mill – *mill* stands for 1000 – of impressions, or CPM). Non-guaranteed selling involves buying and selling digital advertising impressions in real time (real-time buying or RTB). There is a unique ecosystem of intermediaries enabling this exchange, including DoubleClick Ad Exchange and OpenX (Choi et al., 2020). These intermediaries typically rely on auctions for making a market for digital impressions, and the digital marketer needs to assess the value of these impressions in relation to customer and competitor behaviour. As will be clear, regardless of the channels used, digital marketers require excellent customer data if they are to effectively use digital display advertising.

4 Content marketing

Ho et al. (2020) explain that the goal of a content marketing strategy should be a 'strategic marketing approach for creating and distributing valuable, consistent and relevant content to attract and retain' customers across a multitude of platforms to 'deliver engaging relationships, consumer value and measurable success for brands' (Content Marketing Association, 2017). Digital content marketing pursues these goals via digital marketing channels, using a variety of digital content types, including textual, visual, and audiovisual content; as such content marketing may be combined with email marketing for example or as part of the sharing of video content on social media platforms. Box 10.2 provides a framework for executing digital content marketing strategies.

Box 10.2: Content Marketing Framework

As it has become increasingly challenging to gain and maintain attention on digital channels, content marketing has emerged as a very effective means for engaging customers with relevant content. It is critically important to understand that digital content marketing strategies are entirely customer-centric when executed well, they deliver valuable content to the right customer at the time the customer needs that information. This creates value for the customer, building the customer relationship with the brand/firm. The goal should be to provide content to customers that answers their questions or solves problems they may be having at a particular point

(Continued)

in the customer lifecycle for the firm's products and/or services. Content marketing is not easy or low effort; it requires careful planning and execution to be effective. The process is visualised in Figure 10.8.

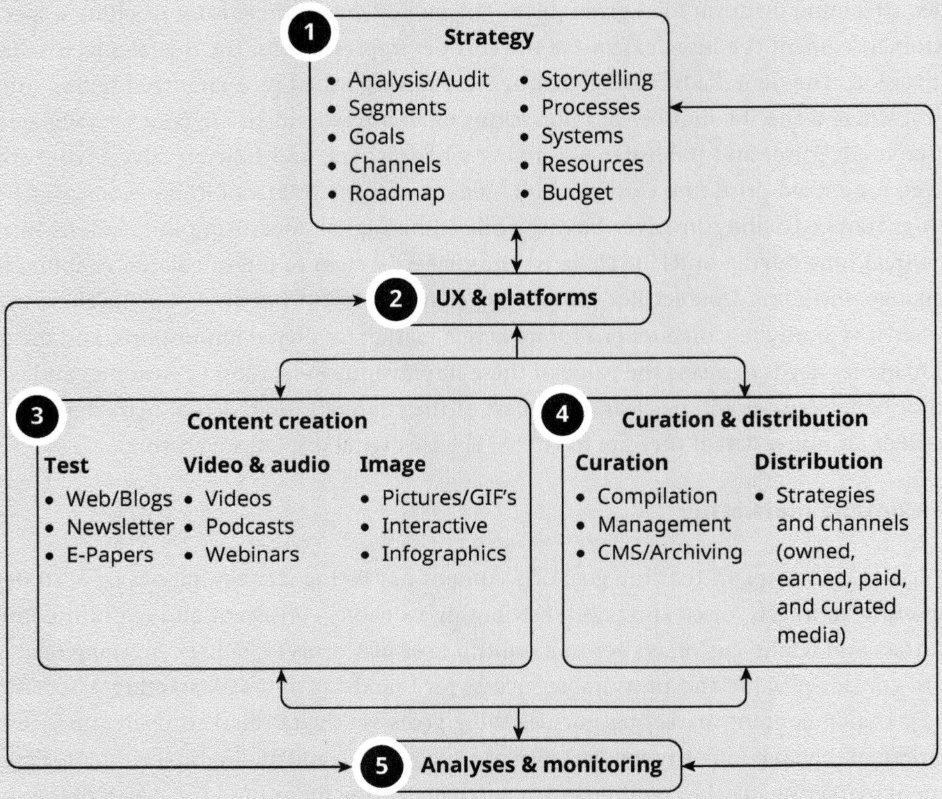

Figure 10.8 Content marketing framework

Source: Peter (2023, 2024)

The content marketing framework consists of five steps: phase 1 is the content marketing strategy, incorporating e.g., a content audit and the definition of the content/storytelling approach, as well as the required resources, followed by phase 2 which is defined as served/managed digital platforms/channels (e.g., the social media websites which the firm wants to use). Phase 3 focuses on the content creation via different formats, and phase 4 will manage/curate the content, and distribute it via, e.g., marketing automation infrastructure (or manually in smaller firms). Finally, phase 5 will analyse the success of the content marketing activities, for instance aligned to the marketing and sales funnel of the organisation (see Figure 10.2).

Content marketing strategies require customer segmentation to allow clear customer needs and goals to be identified. This then allows a communication roadmap to be developed, which supports storytelling, thereby activating customer emotions. If the story is carefully designed to suit specific digital channels, the customer will perceive the firm positively and develop trust in the firm. The format and style of the content must be tailored to the digital channels being used if the storytelling is to be effective and the distribution of this content should be guided by the communication plan that is aligned with the overall roadmap for the marketing strategy. Finally, the firm should actively leverage the data generating potential of the digital channels to develop deeper understanding of their customers' behaviour, allowing positive feedback loops that enable more effective future content marketing initiatives.

Source: Peter (2024)

5 Email marketing

Email marketing is arguably the oldest of the digital marketing competencies. Alex Souchoroukof (2020) summarises in a LinkedIn post how the first email campaign was sent by Gary Thuerk in May 1978 via Arpanet, the forerunner to the internet as we know it today, to 400 email addresses to promote DEC machines. Email marketing has evolved significantly since the late 1970s, not least because of the extensive efforts to reduce spam (unwanted, unsolicited and often criminal bulk) email since the early 2000s (Carmi, 2017).

The result today is an understanding of effective email marketing as a one-to-many and/or one-to-one email communication sending messages to customers (B2B or B2C) that can serve a variety of purposes. Email marketing is effective in directing customers to content and also advertising, for example, as well as serving to build customer relationships by providing value to customers in other ways. Email is highly effective due to its platform/software independence and its ability to reach customers at local, national, regional or even global scales almost instantaneously. At the same time the increasing implementation of technologies to prevent spam emails and also the increasing regulatory emphasis on customer privacy rights can affect the reach of email marketing.

Today, email marketing, whether automated (via marketing automation) or not, is most effective when customers have granted permission to contact them (in some countries, there is a legal requirement for a 'double opt-in', where users first have to register for emails, and then confirm again that they indeed want emails from the organisation), the content sent to customers is personalised to some degree and provides the customer with value regardless of whether the email leads to a sale. This is made possible by the increasing sophisticated marketing automation tools and emerging artificial intelligence tools available to digital marketers for executing email marketing campaigns.

6 Affiliate marketing

Affiliate marketing is a digital marketing competence that relies on partnerships with other organisations/websites to increase the reach of a company's marketing coverage. These relationships can be of a very transactional nature or highly personal and aligned partnerships. Amazon for example has a highly automated online process for becoming an affiliated marketer of products on its site, with online influencers often marketing products they use or promote by including affiliate links in their content and then earning income from any sales that occur via the links to products on the Amazon site. Social media influencers will often promote products or services; they may be paid to do so a specific number of times or earn a commission on any sales that result from their promotion of the products or services.

7 Viral marketing

Viral marketing seeks to take advantage of content sharing that is made especially easy with digital content on social media platforms, but email is also suitable for viral sharing (Peter & Dalla Vecchia, 2021). Viral marketing is similar to word-of-mouth communication (Bampo et al., 2008), but it takes place in a digital environment and thus seeks to initiate/encourage the sharing of content in such a manner that the potential for exponential distribution of the content is possible. Viral marketing when realised is highly attractive as there is an inherent natural selection of the recipients of the content being shared, leading to more targeted communication, with a very high speed of diffusion and higher likelihood of content integrity, while the conversion rate for content with a call to action is likely to be much higher than with mass communication. The effectiveness of a viral marketing strategy is dependent on the 'the social structure of the digital network through which the message is propagated, the behavioural characteristics of its members that facilitate the propagation of the message, and a seeding strategy that initiates the process' (Bampo et al., 2008, p. 274). While content may unexpectedly go viral on social media platforms after 'hitting a nerve', digital marketing managers responsible for viral marketing campaigns must create the content for the viral campaign, seed this content into a social network, and then activate this network to share the intended viral content.

8 E-coupons / promotions marketing

The use of electronic coupons (e-coupons) and promotional marketing online is unlikely to be one of the first digital marketing competencies to come to mind if asked what digital marketing involves, none-the-less this longstanding marketing tactic also has an important place in the digital marketing competencies of an effective digital marketing manager. More specifically e-coupons can be issued by a merchant to attract new customers and/or encourage repeat purchase with existing customers by offering a benefit, which may be a volume or monetary benefit (e.g., a discount). E-coupons are distinguished from traditional paper coupons by all 'processing (e.g., issuing, distributing, and redeeming) being done electronically (Ferrer-Gomila et al., 2018). Effective promotional marketing using e-coupons requires excellent consumer segmentation, as there is clear evidence that consumers differ significantly in their purchasing behaviour with e-coupons (Ren et al., 2021). At the same time e-coupons are still faced by challenges related to consumer privacy and security concerns related to the issuing and redemption of e-coupons (Ferrer-Gomila et al., 2018).

10.2 COMPANY WEBSITE AND SOCIAL MEDIA

Important channels on the internet (web) 1.0 and 2.0 are both company websites as well as social media platforms (see Figure 10.3), next to other channels including portals, emails, mobile apps such as games, digital platforms/intermediaries, and streaming/video apps/services.

10.2.1 Identity and Branding – Importance of Company Websites

A company website, whether still based on Internet 1.0 (Web 1.0) or ideally Internet 2.0 (Web 2.0) principles, remain a critical, even foundational, digital presence for a company in the digital age. The company website represents the online identity and brand of the company (Peter, 2024) and will often be the first digital point of contact with a customer or other stakeholders, allowing other digital channels to be found, but other digital channels will, also more often than not, lead customers and other stakeholders back to the main company website. While the branding on the website is largely in the hands of the company, the opportunity to present products and services is increasingly regulated in jurisdictions like the EU, and it is important for companies to ensure that all product offerings online are communicated in such a manner that they are compliant with applicable regulations for digital/e-commerce activities. This compliance includes the product description and how pricing is communicated.

10.2.2 Marketing on Social Media

Social media platforms (e.g., Facebook, Instagram, LinkedIn, TikTok, YouTube, etc.) represent a very attractive digital marketing channel for companies, given the large number of users on the major platforms and the rich data available to the social media platform operators and their social media advertising solutions. Social media with its social networks and the deep data on users in those social networks is highly suited to targeted digital advertising and viral advertising campaigns. Social media, however, also represents a unique environment for companies to engage their stakeholders with content marketing campaigns, especially given the possibility for two-way communication between the company and its stakeholders (Peter, 2024), but requires a highly responsive engagement from companies that seek to engage stakeholders. This is especially the case when companies seek to build online communities via social media platforms (see Box 10.3). A company should choose the social media platforms to participate in carefully, as each has its unique strengths and weaknesses and unique form of social communities and norms of behaviour. These should match the identity and brand of a company. Not only organic content strategies and marketing campaigns are available to companies; there is also an opportunity for paid social media advertising and affiliate marketing via influencers or brand ambassadors, allowing targeted marketing.

Box 10.3: Community Building

Community building has emerged as a critical activity for companies in the digital age and is mostly associated with social media platforms. Indeed, on social media platforms the establishment of a community around a content creator's channel is essential for the commercial viability of the channel. Online communities are featured by free association. Members can freely join and leave the community, the two-way communication between members and a community founder(s). Often the community founders are a single or small group of content creators that through their work on a specific topic, theme, or issue attract others to join their community. There is no end to the variety and specific nature of online communities, but from the perspective of the digital transformation of a company, a digital community would be associated with the brand, products, or activities of a focal company. As such, establishing such a company / brand centric online community is going to be most interesting, to the stakeholders in that company, typically the customers, employees, and societal stakeholders of the company. It is critical to understand that the communities need to be maintained and developed with active effort and it should be expected that a company would need to make meaningful investments in the establishment and development of a company / brand centric online community. In return, the company can hope for stable and positive relationships with all its stakeholders as a result of deeper insights through exchange with the most motivated stakeholders. Customers and staff can also if desired be mobilised via the community to contribute to co-creation processes, which could lead to better product market fit and improved performance. Such communities are most likely to be built on channels like social media platforms or a company website.

Source: Peter (2024)

10.2.3 Additional Marketing Concepts

There is a range of other/additional marketing concepts and terms, which are covered here for completeness of the strategic action field of digital marketing (Peter, 2024; Peter & Niedermann, 2020):

- **A/B testing** refers to the activity of constantly improving performance ratios by testing various components of a campaign (such as email titles or images) as a version A or version B (in practice, more than two versions will normally be tested).
- **AI in digital marketing** uses artificial intelligence capabilities such as data collection, natural language processing, machine learning, and analytics to drive better business insights, and automate marketing tasks and decisions

- **AIO (AI Optimisation)** involves optimising content not just for traditional search engines like Google, but also for AI models like ChatGPT, Copilot, Gemini, and voice assistants like Alexa or Siri.
- **Ambassador marketing (also influencer marketing)** is a strategy where firms engage individuals who love their brand to act as representatives and promoters (called ambassadors, fans, or influencers).
- **Content distribution (or delivery) network** is a system of interconnected servers strategically located in different geographical regions. Its primary purpose is to deliver web content, such as images, videos, and other types of files, to users quickly, personalised, and efficiently.
- **Go-to-market (GTM)** plan is a document that summarises all (digital) marketing activities of the organisation. It includes a compendium of all campaigns, the definition of the platform/channel, target segments, goals/metrics, milestones, and budgets.
- **Marketing technology stack** (or 'martech stack') is a collection of technologies and tools used by marketers to plan, execute, analyse and optimise their marketing activities, including CRM (customer relationship management) software, content management systems (CMS), email marketing platforms, marketing automation technology, adverting platforms, social media management, and analytics tools.
- **Search generative experience (SGE)** is a search feature by Google that leverages generative artificial intelligence (AI) to enhance search results (since 2024).
- **Video Search Optimisation (VSO)** is the practice of improving the ranking and visibility of video content on search engines and platforms like YouTube.
- **Voice commerce** (or v-commerce) is a technology that enables customers to interact and make purchases using voice commands via voice-enabled devices, such as smart speakers (like Amazon Echo or Google Home) or virtual assistants (like Siri or Google Assistant).

10.3 DIGITAL MARKETING DATA ANALYTICS

There is a rapidly growing appreciation of the potential of artificial intelligence and machine learning (AI/ML) and data analytics for more efficient and effective digital marketing and promotion activities (Basu et al., 2024). The evidence for the positive impact of AI on customer relationship management (CRM), improving consumer experiences and boosting marketing efficiency across the marketing and sales funnel (see Figure 10.2) is growing. At the same time, it is clear that automation for e-commerce (see Section 10.1.2), customer engagement and building brand loyalty is increasingly being adopted, with AI playing an important enabling role. Machine-learning (ML) algorithms are also playing an important role in enabling optimise ecommerce activities, including customer quality management and pricing decisions. Personalisation of marketing efforts is supported by the adoption of artificial intelligence (AI), such as data analytics and algorithmic decision-making, for 'audience segmentation, personalized content delivery, customer behaviour prediction, and cross-channel marketing campaign optimisation' (Basu et al., 2024, p. 9). There is a plethora of terms associated with digital marketing analytics and metrics across various platforms and channels (see Box 10.4 for a selection).

All data analytic techniques are heavily reliant on high data quality and data analytics using digital technologies (see Chapter 6 for the related discussion to data quality). The effectiveness of the adoption of AI/ML approaches for digital marketing is, however, influenced by a range of internal and external factors, including internal management support (attitude towards) and understanding of the new technologies and external competitive pressures, perceived ease of use, perceived usefulness, and perceived benefits (see Chapter 5 for the theories on technology adoption).

Box 10.4: Digital Marketing Metrics

- **Bounce rate:** the number of users who visit the firm's website (or landing page) and then leave (or bounce) without clicking a link, filling out a form, or making a purchase.
- **Click-through rate (CTR):** the number of clicks a paid ad receives per impression (CTR = total clicks on ad : total impressions x 100).
- **Cost per acquisition (CPA):** it calculates the cost to secure a paying customer (which is a successfully converted lead).
- **Cost per click (CPC):** it calculates how much a firm paid when someone clicks on an add (CPC = ad/campaign cost : number of clicks).
- **Cost per lead (CPL):** it measures the cost to capture a lead, that will later be converted into MQLs and SQLs).
- **Cost per mille (CPM):** it calculates the cost a firm pays for every 1,000 impressions of their ad.
- **Conversion rate (CR):** the numerical percentage of users who complete a desired action (CR = number of conversions : total number of users x 100).
- **Customer lifetime value (CLV):** it calculates the amount a customer is most likely to spend during their lifetime with the firm.
- **Customer retention rate (CRR):** it measures the share of customers who return (following completed purchases) to the company to continue purchase products/services.
- **Exit rate:** similar to bounce rate, but the exit rate measures how many users have left a website from a specific page.
- **Marketing qualified leads (MQLs):** the number of leads who are interested in the firm's products/services, but have not yet made a purchase.
- **Page views:** it measures how many pages users have visited on the website.

- **Page views per session:** it measures how many pages a user visits in a single session (website visit).
- **Return on marketing investment (MROI):** it can be calculated as: ((number of leads x conversation rate to customers x average sales price) : cost for marketing) x 100.
- **Sales qualified leads (SQLs):** the number of leads who are vetted and deemed ready to complete a purchase.
- **Session (or visits):**
  - Direct visitors: users who access the website directly by typing the URL (website address) into the browser.
  - Organic visitors: users who access the website via an unpaid search engine traffic (organic/natural search via SEO).
  - Referred visitors: users who access the website from another site that links to the company's website.
  - Email visitors: users who access the website as the result of a marketing email.
  - Social media visitors: users who access the website via a social media platform.
  - Paid visitors: users who access the website as a result of paid ads (e.g., pay-per-click (PPC) advertising, display advertising, or social media ads).

Source: Extract from Adobe (2023)

10.4 WEB 3.0: DIGITAL MARKETING AND NOVEL DIGITAL TECHNOLOGIES

The preceding sub-chapters have discussed digital marketing within the contemporary and implemented Web 1.0 and Web 2.0 experiences of customers. This chapter takes a prospective approach and asks what can be expected in the next development of the digital space, what has come to be known as Web 3.0. Figure 10.9 shows that while the digital channels and digital marketing activities at this time are expected to remain largely unchanged, the underlying enablers of Web 3.0 are expected to shift to three driving technologies: Big Data, blockchain and machine learning (algorithms). These emerging digital technologies are expected to further facilitate key trends around digital marketing, specifically, decentralised, metamodern customer experiences (see Box 10.5 on digital world / the metaverse) and further automation (Plangger et al., 2022), with impacts across all digital platforms and digital marketing capabilities. Web 3.0 envisions a web where users have greater control over their data and digital identities, promoting privacy and security. This will lead, for instance, to extended or new peer-to-peer business models (see Chapter 7).

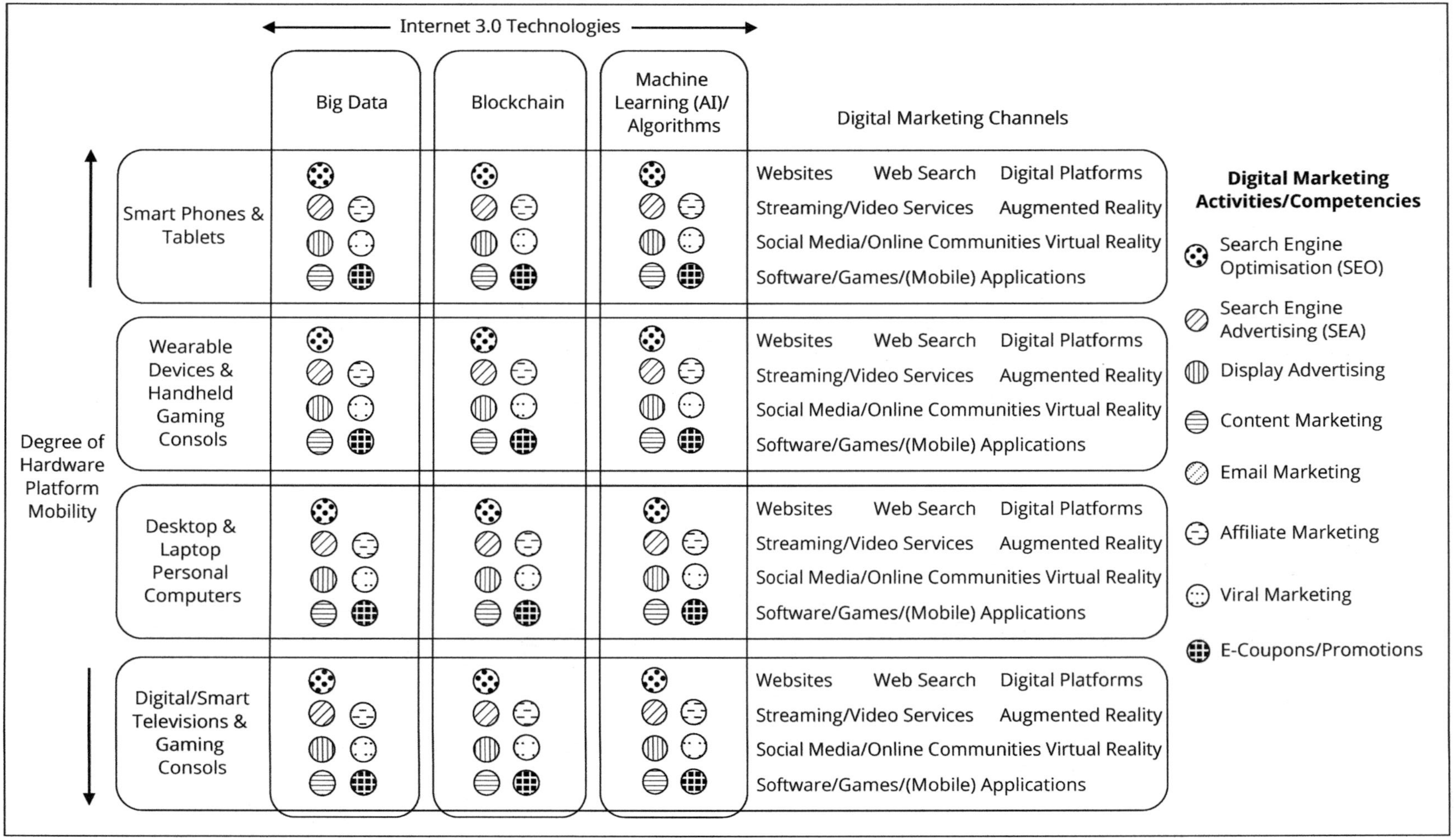

Figure 10.9 Digital marketing platform, channel and competencies matrix for internet (web) 3.0

Source: adapted from Peter (2023, 2024) and Peter & Dalla Vecchia (2021)

Box 10.5: Web 3.0

Digital Worlds and the Metaverse

The virtual environment (or digital world) that has come to be known as the metaverse promises to reduce the friction that humans experience when accessing digital environments, as a result of the dependence of digital experiences and activities on 'gaming consoles, mobile devices, television screens, desktop and laptop computers, virtual reality headsets, and more'. The metaverse, a term coined by Meta and with competitor platforms already in development, promises to reduce this friction between humans and hardware. At the same time, Web 3.0 represents the necessary decentralisation of data and infrastructure needed to realise the metaverse, with blockchain technology as the critical enabling technology of Web 3.0. From a digital marketing perspective, the metaverse (and other digital worlds) offers a new digital space for brand building, providing unique digital only and augmented consumer experiences. Especially in fashion and experience-based service industries the opportunities to engage customers are receiving significant attention, with early explorations in digital fashion arguably leading the way. But non-fungible tokens (NFT) have also already created an entire new digital product category that has allowed new and old brands valuable opportunities for brand building with new generation of consumers.

Source: EY Americas (2022)

10.5 DIGITAL MARKETING AND COMPETITIVE ADVANTAGE

There is growing evidence 'that (the) increasing use of emerging digital technologies to enhance the efficiency and effectiveness of targeted digital marketing and promotions is being harnessed as a competitive advantage' (Andzulis et al. 2012; in Basu et al., 2024, 1). The resource-based view (see Chapter 2) draws attention to the need to understand the digital marketing competencies/capabilities that at a more fundamental level enable the use of digital technologies to create a competitive advantage, where digital marketing capabilities (DMC) can be defined as a 'firm's ability to use digital technology–enabled processes to interact with customers and partners in a targeted, measurable, and integrated way to create new forms of value without regard for distance or time' (Homburg & Wielgos, 2022). Digital marketing capabilities have been found to differ from conventional marketing capabilities (CMC) in terms of their (1) scalability, (2) measurability, (3) interconnectivity, and (4) adaptability (Homburg & Wielgos, 2022). The empirical evidence for DMCs adding value to the firm in addition to the value created by CMCs is emerging and showing support for a distinct contribution by DMCs to value creation and the competitive advantage of firms (Homburg & Wielgos, 2022). Importantly, the likelihood of DMCs and CMCs contributing to value creation in the same firm is dependent on specific organisational orientation, including greater degrees of customer orientation and lower degrees of competitor orientation, or external environmental conditions, such as greater environmental dynamism in terms of rapid changes in customer preferences, competitor actions, and technological change. There is no evidence to suggest that the interaction of DMCs and CMCs contributes to improved performance under greater degrees of inter-functional coordination, though (Homburg & Wielgos, 2022).

10.6 DIGITAL MARKETING AND SUSTAINABILITY

The transformation of marketing by digital technologies has resulted in an even more critical role for data and indeed as a result of the inherent data generating potential of digital technologies, data proliferation and associated data privacy issues have emerged as a critical ethical concern (Quach et al., 2022). There is an inherent tension between attempts by firms to monetise data for greater profitability and consumer data protection, often resulting in a regulatory response to protect the rights of consumers, an example being the EU GDPR. Often, data is fragmented and needs to be aggregated across different actors, these may be internal functions or independent businesses, to enable its full value creation potential to be realised, but again these data aggregation activities are in tension with data privacy concerns (Quach et al., 2022). Similarly to the need to manage tensions in environmental sustainability transitions (Hahn et al., 2015), the digital transformation transition challenges firms' managers to learn to manage these kinds of tensions to ensure a sustainable digital transformation of a firm or business ecosystem.

10.7 CONCLUSION

Digital marketing and digital marketing competencies/capabilities offer valuable new ways for firms to gain customer attention, convert this attention into sales and develop customer loyalty. The chapter introduces the concept of digital marketing as a means to communicate value propositions and capture value through marketing and sales. It emphasises the importance of digital technologies in creating new channels and capabilities for engaging customers. The proposed digital marketing toolkit includes various technologies and platforms, such as e-commerce and marketing automation, which streamline marketing tasks and enhance operational efficiency, together with key digital marketing channels, including company websites, social media, email, and search engines, and digital marketing competencies like SEO, SEA, display advertising, content marketing, email marketing, affiliate marketing, viral marketing, and e-coupons.

Data analytics in digital marketing supports a more successful marketing and sales funnel (see Figure 10.2), based on various metrics (see Box 10.4). New digital technology from the Web 3.0 emphasise decentralisation, blockchain, and AI, resulting in, for example, new digital worlds.

Case Studies

Students can complete the following tasks either based on the focal case study (adapt accordingly), or work on the recommended case study for this chapter (*Switzerland Tourism – cross-media campaign 'The ride of a lifetime'*) and answer the questions below.

1. Which activities were particularly successful in improving the perception of Switzerland as a holiday destination? How could these activities be further optimised?
2. Was the campaign executed using Web 1.0, Web 2.0 or Web 3.0 digital technologies?
3. How could virtual reality add-ons (e.g., virtual tours of Switzerland) be developed to improve the user experience?
4. What are the success factors of influencer marketing with stars (ambassador marketing), and how could this marketing approach be used in the future?
5. What recommendations do you have to other organisations in utilising influencer marketing / ambassador marketing?
6. How could specific target groups be addressed even better in order to take cultural and regional differences into account?
7. What other digital approaches could be used to strengthen public transport as part of the travel experience?
8. What does a possible marketing and sales funnel (see Box 10.1) look like, and what are the key online metrics which Switzerland Tourism should use (see Box 10.4.)?
9. Which technologies (also see Chapter 10.1.2) could help to personalise the travel experience and further increase Switzerland's attractiveness as a travel destination?

Additional cases with student questions for the strategic digital action field of *Digital Marketing* are covered in:

- Adelbodner mineral water – the digital roadmap of a SME (available online).
- Autodesk Asia-Pacific – customer lifecycle management and marketing automation (available online).
- Blackroll – from Product Innovation to International Expansion via E-Commerce (available online).
- BRUGG Lifting and its industrial Internet of Things (IIoT) asset management solution 'PVS' (available in the Appendix).
- Action fields of digital transformation at Synchrony Financial (USA) (available online).
- CRM and sales automation at Transgourmet Switzerland (available online).

You will find a collection of case studies for Strategic Digital Transformation in the Appendix and additional cases online at www.strategic-digital-transformation.com

Exercises

Discuss the following questions in your class, in your group, or assignment

1. Reflect on the importance of social media in a firm's digital marketing strategy, for instance in the example of the opening case study 'Ryan Reynolds' multi-brand social media marketing strategy on X'.
2. Based on a selected industry/business, develop a marketing and sales funnel for the firm (see Figure 10.2).

3 Explain the dominance of 'gatekeeper firms' as per the EU definition, and why this is important in the context of digital marketing (see Figure 10.4).
4 Forming two small groups (2–4 students in each group), assign a pro and contra position to each group and debate whether influencer marketing/brand ambassadors is an important/successful marketing tactic (group 1), or overrated and not necessary (group 2).
5 For the firm selected in exercise 2, evaluate their digital marketing strategy (make assumptions, if required) across the four areas of technology platforms, digital marketing technology, digital marketing channels and digital marketing competencies (see Chapter 10.1).
6 For your select firm in exercise 2, develop a content marketing strategy based on the framework presented in Box 10.2.
7 Describe how you would build and nurture an online community (see Box 10.3) for the firm selected in exercise 2.
8 For your selected firm in exercise 2, ideate how Web 3.0 (focus virtual worlds/the Metaverse) could benefit the firm (see Box 10.5). Provide at least three ideas.

Further Reading List

- Brinker, S. (2024). 2024 Marketing technology landscape supergraphic. Chiefmartec, May, The State of Martech 2024, https://chiefmartec.com/2024/05/2024-marketing-technology-landscape-supergraphic-14106-martech-products-27-8-growth-yoy/.
- Checa, A., Heller, C., Stein, E., & Wilkie, J. (2023). Modern marketing: Six capabilities for multidisciplinary teams. McKinsey & Company, 5 April 2023. Last accessed on 23 January 2025 from www.mckinsey.com/capabilities/growth-marketing-and-sales/our-insights/modern-marketing-six-capabilities-for-multidisciplinary-teams.
- Field, D., Patel, S., & Leon, H. (2018). Mastering digital marketing maturity. BCG, 20 February 2018. Last accessed on 23 January 2025 from www.bcg.com/publications/2018/mastering-digital-marketing-maturity.
- Halim, J., Lin, J., Sutisna, E., Zhang, B., & Menon, L. (2023). Reimagining marketing during recessionary times: How top brands are using marketing data and experimentation to stay connected to consumers. Bain & Company. Last accessed on 23 January 2025 from www.bain.com/insights/reimagining-marketing-during-recessionary-times.
- Meyer, M., & Peter, M. K. (2024). Evolving marketing strategies for Swiss SMEs in the ICT sector: A marketing strategy canvas in support of digital transformation. *International Journal of Technology Marketing*, 18(1), 91–112.

References

Adobe (2023). Digital marketing metrics your business should be using. Adobe Experience Cloud, 10 August, https://business.adobe.com/blog/basics/digital-marketing-metrics.

Andzulis, J. M., Panagopoulos, N. G., and A. Rapp, A.(2012. A review of social media and implications for the sales process. *Journal of Personal Selling & Sales Management*, *32*(3), 305–16.

Audiovisual Identity Database (2024). Audiovisual Identity Database. Last accessed on 12 December 2024 from https://www.avid.wiki/AVID:2024.

Bampo, M., Ewing, M. T., Mather, D. R., Stewart, D., & Wallace, M. (2008). The effects of the social structure of digital networks on viral marketing performance. *Information Systems Research*, *19*(3), 273–90.

Basu, R., Aktar, M. N., & Kumar, S. (2025). The interplay of artificial intelligence, machine learning, and data analytics in digital marketing and promotions: A review and research agenda. *Journal of Marketing Analytics*, *13*, 267–87.

Carmi, E. (2017). Regulating behaviours on the European Union internet, the case of spam versus cookies. *International Review of Law, Computers & Technology*, *31*(3), 289–307.

Choi, H., Mela, C. F., Balseiro, S. R., & Leary, A. (2020). Online display advertising markets: A literature review and future directions. *Information Systems Research*, *31*(2), 556–75.

Colicev, A., Kumar, A., & O'Connor, P. (2019). Modeling the relationship between firm and user generated content and the stages of the marketing funnel. *International Journal of Research in Marketing*, *36*(1), 100–16.

Content Marketing Association (2017). About the content marketing association – definition of content marketing, available at: http://the-cma.com/about-us/.

Content Marketing Institute (2017). What is content marketing?, available at: http://contentmarketinginstitute.com/what-is-content-marketing/.

Dalla Vecchia, M., & Peter, M. K. (2018). Marketing automation: A project framework in support of digital transformation. *Business Information Systems and Technology 4.0: New Trends in the Age of Digital Change*, 117–30.

European Commission (2024). Gatekeepers. Last accessed on 14 December 2024 from https://digital-markets-act.ec.europa.eu/gatekeepers_en.

Eurostat (2024). Digital economy and society statistics – enterprises. Last accessed on 14 December 2024 from https://ec.europa.eu/eurostat/statistics-explained/index.php?title=Digital_economy_and_society_statistics_-_enterprises#Access_to_the_internet.

EY Americas (2022). How metaverse and Web 3 can create real value for your organization. Last accessed on 13 December 2024 from https://go.ey.com/3KZziVa.

Ferrer-Gomila, J. L., Hinarejos, M. F., & Huguet-Rotger, L. (2018). A survey on electronic coupons. *Computers & Security*, *77*, 106–27.

Ghorbani, Z., Kargaran, S., Saberi, A., Haghighinasab, M., Jamali, S. M., & Ale Ebrahim, N. (2021). Trends and patterns in digital marketing research: bibliometric analysis. *Journal of Marketing Analytics*, 1–15.

Hahn, T., Pinkse, J., Preuss, L., & Figge, F. (2015). Tensions in corporate sustainability: Towards an integrative framework. *Journal of Business Ethics*, *127*, 297–316.

Ho, J., Pang, C., & Choy, C. (2020). Content marketing capability building: A conceptual framework. *Journal of Research in Interactive Marketing*, *14*(1), 133–51.

Homburg, C., & Wielgos, D. M. (2022). The value relevance of digital marketing capabilities to firm performance. *Journal of the Academy of Marketing Science*, *50*(4), 666–88.

Ipsos (2022). *ICT User Behaviour Study: Intermediate Report for European Commission Joint Research Centre (JCR)*. Ipsos European Public Affairs, last accessed on 14 December 2024 from https://susproc.jrc.ec.europa.eu/product-bureau/sites/default/files/2022-08/Task%207%20-%20JRC%20ICT%20user%20behaviour%20study%20-%20intermediate%20report.pdf.

Kannan, P. K. (2017). Digital marketing: A framework, review and research agenda. *International Journal of Research in Marketing*, *34*(1), 22–45.

Kupfer, A. K., Pähler Vor der Holte, N., Kübler, R. V., & Hennig-Thurau, T. (2018). The role of the partner brand's social media power in brand alliances. *Journal of Marketing, 82*(3), 25–44.

Maximum Effort (2024a). Home Page. Last accessed on 12 December 2024 from www.maximumeffort.com.

Maximum Effort (2024b). LinkedIn Profile. Last accessed on 12 December 2024 from www.linkedin.com/company/maximumeffort/.

Meyer, M. & Peter, M.K. (2024): Evolving marketing strategies for Swiss SMEs in the ICT sector: A marketing strategy canvas in support of digital transformation, *International Journal of Technology Marketing, 18*(1), 91–112.

Ngai, E. W. (2003). Internet marketing research (1987–2000): A literature review and classification. *European Journal of Marketing, 37*(1/2), 24–49.

Peter, M. K. (Hrsg.) (2017). *KMU-Transformation: Als KMU die Digitale Transformation erfolgreich umsetzen. Forschungsresultate und Praxisleitfaden.* FHNW Hochschule für Wirtschaft, Olten/Schweiz, www.kmu-transformation.ch.

Peter, M. K. (Hrsg.) (2021). *Strategieentwicklung im digitalen Zeitalter: Planung und Umsetzung der Digitalen Transformation.* FHNW Hochschule für Wirtschaft und Strategylab, Olten/Schweiz, www.strategische-transformation.ch.

Peter, M. K. (2023). *Digitaler Masterplan für KMU. So gelingt die digitale Transformation in Ihrem Unternehmen.* Verlag Beobachter Edition & Handelszeitung. Zürich/Schweiz, www.digitaler-masterplan.ch.

Peter, M. K. (2024). *The Digital Transformation Canvas. Develop and implement your digital strategy.* FT Publishing/Pearson, London/UK, www.the-digital-transformation-canvas.com.

Peter, M. K., Kraft, C., & Lindeque, J. (2020). Strategic action fields of digital transformation: An exploration of the strategic action fields of Swiss SMEs and large enterprises. *Journal of Strategy and Management, 13*(1), 160–80.

Peter, M. K., Baumgartner, R., Siscaro, D., & Neher, A. (2025). E-commerce automation: A mixed-method investigation and workshop canvas for e-commerce roadmap development, in: Reis, J. L., Peter, M. K., Reis, L. P., & Bogdanovic, Z., *Marketing and Smart Technologies, Proceedings of ICMarkTech 2023, Volume 2*, Springer, https://link.springer.com/book/9789819736973 (in print).

Peter, M. K., & Dalla Vecchia, M. (2021). The digital marketing toolkit: A literature review for the identification of digital marketing channels and platforms. *New Trends in Business Information Systems and Technology: Digital Innovation and Digital Business Transformation*, 251–65.

Peter, M. K., & Niedermann, A. (Hrsg.) (2020). *Digitales Marketing für KMU. Wie Unternehmen sich digital vermarkten und kommunizieren.* Beobachter Edition & Handelszeitung, Zürich/Schweiz.

Plangger, K., Grewal, D., de Ruyter, K., & Tucker, C. (2022). The future of digital technologies in marketing: A conceptual framework and an overview. *Journal of the Academy of Marketing Science, 50*(6), 1125–34.

Quach, S., Thaichon, P., Martin, K. D., Weaven, S., & Palmatier, R. W. (2022). Digital technologies: tensions in privacy and data. *Journal of the Academy of Marketing Science, 50*(6), 1299–1323.

Ren, X., Cao, J., & Xu, X. (2021). A two-stage model for forecasting consumers' intention to purchase with e-coupons. *Journal of Retailing and Consumer Services, 59*, 102289.

Reynolds, R. (2024). LinkedIn Profile. Last accessed on 12 December 2024 from www.linkedin.com/in/vancityreynolds.

Souchoroukof, A. (2020). History of email marketing. LinkedIn. Last accessed on 31 December 2024 from www.linkedin.com/pulse/history-email-marketing-alexis-souchoroukof.

Schweidel, D. A., Bart, Y., Inman, J. J., Stephen, A. T., Libai, B., Andrews, M., ... & Thomaz, F. (2022). How consumer digital signals are reshaping the customer journey. *Journal of the Academy of Marketing Science*, *50*(6), 1257–76.

Wiraguna, R. T., & Aulia, D. (2024). The influence of sales funnel marketing on brand awareness through social media influencers. *International Journal of Applied Management and Business*, *2*(1), 52–61.

11

SUCCESS FACTORS AND METRICS FOR DIGITAL TRANSFORMATION IMPLEMENTATION

Learning Goals

By the end of this chapter, you should...

- Be able to describe the need for organisation-centric activities, based on identified barriers and risks, while implementing digital transformation.
- Be able to articulate the importance of organisational anchoring of digital transformation and the role of a Chief Digital Officer in realising this anchoring.
- Be able to critically evaluate the implementation of the three implementation success factors (project management, change management, digital leadership) for a specific case organisation.
- Be able to describe the differences in strategic programmes, projects portfolios, and projects for digital transformation implementation.
- Be able to analyse implementation challenges and apply the change management process to support digital transformation and digital internal communication.
- Be able to describe the need for digital capabilities and skills development measures.
- Be able to apply the success metrics of digital transformation (financials, customers, and employees) in a business situation.

The LEGO Transformation Story

In the early 2000s, LEGO – the producer of the famous plastic building-blocks – faced a severe financial crisis. In 2004, the company posted a significant loss. This crisis was partly attributed to a misapplication of digital transformation efforts, where diversification into digital initiatives had distracted the company from its core product – the LEGO brick. Many strategic initiatives were unsuccessful, and the operating model suffered from knowledge silos, hindering collaboration and information flow within the organisation.

The turning point came with the appointment of a new CEO, Jørgen Vig Knudstorp, in 2004 (El Sawy et al., 2020). Under his leadership, LEGO realigned its business model by combining physical products with digital experiences. This strategic shift marked the beginning of LEGO's successful digital transformation journey, that included a number of strategic initiatives (selection):

- Organisational restructuring: to reduce costs and break down company silos, LEGO reorganised itself with fewer business units, resulting in improved collaboration and communication between LEGO's departments. In addition, it moved from functional departments to cross-functional product-based teams.
- Enterprise platform development: LEGO created the LEGO Enterprise platform, a central hub for resource planning, HR, IT, sourcing, and other business functions. This platform became the foundation of LEGO's business processes, allowing for effective planning and execution based on data.
- Supply chain digitalisation: LEGO's new leadership team improved revenues by digitalising supply chain processes, centralising information streams, collaborating with retail customers, and breaking down company silos.

Their CEO, Jørgen Vig Knudstorp, said that they constantly need to identify 'the next upcoming disruptive gaming or consumer-engaging technology that could really impact (their) business and business model' (Andersen & Ross, 2016, p. 9). LEGO's successful transformation thus underscores the critical role of change management in digital transformation initiatives. Several key aspects of LEGO's change management approach contributed to its success:

- Holistic approach: the transformation considered technology, processes, structures, and skills development. This comprehensive approach ensured that all aspects of the organisation were aligned with the new digital strategy.
- Gradual implementation: LEGO announced the transformation well in advance, providing ample time for employees and leaders to understand and adapt to the changes. This gradual approach helped mitigate resistance and allowed for smoother adoption of new processes and technologies.

The transformation fostered a more collaborative organisational culture. Product teams were given full responsibility for delivery, and the reward system was overhauled to incentivise team collaboration and value delivery over individual achievements. In addition, LEGO emphasised continuous learning and development opportunities for employees. This focus on ongoing skill development helped ensure that the workforce could adapt to new technologies and processes. One of LEGO's employee promises is that 'everyone is awesome and we do our best to create a culture where everyone is safe, valued and feel they belong' (LEGO, 2025).

(Continued)

LEGO's digital transformation yielded significant improvements in operations and customer engagement. It went from near bankruptcy to becoming again a successful business, the digitalisation of supply chain processes and implementation of advanced analytics improved operational efficiency, and the integration of physical and digital play experiences created new product possibilities and revenue streams (El Sawy et al., 2020). Finally, various customer engagement initiatives provided valuable insights into consumer preferences, and their cultural transformation fostered a culture of continuous improvement and collaboration among the 25,000 employees, thus driving continues innovation. LEGO's VP of Finance said about their digital transformation that they have just begun and are not yet done: 'it is a journey – not a destination' (Andersen & Ross, 2016, p. 11).

11.0 INTRODUCTION

Carefully planning the implementation of digital transformation is crucial for organisations to successfully navigate the complex process of integrating new business models, technologies, processes, collaboration frameworks, and skills into their operations as discussed with reference to the seven strategic action fields of digital transformation (Chapters 4–10). A well-planned approach ensures that the transformation aligns strategic and operational aspects with business goals, minimises disruptions, and maximises the benefits of digital strategic initiatives (Mahboub & Sadok, 2023). Reasons and important considerations include (1) risk mitigation, as digital transformation involves significant changes to an organisation's processes, systems, and culture. Without proper planning, these changes can lead to, for example, disruptions, financial loss, quality issues, and IT and data security vulnerabilities. Next (2), digital transformation requires resources and substantial investments in technology, employees, and skills development/training. Careful planning allows organisations to allocate resources effectively, ensuring that they have the necessary budget, teams, and infrastructure to support the transformation. And finally (3), one of the biggest challenges in digital transformation is to manage the human aspect of change (i.e., change management). A well-planned implementation strategy should include a change management component to address resistance, build buy-in from stakeholders, and support employees through the transition. This chapter will discuss both the success factors of digital transformation implementation, as well as the main metrics to measure the success of digital transformation, before moving to the practical digital toolkit that will aid this process in Chapter 12.

11.1 IMPLEMENTING DIGITAL TRANSFORMATION

In a study of 14 technology firms, Balakrishnan and Das (2020) analysed the impact of digital transformation towards organisational structures and managerial actions. The study identifies three main categories of DT-related managerial activities for implementation:

1 Organisation-centric activities focused on employee engagement;
2 External stakeholder-centric activities related to partner engagement; and
3 Technology-centric activities aimed at achieving higher growth and economies of scale.

For above mentioned organisation-centric activities (first point from Balakrishnan & Das, 2020), Loonam et al. (2018) revealed three approaches when introducing digital transformation, namely (ibid., p. 106):

1 Recognising the importance of fostering a digital culture;
2 Having a clear understanding of the key critical success factors required to deliver upon digital transformation; and
3 Focusing on the organisation rather than the technology in delivering change.

To implement change (which can be less or more radical), organisations implement processes and activities to guide them through significant changes in a systematic and strategic approach. Kotter (2012) emphasises that change management involves preparing, supporting, and helping individuals, teams, and the entire organisation transition from their current state (before digital transformation) to a desired future state (an organisation capable of achieving competitive advantages in the digital age and delivering profits to its shareholders; see Chapter 9). However, to prepare for the implementation of digital transformation, barriers and risks that might reduce the effectiveness of the strategy must be identified, recognised, and addressed.

11.1.1 Proactively Address Barriers and Risks

Knowing the various barriers to digital transformation is crucial to preparing the various strategic initiatives to be implemented (Agrawal et al., 2020). Strategies and projects relating to digital transformation require a great deal of employee commitment, know-how, time, and motivation. In a Swiss study of small businesses that work on digital transformation (Peter, 2020), half of the surveyed organisations name a lack of time as the biggest barrier to a successful digital transformation. This is followed by a lack of knowledge – almost half of all organisations consider the lack of know-how among managers to be the biggest barrier. The unwillingness to change among employees (27%) and managers (26%) is also significant and shows how important it is to support both managers and employees in the implementation of digital transformation (see Figure 11.1).

Digital transformation also presents some risks that should be considered, with IT security and data protection among the top recognised risks. A shortage of skilled employees (37%) and a fear for possible job losses (34%) are also cited as risks.

A study on internal workplace transformation (Peter, 2019) showed that a large proportion of organisations (70% of small businesses and 52% of large organisations) do not involve their employees in strategy discussions. Only slightly more than a fifth of small businesses and slightly more than a quarter of large organisations use the opportunities and needs identified by their employees to develop modern transformation strategies. Employees should be allowed and encouraged to participate from the very beginning.

Strategy project teams should utilise the findings on barriers and risks to proactively find tactics to overcome these in their own digital transformation implementation. Employees hold a lot of knowledge on the day-today business and their ideas can help to solve problems early on in workshops and through discussions so that your digital transformation can be successfully implemented.

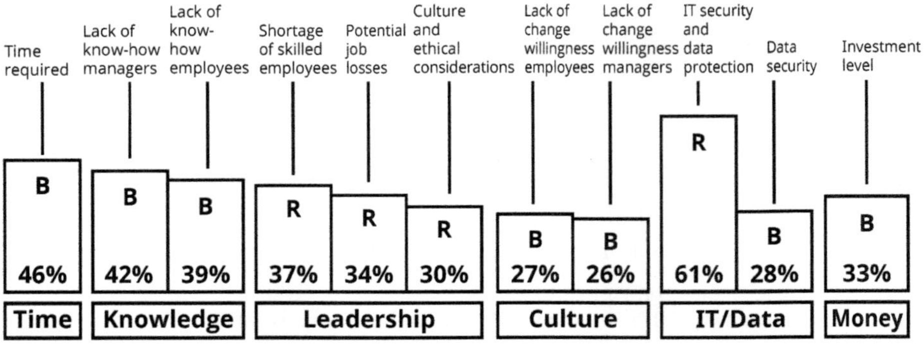

Figure 11.1 Barriers and risks of digital transformation

Note: if barriers (B) and risks (R) are addressed by management at an early stage, transformation strategies and projects can be implemented more successfully.
Source: Peter (2017, 2021, 2023, 2024); Peter et al. (2020)

11.1.2 Organisational Anchoring of Digital Transformation

Both for the development as well as implementation of digital transformation, resources (new departments, project teams and/or individuals) must be provided and organisationally anchored (setup) in the organisation. This is important for various reasons:

- Clarity and accountability: a clear organisational setup for digital transformation helps define roles, responsibilities, and accountability. This ensures that everyone understands their part in the transformation process and how their work aligns with the organisation's overall goals.
- Effective communication: a structured organisation for digital transformation enhances internal communication by establishing formal channels and protocols. This is crucial for implementing programmes and projects, sharing updates, gathering feedback, and making informed decisions quickly.
- Resource allocation: with a defined structure, it is easier to allocate resources efficiently, including budget, teams, and technology. This ensures that the necessary resources are available where they are most needed to drive the transformation.
- Change management: as digital transformation involves significant changes in all action fields; a structured approach helps manage these changes systematically, minimising resistance, and ensuring a smoother transition.
- Measurement and evaluation: a clear organisational anchoring and setup clarifies accountabilities for progress/performance measurement and evaluation to make adjustments to the transformation strategy.

As discussed in Chapter 9, Zoppelletto et al. (2023) revealed that approaches to the organisational setup differ in small businesses/SMEs and large enterprises (see Figure 11.2). In large enterprises, a 'digital transformation conductor' (often called 'Chief Digital Officer' (CDO)) oversees digital transformation, driving a top-down strategy implementation approach, whereas in small businesses, there is a 'digital transformation peer-tutor' approach to digital transformation, characterised by a bottom-up, informal, persuasive, and empathic approach similar to a digital coach or mentor. The Chief Information Officer (CIO) role combines both strategic and operational tasks to oversee the establishment of digital capabilities in the firm as either an evangelist, coordinator, innovator, or advocate for digital transformation (Haffke et al., 2016). However, there is the potential for considerable redundancy between the CIO and CDO roles.

According to the framework from Zoppelletto et al. (2023), the macro level (X-axis on Figure 11.2) looks at the organisation as a whole and its position within the broader industry/society (for instance, the organisation collaborating with strategic partners such as suppliers, or important customers); the meso level encompasses the intermediate structures within an organisation (such as departments and teams) to understand how they interact with each other, and the micro level focuses on individuals (or small groups such as project teams) to understand personal interactions, behaviours, and dynamics.

Large enterprises	Ecosystem/ Business Network	Adopting existing organisational structure and culture (e.g., with a digital transformation project team)	Chief Digital Officer
Small businesses/ SMEs	Business Network/Ecosystem	Adopting existing organisational structure and culture (e.g., with digital internal consultants)	Digital Coach (peer-tutor approach)
	MACRO	MESO	MICRO

Figure 11.2 Options for digital transformation organisational anchoring and setup

Source: own illustration following Zoppelletto et al. (2023)

The proposed organisational anchoring/setup depends on company size and the desired organisational level of anchoring. The implementation of a chief digital officer (CDO) role might be the right option (for large enterprises which want the accountability with one person); whereas a small business/SME might benefit from a network of business partners to obtain digital transformation expertise and project delivery through external parties. In essence, an effective organisational anchoring and setup provides the structural foundation for a cohesive and coordinated digital transformation, ultimately supporting successful implementation together with the success factors of digital transformation.

11.2 SUCCESS FACTORS FOR DIGITAL TRANSFORMATION IMPLEMENTATION

The implementation of digital transformation and new digital technology into all aspects of a business is not just about adopting new tools, but involves a fundamental shift in how organisations operate (internally) and deliver value to their customers (externally). Understanding the success factors of digital transformation implementation is crucial for several reasons.

Digital transformation is inherently complex and multifaceted. It involves changes to all seven action fields, and these changes must be managed cohesively to achieve the desired outcomes. Recognising the success factors (see Figure 11.3) helps organisations navigate this complexity by providing a clear framework for implementation. It ensures that all aspects of the transformation are addressed, from technology adoption to cultural shifts. In addition, agility and flexibility are essential for navigating the dynamic nature of digital transformation. Organisations must be able to adapt quickly to changing circumstances and pivot when necessary. In turn, understanding this factor helps organisations remain resilient and responsive to emerging trends and challenges on an ongoing basis.

As digital transformation has become a crucial strategy for organisations seeking to remain competitive and relevant, the action fields of digital transformation, from customer communication, process adoptions, the implementation of new technology and work practices, drive changes in organisational practices. These changes can be implemented in the form of programmes, consisting of several programmes and projects. In the application of digital transformation, this could be a digital transformation change initiative, projects (activities with defined goals and objectives within a given period and budget), and project portfolios (which allow a more efficient management of a set of projects) (IPMA, 2018). The complexity and scope of digital transformation initiatives/programmes make effective ***project management*** indispensable for their success (see Chapter 11.3).

However, the successful implementation of digital transformation initiatives, programmes, and projects hinges not just on project management planning and executive capabilities, but significantly also on effective change management as 'the successful management of change is crucial to any organisation in order to survive and succeed in the present highly competitive and continuously evolving business environment (By, 2005, p. 369). ***Change management*** is the discipline that guides how an organisation prepares, equips, and supports teams and individuals (both managers and employees) to successfully adopt change in order to drive organisational success and outcomes, and thus plays a critical role in digital transformation. Kurt Lewin's 1947 principle of change, commonly referred to as 'Lewin's Change Management Model', involves a three-step process known as the 'Unfreeze-Change-Refreeze' framework that guides change management efforts in organisation, and can still be applied to digital transformation initiatives (see Chapter 11.4).

With new digital technology emerging on an ongoing basis, it is not only the organisation that must adapt to survive and thrive. As digital transformation changes the way how organisations operate and deliver value to customers, the successful implementation is not solely dependent on the digital transformation initiative, but it hinges significantly on effective digital leadership. ***Digital leadership*** is the practice of guiding and influencing an organisation and its employees (as well as external strategic partners) to harness digital technologies and drive transformative change. Digital leadership (see Chapter 11.5) is an 'enabling' leadership style that supports continual exploration within an organisation to create value for customers using digital transformation (Tanniru, 2017). Digital leadership in digital transformation implementation also links to the concepts in strategic action field *Digital leadership and culture* as discussed in Chapter 9.

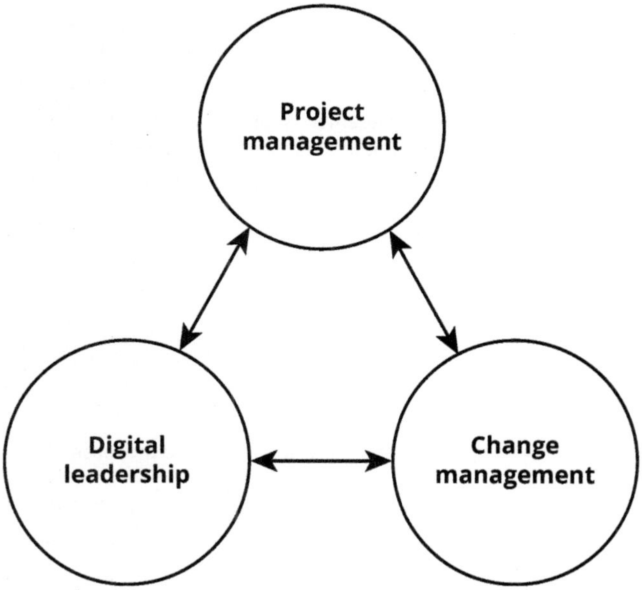

Figure 11.3 Success factors of digital transformation implementation

Source: Peter (2023, 2024)

Therefore, to successfully implement a digital transformation roadmap, programmes and projects must be planned and managed, changes must be communicated and guidance provided, and the leadership and corporate culture must be renewed in line with activities within the action fields of digital transformation:

- **Project management**: the planning, monitoring, and execution of the entire digital transformation roadmap, including its individual programmes/initiatives and projects.
- **Change management**: actively guiding, communicating, and supporting organisations and their employees in the change process of digital transformation.
- **Digital leadership**: inspiring employees in the digital age with a people-centred leadership and rewarding corporate culture.

In a study of manufacturing companies (Vogelsang et al., 2018), the authors identified 614 statements concerning the factors that lead to successful digital transformation. These attributes (see Table 11.1) can be aligned to the identified success factors of project management, change management, and digital leadership.

Table 11.1 Organisational and environmental success factors of digital transformation

Success Factors	Attributes
Project management	• Pilot projects to learn from success and failures. • Use (big) data which enable new ways of value creation. • Provide management support, including the provision of projects with resources, knowledge, and time required. • Provide technology connectivity for seamless data exchange.
Change management	• Foster employee qualifications due to knowledge intense tasks. • Identify customer needs for the mutual trust to build a reliable organisation with the customer. • Enable transparency, which requires trust into data exchange. • Stimulate collaboration as tasks are not solvable alone due to complexity. • Implement standards for quality and processes.
Digital leadership	• Prepare for the future and learn to develop roadmaps/set goals. • Build a culture that allows failures and the sensing of opportunities. • Provide autonomy, including decentral production processes. • Drive usability and ensure a fit between technologies and tasks. • Enable interdisciplinary collaboration and hybrid (cooperative) value creation.

Source: Adapted from Vogelsang (2018, p. 131) and aligned to the three dimensions of project management, change management, and digital leadership

Through a literature review, Morakanyane et al. (2020) also tried to identify digital transformation success factors and attributes. Their research unveiled that the most important success factor is to determine the drivers of digital transformation (e.g., digital technology, new digital skills including leadership skills), followed by the determination of the impacts of digital transformation (for example, to define and determine the expected and realised customer facing impacts, as well as internal organisational impacts). Other success factors include the cultivation of a digital culture and a digital vision, and establishment of a digital organisation.

11.3 PROJECT MANAGEMENT FOR DIGITAL TRANSFORMATION

Project management serves as the backbone of digital transformation implementation by providing a structured approach to planning, executing, and monitoring the various involved components. It includes organising (structuring) the strategic digital transformation into strategic programmes, portfolios, and projects, and requires project management functions to be established including programme and project governance and risk management together with the ongoing measurement and monitoring of implementation progress

11.3.1 Organising the Transformation and Project Planning

Project management is important because it ensures that a clear and cohesive roadmap (plan) is in place, and teams are aligned towards the roadmap. A well-defined project plan outlines the objectives, scope, timelines, and resources required, providing a roadmap for the entire transformation journey. This clarity supports alignment and increases the likelihood of successful digital transformation.

Strategic digital transformation implementation (see Figure 11.4) can be structured into programmes (consisting of several portfolios and projects), projects (activities with defined goals and objectives within a given time/period and budget), and project portfolios (which allow a more efficient management of a set of projects) (IPMA, 2018):

- ***Strategic programmes*** are directly linked to an organisation's vision and strategic objectives. They might have unclear outcomes, a multitude of stakeholders, and unclear timelines. Programmes can consist of formally set-up and managed project portfolios, or individual projects directly linked to the programme.
- A ***project portfolio*** is a set of projects that have one or multiple common factors. They might be grouped around an action field of digital transformation, an important organisational theme (for instance, a strategic priority) or be linked to a specific organisational function (for instance, marketing or HR). Project portfolios allow a more efficient management of a set of projects as they mostly have a dedicated project officer/leader and separate planning and management controls.
- ***Projects*** have clearly defined deliverables that consist of activities with defined goals and objectives within a given time/period and budget. They drive the desired organisational outcomes, such as new products and services, implementation of new digital technology, improved collaboration and communication, faster processes, quality improvements, and cost reductions. It is at the project level where project managers have most impact in driving successful digital transformation implementation.

Depending on factors such as organisational size and resources, and scope of the digital transformation strategic roadmap, an organisation might choose to implement its transformation activities as a strategic programme in combination with a project portfolio (or without), or directly via a set of projects not actively managed in a portfolio (see Box 11.1 for an example).

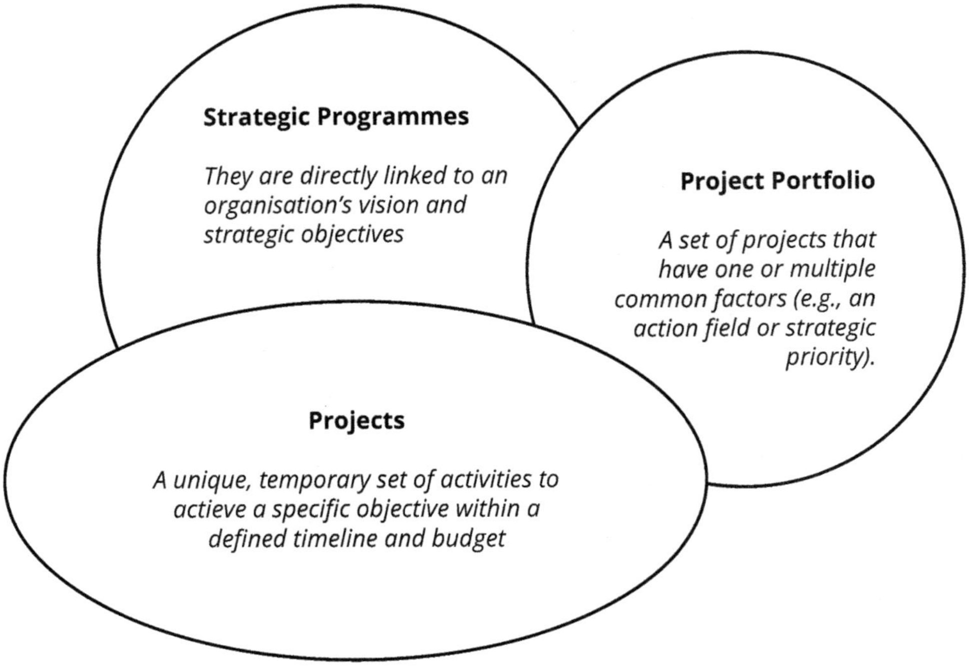

Figure 11.4 Strategic programmes, portfolios, and projects

Source: own illustration following Grundy (1997); IPMA (2018); and Sedlmayer (2017)

Box 11.1: Projects and Programmes

The Gotthard Base Tunnel in Switzerland, the longest and deepest train tunnel in the world, was a ***project***. The team dug a massive hole through the central European alps, applied new technologies, and installed uncountable amounts of materials to finally enable trains to run safely through the alps. It cost a fortune, lasted more than ten years, and endless, often very difficult management decisions had to be taken. Although one might also call it a megaproject, it is a project, not a programme. It was an undertaking with a clear objective and clear to be achieved results: a unique, temporary, multidisciplinary, and organised endeavour to realise agreed deliverables within predefined requirements and constraints.

In parallel to the Gotthard Base Tunnel project, a ***programme*** was conducted to organise the flow of train traffic from Rotterdam (Netherlands) and the industry centres in Germany through the alps to the northern Italian industrial area and the Genoa harbour (the Rhine-Alpine corridor). Many topics had to be tackled, including the traffic flow with the neighbouring countries, upgrade of current and buying of new rolling stock, new customers' offers and timetable, new maintenance concepts and logistics concepts, and an upgrade of access routes in Switzerland and neighbouring countries.

Finally, over 3,900 employees had to be trained in new train management approaches and technologies, while maintaining the current operations. The money and time spent was just a fraction of the cost for the building of the Gotthard base tunnel.

The programme had a completely different approach than the project as it had unclear outcomes, a multitude of stakeholders, unclear timeline etc. But the programme was essential to exploit the tunnel in the most efficient way; and it was essential to fulfil the decision of the Swiss nation which agreed to the enormous investment. The objective was never to have a tunnel up and running, but to relocate goods transport across the country on rail, away from the roads. A typical programme is set up to achieve strategic goals and is thus directly linked to an organisation's strategy.

Source and reprinted with permission: Sedlmayer (2017)

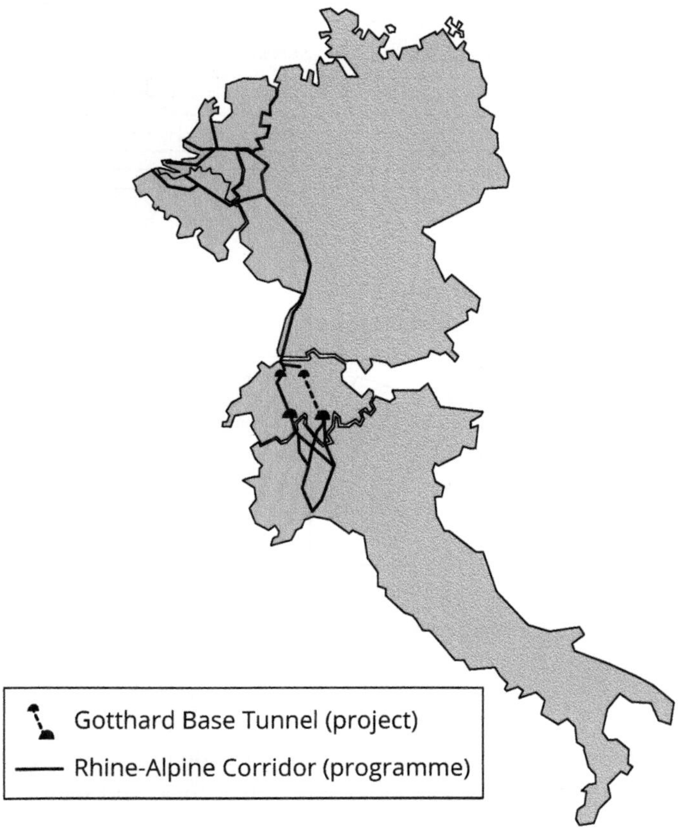

Figure 11.5 Projects and programmes (example)

Source: own illustration following Sedlmayer (2017)

At the project level, the planning procedure may consist of the following steps (Peter, 2024):

- Create work packages: how can individual goals and project tasks be grouped into work packages?
- Create a breakdown of the work structure: how do the individual work packages fit together?
- Identify project activities: what is being done in detail, and in which sequence?
- Create a schedule: by when must which work package be completed?
- Allocate resources and costs: which employees, external consultants, machines, and so on are brought into the project and at what cost?
- Set milestones as control points: into which phases and with which intermediate goals can the project be divided?

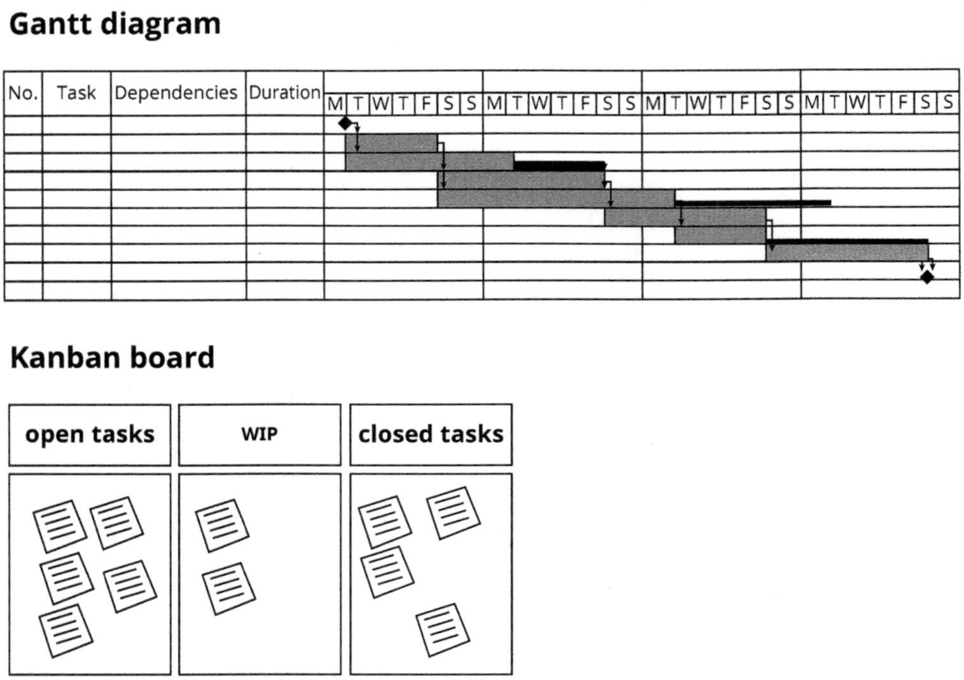

Figure 11.6 Gantt Charts and Kanban Boards

Source: Peter (2023, 2024)

Today, projects are being planned and completed via a hybrid project management approach consisting of the Waterfall planning method (through a linear and sequential step-by-step process), and an agile method for the design, development, and implementation of the project. Agile methods include for instance the design thinking method, or agile software development methods such as Scrum (a term derived from Rugby where team restart the play after a stoppage) that include short sprints or iterations of 1-4 weeks.

To visualise a project plan, for smaller and less complex projects, the so-called Gantt charts (bar charts named after the inventor Henry Gantt) can be used to maintain a chronological overview. Another visualisation type used for agile project management (such as Scrum) is Kanban (see Figure 11.6). This is a table with three columns: 'open tasks', 'work in progress' and 'closed tasks' (additional columns can easily be added as needed). The various tasks then move through the processing of the work packages. The visualisation of the workflow provides clarity, and possible bottlenecks and problems quickly become visible (with appropriate project planning software, even more complex representations and dashboards can be created automatically).

To support project planning and management, a set of software tools for various functions are available at low cost (for instance, via apps hosted in the Cloud). Important features are planning, communication and collaboration, documentation, resource and risk management (see Box 11.2).

Box 11.2: Features in Software Tools/apps to Support Project Management

- **Planning**: a good project management tool, such as Jira, Microsoft Project, Monday, Padlet, Trello, or Zoho, allows a project manager to plan and assign tasks to team members and define deadlines. It helps to set priorities and meet deadlines. In addition, it creates notifications when the project is approaching the planned completion date, but certain activities have not yet been completed.
- **Communication and collaboration**: project management tools have a dashboard that allows the project manager to track the team and the progress of the project. Team members can access each other's work through the dashboard. Other features required for collaboration in a project management tool include status sharing, commenting, tracking of edits, and version history.
- **Documentation:** information on planned and completed tasks, resource data, billing information, and so on is important. However, manually documenting these can be tedious and error-prone. Therefore, project management tools often include a documentation function that makes it possible to store all project information in one place and make it accessible to the relevant stakeholders.
- **Resource management**: by optimising resources (material goods, labour, expenses, etc.), the duration as well as the costs of a project can be significantly reduced. An efficient resource management function in project management helps to create a complete overview of the total project costs. It shows who has worked on the project, how many hours and at what hourly rate, and what other costs have been incurred. The overview helps with budget control as well as resource planning for the coming months.
- **Risk assessment:** due to unforeseen events, there may be IT problems, changes in the project team or the economic situation, and project management must be able to calculate or map these types of risks (e.g., the duration/progress/deadline/budget of a project). As a rule, the risks are marked as such, described, and the likelihood of their occurrence is calculated with their possible consequences. It is then also possible to become aware of the risks, to prepare for them and to better deal with them in future.

Source: Peter (2023, 2024)

11.3.2 Programme and Project Portfolio Governance

Programme and project governance is a framework that guides the management and control of a programme/portfolio, which consists of multiple related projects aimed at achieving a common strategic goal. This framework ensures that the programme aligns with organisational strategic objectives, follows best practices, and delivers value to stakeholders.

Ul Musawir et al. (2020) define governance as 'widely recognised to be among the most critical factors for successful project delivery and benefits realisation' for organisational strategy implementation. In their literature review, they propose the following definition of project governance (Ul Musawir et al., 2020, p. 7):

- It is a system (comprising of frameworks, structures, processes, policies, responsibilities, accountabilities, and relationships) by which a project is directed, controlled, and held to account.
- It simultaneously allows for the encompassment of all governance elements involved in the direction and control of projects, which may include programme management, portfolio management, organisational project management, senior management, and organisational governance depending on the project context.
- It should not be viewed as 'residing' at a particular level in the organisation, but rather as a system involving all elements that pertain to the governance of a particular project.

In practical terms, programme governance includes strategic alignment, leadership and stakeholder management, communication and collaboration, and monitoring and risk management:

- **Strategic alignment:** to ensure that programme's goals and objectives support the organisation's strategic direction and priorities.
- **Stakeholder management:** to identify and involve all relevant stakeholders throughout the programme's lifecycle.
- **Leadership and decision-making**: to establish a clear governance structure with defined roles, responsibilities, and authorities that provides a decision-making process that is transparent, efficient, and accountable.
- **Monitoring and resource management**: to continuously monitor and adjust the programme to maintain alignment with both external market driven as well as internal organisational changes, and to allocate resources to the changing nature of a strategic programme.
- **Communication and collaboration**: to ensure effective communication and collaboration with stakeholders to address their needs and concerns.
- **Risk management**: to identify and manage potential risks to the programme, and to develop and deploy contingency plans and mitigation strategies to address potential issues.
- **Performance review and monitoring**: establish OKRs (objectives and key results) and KPIs (key performance indicators) to measure the programme's progress and success (see Chapter 11.6).

By providing a structured approach to managing programmes, programme governance helps organisations achieve their strategic objectives, optimise resource use, and deliver value to stakeholders.

11.3.3 Conclusion

Project managers act as the central point of contact, facilitating clear and consistent communication among all parties. This ensures that everyone is aligned, understands their roles and responsibilities, and can provide input and feedback throughout the project. Transparent communication also helps build trust and buy-in from stakeholders, which is crucial for the successful implementation of digital initiatives. In addition, project management provides a framework for measuring and monitoring progress. Digital transformation is an ongoing process that requires continuous evaluation to ensure that objectives are being met. Project managers therefore utilise a management system with metrics to track progress, identify areas for improvement, and make data-driven decisions (see Chapter 11.6). This ongoing monitoring helps ensure that the project stays aligned with organisational goals and can adapt to changing circumstances.

Overall, project management is a critical component of digital transformation projects. It provides the structure, discipline, and oversight needed to navigate the complexities and challenges of these initiatives. By ensuring clear planning, effective communication, efficient resource management, and continuous monitoring, project management helps organisations achieve their digital transformation goals and drive sustainable growth in the digital age. Without robust project management, digital transformation projects are more likely to encounter obstacles, miss deadlines, and fail to deliver the desired outcomes.

11.4 CHANGE MANAGEMENT FOR DIGITAL TRANSFORMATION

Digital transformation is inherently disruptive. It involves significant changes to processes, technologies, and organisational structures. Such changes can create uncertainty and resistance among employees. Effective change management helps mitigate this resistance by preparing and supporting employees through the transition. By addressing the human side of change, change management ensures that employees are not just passive recipients of digital transformation and new technologies, but active participants in the transformation journey.

11.4.1 The Change Management Process

Change management is therefore a process for preparing and implementing organisational change driven by digital transformation. The more strategies, programmes, and projects change the basic conditions (operating model) in the organisation, the more the managers and employees must change as well. Change management is an instrument for steering change processes in the organisation in which stakeholders are actively involved. A change management process often includes strategies to help teams implement an organisational change step-by-step, introducing the change as a pilot project in one part of the organisation or to ensure support for key stakeholders before introducing a new initiative (By, 2005; Peter, 2024).

The roots of the change process date back to the 1940s and it was described by the social psychologist Kurt Lewin (1947). In his theory, he assumes that a change process goes through three stages: unfreeze – change – refreeze (see Box 11.3). Lewin explained (1947, p. 32) that 'in discussing the means of bringing about a desired state of affairs one should not think in terms of the "goal to be reached" but rather in terms of a change "from the present level to the desired one"'. It is therefore a matter of breaking the current state, bringing about a movement and consolidating the newly achieved state. If we apply this model to digital transformation, we could adapt Lewin's formula as follows: unfreeze – transform – remain agile (Hussain et al., 2018; Peter, 2017).

Box 11.3: Kurt Lewin's Change Management Model

Kurt Lewin's (1947) principle of change, known as Lewin's Change Management Model, involves a three-step process known as the 'Unfreeze-Change-Refreeze' framework (Figure 11.7):

- **Unfreeze (preparation for change):** this initial stage is about preparing the organisation or teams for change. It involves breaking down the existing status quo before building up a new operating model. The goal is to get people to recognise and accept that change is necessary.
- **Change (transformation/transition):** the actual transition (digital transformation) from the old to the new operating model takes place. This is often a period of confusion, learning, and transition as managers and employees begin to learn and adapt to the new processes, technology, structures, and behaviours (operating model).
- **Refreeze (setting the new state and remain agile):** once the change has been implemented and the new operating model has been adopted, the final stage is about making these changes stick. To ensure lasting change, it's important to remain agile and being able to adapt to changing circumstances.

Lewin's framework emphasises the importance of preparing for change, managing the transformation, and reinforcing the new operating model to ensure it is anchored in the organisation.

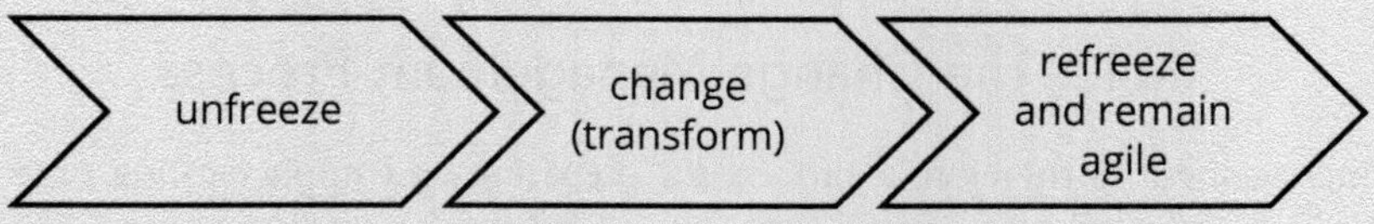

Figure 11.7 Kurt Lewin's change process adapted to digital transformation

Source: own illustration adapted from Lewin (1947)

The aim is to achieve a state that allows a certain flexibility in terms of the new operating model, which is change itself. With that, digital transformation is not just a change process, but a new reality that will endure for the time being, at least.

As mentioned earlier, Kotter (2012) created a popular change management method, which also highlights that organisations shall demonstrate the urgency to employees and to make it clear how important it is to change (the 'unfreeze' stage), to build a leadership team to lead, coordinate, and communicate organisational change based on a strategic vision and initiatives to outline how the future will be different from the past, and implement these initiatives (programmes and projects; the actual 'change/transform' stage), and to consolidate changes in the culture until they are strong enough to replace old habits (the 'refreeze' stage).

11.4.2 Project Communication and Skills Development

Communication is the most important part of change management (Peter, 2024). Clear, consistent, and transparent communication helps to align everyone in the organisation around the transformation goals. It helps employees understand the reasons behind the change, the benefits it brings, and their role in the process. Effective communication reduces uncertainty and builds trust, making employees more likely to embrace the changes.

It is important to inform those affected and to solicit their support. The primary goal is to constructively communicate the change project, starting with the management and extending to the employees. First, the willingness to change must be awakened among the managers. It is a matter of taking their fears seriously and preparing them for their task of smoothing the change for their employees. The better the managers can transform the employees' concerns and frustration into motivation, the faster the organisation's goal can be achieved (By, 2005).

Training courses and workshops can help solidify internal corporate communications and empower managers to communicate with their colleagues in a way that aligns with the organisation's goals. In workshops, managers can work with senior management and communication officers to develop consistent, unambiguous team messages. Afterwards, the whole organisation must be informed about the change. At a staff meeting and in a way that staff will understand, management must explain why the change is necessary. Often, employees do not understand the information right away because their emotions and fear of the future get in the way. In a situation such as this, internal corporate communication has the task of preparing the messages from the strategy meeting for quick dissemination via suitable information channels in a way that presents the background in an understandable way to the target group. It is important to avoid speculations and rumours. Communication must be maintained throughout the entire change process. It is essential to inform staff on where the organisation or the team stands in the change process and assure them that it is worth the effort.

As change processes usually affect the whole organisation, they also require a new leadership culture, which organisations like to call a 'change leadership programme'. In this process, principles that are to guide managers' actions in future are outlined and communicated.

These principles are based on the challenges of the change process and are intended to help management prepare the team for the increasing complexity of market requirements.

Moreover, change management involves training and development. Digital transformation often requires managers and employees to acquire new skills and competencies (see Chapter 11.5.1). Through targeted training programmes, the organisation can support employees, so they are equipped with the necessary knowledge and skills to effectively use new digital technologies and adapt to the new operating model / new processes. This not only enhances their productivity but also boosts their confidence and morale, making the transition smoother.

11.4.3 Conclusion

Change management helps in aligning the transformation with the organisation's strategic intent, culture and values. Every organisation has its unique culture, which shapes how changes are perceived and adopted. By understanding and aligning with the organisational culture and operating model, change management ensures that the transformation is not just a top-down mandate, but a shared vision embraced by everyone. This cultural alignment is vital for sustaining the changes and embedding them into the organisation's DNA.

Change management addresses the human aspects of change, ensuring that employees are prepared, engaged, and supported throughout the transition. By fostering effective communication, training, stakeholder engagement, cultural alignment, and continuous improvement, change management paves the way for a smooth and successful digital transformation. Without effective change management, even the best-designed digital transformation initiatives might not deliver their objectives, as they fail to gain the necessary buy-in and support from those who are most impacted by the changes (namely, both managers and employees). Therefore, integrating change management into digital transformation programmes and projects is not just beneficial, but essential for achieving long-term success and driving organisational growth in the digital age.

11.5 DIGITAL LEADERSHIP

Digital transformation requires a new leadership culture. In particular, increasing digitalisation requires a stronger focus on people in order to get employees excited about the digital roadmap (Peter, 2024). If an organisation wants to convince and motivate their employees, they will have to develop a collaborative leadership style: instead of domination and control, digital leadership is about networking and trust. Instead of demanding performance, options are offered.

Digital leaders should see themselves, first and foremost, as facilitators, mediators, and networkers. The focus should increasingly fall on people and on their needs. It is important to establish consistent corporate values and a corporate culture that offers trust and security. This is one of the core tasks of digital leadership. It serves to create an environment that builds team spirit, shows them the common goal and, at the same time, leaves enough room for self-development.

11.5.1 Developing Skills for the Digital Age

Effective digital leadership involves the development of digital capabilities and skills within the organisation. Together with their employees, digital leaders identify the skills gap, with the insights used to plan and invest into training and development programmes to ensure that employees (and managers) are equipped with the necessary knowledge and tools to thrive in the digital age. This focus on capability building not only enhances individual performance but also strengthens the overall organisational capacity to manage and leverage digital technologies.

Digital Leadership Skills

The skills and characteristics that digital leaders require nowadays include the ability to manage heterogeneous and geographically dispersed teams (e.g., employees working from home or outsourced teams) through appropriate team-building measures (see strategic action field of *Digital leadership and culture* in Chapter 9). Digital leaders must be able to build a successful team from a group of diverse people. Leaders should also be agile and flexible in adapting to change. They must be able and willing to react quickly to new situations, and to build and expand networks, set the direction, and encourage employees to be creative and innovative.

Eberl and Drews (2021) identified the components (or values) of digital leadership in a literature review, and identified them to be diversity and inclusion, sustainability, trust, freedom to experiment, openness, transparency, employee focus, and customer centricity. As a result, they determined the 'key ingredients' of digital leadership across three levels:

1 The organisational level, including availability of a company vision, values, culture, governance, decisions, and structure;
2 The digital leader's skills, roles, and leadership style; and
3 The individual level of the organisation on how the team member (employee) experiences people management, knowledge levels, as well as collaboration and communication (in e.g., virtual teams).

Organisations must have the courage to experiment with new approaches and to share these experiences with others. This includes, among other things, the willingness to fail. Leadership programmes are evolving from technically focused training to development processes in which leaders (and employees) take ownership. Only when leaders have personally experienced development and new tools can they pass them on to their team. Innovative ideas emerge through the networking of people from different business areas, generations, and cultures. The more perspectives come together, the greater the potential for continued innovation. In this, the most important skill is daring to take a step forward and trying out new approaches.

Digital Capabilities and Skills Development

With the shift towards the fourth and fifth industrial revolutions, the search for digital talent is also intensifying. At the same time, many existing job profiles are also changing.

Certain professions are disappearing altogether, while completely new job profiles and roles are emerging that offer a wide range of opportunities but require a variety of digital skills. If organisations invest in developing those digital skills, they can remain competitive, retain talent long-term and successfully design digital transformation.

For employees, the most important digital skills include the ability to work with communication technologies, collaboration software and apps, data management and data security, and software solutions to increase productivity. Training solutions should be designed to support the goals of the individual participants and enable them to build or deepen one or more skills within their existing roles. The focus of the training should always fall on the employees and their current needs and interests.

According to a European small business association (European Digital SME Alliance, 2024), the three top priorities for skills development are now in the areas of:

- Artificial intelligence (AI);
- Green (environmental/sustainability) and digital skills; and
- Digital resilience and cybersecurity skills.

This aligns with the 'Future of Jobs Report' from the World Economic Forum (WEF, 2025), which surveyed 1,000 leading global employers (organisations) to provide a perspective on the transformation of work and impact to jobs and skills (see Box 11.4).

Following a skills assessment that identifies gaps and provides input for a corporate skills development programme, new capabilities in the form of up-skilling and re-skilling can be developed via internal company training programmes, public–private partnerships with educational/academic institutions, micro-credentials from various (online) providers, on-the-job training and customised training (delivered by, for example, IT service partners) (European Digital SME Alliance, 2024).

Box 11.4: World Economic Forum Future of Jobs Report

According to WEF (2025), skill gaps are considered the biggest barrier to business transformation by 63% of employers (identifying them as a major barrier over the 2025-2030 period). As a consequence, 85% of employers will prioritise upskilling, 70% expect to hire staff with new skills, 40% plan to reduce staff as their skills become less relevant, and 50% plan to transition staff from declining to growing roles. AI (86%) and robotics and autonomous systems (58%) are regarded as those technology trends over the 2025–2030 period that primarily drive digital transformation. They surveyed organisations anticipate the following jobs to the the fastest growing (top 5):

1. Big Data Specialists
2. FinTech Engineers
3. AI and Machine Learning Specialists

4 Software and Applications Developers
5 Security Management Specialists

The fastest declining jobs are those in process-driven roles such as Postal Service Clerks, Bank Tellers and Related Clerks, Data Entry Clerks, Cashiers and Ticket Clerks, and Administrative Assistants and Executive Secretaries.

Core skills for the digital age are (WEF, 2025):

- Analytical thinking
- Resilience, flexibility, and agility
- Leadership and social influence
- Creative thinking
- Motivation and self-awareness
- Technological literacy

11.5.2 Digital Internal Communication

For sustainable digital transformation, digital internal communication refers to the use of digital tools and platforms to facilitate the exchange of information, ideas, and collaboration within an organisation in support of digital leadership. It encompasses a wide range of activities with a focus on trust building, which includes the development and implementation of digital competencies and skills. Digital internal communication is designed to keep employees informed, engaged, and connected, regardless of their physical location. By leveraging digital technologies, organisations can ensure that their workforce remains cohesive and aligned with the organisation's strategic goals and values.

A research project from Wuersch et al. (2023, 2024) explored digital internal communication at the nexus between digital transformation and internal communication. Based on an integrative review of the existing literature, digital internal communication can be explained as a socio-technical organisational system and as a people-focused phenomenon, which is linked to competency development and trust-building. The conceptual model (see Figure 11.8) can be used by organisations to reflect their current strategies as well as leadership development and skills building in a digital workplace environment.

The analysis revealed that 'developing competencies', inherent on the intrapersonal, interpersonal, and organisational communication levels, sits at the heart of digital internal communication. The study has also shown that competency development leads to digital trust-building. Digital trust, in turn, is the all-embracing mantle of intrapersonal processes, interactions, and relationships, and organisational functioning and success in a digital space. Overall, DIC contributes to the creation and reproduction of socially constructed organisations.

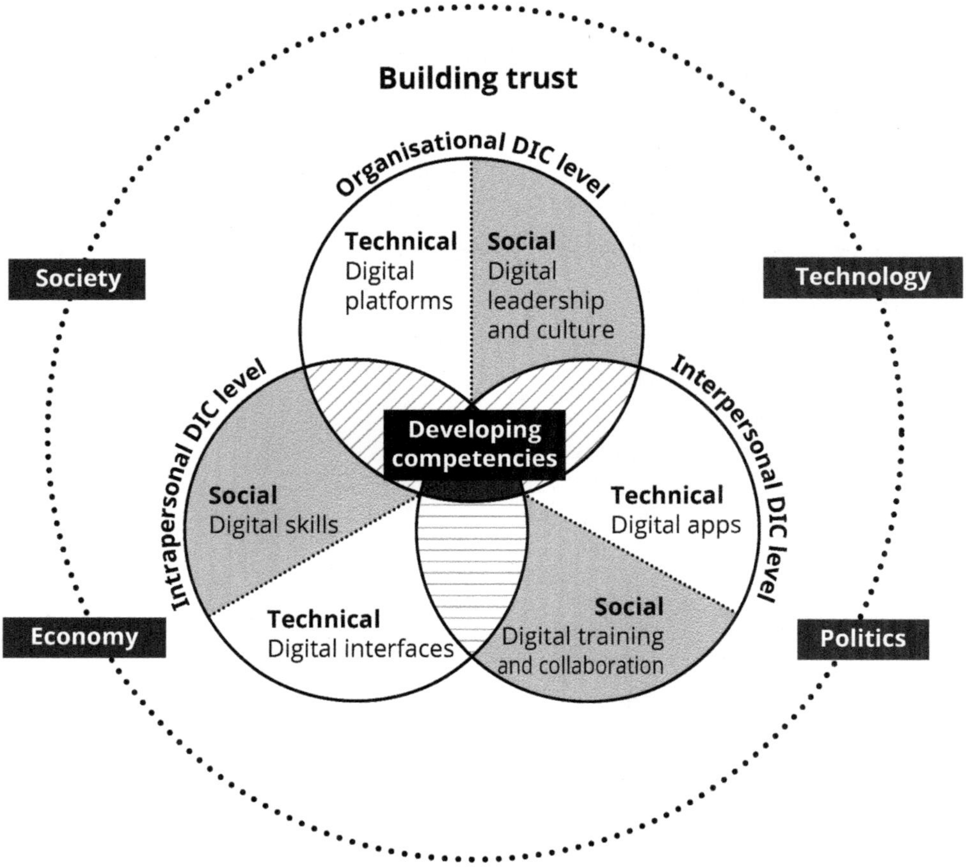

Figure 11.8 Conceptual model for digital internal communication

Source: Wuersch et al., 2023

11.5.3 Conclusion

Digital leadership provides a clear vision and direction. In the face of technological disruption, organisations need a compelling vision that aligns with their strategic goals. Digital leaders articulate this vision, ensuring that all stakeholders understand the purpose and benefits of the transformation. This clarity fosters alignment and commitment across the organisation, driving the collective effort towards common objectives. In order to build a collective effort and culture of (digital) innovation, digital transformation requires a shift in mindset, encouraging experimentation and embracing change. Digital leaders create an environment where innovation can flourish by promoting a culture that values creativity, risk-taking, and continuous capabilities and skills development, leading to organisational learning. They empower employees to explore new ideas, test new technologies, and learn from failures, thus driving the organisation towards their strategic, competitive goals.

Finally, digital leadership is also essential for ensuring ethical and responsible use of technology and AI. As organisations embrace digital transformation, they must navigate complex issues related to data privacy, cybersecurity, and ethical use of AI. Digital leaders set the value framework for digital internal collaboration and communication, ethical behaviour; establish robust governance frameworks, and ensure compliance with relevant regulations. This commitment to digital, ethical leadership builds trust with customers and stakeholders, which is crucial for long-term success in the digital age.

11.6 SUCCESS METRICS OF DIGITAL TRANSFORMATION

Measuring and monitoring progress is vital in long-term, strategic digital transformation programmes. In many organisations, the budgets allocated to digital transformation are massive (i.e., if digital transformation programmes and projects fail, their impact to the long-term success/competitiveness are substantial). Organisations must therefore continuously track progress and make necessary adjustments.

The difficulty with measuring digital transformation success, however, is that a holistic and strategic digital transformation takes several years to implement. Management may lose focus, energy, or interest in the transformation projects, or executives and project members may leave the organisation, causing initiatives to stall. If an organisation is serious about strategic digital transformation, outlining projects and releasing budgets, it must also establish and use a long-term transformation management system comprising of key metrics.

Transformation management can be carried out in two ways (Peter, 2024). First, based on the progress of the project. The digital roadmap or the digital strategy consists of several programmes and projects. Their progress can be measured, for example, with project reports or a traffic-light system.

Second, key strategic success metrics are continuously measures, reviewed, and discussed. These are:

- ***Financials***: is the organisation making more money? Is profitability increasing? This is most often measured by revenue and profit growth, profit margins, or return on investment (ROI) metrics.
- ***Customer focus***: does the organisation make customers more successful and does this bind them to the organisation? This is often measured with customer surveys, social media customer reviews, or customer (net) promotor scores.
- ***Employee focus:*** does the organisation create a modern working environment that is appreciated by its employees? This is often measured via employee opinion surveys.

In addition to the above key success metric, sustainability (see Chapter 3) is an emerging, additional key success metric.

Important concepts to measure financial, customer, and employee relevant metrics (Petzold, 2024) are Objectives and Key Results (OKR) and Key Performance Indicators (KPI):

- Objectives and key results (OKR) form a goal-setting framework consisting of qualitative strategic goals (= objectives and quantitative metrics as key results). With OKRs, organisations can define measurable goals and track their impact/outcomes with a clear focus on strategy implementation.

- Key performance indicators (KPI) are a type of (relative or absolute) performance measurement. KPIs evaluate the success and health of an organisation or a specific programme or project. KPIs provide a focus for strategic and operational improvements and create an analytical basis for decision-making to focus attention on what matters.

Organisations that effectively implement their digital strategies gain digital competitive advantages that can be measured using OKRs and KPIs (see Figure 11.9). Specifically, the

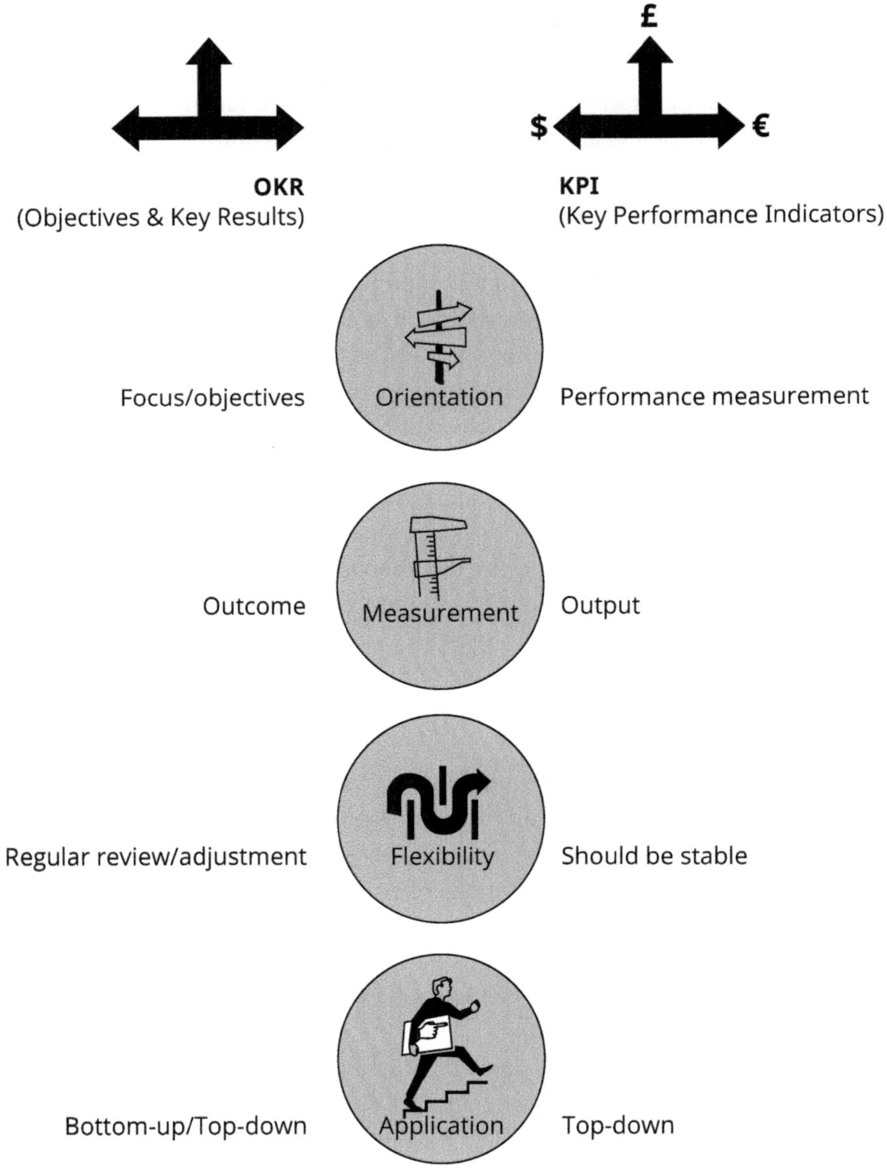

Figure 11.9 Objectives and key results (OKR) and key performance indicators (KPI)

Source: own illustration following Petzold (2024)

focus is on linking the corporate strategy with the digital transformation programme. This includes planning, agile implementation and measurement of the goals and results of output-impact-outcome through coordination and synchronisation with these frameworks.

Organisations should embed financial, customer, and employee metrics (and if possibly, sustainability metrics) in their leadership principles and culture, and leaders and employees should use feedback from the market and the business to continuously improve and develop the digital transformation roadmap.

11.7 CONCLUSION

To successfully and sustainably implement digital transformation strategies across the seven action fields, resources must be allocated, risks must be managed and mitigated, and the change process carefully planned across an organisations' employees and business partners in the context of new digital technology (see Box 11.5). The first step in successful digital transformation implementation is to identify and proactively address potential barriers and risks, followed by a discussion regarding the most suitable (efficient and cost-effective) organisational anchoring of digital transformation.

Box 11.5: How Long Does a Digital Transformation Strategy Take to Implement?

Depending on the size of the organisation, the industry, the culture, and the maturity of the organisation, business strategies are designed to last between two and six years. Digital transformation, which is at the heart of business strategy in the digital age, takes just as long. In a small business, the digital roadmap is planned and outlined for two to three years. In this stretch of time, an SME can plan and implement many strategic initiatives and digital projects. In a large enterprise, the transformation takes longer due to, for example, the complexity of the organisation or IT infrastructure, leadership challenges, culture, and resistance. Usually, the digital strategy is designed for a period of four to six years, although a sustainable digital transformation can take longer. Therefore, organisations should plan for the future (long-term) and think about how many projects they can and want to implement to achieve a competitive position in the market.

Source: Peter (2023, 2024); Peter & Jarratt (2015)

The main success factors that determine the achieved maturity level following a digital transformation strategy update are:

1 **Project management** to structure the strategy into manageable programmes, project portfolios and projects, and to establish a sound programme and project governance to monitor progress;
2 **Change management** to support an organisation in its endeavour towards the intended objectives across the three phases of unfreeze, change/transform, and

refreeze/remain agile, and to actively communicate project steps, challenges, and benefits; and

3 **Digital leadership** with new leadership paradigms, the development of (digital) skills as required by the renewed organisation, and the establishment of a new digital internal collaboration and communication framework.

The three metrics that allow performance monitoring and risk management are the financial metrics alongside customer and employee metrics. Most recently, sustainability metrics are emerging as a fourth success metric for digital transformation. Of course, the planning and implementation of strategic digital transformation must be based on a defined and communication method that can leverage tools: the digital toolkit (as presented in Chapter 12) will build the bridge from theory and frameworks to business practice. Only by planning for, and implementing the three success factors along a pre-defined method, and monitoring progress, digital transformation can be implemented successfully for the long run.

Case Studies

Students can complete the following tasks either based on the focal case study (adapt the questions, as required), or work on the recommended case study for this chapter (*Digital transformation of the city of Lucerne*) and answer the questions below.

1 What risks and barriers can you identify when renewing (digitally transforming) a government organisation (also see Section 11.1.1)?

2 What are the differences between the digital transformation of a business and government (or not-for-profit) organisation?

3 How would you prepare the City of Lucerne for their digital transformation in the three areas of project management, change management, digital leadership (see Chapter 11.2)? How would you recommend the City of Lucerne invest into these three areas?

4 Is the Smart city Lucerne strategy map (2021) a strategic programme or a project portfolio (see Section 11.3.1)? Explain your rationale.

5 What are the benefits of the digital maturity assessments? Why would you recommend this approach to another organisation (see Chapter 12)?

6 What are the tasks of the Chief Digital Officer (CDO) at the city of Lucerne? Define at least ten tasks/deliverables (see also Chapter 11.1.2)?

7 What other activities could CDO Urs Truttmann initiate to advance digital transformation in the city's administration?

Additional cases with student questions for the *implementation of digital transformation* are covered in:

- BRUGG Lifting and its industrial Internet of Things (IIoT) asset management solution 'PVS' (available in the Appendix).
- CRM and sales automation at Transgourmet Switzerland (available online).

- From limited budget to limitless potential: the digital journey of OSHE@UTMKL (available online).
- Valuu: a corporate start-up for digital business model innovation (available in the Appendix).

You will find a collection of case studies for strategic digital transformation in the Appendix and additional cases online at www.strategic-digital-transformation.com

Exercises

Discuss the following questions in your class, in your group or assignment:

1. Discuss the barriers and risks associated with digital transformation in light of Lego's transformation story (see opening case study and Section 11.1.1). Identify at least three barriers/risks and explain how to overcome these.
2. Discuss why Lego's VP of Finance said that digital transformation is a '(...) journey – not a destination' (see opening study case). What does he mean by that?
3. Explain the role of Chief Digital Officer (CDO) (see Section 11.1.2). What are the deliverables (tasks) of a CDO in a large organisation? List and describe at least five tasks.
4. Based on a selected industry/business, try to define strategic activities of the firm to innovate and digitally transform, and categorise them into the following three groups: strategic programmes, projects portfolios and projects (see Section 11.3.1).
5. Forming two small groups (2–4 students in each group), assign a pro and contra position to each group and debate whether change management (and it's 'unfreeze – change – refreeze/remain agile' process) is important (group 1), or overrates and not necessary (group 2) for the digital transformation of firms.
6. For your firm selected in exercise 4, develop a programme of digital capabilities and skills building in the firm (make assumptions, where required). Define at least five potential activities.
7. For the firm selected in exercise 4, define how it could measure digital transformation success with the three metrics of financials, customers, and employees (make assumptions, if required). Define at least three examples for each metric.

Further Reading List

- El Sawy, O. A., Kræmmergaard, P., Amsinck, H., & Vinther, A. L. (2020). How LEGO built the foundations and enterprise capabilities for digital leadership. *MIS Quarterly Executive*, June, 15:2, 141-166.
- European Commission (2022). DigComp Framework. DigComp 2.2, https://joint-research-centre.ec.europa.eu/scientific-activities-z/education-and-training/digital-transformation-education/digital-competence-framework-citizens-digcomp/digcomp-framework_en.
- Mahboub, H., Sadok, H., Chehri, A., & Saadane, R. (2023). Measuring the digital transformation: a key performance indicators literature review. *Procedia Computer Science*, 225, 4570–9.

- WEF (2025). The Future of Jobs Report 2025. World Economic Forum, 7 January, www.weforum.org/publications/the-future-of-jobs-report-2025/.
- Wuersch, L., Neher, A., & Peter, M. K. (2023). Digital internal communication: An interplay of socio-technical elements. *International Journal of Management Reviews*, 25(3), 614–39, https://doi.org/10.1111/ijmr.12323.

References

Agrawal, P., Narain, R., & Ullah, I. (2020). Analysis of barriers in implementation of digital transformation of supply chain using interpretive structural modelling approach. *Journal of Modelling in Management, 15*(1), 297–317.

Andersen, P., & Ross, J. W. (2016, March). Transforming the LEGO Group for the digital economy. In ICIS, *MIT Sloan Management, Center for Information Systems Research*, CISR WP no. 407.

Balakrishnan, R., & Das, S. (2020). How do firms reorganize to implement digital transformation?. *Strategic Change, 29*(5), 531–41.

By, R. T. (2005). Organisational change management: A critical review. *Journal of Change Management, 5*(4), 369–80.

Eberl, J. K., & Drews, P. (2021). Digital leadership-mountain or molehill? A literature review. *Innovation through Information Systems.* Volume III (A collection of latest research on management issues), 223–37.

El Sawy, O. A., Kræmmergaard, P., Amsinck, H., & Vinther, A. L. (2020). How LEGO built the foundations and enterprise capabilities for digital leadership. *MIS Quarterly Executive*, June, 15:*2*, 141–66.

European Digital SME Alliance (2024): *Skills for Digital Leadership*. European DIGITAL SME Alliance, September.

Grundy, T. (1998). Strategy implementation and project management. *International Journal of Project Management, 16*(1), 43–50.

Haffke, I., Kalgovas, B. J., & Benlian, A. (2016). *The Role of the CIO and the CDO in an Organization's Digital Transformation*. Thirty Seventh International Conference on Information Systems, Dublin.

Hussain, S. T., Lei, S., Akram, T., Haider, M. J., Hussain, S. H., & Ali, M. (2018). Kurt Lewin's change model: A critical review of the role of leadership and employee involvement in organizational change. *Journal of Innovation & Knowledge, 3*(3), 123–7.

IPMA (2018): *IPMA Reference Guide. ICB4 in Agile World*. Version 2.3. International Project Management Association (IMPA). Zurich, Switzerland.

Kotter, J.P. (2012): *Leading Change*, Harvard Business Review Press, Boston/USA.

LEGO (2025): *Lego Jobs*, www.lego.com/en-us/careers, accessed 8 January 2025.

Lewin, K. (1947) Frontiers in group dynamics: Concept, method and reality in social science; social equilibria and social change. *Human Relations, 1*(5).

Loonam, J., Eaves, S., Kumar, V., & Parry, G. (2018). Towards digital transformation: Lessons learned from traditional organizations. *Strategic Change, 27*(2), 101–9.

Mahboub, H., & Sadok, H. (2023). Implementing enterprise digital transformation: A contribution to conceptual framework design. *Nankai Business Review International, 14*(1), 35–50.

Morakanyane, R., O'Reilly, P., McAvoy, J., & Grace, A. (2020). *Determining digital transformation success factors*. Proceedings of the 53rd Hawaii International Conference on System Sciences (pp. 4356–65). HICSS.

Peter, M. K. (Hrsg.) (2017). *KMU-Transformation: Als KMU die Digitale Transformation erfolgreich umsetzen. Forschungsresultate und Praxisleitfaden*. FHNW Hochschule für Wirtschaft, Olten/Schweiz, www.kmu-transformation.ch.

Peter, M. K. (Hrsg.) (2019): *Arbeitswelt 4.0: Als KMU die Arbeitswelt der Zukunft erfolgreich gestalten*. Forschungsresultate und Praxisleitfaden. FHNW Hochschule für Wirtschaft, Olten/Schweiz.

Peter, M. K. (Hrsg.) (2021). *Strategieentwicklung im digitalen Zeitalter: Planung und Umsetzung der Digitalen Transformation*. FHNW Hochschule für Wirtschaft und Strategylab, Olten/Schweiz, www.strategische-transformation.ch.

Peter, M. K. (2023). *Digitaler Masterplan für KMU. So gelingt die digitale Transformation in Ihrem Unternehmen*. Verlag Beobachter Edition & Handelszeitung. Zürich/Schweiz, www.digitaler-masterplan.ch.

Peter, M. K. (2024). *The Digital Transformation Canvas. Develop and implement your digital strategy*. FT Publishing/Pearson, London/UK, www.the-digital-transformation-canvas.com.

Peter, M. K., & Jarratt, D. G. (2015). The practice of foresight in long-term planning. *Technological Forecasting and Social Change*, *101*, 49–61.

Peter, M. K., Kraft, C., & Lindeque, J. (2020). Strategic action fields of digital transformation: An exploration of the strategic action fields of Swiss SMEs and large enterprises. *Journal of Strategy and Management*, *13*(1), 160–80.

Petzold, R. (2024): *KPI und OKR in der digitalen Transformation. Strategien für die Planung, Umsetzung, Steuerung sowie Messung der Ergebnisse und Wirkung*. FHNW Hochschule für Wirtschaft, Olten/Schweiz.

Sedlmayer, M. R. (2017). Programmes are not just big projects, *IPMA*, 29 September, https://ipma.world/programme-not-just-big-projects/.

Tanniru, Mohan (2017). Digital Leadership. *AMCIS 2017 Proceedings. 79*. https://aisel.aisnet.org/amcis2017/TREOs/Presentations/79

Ul Musawir, A., Abd-Karim, S. B., & Mohd-Danuri, M. S. (2020). Project governance and its role in enabling organizational strategy implementation: A systematic literature review. *International Journal of Project Management*, *38*(1), 1–16.

Vogelsang, K., Liere-Netheler, K., Packmohr, S., & Hoppe, U. (2018). Success factors for fostering a digital transformation in manufacturing companies. *Journal of Enterprise Transformation*, *8*(1-2), 121–42.

WEF (2025): *Future of Jobs Report 2025. Insight Report*, January. World Economic Forum, Geneva/Switzerland.

Wuersch, L., Neher, A., & Peter, M. K. (2023): Digital internal communication: An interplay of socio-technical elements. *International Journal of Management Reviews*, doi.org/10.1111/ijmr.12323.

Wuersch, L., Neher, A., Maley, J. F., & Peter, M. K. (2024). Using a digital internal communication strategy for digital capability development, *International Journal of Strategic Communication*, *18*(3), 167–88.

Zoppelletto, A., Orlandi, L. B., Zardini, A., Rossignoli, C., & Kraus, S. (2023). Organizational roles in the context of digital transformation: A micro-level perspective. *Journal of Business Research*, *157*, 113563.

12

TRANSFORMATION IN PRACTICE – DIGITAL TRANSFORMATION TOOLKIT

Learning Goals

By the end of this chapter, you should...

- Be able to apply theory into practice via the *Digital Transformation Toolkit* for implementation of digital transformation concepts.
- Be able to describe the ten project steps for digital transformation and develop a digital transformation project plan for an organisation.
- Be able to describe the activities in each of the ten project steps for digital transformation process for an organisation.
- Be able to analyse and evaluate the ACT method (Analyse, Create, Transform) for a specific organisation.
- Be able to evaluate and prioritise candidate digital projects.
- Be able to document a digital roadmap/digital transformation strategy based on the inputs from managers, employees, investigations, and workshops.
- Be able to critically evaluate the tools/templates from the *Digital Transformation Toolkit*.

Digital Transformation in Practice at Synchrony (USA)

Synchrony Financial is a consumer financial services company based in the USA, offering a wide range of credit products (including credit cards) through its digital financial ecosystem. With a history dating back to 1932, Synchrony has evolved into a leader in consumer financing, managing over 70 million active customer accounts across more than 480,000 partner locations and processing over 240 million transactions per month (Chaudhuri, 2025). Synchrony's corporate strategy leverages deep industry expertise, advanced data analytics, and a dynamic technology platform to deliver value to customers and partners. Key strategic initiatives include the expansion of digital capabilities (investing in digital platforms to enhance the customer experience and streamline operations), partnership growth (expanding partnerships across various industries to diversify revenue streams), innovation and technology (developing new financial products and services to meet evolving consumer needs), as well as sustainability and social responsibility (implementing sustainable practices and supporting community initiatives).

Across its digital transformation programme and project portfolio, over many years Synchrony has successfully planed and implemented various digital strategy projects across the seven action fields of digital transformation:

1 **Customer centricity**: driven by data analytics and insights, Synchrony focuses on both B2B and B2B2C models, prioritising the customer experience.
2 **New digital technologies**: development of proprietary technology like SyPI, which integrates credit capabilities into partners' mobile apps.
3 **Data and the cloud**: building a data lake to leverage rich data sets for strategic and operational purposes.
4 **New strategies and business models**: launching a unified digital marketplace to enhance the B2B2C (business-to-business-to-consumers) offering.
5 **Operational excellence / process management**: implementing technology-driven process management capabilities for efficiency and agility.
6 **Digital leadership and culture:** promoting a hybrid work model and fostering a supportive work environment.
7 **Digital marketing:** utilising an extensive marketing technology stack and digital channels to strengthen marketing capabilities.

In the future, Synchrony will continue to drive its digital transformation agenda by leveraging AI capabilities. Most recently, a hackathon identified AI opportunities such as risk management, credit limit management, fraud prevention, and personalised shopping experiences. The integration of generative AI into Synchrony's marketplace is one of the first tangible results from these efforts. Digital transformation in practice requires a holistic view of all action fields, and a planning method that is well-structured and clear to all stakeholders of the firm (in addition, the three success factors of project management, change management and digital leadership as outlined in Chapter 11).

Source: Sudip Chaudhuri (2025): Case study 'Action fields of digital transformation at Synchrony Financial (USA)' (case study available online)

12.0 INTRODUCTION

In a dynamic market environment driven by new digital technologies, it is important to develop and continuously optimise successful competitive strategies for the digital age. This chapter focuses on the traditional strategy development process of analysis, strategy formulation, implementation, monitoring, and optimisation to provide a practical approach to realising digital transformation projects by drawing on the seven action fields of digital transformation (Chapters 4–10). Such a practical strategic digital transformation method for the fourth/fifth industrial revolutions needs to offer a practice-oriented structure for understanding the market and one's own firm's situation (*Analyse*), designing strategic digital capabilities, competencies, and innovations (*Create*), and implementing, continuously evaluating, and optimising them (*Transform*), in order to ensure the firms' sustainable success, while ensuring strategic flexibility.[1]

This chapter will 'transform' the theory (from Chapters 1–11) into business practice, based on a practical digital transformation toolkit centred around the ACT method (see Box 12.1), a strategy development method developed in Switzerland over the past five years (Peter, 2021, 2023, 2024). This chapter therefore is purposefully not theory-led, but more practical in its nature, allowing students and practitioners (e.g., business leaders/owners, CDOs/CIOs as well as strategy, digital innovation and project managers) to plan and implement their own digital transformation in ten steps, as described in Chapter 12.2.

Box 12.1: ACT Method (Analyse, Create, Transform)

- **Analyse:** market analysis with topics such as customer expectations, competitors, environmental factors, technology trends, and the firm's own digital maturity.
- **Create:** developing and shaping the vision as well as strategic core competencies, business models, working environments, and digital channels.
- **Transform:** implementation of the strategy roadmap with a new market positioning, new ideas/products and ongoing evaluation, selection and optimisation of options to improve strategic flexibility.

Figure 12.1 ACT method

Source: Peter (2021, 2023, 2024)

[1]This chapter is based on previously published research in Peter 2017/2021/2023/2024.

12.1 ACT METHOD (ANALYSE, CREATE, TRANSFORM)

Most businesses, if at all, use the traditional process of strategic development (analysis, formulation, implementation, monitoring, and optimisation). In light of the fourth/fifth industrial revolutions, for many years now, some organisations have used the seven action fields of digital transformation as a navigation aid/checklist, in order to capture all relevant topics for the development of an effective digital competitive strategy. Based on understanding changing customer needs, the potential and risks of new digital technologies and the strategic use of data, strategies and business models that ensure or increase the competitiveness of businesses in the digital age can be developed. The traditional strategy development process has therefore been expanded to include the strategic action fields of digital transformation. Acknowledging that many small businesses (see Chapter 1) often have no (digital) strategies, the ACT method was developed to provide a practical basis for developing corporate strategies in the digital age in ten steps. It is, however, still based on the core elements of strategic planning (e.g., Cesnovar, 2006; Mintzberg, 1994).

Each phase of the ACT method is linked to the strategic action fields of digital transformation with the respective related, strategic topics. The approach taken with the ACT method is based on design science research, an approach for academically rigorous research that develops solutions to business and management practice problems, developed by the field of information systems (Hevner et al., 2004). The approach includes four elements that enable the development of new solutions (innovations, products) to solve practice problems (Hevner et al., 2004; Kuechler & Vaishnavi, 2008; Venable, 2006). Kuechler and Vaishnavi (2008, p. 489) formulate the approach as 'learning through the act of building' – solutions are built in a learning process that integrates academic and practice knowledge and experience. The four elements include:

1 Analysis of the environment or problem diagnosis (people, organisations, technologies);
2 Development and construction (technology innovations, products, processes, systems);
3 Justification and evaluation of the solution (field studies, surveys, experiments, simulations); and a
4 Knowledge base (methods, models, instruments).

Based on design science research, the ACT method (Peter, 2020) provides the knowledge base to analyse the environment (*Analyse*), develop/build solutions (*Create*), and continuously justify and evaluate them in an agile environment during implementation (*Transform*). The method simplifies the traditional strategy development process, with a focus on digital transformation topics and strategic questions.

12.1.1 Analyse – Obtaining and Using Data

Analysis tools support organisations with the groundwork of the strategy process, enabling managers to understand and discuss strategic issues based on internal and external information and analysis. Knowledge gaps and strategic uncertainty in the strategy process can then be reduced by identifying threats and opportunities to the strategic transformation process. In this way, organisations can use their strengths to exploit opportunities and reduce weaknesses to cope with threats. In many organisations, IT solutions are also used to utilise an organisation's data for strategic decision-making. Topics in the *Analyse* phase include:

- Customer expectations;
- Competitive dynamics;
- Environmental factors;
- Technology trends; and
- Data about and used in the current product and service portfolio.

With the analysis, the organisation can gather and present relevant basic information in an understandable way and, on that basis, make strategic decisions.

12.1.2 Create – Building Capabilities and Creating Innovations

With the increasing pace of market changes and new digital technologies, the pressure on organisations to develop (create) new strategies and innovations is growing. The findings from the *Analyse* phase are used in this process. Innovations are vital for organisations to maintain their competitive edge, but to be able to design innovations, organisations need to develop the skills that enable them to use technology strategically and to collaborate strategically with partners. Co-creation describes a concept that in dynamic markets, through interaction and experimentation, creates the link between strategic focus and strategic flexibility. Co-creating value with customers, suppliers, competitors, and other partners shapes and forms new markets based on their needs and requirements in a dynamic, digital market environment.

The topics in the *Create* phase include:

- (Digital) Vision;
- Core capabilities;
- Business models;
- Ecosystems with customers and partners;
- Market positioning;
- Customer experience/journey;
- New work;
- New business processes/process automation;
- Digital marketing.

In this way, contemporary digital strategies and business models are created, which are implemented by means of activities, enabled by new capabilities, infrastructures, networks, products, and services, and that create new value for customers and the organisation.

12.1.3 Transform – Implementing, Testing, and Optimising Strategies

In fast-moving markets, the strategy and its implementation plan must be continuously monitored, tested, and adjusted – both before and during implementation. Assessments are carried out to test the changes in the market and in the organisation itself, as well as their impact on the strategy. In addition, feasibility and efficiency are continuously tested and optimised. This phase should test whether the strategy delivers the desired return, whether the growth targets are achieved, the necessary resources (staff, finances) are available, and any plans are coordinated and realistic. The plans include marketing, production, human resources, finance, and leadership concepts. Therefore, the *Transform* phase includes the topics:

- Ideas and products;
- Strategic flexibility; and
- Process transparency and efficiency.

Here the concept of 'stress testing' is used, in which new business models and innovations should be tested. This is particularly important in order to continuously assess the organisation's agility and strategic flexibility. In stress testing, organisations evaluate their strategy in the context of scenarios, possible crises, new laws, and/or technologies. This testing provides insights and a more robust strategy, so that the organisation can react in a more agile way to market changes. The results lead to further analyses and, afterwards, an adjustment of strategy.

Box 12.2: Empirical Studies Supporting the ACT Method

The first foundational study on digital transformation from a survey of Swiss organisations with 2,590 study participants helped to identify the seven strategic action fields of digital transformation (Chapters 4–10) (Peter, 2017; Peter et al., 2020). The second large study with 1,812 study participants further examined the data from the first study and identified 35 strategic topics (Peter, 2021): It identified and surveyed the five most frequently mentioned strategic topics for each of the seven action fields of digital transformation (7 action fields, x each with the 5 most often cited strategic topics = 35 topics). Most importantly, the study clearly validated that organisations are active in all seven action fields and allowed the 24 most important strategic topics in the digital age to be identified. All strategic topics derived from the first study, according to which in the second study were implemented (or currently worked on) in over half (>49%) of the sample, were defined as 'best practice' and therefore embedded in the ACT method in the respective strategic action field (see Figure 12.2).

(Continued)

The hypothesis for other firms is that if half or more of the sampled organisations are working on a topic, then this topic should be at least discussed (or in the best case, elaborated) in any other organisation as well.

Visit www.strategic-digital-transformation.com to access the toolkit.

Source: Peter, Lindeque, Savoy, & Tonazzi (2021)

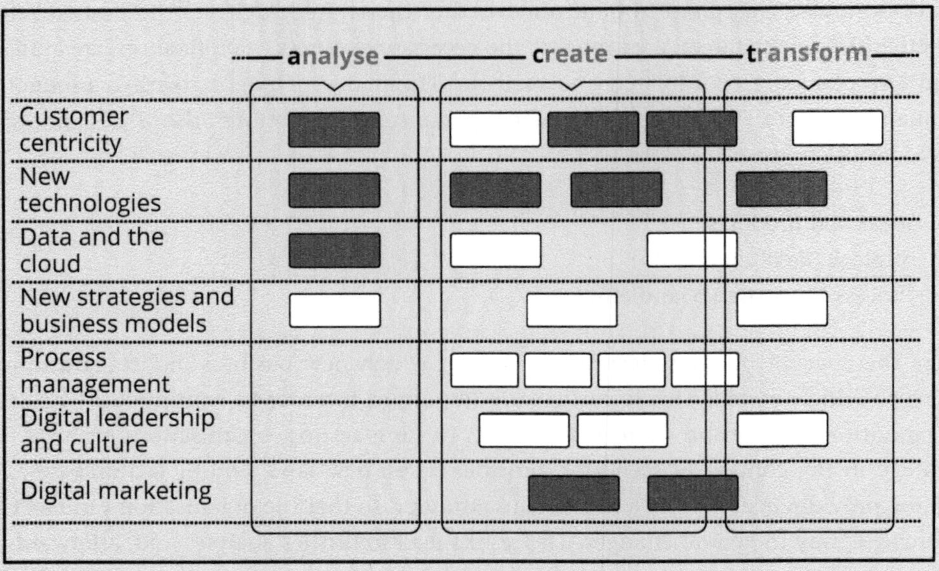

Figure 12.2 ACT and the strategic action fields of digital transformation

Source: Peter (2017, 2021, 2023, 2024)

12.2 DIGITAL TRANSFORMATION WITH ACT IN TEN STEPS

Using the ACT (Analyse, Create, Transform) method, an organisation therefore can ensure that they cover the 24 most important strategic topics for the future digital strategy. The organisation will develop the digital transformation strategy in the three ACT phases as separate workshops and in ten strategy steps. Before and between the workshops, there are various pre- and post-processing activities: these are described in the ten steps that follow (see Chapter 12.3 for the *Digital Transformation Toolkit* and links to download the toolkit materials). The ten step ACT strategy development process is the primary applied strategy design process that emerged from the multi-year research process described in Box 12.2 (see Figure 12.3).

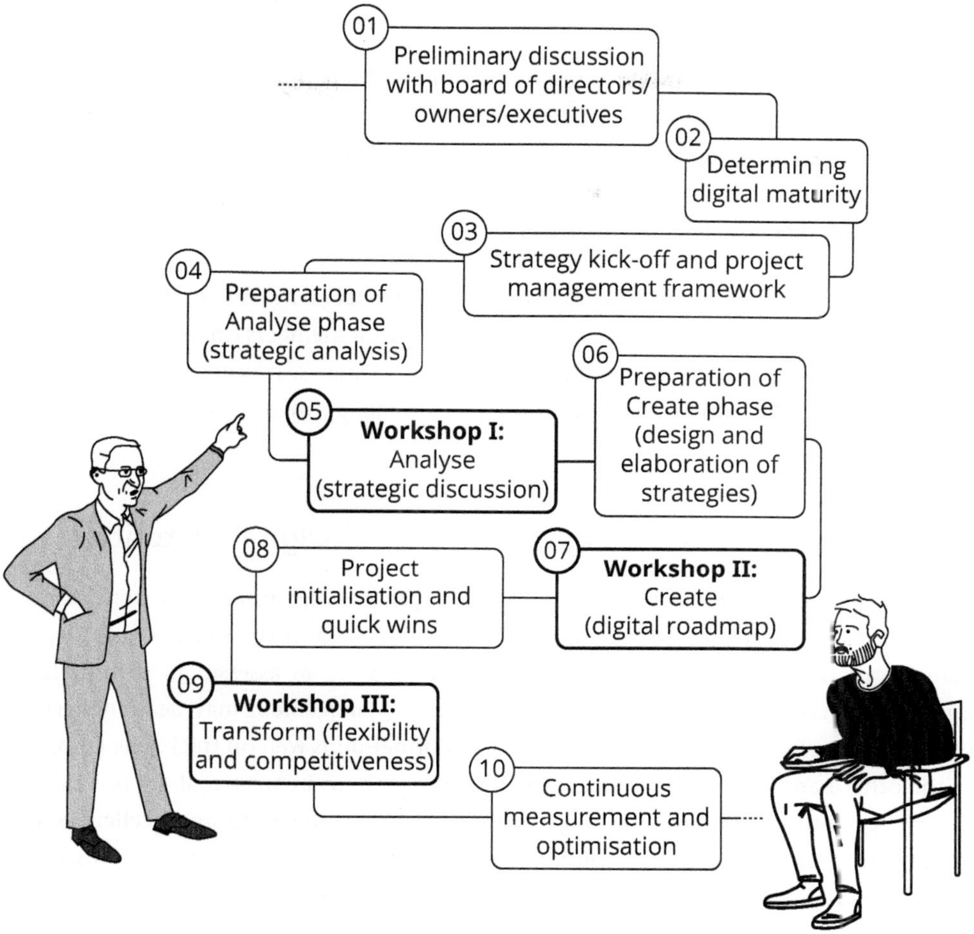

Figure 12.3 Ten steps of digital transformation projects

Source: Peter (2021, 2023, 2024)

Step 1: Preliminary Discussion with Board of Directors/Owners/Executives

In a semi-structured discussion or mini-workshop with the board of directors, owners, and/or executive management (top-down approach), the person in charge of the digital transformation programme (e.g., a strategy manager/consultant or newly appointed CDO) can elicit and outline the first important strategic questions and issues for a specific firm. Typical questions for the initiators and stakeholders of the new strategy are, for example:

- What new digital technology is impacting your industry/business the most?
- What is not running optimally in terms of the business, processes, products and services?

- What do the managers often think about when receiving complaints from customers, business partners, or employees?
- Which departments or product groups are often underperforming?
- What topics should the business discuss/cover in a strategy workshop?
- For which strategy topics does the business normally not take enough time (or which topics are not dealt with sufficiently)?
- Who should be involved in the strategy development process?

Step 1 is important for obtaining buy-in from senior management, but also to help scope the digital transformation programme and identify those team members (managers and employees) who should participate in the kick-off workshop in step 3. It is an important first step towards realising the 'unfreeze' phase in the change management process (see Chapter 11 and Box 11.3).

Step 2: Determining the Degree of Digital Maturity

Often, organisations will have carried out partial aspects of digitalisation or strategic digital transformation. Therefore, not all topics need to be tackled in the same way or depth. A maturity analysis to determine a firm's digital maturity is an assessment of how far the organisation has come in their digital achievements. Management may be convinced that it has already achieved a lot and that digital transformation is well on track. The employees, on the other hand, may still see a lot of potential – perhaps in areas that are not currently on management's radar. Determining digital maturity is therefore an excellent starting point on the path to digital transformation. Following the survey, the evaluations are presented and discussed by the board of directors and management as well as by the individual project teams and departments. Through this discussion, a common understanding of the situation, the topics, and the perceived digital maturity is developed, thereby supporting the 'unfreeze' phase of the change management process. The analysis can be designed as an online survey and is, ideally, based on the seven action fields of digital transformation (see Box 12.3). The answers to the questions and its subsequent evaluation in the form of lists, bar charts or spider diagrams produces meaningful results for presentation and discussion. The resulting evaluation of the results enables the organisation to answer many important questions, such as:

- How competitive is our organisation in the digital age?
- How far have we progressed with our digital transformation?
- Why do we assess our progress as low/medium/high?
- Have we started or already completed projects in all action fields, and where is potential present?
- Where do we have to do more or show a higher degree of maturity?

Box 12.3: The 'Digital Strategy Check'

The Digital Strategy Check is based on the seven action fields of digital transformation and helps to determine an organisation's digital maturity in the form of a maturity analysis based on 24 strategic questions of the ACT method. If, during the strategy process, organisations want to take the opinions of their employees into account (bottom-up approach), several employees (or all employees in a smaller business) can complete the digital strategy check as well. In this way, the organisation receives an individual evaluation across the entire firm and all departments.

Visit www.digital-strategy-check.com to complete a free digital strategy assessment.

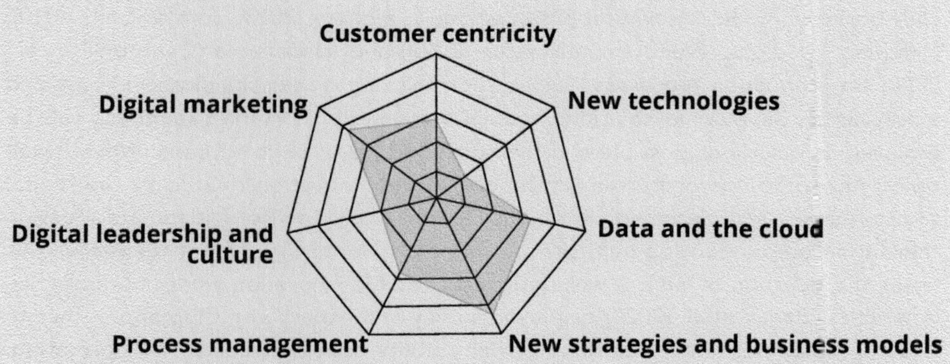

Figure 12.4 Digital Strategy Check maturity assessment

Source: Peter (2017, 2021, 2023, 2024)

Step 3: Strategy Kick-Off and Project Management Framework

In a first large workshop, the topics that were identified by the board of directors, owners, and management are presented and discussed in combination with the results of a maturity analysis or the 'Digital Strategy Check'. The participants (identified/defined in steps 1 and 2) should develop and document goals, topics, tasks, project teams, deadlines, and the process for strategy development to define the scope of the firm's strategic digital transformation. In the ACT method, these three initial process steps (1–3) now lead to *Gate 1* (Digital Strategy Check and strategy kick-off, see the template in Chapter 12.3), an initial project management framework (see Chapter 11.3).

Step 4: Preparation of Analyse Phase (Strategic Analysis)

Some tasks defined during the strategy kick-off (step 3) need to be completed in preparation for the first workshop. These include, for example, an updated competitor analysis, the evaluation of the customer experience/journey, and customer feedback (see Chapter 4), to identify new digital technology based on the technology radar template (see Chapter 5), to create an overview of all data (see Chapter 6) that could be used operationally (for instance for process automation) or strategically (for instance, to build new business models and ecosystems).

Box 12.4: The Power of Well-Designed Workshops for Strategic Innovation

Design thinking approaches to strategy innovation processes are strongly associated with business model innovation (Osterwalder & Pigneur, 2013; Zott & Amit, 2010), including for digital (Vendraminelli et al., 2023) and sustainable (Centobelli et al., 2020) transformation processes. Such design thinking places significant reliance and emphasis on developing solutions in such a manner that market feedback can be achieved as quickly as possible and then captured on an ongoing basis. When developing new offerings or pursuing business model innovation related to the digital transformation, well designed workshops can serve as a tool for initiation of a design thinking strategic development process ahead of capturing market feedback. This raises the question of what a well-designed strategic innovation workshop looks like in practice. Barjak et al. (2022) employed survey and expert workshop approaches to develop customer segments for electricity utility business model transformation, showing that expert workshops with diverse participants representing the appropriate internal and external stakeholders in the focus of the workshop can lead to results that are very well aligned with the insights of far more resource intensive survey-based evidence. Ideally the process is also iterative and allows workshop participants time within and across a series of workshops to contribute their insights. By ensuring diverse participants (i.e., experience and knowledge) and an iterative approach, the inherent subjectivity of the workshop approaches is counteracted, leading to better results. The use of canvases and other similar tools enables expert workshops to stay focused and develop useful insights.

Step 5: Workshop I: *Analyse* (strategic discussion)

In this phase, through a bottom-up approach, all strategic action fields will be discussed with all employees (in small businesses) or a selected group of employees (representing all departments and functions/roles in a large enterprise). The recommended tool in this phase is the *Workshop canvas for digital transformation* (see Box 12.4 and 12.5), which allows an engagement across all important topics of a digital strategy. Employees and managers are being invited to discuss the current challenges in each action field and ideate/brainstorm potential strategic projects to capture future value to enable growth and build a competitive position for the firm in the digital age.

At this point of time, the ACT method also suggests four specific strategic topics (market analysis, customer expectations, technology trends, and strategic data) to be discussed specifically, in addition to the findings from the bottom-up workshops with the canvas tool as presented in Box 12.5, thereby allowing ideas and opportunities to be documented and summarised. In turn, preparatory tasks for step 6 in the strategy development process are outlined.

Box 12.5: Workshop Canvas for Digital Transformation

The workshop canvas for digital transformation delivers quick results. In a one-day workshop, the team covers the seven action fields of digital transformation with the help of predefined topics and questions in order to compile and describe challenges, opportunities, and project ideas. In this way, the organisation's management is intentionally using the collective knowledge of the organisation (see Figure 12.5) and ensures that the experiences, ideas, and suggestions for improvement from those employees who spend their days working in the store, factory, or in the field are also incorporated into the strategy development process. The results from the workshops are documented and the completed workshop canvas is recorded in a photo log or screenshot when workshopped with virtual teams. Then, the results are communicated to those within the organisation and the employees, with participants thanked for their energy and ideas. See Chapter 12.3 for the *Digital Transformation Toolkit* and links to download the toolkit materials. The diversity of inputs (i.e., knowledge and expertise) can be managed by expanding or constraining the internal and external stakeholders that are involved in the process. The more stakeholders that are involved, the more likely the work will require more time and coordination effort.

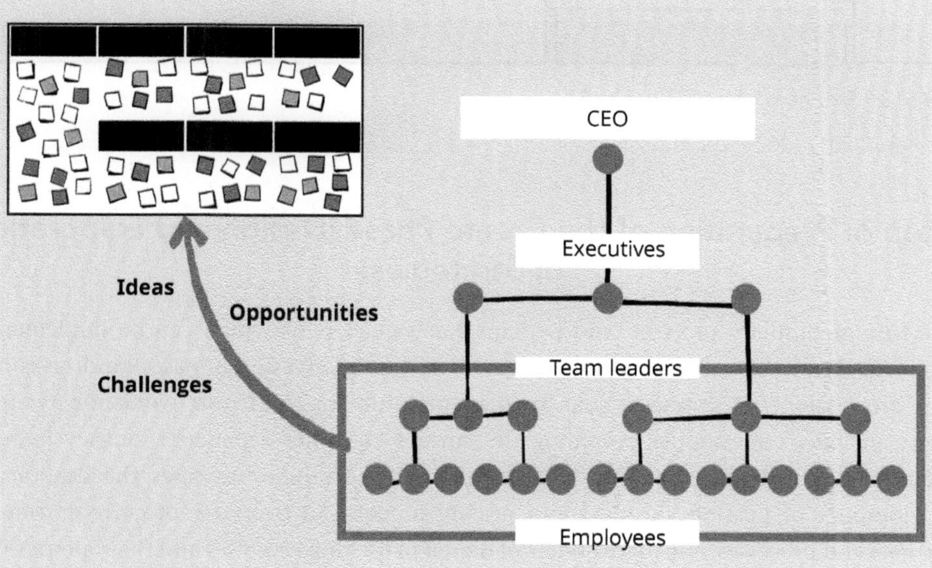

Figure 12.5 Ideation with the digital transformation canvas (bottom-up approach)

Source: Peter (2017, 2021, 2023, 2024)

The completion of step 5 leads to *Gate 2* which is mostly concluded (documented) in the form of a SWOT analysis (see example Figure 12.6), which summarises the identified strengths, weaknesses, opportunities and threats from the *Analyse* phase.

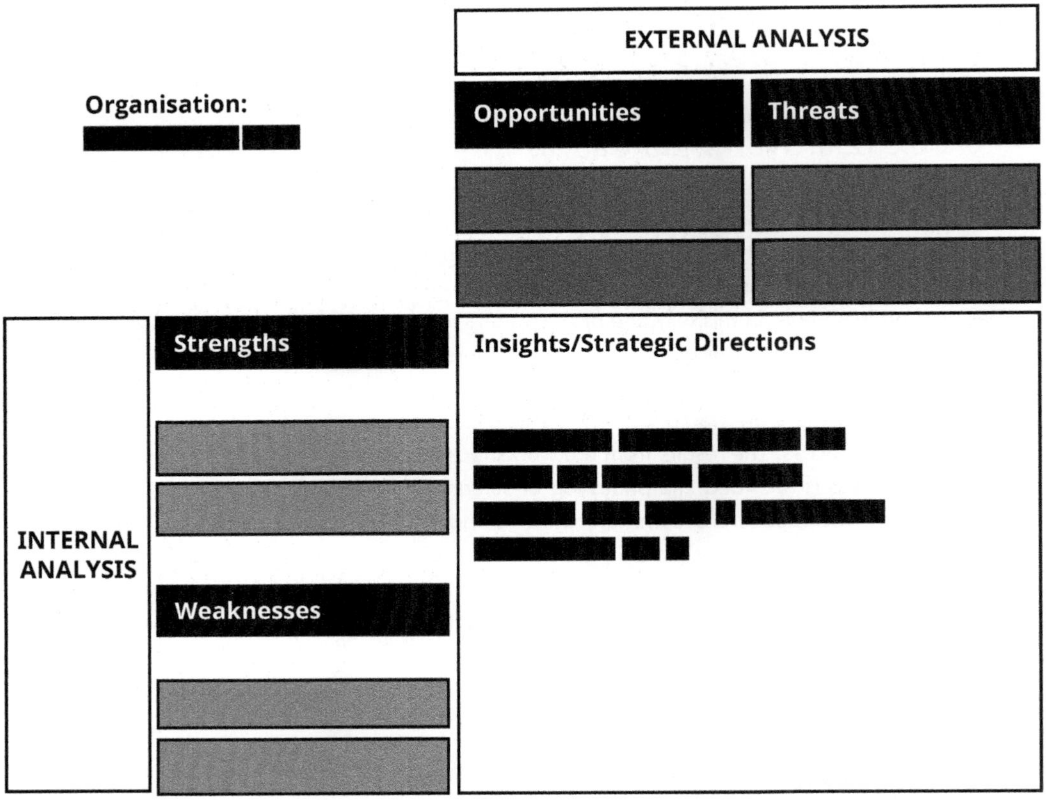

Figure 12.6 Example of SWOT analysis

Source: Peter (2017, 2021, 2023, 2024)

Step 6: Preparation of the Create Phase (Design and Elaboration of Strategies)

The first preliminary projects (and perhaps some quick-wins which can be implemented immediately, without the need for separate business or investment cases) and tasks may arise from the *Analyse* phase (step 5) in preparation for the *Create* workshop (step 7). These include, for example, recording the current customer experience/journey in more detail to identify digital technology implementation opportunities/use cases, the ideation and development of possible business and pricing models, an overview of current strategic partners and processes, and an overview of digital marketing activities and their metrics. The list of deliverables/tasks in this step 6 is a result of the SWOT analysis, that automatically led to activities for the project team.

Step 7: Workshop II: *Create* (Digital Roadmap)

The *Create* phase topics are a result of project ideas from step 5 and further analysis and preparation work in step 6. All strategic topics (project ideas or candidate projects) shall now be discussed, prioritised, and added to the digital roadmap (a digital strategy document). This requires one or multiple workshops (in the form of both bottom-up and top-down discussions). In this phase, the digital vision, the digital transformation programme, project portfolios and individual strategic projects are documented.

The project ideas (candidates) from steps 5/6 are collected and categorised by topic. For this purpose, the business can use the action fields for categorisation or create new, organisation-specific categories. Often, ideas are grouped into 'possible projects'. The project ideas are now discussed by the project team and by management. Afterwards, management can discuss and prioritise the proposals (project ideas/candidates). Answering the following questions will help:

- What kind of organisation will we become?
- Which products and services will be offered in a new way?
- How quickly and how intensively should the transformation be carried out?
- Do we see opportunities in these project ideas for digital transformation?
- Do the project ideas fit our business/strategies so far? If not, would these be good ideas for testing and further developing the organisation?
- Do we have a need for this change?
- Will we capture more value and put our business into a more competitive position?
- What is the implementation cost? Can we bear the risk?
- Do we have the knowledge and the finances to do this?
- Who in the organisation can lead and implement the projects?

To support conversations, project ideas can be visualised in a 2x2 matrix (see Figure 12.7 for an example), for instance with the two dimensions of business impact (how much impact do we expect from the idea/project?) and feasibility (do we have the market/customers, knowledge and resources/finances to implement the idea/project?).

As a next step, all strategic initiatives and strategic projects will be documented with goals, responsibilities, project budgets, and deadlines:

- **Goals**: what measurable successes (quantitative, such as process speed, cost reduction or sales growth, or qualitative, such as customer/employee satisfaction or product quality) are to be achieved with the initiative/project?
- **Responsibilities**: who leads the initiative/project and is assigned the appropriate tasks, responsibilities, and capabilities?
- **Budgets**: what investment and operating budgets are available for the initiative/project?
- **Deadlines**: when does the initiative/project start and end, and what are the key milestones that need to be met (e.g., due to reliance on other initiatives)?

A template digital roadmap together with a small business example is available in Chapter 12.3 (*Digital Transformation Toolkit*).

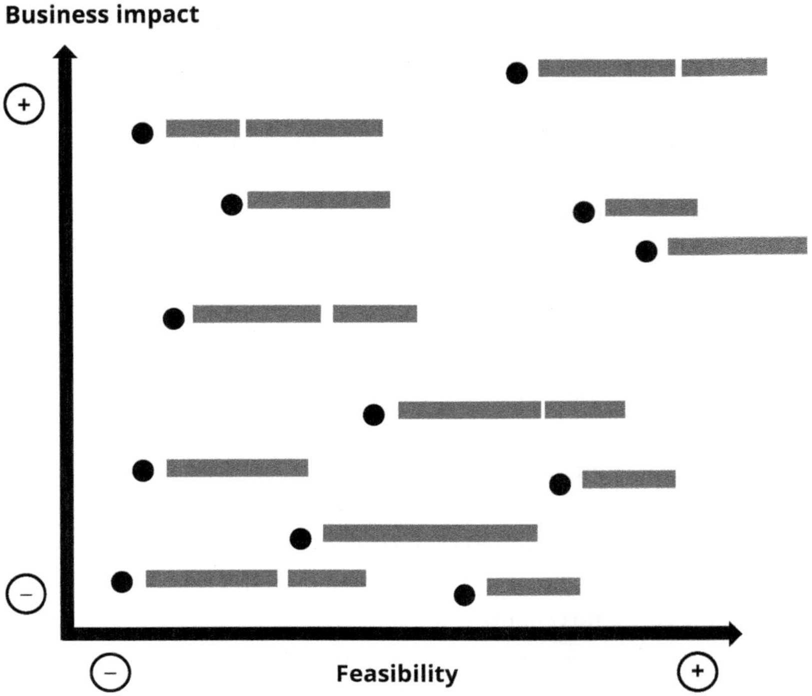

Figure 12.7 Assessment matrix for digital project candidates

Source: Peter (2017, 2021, 2023, 2024)

The final step of phase 7 is the development and definition of performance indicators (OKR and/or KPI, see Chapter 11.6) to measure and control progress in strategy implementation and assess critical success factors in the *Transform* phase. This therefore leads to *Gate 3*, the digital roadmap with key metrics for the successful implementation and monitoring of digital transformation. For a SME implementation see Box 12.6.

Step 8: Project Initialisation and Quick Wins

After the digital strategy/roadmap has been approved by the board of directors/owners, the implementation of an effective transformation starts with various project kick-offs and the execution of those activities that can be completed quickly and deliver quick results (including quick-wins). In most cases, the pre-approved strategy projects (grouped in project portfolios) of the digital roadmap still require a separate business case (or investment case) which involves management/board approval before implementation.

A strategic project committee (in the form of a 'digital office' or more traditionally, a 'project management office' (PMO)) is convened to support and control progress. In this phase, all success factors of digital transformation – project management, change management, and digital leadership (see Chapter 11.2) – must be established, including:

- Organisational anchoring of digital transformation (Section 11.1.2);
- Programme and project portfolio governance (Section 11.3.2);
- Skills development and training (Section 11.5.1);
- Digital internal communication (Section 11.5.2); and
- Monitoring of digital transformation performance (Section 11.6).

This step is the dawn of the 'change/transform' phase as per the change management process (see Chapter 11 and Box 11.3).

Box: 12.6: Small Business Example of the ACT Method Implementation

The following example illustrates the implementation of the ACT method in a small business setting.

Month 1

The need for a digital transformation strategy is the main item on the agenda for the board of directors and the executive team meeting of a small manufacturing business (step 1). After an initial assessment, it is decided that all employees will be asked to participate in the digital maturity assessment (step 2). The CEO writes an email to all employees explaining the idea of a digital roadmap and asks them to participate in the survey.

Month 2

In the strategy kick-off (step 3), the results of the 'Digital Strategy Check' are discussed and the project team is appointed. At the same time, preparatory tasks are outlined, which some employees will work on until the end of the month (step 4). These include a competitor analysis and a discussion with the external IT service provider to determine the latest technology trends and availability. The CEO attends all individual team meetings to explain the next steps of the strategy development process to the employees and to answer questions.

Month 3

In a two-day workshop, the strategic questions of the *Analyse* phase are discussed, along with an ideation workshop based on the workshop canvas with the seven action fields. The first project ideas emerge (step 5). This leads to further tasks for the CEO's project team so that, in the next workshop, the first strategy ideas can be discussed (step 6). The CEO gives the teams two weeks. In a video message, the CEO explains to the employees all that was discussed in the *Analyse* strategy workshop and what will happen next.

(Continued)

Month 4

In the second workshop (*Create*), the CEO and the management team review the various inputs from the *Analyse* workshop and subsequent tasks (step 7). The workshop covers the topics of business and pricing models, leading to new data-driven services and a new market position, the development of an ICT roadmap including cybersecurity measures, a new work framework to push digital leadership and culture, and a digital marketing strategy. All project ideas are being discussed, prioritised, and allocated to teams/departments.

Month 5

Four months after the start of the digital transformation programme, the first projects start (step 8). Several quick win projects are identified that are already being implemented. More projects are launched in the coming weeks, some with external partners. The CEO visits all departments, presents the projects, and makes sure that the teams understand the strategy and are motivated to implement the first projects.

Month 8

Three months later, following intensive project work, management and the project team meet for a one-day *Transform* workshop (step 9). The project's progress is discussed, corrective measures are introduced, and they explore how digital transformation can further be strengthened with increased flexibility and faster processes (step 10). At this point, the CEO sends out a survey to all employees to see if they understand the strategy and projects. The CEO also wants to know which new digital capabilities the training programme should be offering and if employees are satisfied with the digital strategy and roadmap.

This example of small business digital transformation shows that, even in small firms, digital transformation only starts to show results after a year. But the CEO now has a strategy for the digital age which the business can follow. This increases the flexibility and competitiveness of the firm and, at the same time, brings a breath of fresh air, new energy, and new opportunities for the entire team.

Source: Peter (2023, 2024)

Step 9: Workshop III: Transform (Flexibility and Competitiveness)

After a few months, the *Transform* workshop is held with the strategy team and the board of directors, owners, and management. In this workshop, the progress of the strategy implementation is analysed on the basis of the project reports from the digital office/project office and based on the defined success metrics (OKRs and/or KPIs) of digital transformation (Chapter 11.6). In addition, further strategic topics of the *Transform* phase – such as the current state of strategic flexibility, additional new customer-centric ideas and products, data availability, and to foster transparency via technology in business processes – are discussed to achieve future sustainable and competitive market positions. This step is the start of the 'refreeze/remain agile' phase as per the change management process (see Chapter 11 and Box 11.3).

Step 10: Continuous Measurement and Optimisation

In a type of control loop, all initiatives from the digital transformation roadmap are continuously measured and optimised. In dynamic markets driven by new digital technologies, the *Analyse* phase is now being reactivated. The findings flow into the current strategy stage (or the implementation plans) and form the basis of the next version of the updated business strategy. Depending on the organisation, the industry, the competitive situation, the need for innovation and projects for an updated digital roadmap, the organisation might now restart process step 1 – ideally, at least once a year (or every second year). In organisations with agile management and working methods, this is a continuous and parallel process

The *Digital Transformation Toolkit,* as presented in the next section, provides tools and templates for business practice that are market tested in hundreds of organisations and enable firms to succeed with the ACT method across the ten steps for digital transformation strategy planning and implementation.

12.3 DIGITAL TRANSFORMATION TOOLKIT

As a result of research projects with thousands of participants, five continuously developed and improved, practice-validated tools/templates have emerged which are available for organisations to start their strategic digital transformation (Peter 2017, 2021, 2023, 2024; Peter et al., 2020; Peter & Lindeque, 2026a–d):

- The ACT method – overview;
- The ACT method – checklist;
- The Digital Strategy Check – free online tool;
- The Workshop Canvas for Digital Transformation; and
- The Digital Roadmap – template and small business example.

1 The ACT method – overview

The ACT (Analyse, Create, Transform) method ensures that the 24 most important strategic topics (and questions for workshops) are covered in the digital transformation strategy. The three phases are completed as separate workshops and in ten strategy steps. This overview/canvas can be used to discuss the 24 strategic questions with the transformation project team; it allows ACT to be used to identify the challenges, opportunities and project ideas for a holistic strategy towards a competitive position for the fourth/fifth industrial revolutions.

→ Free download of the PDF template: www.strategic-digital-transformation.com/ACT-method

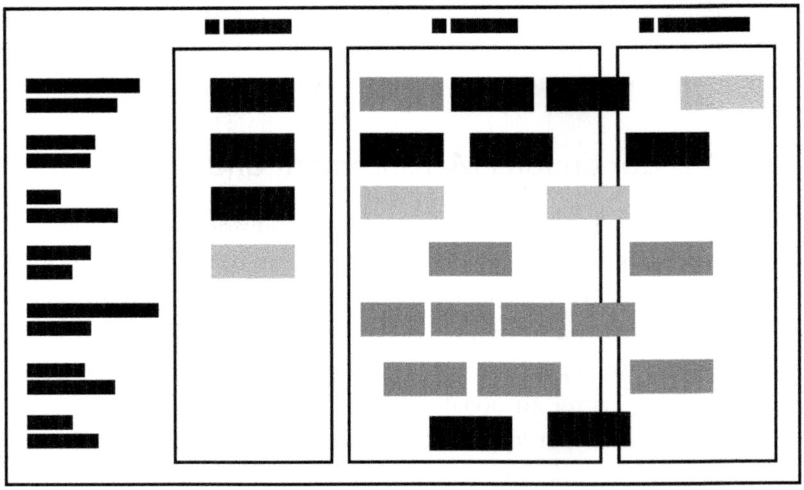

Figure 12.8 The ACT method – overview

Source: Peter (2017, 2021, 2023, 2024)

2 The ACT method – checklist

A digital transformation project team can use this detailed checklist to develop a holistic digital strategy towards a digital roadmap, as all 24 strategic topics are discussed in detail in the form of a question for a firm's strategy workshops. Each question is explained with a description and the practical tip provides simple advice on how to implement the topic in the organisation. Based on a small business example (Alexandra's Bikeshop), the checklist provides a navigation aid to incorporate the ACT strategy topics in the digital transformation of the organisation.

→ Free download of the PDF template: www.strategic-digital-transformation.com/ACT-checklist

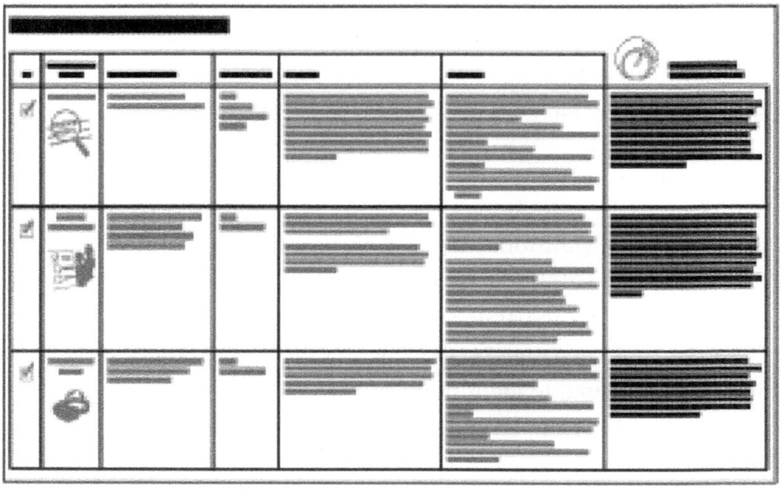

Figure 12.9 The ACT method – checklist

Source: Peter (2017, 2021, 2023, 2024)

3 The Digital Strategy Check – free online tool

The free *Digital Strategy Check* helps to determine the digital maturity of an organisation with the 24 digital strategy questions of the ACT method. It provides an initial assessment of an organisation's digital posture and opportunities for the digital roadmap. In less than ten minutes, the 24 questions can be answered, resulting in an assessment right away online and as a free downloadable PDF.

→ Free digital maturity assessment: www.digital-strategy-check.com

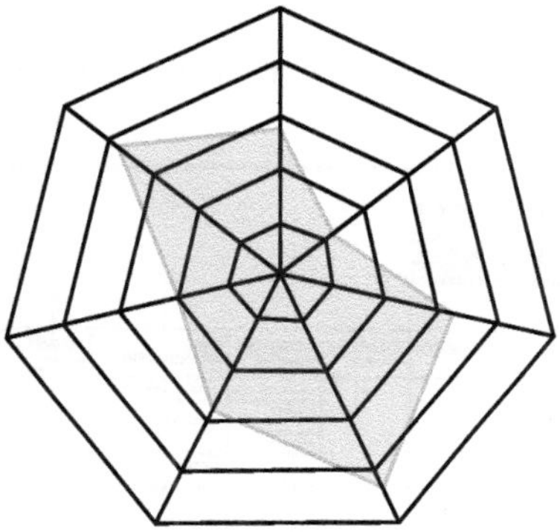

Figure 12.10 The Digital Strategy Check – free online tool

Source: Peter (2017, 2021, 2023, 2024)

4 The Workshop Canvas for Digital Transformation

The Workshop Canvas for Digital Transformation delivers quick results via its bottom-up approach of collaboration with the project team (or the entire organisation) to activate the collective knowledge of the firm. In a one-day workshop, the seven action fields of digital transformation are completed step by step with the help of questions to identify and debate challenges, opportunities, and project ideas with the team. In this way, the business will quickly receive input for the development of the digital transformation strategy.

→ Free download of the PDF template: www.strategic-digital-transformation.com/workshop-canvas

Figure 12.11 The Workshop Canvas for Digital Transformation

Source: Peter (2017, 2021, 2023, 2024)

5 The Digital Roadmap – template and small business example

This template can be used to document and present all strategic initiatives and projects on the digital roadmap. The digital roadmap helps an organisation to obtain an overview: It is a strategic management tool, that forms the basis for internal communication (e.g., towards employees and strategic partners) and is an important control/monitoring instrument. Every month (or at least once a quarter), management should discuss the transformation progress with the project team/employees and document successes and changes to the plan. Again, there is an example of a small business (Alexandra's Bikeshop) included.

→ Free download of the PDF template: www.strategic-digital-transformation.com/roadmap

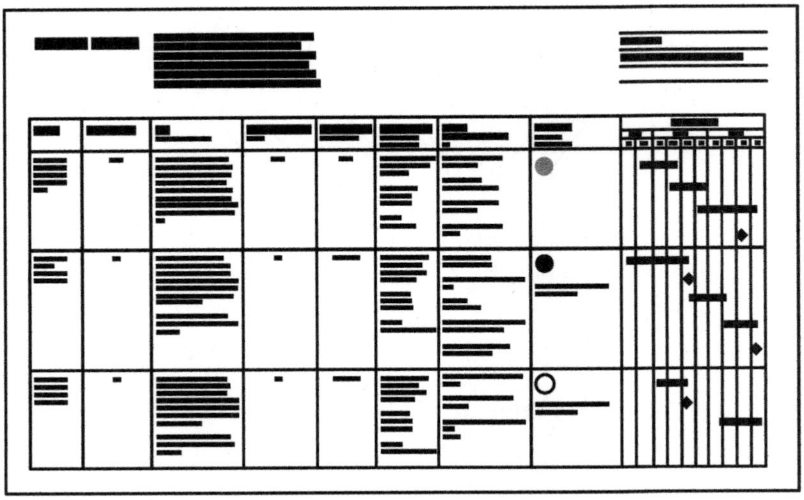

Figure 12.12 The Digital Roadmap – template and small business example

Source: Peter (2017, 2021, 2023, 2024)

12.4 CONCLUSION

This final chapter (Chapter 12) focuses on transforming the theoretical foundations for strategic digital transformation (from Chapters 1 to 11) into practical applications and tools using the ACT method (Analyse, Create, Transform). This text can be used as an input into such a strategy development process, providing the intellectual rigour to support the practice insights and relevance of business experience and knowledge. This method is designed to help businesses develop and implement digital transformation strategies that are academically rigorous and practically relevant as efficiently and effectively as possible. An example of such a holistic digital transformation across all seven action fields is presented in the opening case.

The ACT method simplifies traditional strategy development processes by focusing on digital transformation topics. It consists of three phases / workshops:

- **Analyse**: conducting market analysis, understanding customer expectations, competitive situations, environmental factors, technology trends, and digital maturity.
- **Create**: developing strategic capabilities, business models, digital channels, and innovations based on the findings from the Analysis phase.
- **Transform**: implementing, testing, and optimising strategies to ensure flexibility and competitiveness.

For a successful transformation, this chapter presents ten steps for developing and implementing a digital transformation strategy using the ACT method. The *Digital Transformation Toolkit* in Chapter 12.3 offers practical tools and templates to support this process, and to apply it in respect to a case study (in a university setting) or directly in business practice.

Case Studies

For this chapter, students should complete the following tasks based on the focal case study from week 1 / Chapters 1–3. Below tasks can be completed either individually or in a group of 3–5 students as the final project for the course/textbook.

1. Develop a project plan that includes the ten project steps (see Chapter 12.2). For each step, define who is involved, what should be done, how long it will take, what the deadlines are, and what the critical success factors are to succeed with the digital transformation initiative.
2. As per above task no. 1, define how long it will take to develop the digital roadmap/ digital transformation strategy before implementation can start. Analyse if – for the size and type of business and the current competitive market situation – this is too short, just right, or too long.
3. Define the questions which you would ask during a preliminary discussion with the board of directors/owners/executives of the organisation (Step 1 as per Chapter 12.2): define at least ten questions which you would ask in order to identify the importance/ scope of the digital transformation initiative of the business.
4. Complete the online digital maturity assessment (see Box 12.3) for the organisation on www.digital-strategy-check.com (make assumptions, if required). Critically analyse the findings and explain/describe where (in which strategic action field or for which topics) the organisation should prioritise digital transformation projects.
5. For the focal case organisation, review their website and social media profiles, the websites of competitors, collect documents online, and with the collected information, describe strategic opportunities, barriers/challenges, and proposed steps to overcome these for each phase of the ACT method (Analyse, Create, Transform).
6. In your group, use the workshop canvas for digital transformation (see Box 12.5 and Chapter 12.3) to review (1) potential barriers/challenges and (2) identify strategic digital opportunities across the seven action fields of digital transformation. Document your findings.

7 Review your digital transformation ideas (digital project candidates) from task no. 6.2 regarding business impact and feasibility (see Figure 12.7). Which projects would you want to support?
8 With the input from tasks nos 6 and 7, develop the digital roadmap for the case organisation based on the template in Chapter 12.3 (The Digital Roadmap, Figure 12.12).
9 Finally, critically review your work in tasks nos 1–8: which activities were the most valuable/meaningful, and which activities did not result in great output? Please explain/describe why you made this evaluation.

Optionally, the final project could be documented and presented as a slide deck (or in any other professional form of an impactful presentation in an actual business situation).

You will find a collection of case studies for Strategic Digital Transformation in the Appendix and additional cases online at www.strategic-digital-transformation.com.

Exercises

Discuss the following questions in your class, in your group, or assignment:

1 Discuss the degree of digital transformation in the opening case (Digital Transformation in Practice at Synchrony (USA)): is Synchrony a digitally mature business? Critically review your evaluation/answers.
2 Visit www.digital-strategy-check.com to complete a free digital strategy assessment (see Box 12.3) for a company which you know (or are a customer of). How do you evaluate the results, and where should the business invest as part of their digital transformation endeavour?
3 Review the ten steps of a digital transformation project (see Chapter 12.2) and discuss if the suggested process is complete. Identify and describe at least three additional activities/steps that could be implemented.
4 Forming two small groups (2–4 students in each group), assign a pro and contra position to each group and debate the degree to which a bottom-up approach is important (group 1), or a top-down approach is more meaningful (group 2) in the context of digital transformation across the ten project steps as per Chapter 12.2.
5 Critically evaluate the five tools as presented in the *Digital Transformation Toolkit* (Chapter 12.3): describe which tool you would use, and why, but also identify at least three additional tools that you could use during a digital transformation project.

Further Reading List

- Peter, M. K. (2024). *The Digital Transformation Canvas. Develop and Implement Your Digital Strategy.* FT Publishing/Pearson, London/UK, www.the-digital-transformation-canvas.com.
- Peter, M. K. (2024). Digital Strategy Check, www.digital-strategy-check.com
- Peter, M. K., & Lindeque, J. (2026). The ACT method – overview, www.strategic-digital-transformation.com/ACT-method.

- Peter, M. K., & Lindeque, J. (2026). The ACT method – checklist, www.strategic-digital-transformation.com/ACT-checklist.
- Peter, M. K., & Lindeque, J. (2026). The Workshop Canvas for Digital Transformation, www.strategic-digital-transformation.com/workshop-canvas.
- Peter, M. K., & Lindeque, J. (2026). The Digital Roadmap – template and small business example, www.strategic-digital-transformation.com/roadmap.

References

Barjak, F., Lindeque, J., Koch, J., & Soland, M. (2022). Segmenting household electricity customers with quantitative and qualitative approaches. *Renewable and Sustainable Energy Reviews, 157*, 112014.

Centobelli, P., Cerchione, R., Chiaroni, D., Del Vecchio, P., & Urbinati, A. (2020). Designing business models in circular economy: A systematic literature review and research agenda. *Business Strategy and the Environment, 29*(4), 1734–49.

Cesnovar, T. (2006). The impact of strategic management on business outcomes – empirical research, *Journal of East European Management Studies, 11*(3), 227–43.

Hevner, A. R., March, S. T., Park, J., & Ram, S. (2004). Design science in information systems research, *MIS Quarterly*, S. 75–105.

Kuechler, B., & Vaishnavi, V. (2008). On theory development in design science research: Anatomy of a research project, *European Journal of Information Systems, 17*(5), 489–504.

Mintzberg, H. (1994). *The Rise & Fall of Strategic Planning*. Prentice Hall International, London.

Osterwalder, A., & Pigneur, Y. (2013). Designing business models and similar strategic objects: The contribution of IS. *Journal of the Association for Information Systems, 14*(5), 237.

Peter, M. K. (Hrsg.) (2017). *KMU-Transformation: Als KMU die Digitale Transformation erfolgreich umsetzen. Forschungsresultate und Praxisleitfaden*. FHNW Hochschule für Wirtschaft, Olten/Schweiz, www.kmu-transformation.ch.

Peter, M. K. (Hrsg.) (2021). *Strategieentwicklung im digitalen Zeitalter: Planung und Umsetzung der Digitalen Transformation*. FHNW Hochschule für Wirtschaft und Strategylab, Olten/Schweiz, www.strategische-transformation.ch.

Peter, M. K. (2023). *Digitaler Masterplan für KMU. So gelingt die digitale Transformation in Ihrem Unternehmen*. Verlag Beobachter Edition & Handelszeitung. Zürich/Schweiz, www.digitaler-masterplan.ch.

Peter, M. K. (2024). *The Digital Transformation Canvas. Develop and Implement Your Digital Strategy*. FT Publishing/Pearson, London/UK, www.the-digital-transformation-canvas.com.

Peter, M. K., Kraft, C., & Lindeque, J. (2020). Strategic action fields of digital transformation: An exploration of the strategic action fields of Swiss SMEs and large enterprises. *Journal of Strategy and Management, 13*(1), 160–80.

Peter, M. K., & Lindeque, J. (2026a). The ACT method – overview, www.strategic-digital-transformation.com/ACT-method.

Peter, M. K., & Lindeque, J. (2026b). The ACT method – checklist, www.strategic-digital-transformation.com/ACT-checklist.

Peter, M. K., & Lindeque, J. (2026c). The Workshop Canvas for Digital Transformation, www.strategic-digital-transformation.com/workshop-canvas.

Peter, M. K., & Lindeque, J. (2026d): The Digital Roadmap – template and small business example, www.strategic-digital-transformation.com/roadmap,

Peter, M. K., Lindeque, J., Savoy, V., & Tonazzi, M. (2021). *Die digitale Toolbox – Prozess und Vorlagen zur Anwendung der «ACT-Methode»*, in: Peter, M. K. (Hrsg.), Strategieentwicklung im digitalen Zeitalter: Planung und Umsetzung der Digitalen Transformation. FHNW Hochschule für Wirtschaft und Strategylab, Olten/Schweiz.

Venable, J. (2006). A framework for design science research activities, *Proceedings of the 2006 Information Resource Management Association Conference* (Khosrow-Pour, M., ed.), Washington, DC, 24–26 May, IRMA, Hershey, PA.

Vendraminelli, L., Macchion, L., Nosella, A., & Vinelli, A. (2023). Design thinking: Strategy for digital transformation. *Journal of Business Strategy*, *44*(4), 200–10.

Zott, C., & Amit, R. (2010). Business model design: An activity system perspective. *Long Range Planning*, *43*(2–3), 216–26.

APPENDIX: CASE STUDY COLLECTION

The Appendix includes all referenced case studies. Additional case studies are available on the book's website.

Visit www.strategic-digital-transformation.com for:

- Videos from case organisations (case introductions, promotional clips, and interviews).
- Slide decks for each case (case summaries and illustrations).
- Slide decks with the most important concepts, tables, and illustrations for each chapter.
- The *Digital Transformation Toolkit* with workshop templates and checklists.

The authors would like to express their gratitude to all participating organisations and to the contributors (authors and interview partners) of the case studies.

CASE STUDIES IN THE BOOK

BRUGG Lifting and its Industrial Internet of Things (IIoT) Asset Management Solution 'PVS'

BRUGG Lifting is a global producer of elevator ropes, lifting technology and architectural ropes.

- Countries: China, Switzerland (HQ), USA
- Strategic action fields of digital transformation
- New digital technologies
    - Data and the Cloud
    - New strategies and business models
    - Digital marketing
- Website: www.brugglifting.com
- Author: Marc K. Peter
- Other contributors: Raphael Schifferle

City of Lucerne / Stadt Luzern: Digital Transformation of the City of Lucerne

The city of Lucerne is the administrative governing organisation of the Swiss city with 85,000 residents.

- Country: Switzerland
- Strategic action fields of digital transformation
    - Digital leadership and culture
    - New strategies and business models
- Website: www.luzern.ch
- Author: Marc K. Peter
- Other contributors: Urs Truttmann, Damaris Hostettler

Switzerland Tourism: Cross-Media Campaign 'The Ride of a Lifetime'

Switzerland Tourism is the national organisation that promotes Switzerland as a travel destination worldwide.

- Country: Switzerland
- Strategic action fields of digital transformation
    - Customer centricity
    - Digital marketing
- Website: www.myswitzerland.com
- Author: Dominic Stöcklin
- Other contributors: n/a

Valuu: A Corporate Start-Up for Digital Business Model Innovation

Valuu is a digital corporate start-up of Swiss retail bank PostFinance that has revolutionised digital end-to-end mortgage processes between 2019 to 2024.

- Country: Switzerland
- Strategic action fields of digital transformation
  - New strategies and business models
  - New digital technologies
- Website: www.postfinance.ch
- Author: Marc K. Peter
- Other contributors: Thomas Jakob, Michael Gaschen

CASE STUDIES AVAILABLE ONLINE

Adelbodner Mineral Water – The Digital Roadmap of a SME

Adelbodner is a traditional small business which bottles high-quality mineral water directly from the spring in the Swiss mountains.

- Country: Switzerland
- Strategic action fields of digital transformation
    - Customer centricity
    - New digital technologies
    - Data and the cloud
    - New strategies and business models
    - Operational excellence / process management
    - Digital leadership and culture
    - Digital marketing
- Website: www.adelbodner.ch
- Author: Marc K. Peter
- Other contributors: Patrick Marti

Autodesk Asia-Pacific: Customer Lifecycle Management and Marketing Automation

Autodesk is an American multinational software corporation that provides software products and services for various industries.

- Countries: USA (HQ), Asia-Pacific
- Strategic action fields of digital transformation
    - Customer centricity
    - Digital marketing
- Website: www.autodesk.com
- Author: Ljubica Radoicic
- Other contributors: Marc K. Peter

IT Portfolio Management and Corporate Knowledge: Colloquial Enterprise Architecture Management

Colloquial is an IT enterprise architecture tool that makes it easy to capture, visualise, and maintain business knowledge.

- Country: Australia
- Strategic action fields of digital transformation
    - New digital technologies
    - Operational excellence / process management

- Website: www.colloquial.io
- Author: Luke Houghton
- Other contributors: n/a

Blackroll – From Product Innovation to International Expansion Via E-Commerce

Blackroll produces foam rollers and other fitness tools designed to improve muscle relaxation, posture, and overall physical well-being.

- Countries: Germany, Switzerland (HQ)
- Strategic action fields of digital transformation
  - New strategies and business models
  - Digital marketing
- Website: www.blackroll.com
- Author: Marc K. Peter
- Other contributors: Marius Keckeisen

Sulzer – Strategic Leadership In Sustainable, Digital Tech-Enabled Value-Adding Services

Sulzer is a global leader in fluid engineering and chemical processing applications.

- Country: Switzerland (HQ) - with 180 manufacturing facilities and service centres across the globe
- Strategic action fields of digital transformation
  - New digital technologies
  - New strategies and business models
- Website: www.sulzer.com
- Author: Marc Heggemann
- Other contributors: Marc K. Peter

Action Fields of Digital Transformation at Synchrony Financial (USA)

Synchrony Financial is a consumer financial services company, offering a wide range of credit products through its digital financial ecosystem.

- Country: USA
- Strategic action fields of digital transformation
  - Customer centricity
  - New digital technologies
  - Data and the cloud
  - New strategies and business models
  - Operational excellence / process management

  - Digital leadership and culture
  - Digital marketing
- Website: www.synchrony.com
- Author: Sudip Chaudhuri
- Other contributors: Marc K. Peter

CRM and Sales Automation at Transgourmet Switzerland

Transgourmet is a delivery and cash+carry wholesale company.

- Country: Switzerland
- Strategic action fields of digital transformation
  - Data and the cloud
  - New digital technologies
  - Operational excellence / process management
  - Digital marketing
- Website: www.transgourmet.ch
- Author: Christian Zimmerli
- Other contributors: n/a

From Limited Budget to Limitless Potential: The Digital Journey of OSHE@UTMKL

Universiti Teknologi Malaysia (UTM) is a premier research university in Malaysia, renowned for its innovation and technical expertise.

- Country: Malaysia
- Strategic action fields of digital transformation
  - Operational excellence / process management
  - New digital technologies
  - Digital leadership and culture
- Website: www.utm.my
- Author: Mohamad Syazli Fathi
- Other contributors: n/a

Additional case studies are available on www.strategic-digital-transformation.com.

CASE STUDY A: BRUGG LIFTING AND ITS INDUSTRIAL INTERNET OF THINGS (IIOT) ASSET MANAGEMENT SOLUTION 'PVS'

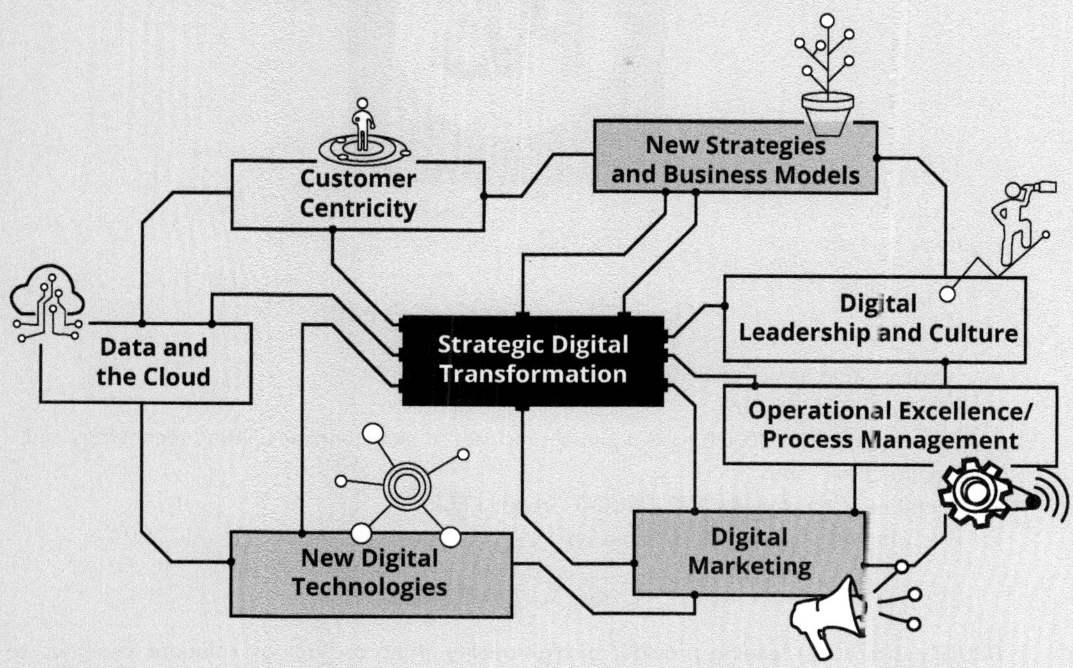

Figure A.1 BRUGG Lifting seven action fields

BRUGG
Lifting

Figure A.2 BRUGG Lifting logo

Figure A.3 PVS logo

Case Organisation Profile

- Organisation name: BRUGG Lifting
- Country: Switzerland
- Description: BRUGG Lifting is a global producer of elevator ropes, lifting technology and architectural ropes
- Number of employees: 230 (BRUGG Group: 1,800)
- Website: https://brugglifting.com/en

Case Organisation

BRUGG Lifting is a leading provider of high-quality lifting technology solutions designed to handle demanding loads in various industries. The company operates predominantly in the manufacturing of wire and steel ropes, textile slings and special lifting equipment. Headquartered in Birr, Switzerland, BRUGG Lifting has a strong global presence (with manufacturing sites and offices in China and the USA) and a reputation for reliability, safety, and innovation. Products include:

- *Wire and steel ropes*: renowned for their durability and strength, these ropes are used in different lifting and transportation applications.
- *Textile slings*: these include a wide variety of synthetic slings that provide flexibility and ease of handling for various lifting tasks.
- *Special solutions*: the company also develops custom lifting solutions tailored to specific industry requirements, such as the PVS solution.

The roots of BRUGG Lifting can be traced back to the late 19th century (the company was incorporated in 1886), making it an established and experienced player in the lifting technology industry. Over the years, the company has continuously evolved by embracing technological advancements and expanding its product offerings. Today, it stands as a key division within the BRUGG Group, a conglomerate with diverse activities spanning heating technology, natural hazard protection, process control, and more. The BRUGG Group has over 1,800 employees across 35 subsidiaries (Brugg, 2025).

At the core of BRUGG Lifting's success (one of the many subsidiaries) is its commitment to innovation and quality. The company continuously invests in research and development to introduce new, efficient, and safe lifting technologies. BRUGG Lifting adheres to stringent quality standards, ensuring that all products meet international safety regulations and customer expectations. One of these initiatives – the PVS solution – is an Industrial Internet of Things (IIoT) solution, driven by LoRaWAN (but also usable with NFC tags), a popular LPWAN (low-power wide-area network) technology.

The Internet of Things (IoT) and LPWAN Technology

Low-power wide-area network (LPWAN) is a wireless communication technology designed for (relative) long-range communication (e.g., within a building or a region) at low bit rates among connected devices, particularly for Internet of Things (IoT) applications.

The Internet of Things (IoT) is a network of interconnected physical devices that collect, share and analyse data across the internet. These devices range from everyday household items, like smart refrigerators and thermostats, to industrial machinery and urban infrastructure. The core idea of IoT is to make objects 'smart' by embedding them with sensors (such as a LPWAN sensor), processors and communication infrastructure, thereby enabling them to interact with each other, with humans and computers. These sensors can collect data from the environment, such as location, temperature, humidity, motion, light, and more.

Applications of IoT are, for instance, smart homes (energy management, home security, automated lighting, etc.); industrial IoT (IIOT) including predictive maintenance, supply-chain management and optimisation, and automation; healthcare (remote monitoring of, for example, smart medical equipment and patients, chronic disease management); smart cities (for example traffic management, public safety, and environmental monitoring); and agriculture (for example livestock monitoring and optimised irrigation, fertilisation, and pest control).

LPWAN has many capabilities, such as its ability to provide connectivity while consuming minimal power, making it ideal for scenarios where devices need to operate on small batteries for extended periods. The primary features of LPWAN are:

- *Long range*: capable of covering distances from a few kilometres in urban areas/cities to over 10 km in rural settings/in the countryside, and even further under optimal conditions.
- *Low power consumption*: designed to function on minimal power, allowing devices to run for many years on small batteries.
- *Low data rate*: typically supports data rates ranging from 0.3 kbps to 50 kbps.
- *Cost-effective*: infrastructure and operational costs for LPWAN networks are relatively low, making it an interesting investment case, and facilitating large-scale deployments.
- *Scalability*: able to support a vast number of devices on a single network.

There are several competing standards and technologies in the LPWAN space, each with its unique advantages and use cases. One of them is LoRaWAN (long-range wide-area network), a popular LPWAN technology, which uses a proprietary modulation called LoRa (long range) for communication. It is widely adopted for its (relative) long-range capabilities and low power consumption.

For its project, BRUGG Lifting prepared an overview of available LPWAN technologies (including LoRaWAN) (see Figure A.4).

LoRaWAN, utilised by PVS, is provided by commercial organisations (e.g., telecommunication providers) and community networks such as LORIOT and The Things Network (see 'Additional information').

Network coverage

	Sigfox	LoRaWAN	Mioty	Wirepas	NB-IOT	LTE-M
Worldwide	Good	Very good (thanks to the community network, which can be expanded independently as required)	Unknown: as far as can be seen, currently only private networks can be used	Unknown: as far as can be seen, currently only private networks can be used	Good	Relatively good
Europe	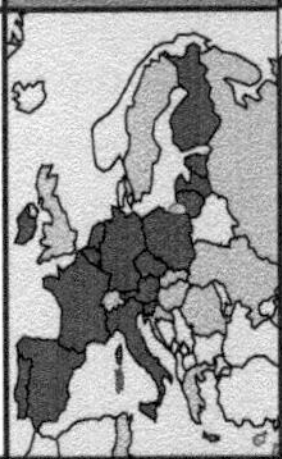	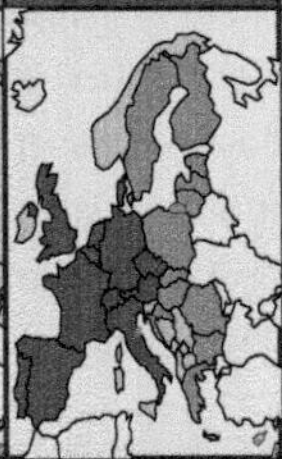	Unknown: as far as can be seen, currently only private networks can be used	Unknown: as far as can be seen, currently only private networks can be used	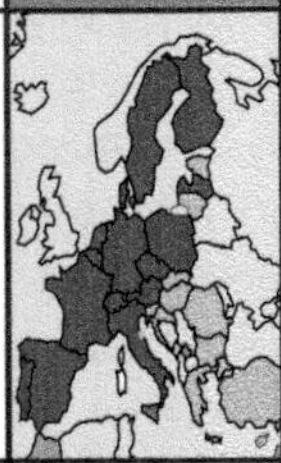	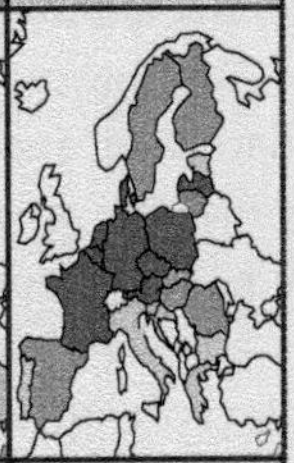
Reach	Very large (3–10 km a city, 30–50 km in the countryside)	Very large (3–10 km in a city, 30–50 km in the countryside)	Large (5 km in a city, 15 km in the countryside)	Medium (approx. 5 km)	Medium (1 km in a city, 10 km in the countryside)	Medium (1 km in a city, 10 km in the countryside)

Figure A.4a Overview of LPWAN technologies and their network coverage (PVS, 2023)

Data transmission

	Sigfox	LoRaWAN	Mioty	Wirepas	NB-IOT	LTE-M
Transmission rate	0.1–0.6 Kbit/s	0.3–50 Kbit/s	0.5 Kbit/s	115 Kbit/s	Limited to max. 250 Kbit/s down- and upload	Approx. 1'000 Kbit/s
Latency	High [a few seconds]	Medium [approx.400 ms for short, several seconds for long distances]	Average [less than 400 ms]	Average [10-900 ms]	High [1'600-10'000 ms]	Low [10–15 ms]
Penetration of walls	Good	Good	Good	Unknown	Good	Good

Figure A.4b Overview of LPWAN technologies and their data transmission (PVS, 2023)

Other criteria

	Sigfox	LoRaWAN	Mioty	Wirepas	NB-IOT	LTE-M
Battery life	Approx. 10 years	Approx. 10 years	Approx. 15–20 years	Approx. 5 years	Approx. 10 years, only if motionless	Approx. 10
Provider and running costs	CHF 7-12/year/ device, depending on the number of upand downlinks with Heliot	Loriot [global], CHF 0.-, Community network The Things Network, CHF 0.-, Community network Swisscom, Switzerland, CHF 10.20/year/ device	Behr Technologies Inc. with the MYTHINGS platform. Prices are not published.	Licence costs for use with Wirepas. Prices are not published.	1 €/year/ device for 500 MB or 10 years with 1 NCE	1 €/year/ device for 500 MB on 10 years with 1 NCE
Future security and market maturity	Market share according to IoT Analytics 2021 at 3%	Market share according to IoT Analytics 2021 at 36% According to the 2021 annual report of the LoRa Alliance growing strongly	Still very new, far as can be seen network	Still very new, as far as can be seen IoT only private network Analytics 2021 networks usable.	Market share as according to Only private networks usable. at 47%	Market share according to IoT Analytics 2021 at 10%

Figure A.4c Overview of LPWAN technologies and various other criteria (PVS, 2023))

For digital transformation, LPWAN is an important technology that addresses the need for long-range and low-power communication in the IoT (and IIoT) landscape. Its ability to support large-scale deployments at a low cost makes it invaluable for various industries and digital transformation initiatives.

The PVS Asset Management Solution

PVS stands for 'Produkte-Verwaltungs-Software' (in English: product management software). PVS was originally developed and used as an internal database at BRUGG Lifting in 2016. Due to its successful operation and the positive response from customers, it was decided to launch PVS as an independent corporate start-up in 2021, offering its product management software to customers outside the BRUGG Lifting network. This meant that companies that use the PVS solution are not obliged to purchase any lifting equipment or other services from BRUGG.

PVS focuses on providing a high-quality and efficient asset management solution and strives to provide customers with maximum flexibility and value. The PVS solution can, for instance, be used to monitor leased resources and devices (e.g., building equipment). In order for customers to take advantage of the opportunities offered by IoT technology, i.e., to track their own products/equipment, BRUGG developed special sensors that can be used to display the GPS position (via LoRaWAN) of all managed devices directly in the PVS solution.

In addition to an implementation of PVS with LoRaWAN sensors (for asset tracking), it can also be used with NFC (near field communication) tags that are based on RFID (radio frequency identification) technology (Apple's AirTag is also an NFC technology solution). Information about assets that have a sensor or tag can also be accessed via a QR (quick response) code attached on the sensor/tag itself. With that, the asset can be identified easily and the relevant documents (e.g., manuals, test protocols, or warranties) can be accessed via the PVS website or app.

Since its launch in 2016, it has managed more than 180,000 assets (e.g., wire and steel ropes for lifts or bridges). The main driver for PVS in the market is the (regulatory) need that important equipment (such as steel ropes in lifts) must be periodically audited, maintained, repaired, documented, and logged in a quality management system. However, in many organisations, these resources/infrastructures, test data, and protocols are still recorded in paper form or in spreadsheet tables. In addition, it takes time for technical experts to read an identification number on a tag and enter it into a system (e.g., an online platform) in order to be able to access the related documents of an asset/equipment.

The PVS solution and its app revolutionise asset management (or device management) through seamless digital management processes. It provides a quick and unique identification of an asset (for instance, via the NFC tag) and its location (via a LoRaWAN sensor), and all assets can then be managed centrally on the PVS platform or via an app on mobile phones.

The PVS database itself can be hosted locally or in the cloud (on Microsoft Azure Cloud). The presentation layer of the app was developed via KendUI, the application layer was developed via C-Sharp in .Net6.

In 2023, the PVS team redefined the solutions' value proposition:

> 'The PVS app for automated equipment and machine asset management improves operational efficiency by streamlining equipment administration processes, reducing the machine maintenance costs, and ensuring safety of both the machines and personnel.
>
> It automates troublesome manual processes and offers real-time visibility into equipment operations from anywhere at any time.'

The following key benefits were articulated:

- PVS provides a 'single source of truth' for the management of the complete equipment lifecycle of an organisation.
- It provides real-time visibility from anywhere at any time.
- It is easy to install, configure, and use the solution.
- It provides security via a granular rights and access management system.

However, while the PVS technology was mature and fulfilled its product value propositions and key benefits, it experienced a challenging and competitive market that would limit its success regarding commercial outcomes.

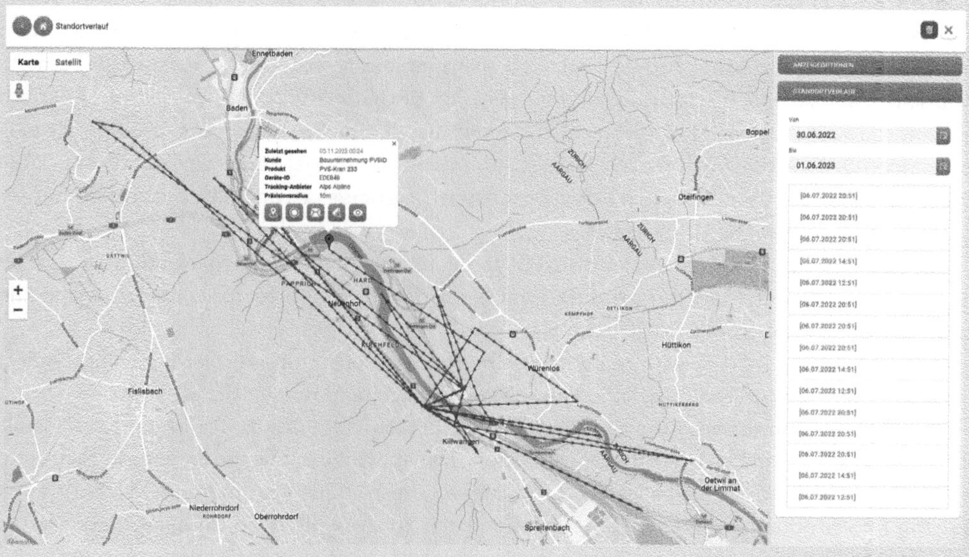

Figure A.5 Example of geographical tracking (geotracking) of a device (in this case, a building tool) (PVS, 2022a)

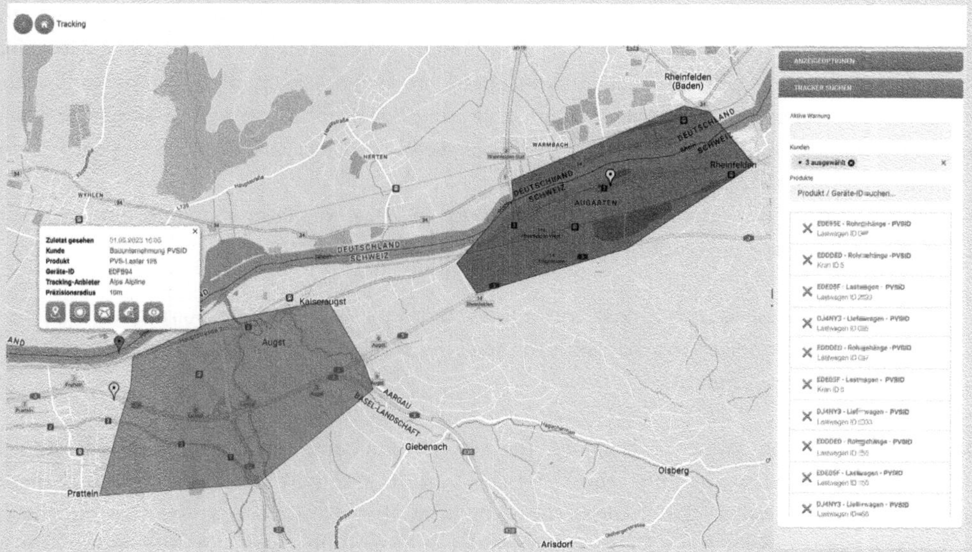

Figure A.6 Example of geographical tracking (geotracking) based on a defined geofence (a geofence is a virtual geographic boundary that enables software to alert the organisation if an asset/equipment enters or leaves a particular area) (PVS, 2022a)

Commercial Strategy

BRUGG Lifting invested a couple of million CHF/USD into the project, but only a fraction of it has been recouped to date. However, while the ROI (return on investment) is low, it has enabled BRUGG Lifting to equip all of its products with a PVS NFC tag and thus provide a competitive differentiator, as it allows its customers to track the purchased products/equipment (e.g., wire and steel ropes), but also to more easily access the related documents, including manuals and test protocols. Internally, for BRUGG Lifting, its five technical experts/inspectors review around 600 technical customer installations per year and provide a quality assurance (QA) certificate for each installation in line with legal requirements (Peter, 2024). The PVS solution thus also provides process efficiencies, especially around document management for BRUGG Lifting itself.

In addition to the internal use at BRUGG, today, more than 9,000 organisations, cities, and municipalities benefit from the product's value propositions and features, and manage their resources purchased from BRUGG with PVS.

However, it is a market with many solutions from various competitors, including OnTrack by Hilti, One Key by Milwaukee Tool, GuardMe by Bosch, and many others.

In order to commercialise the product, BRUGG initially ran POC (proof of concept) installations with ten customers from the construction, transportation, fall protection, infrastructure maintenance, and public administration industries. These POC customers were important to test the PVS product and improve the solution prior to the official go-to-market launch. They also provided an initial reference (e.g., via case studies) to other organisations that were interested in purchasing the PVS solution.

BRUGG Lifting priced its solution both cost-based ('what is the total cost of the product so we can sell it above that?') and value-based ('how much would a customer be willing to pay given its benefits?') and developed bundles and a tiered pricing model (basic, professional, premium). The go-to-market plan included both a sales and marketing strategy. For sales, the strategy included the definition of target segments, customers, and countries with clear objectives. Marketing planning activities included the development of buyer personas, customer journeys, a competitor analysis, and marketing collateral. A marketing and sales funnel was defined, including lead nurturing activities as well as a 'CRM quote to order' process, and a 'subscription order to cash' process.

The tiered pricing model from the initial launch in 2021 was later modified, and two subscription models were developed (PVS, 2022b):

- PVS.PLUS for individual business customers, starting at CHF/USD 69 per month.
- PVS.PRO for organisations that want to resell the service to their customers, starting at CHF/USD 299 per month.

Despite the relatively low price point for the solution, its commercial success was limited. In various business review meetings, the PVS team tried to identify the reasons for the challenging financial situation. In 2022, they reported that the team's focus was too heavily on technical aspects, and it lacked a business model and marketing activities that were centred on lead generation. In 2023, in a business review meeting, the team reported that there were some customer complaints from a new release, but that the main issue was that there was 'simply not enough marketing budget and sales resources to push the solution globally'.

At the end of 2023, the BRUGG Lifting's senior management stopped the project due to financial/cost control risks and appointed a new leadership team. Following a strategy workshop in 2024 (Peter, 2024), the PVS go-to-market plan was redefined. It included new value propositions for each industry/use case, a module-based grouping/structuring of the various features of PVS, a new approach to packages and bundles, and a refined customer segmentation with new priorities (i.e., BRUGG Lifting existing customers).

The BRUGG Lifting case study showcases the challenges of developing new technology-based solutions and using digital technology for new business ventures, in combination with the benefits of streamlined processes (internally) and an improved competitive position (externally).

PVS Roadmap and Outlook

1 How important is IoT/IIoT technology for BRUGG Lifting?

For BRUGG Lifting, IoT technology is extremely important as it allows us to increase our process efficiencies. We already have an ERP (enterprise source planning) system and automated production processes and, with IoT, these technologies allow us to increase efficiencies and the quality of our products and reduce the overall cost. With the achieved time savings, we can focus more on innovation and customer service, for instance via modified roles (and position descriptions) for our team members that enables them to now spend more time on customer projects, which further drives the customer experience.

2 How did the market react to the new PVS go-to-market plan in 2024?

The new go-to-market plan puts our existing 3,000+ B2B customers in the centre of our activities as our strategy is now to primarily up-sell the PVS solution to our existing customers. It is also worthwhile to mention that, internally, our teams are now very motivated to focus on our existing customers, and support them with PVS.

3 Did you identify any market challenges for the successful commercialisation of the PVS solution?

One of the identified market challenges is the PVS brand. The current name is difficult to use in marketing because it lacks a clear unique selling proposition (USP). In addition, PVS is already used as a generic abbreviation/buzzword in many areas, which makes targeted (digital) marketing even more difficult.

4 What are the PVS priorities in 2025/26 on the technology roadmap?

Our focus is to stabilise and secure the PVS platform. Based on new cybersecurity requirements (and a new framework) from the BRUGG Group, one of our priorities now is to protect the IT infrastructure and PVS customer data. In addition, we are going to develop a pilot platform which allows new customers to test the PVS solution as part of a free trial for 30 days. As much as possible needs to be automated on the pilot platform. And, finally, the PVS platform requires a self-serve function for customers to manage and purchase additional licences directly on the platform, without the (manual) involvement of our sales teams.

5 What are the PVS priorities in 2025/26 on the commercial/GTM roadmap?

One of our four priorities is the development and implementation of a PVS reseller strategy. However, our main priority is to further train our technical and sales teams so

(Continued)

they can pitch, demo, sell, and implement the PVS solution. We need to achieve a state in which all employees have the same knowledge level. This is important as our business has many touch points: we need to ensure that the customer experience is the same across all channels, teams, and channels.

Finally, we will review the PVS brand (as mentioned before) and continue to push the PVS solution via digital marketing activities including blog posts and e-direct mails. But as we are now focusing on existing customers (up-selling the PVS solution) rather than to sell to new markets, our internal sales and customer service teams have become our number one go-to-market priority.

6 Are there other plans for technology projects at BRUGG Lifting?

At the end of 2024, we updated our digital transformation roadmap which is based on the five pillars of Smart Factory, Smart Customer Experience, Smart Products, Digital Enablement and Global IT. Technology projects worth mentioning are the ERP cloud project (as every production machine will be connected to cloud-based IoT platforms to reduce, for example, production risks and for predictive maintenance) and a new e-commerce customer portal (which will provide product information, but also allows customers to purchase directly via the digital channel).

Digital transformation and new digital technology is also important, as BRUGG Lifting will expand into new geographical regions in the not too distant future.

Interview 1, 2025
Raphael Schifferle
Global Chief Marketing Officer (CMO) at BRUGG Lifting

Image A.1 Raphael Schifferle, Global Chief Marketing Officer (CMO) at BRUGG Lifting

Student Questions

Discuss the following questions in your class, in your group, or assignment:

Strategic action field 'New Digital Technologies':

1 What are the challenges when developing solutions/products based on new technologies (i.e., technologies that an organisation previously did not use)?
2 What are the challenges when introducing a new technology to the market?
3 What are the benefits of a POC (proof of concept) test installation on a customer's site / in the customer's work environment?
4 What is the link between new digital technologies and cybersecurity. Why does cybersecurity need to be considered in light of new digital technology?
5 Why and how can new (digital) technology support the competitiveness of an organisation with existing products and services?
6 Why is the definition of a business model important for new technology-based solutions/ products?
7 Why do organisations need to balance technology versus go-to-market (sales and marketing) investments?

Strategic action field 'Data and the Cloud':

1 What is the value of data in an organisation; and how important are customer, product, and usage/transaction data (and why)?
2 What data can BRUGG collect wits its sensors? Provide an overview of data categories with examples for each category.
3 Should this data be stored and made available via an IaaS (Infrastructure-as-a-Service), PaaS (Platform-as-a-Service) or SaaS (Software-as-a-Service) Cloud solution? Describe the reasons for your choice.
4 How can BRUGG use this data for process improvements, including automation/ digitalisation, efficiency increase, and cost reduction?
5 How can BRUGG use this data strategically to build, for instance, new service offerings, strategic partnerships with other organisations (e.g., an ecosystem or digital platform) or expand into new industries?
6 How can BRUGG protect this data from unauthorised access or use from an organisational and technological point of view?
7 What skills are required for BRUGG or any other organisation to use data operationally (for e.g., automation) and strategically (e.g., to build new services)?

Additional Information

Suggested further information can be found at the following:

- Brugg Lifting website: https://brugglifting.com/en
- LoRa Alliance: https://lora-alliance.org
- LORIOT: www.loriot.io
- The Things Network: www.thethingsnetwork.org

- PVS promotional video 'Workday' from 2023: https://strategic-digital-transformation.com
- PVS product website: www.pvsid.com/en

Author

Professor Marc K. Peter, HES-SO Valais-Wallis School of Management, Switzerland; Charles Sturt University, Australia; University of Rochester/Simon Business School, USA

Acknowledgements and Authorisation

The authors would like to thank Raphael Schifferle, Global Chief Marketing Officer (CMO) at BRUGG Lifting for his support in providing this case study. The BRUGG Lifting PVS case study and the use of artwork/logos/illustrations was authorised by BRUGG Lifting on 27 January 2025.

References

Brugg (2025) BRUGG Group. Brugg (accessed 15 January 2025), available at: https://brugglifting.com/en/about-us/brugg-group/

Interview 1 (2025) Discussion on 27 January 2025 between Raphael Schifferle and Marc K. Peter.

Peter, M. K. (2024) Brugg Lifting PVS Strategy Workshop, 14 February. BRUGG Lifting, Birr/Switzerland.

PVS (2022a) IoT Überblick. White paper. Brugg Lifting, Birr/Switzerland.

PVS (2022b) Manage, organise and document products, processes, functions and services. Pitch deck, Brugg Lifting, Birr/Switzerland.

PVS (2023) Einfaches und kostengünstiges Geo-Tracking von Betriebsmitteln mit IoT. White paper. Brugg Lifting, Birr/Switzerland.

PVS (2025) PVS product website. Brugg Lifting (accessed 15 January 2025), available at: www.pvsid.com/en/.

CASE STUDY B: DIGITAL TRANSFORMATION OF THE CITY OF LUCERNE

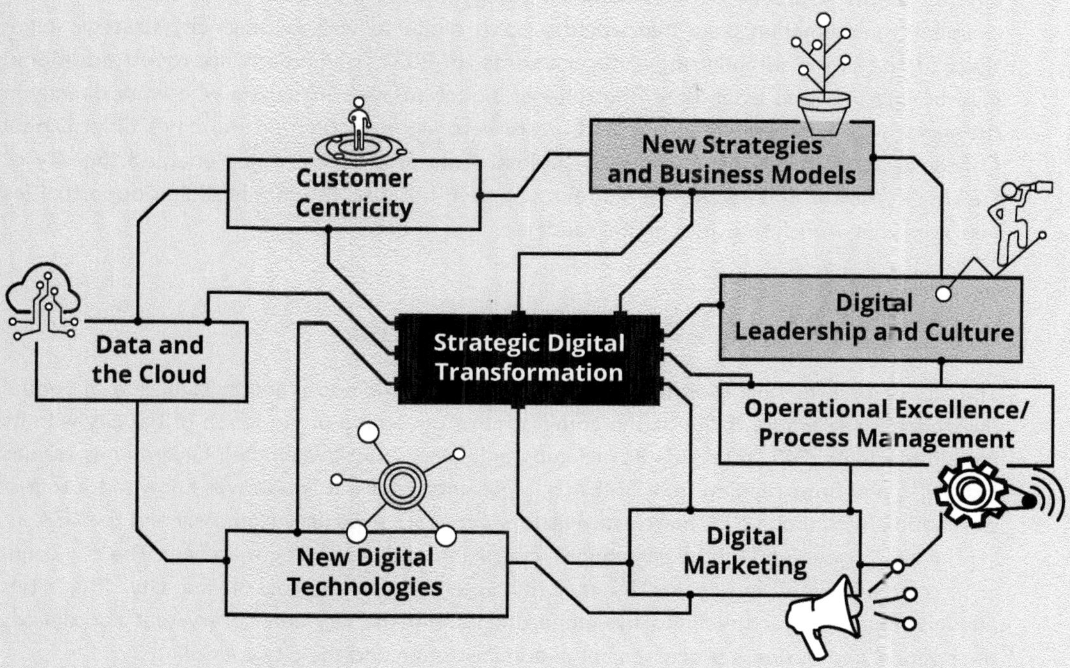

Figure B.1 City of Lucerne seven action fields

Figure B.2 Logo Stadt Luzern

Case Organisation Profile

- Organisation name: City of Lucerne
- Country: Switzerland
- Description: the city of Lucerne is the administrative governing organisation of the Swiss city with 85,000 residents (245,000 residents including adjoining councils/suburbs)
- Number of employees: approximately 1,700
- Website: www.luzern.ch

Case Overview

Following completion of an initial e-government strategy in 2010, the parliament of the Swiss city of Lucerne approved a revised digital strategy in 2019 that enabled the establishment of a digital transformation team that would support digital as well as smart city strategic initiatives of the city's administrative departments. In 2021, parliament approved additional investments that also established the roles of digital business managers who work directly in the various government departments but are centrally managed via the city's Chief Digital Officer (CDO). Various digital maturity assessments at different times enabled the city of Lucerne to better understand the current situation, but also to identify digital opportunities and, with that, enrich the city's digital roadmap.

The City of Lucerne

The city of Lucerne, incorporated in the 9th century, is the social and cultural hub of central Switzerland (see Figure B.3). It is the administrative governing organisation of the city with its 85,000 residents (245,000 residents including adjoining councils/suburbs). Lucerne has various industries and firms ranging from SMEs to larger enterprises. It is also well-known as a tourist destination (with around 1.4 million day-visitors per year), especially from Asia and the USA.

The city is governed by the city council, consisting of five full-time members. The city council is elected every four years by majority vote by the citizens of the city. The city's administration is structured into five departments and the city chancellery that coordinates the political and business processes in the administration and the city council.

Figure B.3 Lucerne in 1642 (City Archives of the City of Lucerne, 2024)

The Initial e-Government Strategies of 2010 and 2016

Back in 2010, the city of Lucerne created its first e-government strategy together with the canton of Lucerne as well as councils/municipalities. In 2016, the strategy was revised in light of various advancements and publications regarding Swiss e-government initiatives and standards (E-Government Standards, 2014).

The objectives and key principles of the 2010/16 Lucerne e-government strategies were to (City of Lucerne, 2019):

- take a joint and coordinated approach to the development of an e-government system so the canton (state), city, and other councils would collaborate and align their digital roadmaps
- implement a customer and service-oriented e-government strategy
- optimise and standardise processes in a consistent way
- reduce redundant data storage.

The Establishment of the Digital Transformation Team in 2019/20

In January 2019, a project team of the city of Lucerne government presented their report and request for funding of a digital transformation team to the city parliament (City of Lucerne, 2019). The document included the city's vision for a digital e-government strategy, objectives, a three-year roadmap (2019–21), and the proposed organisational set-up. In May 2019, parliament approved the digital initiative with some amendments.

The document referenced the city's overall 2019 to 2028 strategy that included the following strategic initiative and objectives (City of Lucerne, 2019):

- Strategic initiative:
  - To advance digital transformation: the city of Lucerne is leading digital transformation in Switzerland.
- Objectives:
  - All services of the city of Lucerne are available on a customer portal in digital form, easy and secure, transparent and personalisable, tailored to various stakeholder groups.
  - The city of Lucerne will benefit from a large digitalisation network/community, centred on its smart city initiative.

In the report, the project team analysed the digital maturity of the city's administration, conducted via a survey in 2018 among employees:

- The majority of administrative services provided by the city of Lucerne in the area of e-government are, according to the survey, government services provided to stakeholders (2/3 of tasks) and repetitive, internal administrative tasks (1/3).
- The survey was therefore primarily focused on the quality of the services area with the inclusion of digital support activities.
- Services provided by the city of Lucerne can be divided into three categories:
  - Mandatory services: these services must be utilised by stakeholder groups of the city such as registration services for relocations (mandated legal tasks). With digital initiatives, improvements could be made in individual areas.

  - Services in the event of a specific need/an incident: these are services (e.g., to request an inheritance certificate or register children for school) that are used only when stakeholders require them and are the most voluminous service category. The internal stakeholders (government departments) expect digitisation to support internal collaboration.
  - Supporting services: these are primarily city-internal and cross-sectional in nature (for instance, quality assurance) and opportunities are identified in individual, targeted cases.

The city's digital roadmap (see box also) included, among others, the development of:

- overarching leadership and monitoring tools
- digital projects and activities related to the focus areas
- digital infrastructure
- governance structure
- project portfolio management
- risk management
- government business model with digital services and a data catalogue
- stakeholder analysis
- cultural components
- data security
- public relations and communications.

For most areas, the document provided an overview of current and ongoing digital projects and activities. It also proposed the establishment of a strategic project unit and a digital transformation team (team DIGI) that would be in charge of the following activities:

- development of the digital strategy
- project portfolio management of digital projects
- project management support for the various government departments
- innovation support and partner management
- data security and public relations/communications.

The team of six employees would be led by a Chief Digital Officer (CDO) who supports all government departments, would collaborate and co-create with them, and would also represent the city regarding digital activities to external stakeholders. Organisationally, the CDO reports to the head of the Department of Education (one of five departments of the city's administration), but also leads and/or coordinates the digital roadmap for all of government.

In order to support the implementation of the digital strategy, additional roles would be created for the centralised IT department, city chancellery, finance and communication departments.

A budget of CHF 2.1 million for IT infrastructure investments, CHF 1 million for digital projects, and CHF 520,000 for salaries of the DIG team (4 FTE) was proposed.

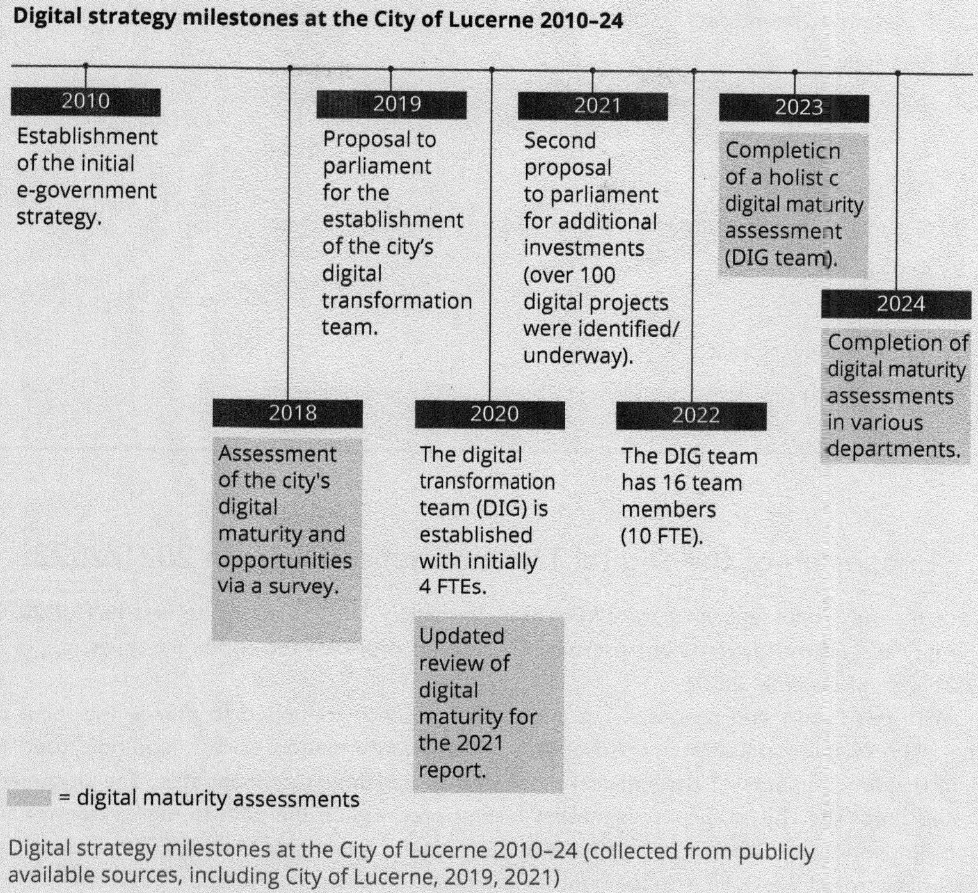

Figure B.4 Digital strategy milestones at the City of Lucerne 2010–24 (collected from publicly available sources, including City of Lucerne, 2019, 2021)

The City of Lucerne Digital Transformation Initiative

The proposal of 100+ pages to parliament was structured as follows (simplified version (City of Lucerne, 2019)):

I *The current situation*

1 Digitalisation and digital transformation

2 Digital transformation in the public sector

II *Digital strategy of the city of Lucerne*

1 Focus areas

1.1 E-government

(Continued)

1.2 Open government data
1.3 Smart city
1.4 Work smart
2 Vision and objectives
3 Digital roadmap
4 Organisational structure and collaboration
5 Activities
6 Budget
7 Return on investment
8 Funding sources

Expansion of the Digital Transformation Team in 2021/2022

With the successful launch of the digital transformation (DIG) team in the first half of 2020, the city of Lucerne government presented a second proposal for additional investments in 2021 (City of Lucerne, 2021).

With this report and proposal, the Lucerne city council continued to pursue the focus of the 2019–28 municipal strategy 'Advancing digital transformation' and, in addition, tried to fulfil the requirements of the political motions and parliamentary mandates. The document stated that, 'The city of Lucerne is making further progress on the path to digital transformation. Important plans and projects have already been implemented since 2020, including a city-wide project portfolio management for digitalisation projects, the open government data strategy with the first published data sets on the national opendata.swiss platform, the "Dialogue Lucerne" participation platform and active collaboration on the cantonal service portal, to name but a few (see Figure B.6). The digital transformation poses challenges for the administration – also in terms of flexibility and rapid action – and will not be completed with this report and proposal.'

The drivers for this second proposal were not only the already identified 107 digital projects across various departments, but also several new identified investment areas through the digital team at the city of Lucerne.

The following objectives were presented to parliament (City of Lucerne, 2021):

- Adjust, further develop and pioneer the path of digitalisation and digital transformation embarked upon in 2019, with reference to the ongoing projects and measures as well as the political demands
- Sharpen the city's digital strategy
- Showcase the development of the city of Lucerne as a smart city
- Provide the necessary human resources.

All investments would be aligned with the focus areas presented in 2019, namely e-government, open government data (OGD), work smart (new work), and the smart city (see illustration).

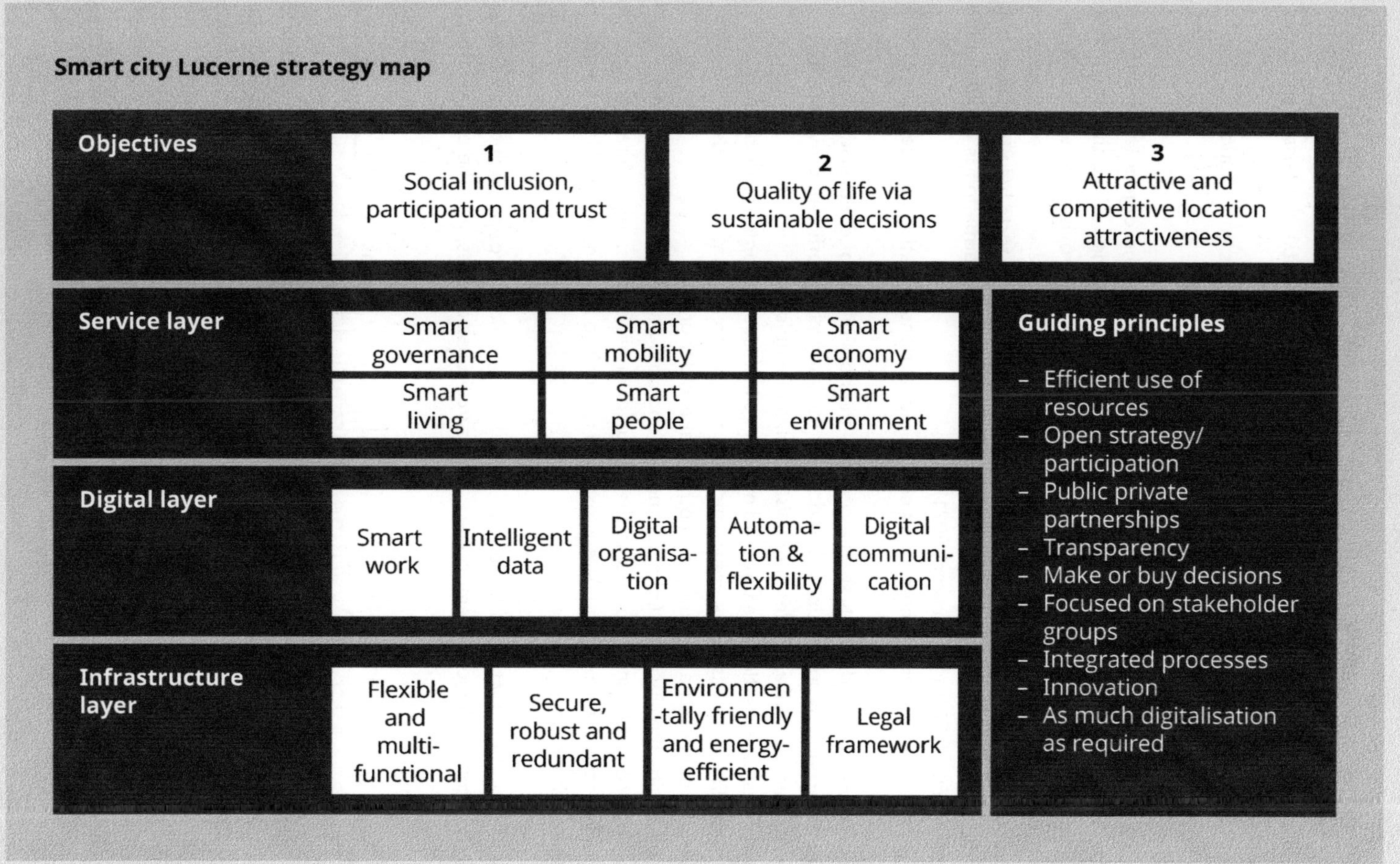

The Smart City Strategy Map of the city of Lucerne includes five components consisting of objectives, layers and guiding principles (City of Lucerne, 2021, p. 40)

Figure B.5 The Smart City Strategy Map of the city of Lucerne includes five components consisting of objectives, layers, and guiding principles (City of Lucerne, 2021, p. 40)

Three action fields were articulated that would form the basis for the city's digital strategy:

1. *Administrative digitalisation* with processes and workflow tools with a primary internal impact (e.g., accounts payable workflow, HR digital).
2. *Digitalisation of external services*, i.e., to the population (residents), businesses and other stakeholders (e.g., service portal, Dialogue Lucerne).
3. *Digitalisation of urban infrastructure* as the basis for new services and solutions (e.g., public WLAN, traffic management).

Based on the experience of one and a half years of activities in the digital team and new insights, the digital vision was further elaborated. The city thus aims to 'identify and implement the opportunities of digital transformation to optimise the provision of services while considering social changes'. The city shall use digitalisation 'to increase resource efficiency as well as the quality of work and life (...) Innovative pilot projects and tests help to ensure that the opportunities and risks are recognised, and that digital transformation is implemented quickly and effectively' (City of Lucerne, 2021).

Guiding principles aligned to the action fields of digital transformation included:

- Under the premise of 'digital first', the city uses the possibilities of digitalisation, in particular technology, innovations, and data for the integral and efficient provision of services as an *attractive, modern administration, and employer.*
- The city uses digitalisation in a targeted manner to increase *customer centricity and service quality* as well as active communication, taking into account the needs of the population, politics, the economy, and other stakeholder groups.
- As a smart city, the city uses *digital technology and data-based activities* to make a sustainable contribution to optimising the design of public spaces, using infrastructure more efficiently and conserving resources while taking into account the needs of nature and the environment.

It presented the above activities in light of various stakeholder groups, including citizens/residents, the economy/employment, politics, society/culture/activities, and the environment.

Action Fields of Digital Transformation for Government Organisations

The new digital strategy was linked to the seven action fields of digital transformation (Peter et al., 2020, 2024). The 'Digital Transformation Canvas' was used as a basis for outlining the tasks regarding the digital transformation of the city's administration, where five action fields would be covered in the city's digital strategy, while responsibility for action field 'digital leadership and culture' was allocated to the HR (human resources) team, and digital marketing to the city's communication team/chancellery.

For government organisations, it is recommended to work with the following seven action fields (Peter et al., 2024):

- customer centricity
- new technologies

- data and the cloud
- digital / e-government strategies (instead of new strategies and business models)
- process management
- digital leadership and culture
- digital communication (instead of digital marketing).

In a critical reflection, the report provided an assessment of the city's digital maturity and stated, among things:

- Digital transformation is not a project with a defined start and end, but should be seen as an ongoing task.
- The complexity of digital transformation and its issues requires a conscious culture of error and courage that allows new approaches to solutions to be tested, and also permits occasional failures.
- As a public administration is fundamentally based on politically defined goals and tasks and implements and executes these with taxpayers' money, pilot tests and 'experiments' have so far been carried out cautiously within the scope of the available possibilities.
- While the goal is often clear, the expected end result often cannot be conclusively defined and must always be adapted to new findings and changing situations over the course of the project.
- In contrast to traditional projects, the resources requirements for an agile project are not fully known.
- The roles of those involved can change over time. A hierarchical understanding of leadership can contradict the agile approach.
- As there is no best or good practice for complex issues, solutions must be developed in-house. Ready-made solutions cannot yet be purchased on the market.
- Differing legal requirements prevent the implementation of joint (including digital) solutions between cities, cantons/states, and the federal government.

The new proposal presented various digital investment areas, most importantly, the extension of the DIG team with the establishment of digital project managers and digital business managers who would work in the matrix organisation to support the various government departments to drive their digital agendas (see box).

Digital Managers Who Support the City's Digital Transformation

Five guiding principles were defined for the role of digital business manager (City of Lucerne, 2021):

1. The digital managers are located in the respective government departments but support each other for the management of digital transformation projects across directorate boundaries.
2. DIG digital managers are part of a virtual digital project manager pool and provide coaching and advise on digital projects. This includes the application of project management methodologies and agile project management principles.

(Continued)

3 The digital managers exchange information monthly and regularly take part in ongoing development/training (internal and external) and thus become digital ambassadors in their allocated departments.
4 The digital project manager pool is intended to ensure that the departments' digital projects are being implemented successfully through the correct application of the right project method and that the digital managers can effectively fulfil their role as consultants and transformers within the departments.
5 The digital managers are employed by the respective department, whereby the Chief Digital Officer can provide support in defining and assessing the technical requirements and can participate in the interviews with candidates.

Figure B.6 Example of citizen participation on the 'Dialogue Lucerne' platform: posts regarding broken streetlights and lose tiles (City of Lucerne, 2024c)

It was proposed to hire an additional nine employees, mostly digital project managers, but also to provide admin support and internal and external communication activities (5.8 FTE), driving the annual cost of the digital team to CHF 1.8 million per year. With the plan for a 10-year investment proposal, parliament was asked to approve almost CHF 14 million to fund the digital services team. It approved the investment strategy in November 2021.

Digital Assessments and Progress in 2023/2024

In 2022, the digital team was expanded as part of the approved investment budget and structured as shown in Figure B.7 (City of Lucerne, 2023).

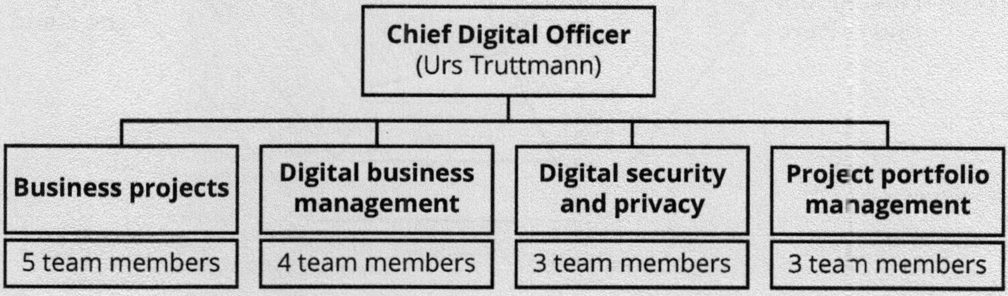

Figure B.7 Organisational structure of the city of Lucerne's digital transformation team (DIG) as of November 2023

As the team embarked upon its four-year anniversary at the end of 2023, CDO Urs Truttmann, together with digital business manager Damaris Hostettler, wanted to review both the team's and the digital initiatives' progress (and how they reflect their progress with the associated departments) in the form of a digital maturity assessment. An external consultant was hired to complete seven interviews in addition to an assessment of the team's digital maturity with the digital strategy check (see chapter 12 of the textbook).

The interviews covered the following set of questions (Peter, 2023):

1 What is your role and what goals do you need to achieve?
2 What are the objectives of Lucerne's digital strategy and smart city strategy map?
3 Who is responsible for the successful implementation of the digital strategy/smart city roadmap?
4 What methods and tools do you use for the digital transformation of the city?
5 What has been achieved so far in the seven fields of action of digital transformation?
6 What have you personally achieved so far; and what are you proud of?
7 If you were to have a coffee with the mayor, what obstacles can he remove for you so that you are more successful as a team?

A total of 13 team members (out of 16 in the DIG team) completed the digital maturity assessment with the results per action field shown in Figure B.8.

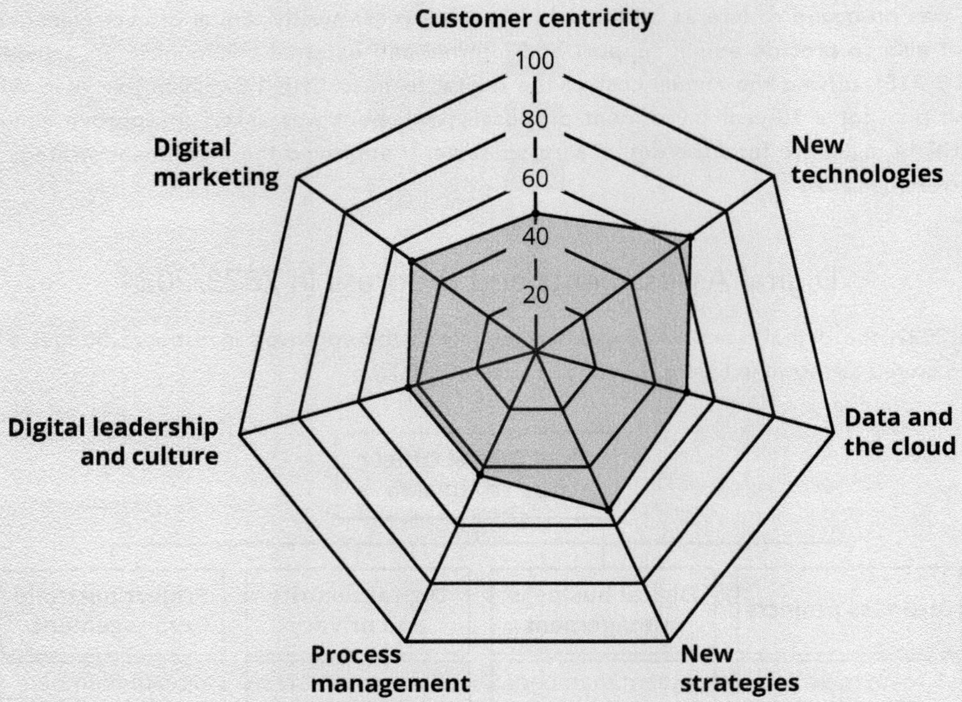

Figure B.8 Perceived digital maturity of the city of Lucerne digital transformation team (November 2023, n=13). Visit www.digital-strategy-check.com for your own digital assessment

During a workshop, the DIG team discussed and challenged the findings from interviews and the digital maturity assessment, provided examples, and further elaborated on the various points. Four recommendations emerged from the findings and discussions:

1 *Strategy (digital strategy city of Lucerne and the smart city strategy map)*
   - Revise and potentially merge the two strategy documents/roadmaps via a top-down and bottom-up approach with a series of strategy workshops.
   - Invite the internal success factor and enabler, central IT services, to participate in all workshops.
   - Develop a communication framework to drive/enable internal change management.

2 *Action fields of digital transformation*
   - Customer centricity: better define employees' understanding of customer orientation both internally and externally.
   - New technologies: identify relevant digital technology in collaboration with central IT services.
   - Data and the cloud: as data will be a priority in 2024, develop a data charter.
   - New strategies: identify and develop new (digital) services for each department.
   - Process management: continue to implement projects as part of ongoing digitalisation efforts.

- Digital leadership and culture: invest in further training and communication to build digital skills and internal resilience for the DIG team.
- Digital marketing: as communication will be a priority in 2024, develop a communication framework.

3 *Collaboration*

- Ongoing communication of the digital roadmap and current projects.
- Better define responsibilities.
- Potentially establish a 'digital council' with members from parliament and departments.
- Improve collaboration with central IT services.

4 *Digital transformation team (DIG)*

- Develop a team vision/charter to share experiences and knowledge, and to provide support to colleagues.
- Develop an internal digital strategy/roadmap with enabling projects.
- Develop a digital transformation method and toolbox.

In 2024, the DIG team achieved numerous milestones and completed projects. CDO Urs Truttmann summarised the team's achievements as follows (interview, 2024):

1 *A revised digital strategy for the city of Lucerne*

The redevelopment of the digital strategy and smart city roadmap started at the end of 2024 with the goal to present a holistic, new digital strategy in 2025. It was agreed that, twice a year, a digital strategy board, consisting of representatives from the administration and politicians, will review and update the digital roadmap.

2 *The establishment of a digital business manager in all five departments*

All five government departments have a digital business manager (DBM) who supports digital strategy development and implementation. According to the CDO, the results vary by department. In some, an entire digital strategy was developed, which links to clearly defined digital initiatives. Those responsible managers in the organisational units used the role of the DBMs very differently, with more or less success, to tackle digital transformations in their areas of responsibility. The results, i.e., impact, range from 'great' to 'not so great'.

3 *Collaboration with IT*

The city's IT strategy was updated in 2024, and the digital team with CDO Urs Truttman was invited to collaborate in its development. The city hired a data architect who will support both teams, IT and DIG, to advanced digital initiatives and support the data strategy from 2025 onwards.

4 *Internal and external communication of digital activities*

Project-related communication activities were implemented throughout 2024, and the team developed a communication framework on how the DIG team will communicate from 2025 onwards. According to the CDO, there is still a lot of room for improvement for internal digital communication to understand how to push digital transformation internally and culturally as it was recognised that not all employees are aware of the DIG's team service and support offering.

In addition, the DIG team utilised the digital maturity assessment in other departments, such as for the Department of Building's real-estate management team, to enable discussions and strategic debates (see Figure B.9). As an example, 40 employees completed the assessment in February 2024 (Digital Strategy Check, 2024).

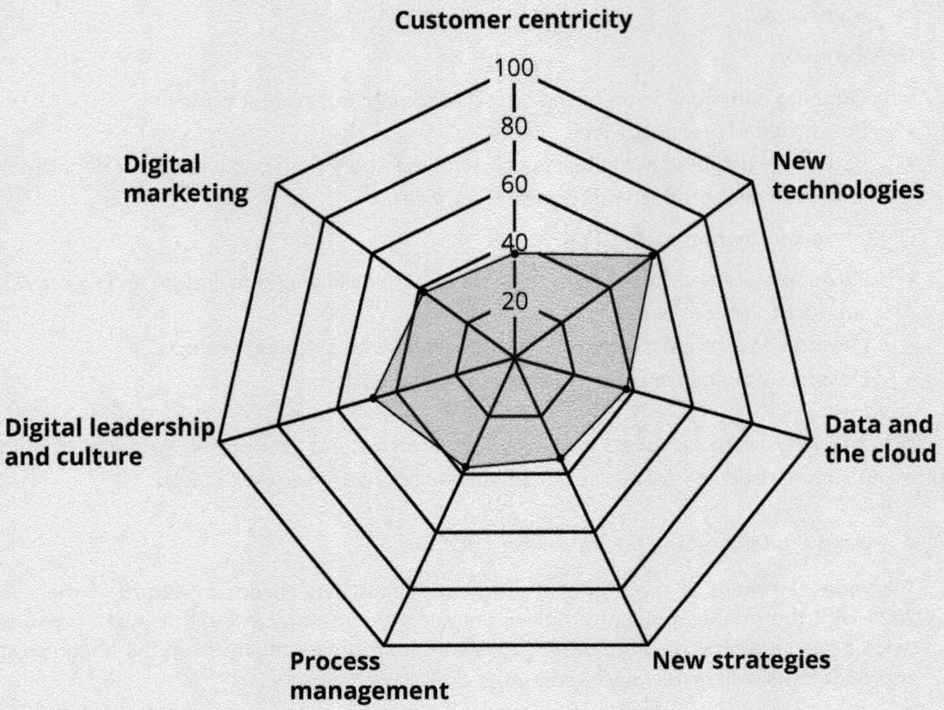

Figure B.9 Perceived digital maturity of the city of Lucerne Department of Building's real estate management team (February 2024, n=40). Visit www.digital-strategy-check.com for your own digital assessment

The perceived digital maturity of the exemplary presented internal stakeholder/customer of the DIG team (of the Department of Building) is higher in all dimensions except for leadership and culture, where DIG is higher, than the perceived digital maturity of the DIG's team members themselves.

The DIG team continues to guide, implement, and support the city's digital transformation roadmap to support advancement and societal transformation in the communities in which they serve (see box with an interview with the city's CDO).

Interview with CDO Urs Truttmann

(Interview, 2024)

How has the city's digital strategy progressed since the DIG team's inception in 2020?

Today, digital transformation is not just regarded as a trend or something short-lived, but as an important success factor for the city's transformation in order to remain competitive as an administrative public sector organisation.

What barriers did you encounter and how did you address them?

The main barrier, based on my experiences and insight from the past years, is the resistance for change in middle management. There is a lot of opportunity to better embrace middle management and support them to be able to achieve digital advancement. It might require a higher degree of political pressure to succeed in digital transformation. Strategy development in the digital age cannot be a static tool but must be dynamic.

Following the workshop to review the DIG team's maturity and effectiveness in 2023, what activities were implemented?

In addition to our new initiatives that include a revised digital strategy for the city of Lucerne, the new IT strategy and stronger internal and external communication of digital activities, we are now trying to implement a sociocracy-based collaboration framework. The first circle with the goal to establish a new leadership framework was created in 2024 with the goal to implement a holacracy system in 2025. The challenge, however, will be to understand how to run a dual leadership framework in a public-sector organisation, where hierarchical frameworks are still more dominant.

What are the key success factors for digital transformation in a government organisation?

It is most certainly the human factor – the employee – who wants to change an organisation and drive digital transformation. Identifying those who enable change is crucial. In addition, customer centricity is a success factor as we should constantly ask ourselves if customers can benefit from an investment. With this in mind, digital transformation implementation might be faster.

Image B.1 Chief Digital Officer Urs Truttmann

Student Questions

Discuss the following questions in your class, in your group or assignment:

Strategic Action Field 'Digital Leadership and Culture':

1 What are the challenges and barriers (including cultural ones) for digital transformation in an organisation; and specifically, in a government organisation?
2 How would you describe the city of Lucerne's effort and progress regarding digital transformation?
3 How could an organisation (such as the city of Lucerne) modify/enrich its technical, social and spatial dimensions to foster digital transformation? Provide five ideas/recommendations for each dimension.
4 Identify two government stakeholder groups and describe three digital services for each group that might provide value and efficiency gains. What digital skills are required to provide these digital services?
5 Would you recommend Scrum as an agile project and work method to the city of Lucerne? Describe why you would (or would not) recommend Scrum.
6 Overall, what are the digital skills which employees require for successful digital transformation in an organisation? Define at least eight skills and provide a rationale for your choice.
7 What are your takeaways from this case regarding digital culture and leadership? What were the key activities at the City of Lucerne that enabled cultural and leadership change?

Digital transformation implementation:

1 What risks and barriers can you identify when renewing (digitally transforming) a government organisation?
2 What are the differences between the digital transformation of a business and government (or not-for-profit) organisation?
3 How would you prepare the City of Lucerne for their digital transformation in the three areas of project management, change management, digital leadership? How would you recommend the City of Lucerne invest into these three areas?
4 Is the Smart city Lucerne strategy map (2021) a strategic programme or a project portfolio? Explain your rationale.
5 What are the benefits of the digital maturity assessments? Why would you recommend this approach to another organisation?
6 What are the tasks of the Chief Digital Officer (CDO) at the city of Lucerne? Define at least ten tasks/deliverables.
7 What other activities could CDO Urs Truttmann initiate to advance digital transformation in the city's administration?

Additional Information

Suggested further information can be found at the following:

- City of Lucerne official website: www.luzern.ch
- Lucerne tourism website: www.luzern.com/en/
- Lucerne's digital dialogue/project platform: https://dialogluzern.ch/

- City of Lucerne tourism video: www.YouTube.com/watch?v=Nd69JuLqIUo
- Digital transformation strategy of Switzerland: https://digital.swiss/en/
- E-government strategy of Switzerland: www.digital-public-services-switzerland.ch/strategy
- Swiss open data platform: https://opendata.swiss/en
- Interview with CDO Urs Truttmann: www.strategic-digital-transformation.com

Author

Professor Marc K. Peter, HES-SO Valais-Wallis School of Management, Switzerland; Charles Sturt University, Australia; University of Rochester/Simon Business School, USA

Acknowledgements and Authorisation

The authors would like to thank Urs Truttmann (Chief Digital Officer of the City of Lucerne) and Damaris Hostettler (Digital Business Manager) for their support in providing this case study.

The City of Lucerne case study and the use of artwork/logos/illustrations was authorised by the City of Lucerne on 28 November 2024.

References

City Archives of the City of Lucerne (2024) Stadtarchiv Bildgalerien, available at www.stadtluzern.ch/dokumentebilder/bildergalerien/6 (accessed 27 September 2024).

City of Lucerne (2019) Stadt Luzern digital: Digitalstrategie der Stadt Luzern: Bericht und Antrag an den Grossen Stadtrat von Luzern vom 22. Januar 2019 (StB 30), Stadt Luzern, Lucerne/Switzerland.

City of Lucerne (2021) Digitalstrategie und Smart City Luzern: Bericht und Antrag an den Grossen Stadtrat von Luzern vom 30. August 2021 (StB 620), Stadt Luzern, Lucerne/Switzerland.

City of Lucerne (2023) Organisational structure of the DIG team, November, Stadt Luzern, Lucerne/Switzerland.

City of Lucerne (2024a) City of Lucerne, available at www.luzern.ch (accessed 26 September 2024).

City of Lucerne (2024b) Lucerne Tourism, available at www.luzern.com/en/ (accessed 26 September 2024).

City of Lucerne (2024c) Dialogue Lucerne, available at https://dialogluzern.ch/assemblies/schadenmelden/f/498 (accessed 25 October 2024).

Digital Strategy Check (2024) Digital Strategy Check, available at www.digital-strategy-check.com (accessed 26 September 2024).

E-Government Standards (2014) Architektur E-Government Schweiz: Grundlagen (eCH-0122), www.ech.ch/de/ech/ech-0122/2.0.0.

Interview (2024) Discussion on 15 October 2024 between Urs Truttmann and Marc K. Peter.

Peter, M. K. (2023) Assessment der Dienstabteilung Digital der Stadt Luzern, *Strategylab*, 29 November, Rotkreuz/Switzerland.

Peter, M. K. (2024) *The Digital Transformation Canvas: Develop and Implement Your Digital Strategy*. London/UK: FT Publishing/Pearson.

Peter, M. K., Kraft, C., and Lindeque, J.P. (2020). Strategic action fields of digital transformation: an exploration of the strategic action fields of Swiss SMEs and large enterprises, *Journal of Strategy & Management*, 13(1), 160–80.

Peter, M. K., Maier, K. L., Lindeque, J. P., and Sollberger, A. (2024) Digitale Maturitätsanalyse und Workshop-Canvas 'Digitale Transformation für die öffentliche Verwaltung': Potenziale, Ideen und Projekte für den digitalen Masterplan, Hochschule für Wirtschaft FHNW & Myni Gmeind, May, Olten/Switzerland, www.gov-digital-check.ch.

CASE STUDY C: SWITZERLAND TOURISM – CROSS-MEDIA CAMPAIGN 'THE RIDE OF A LIFETIME'

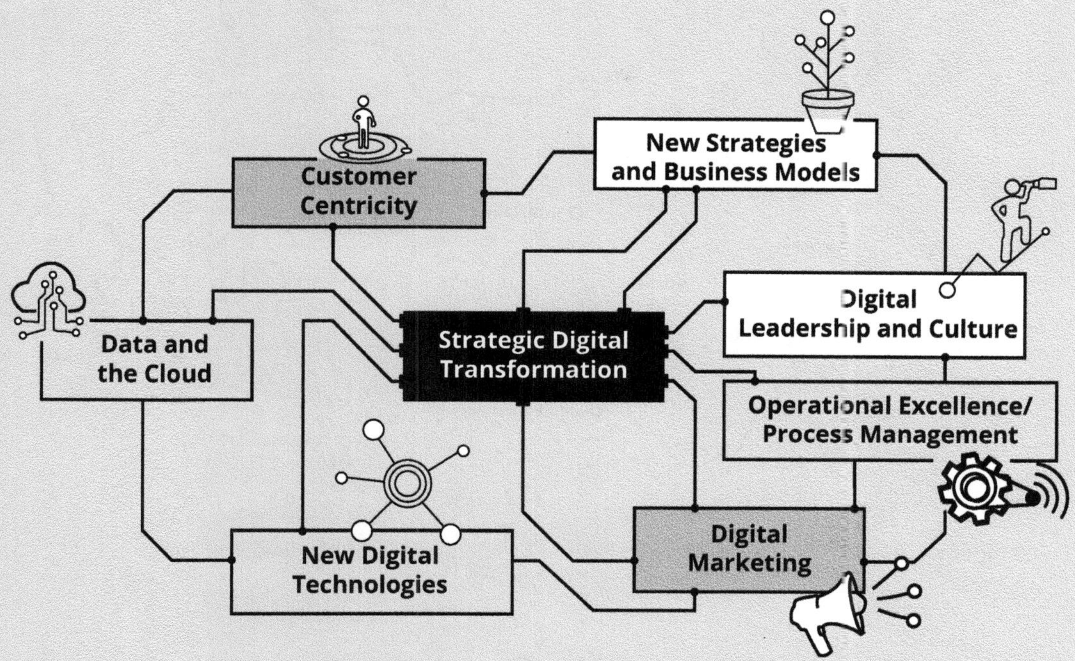

Figure C.1 Switzerland Tourism seven action fields

switzerland

Figure C.2 Switzerland Tourism Logo

Case Organisation Profile

- Organisation name: Switzerland Tourism
- Country: Switzerland
- Description: Switzerland Tourism is the national organisation that promotes Switzerland as a travel destination worldwide.
- Number of employees: 280
- Website: www.myswitzerland.com/

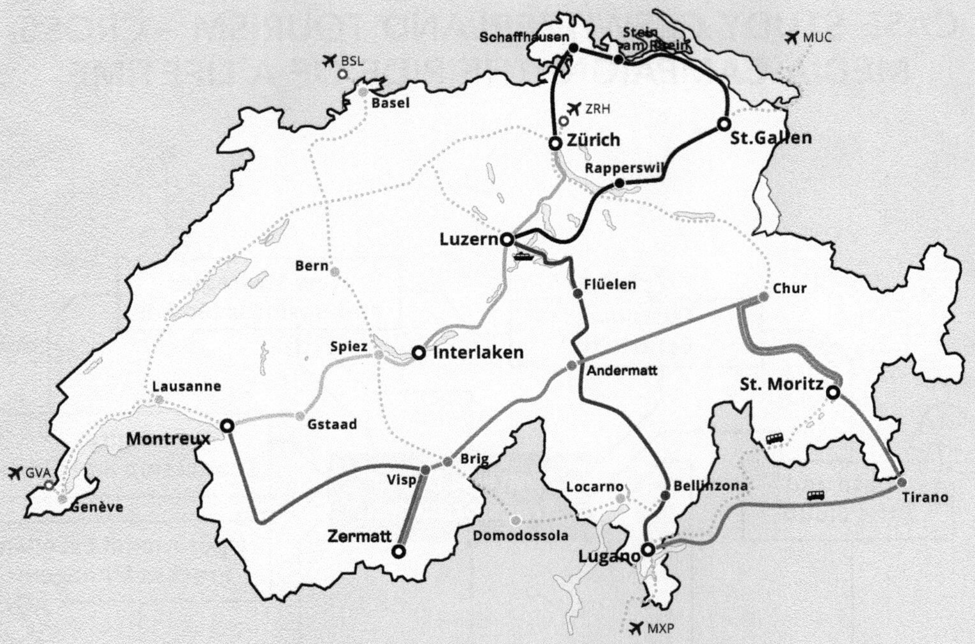

Figure C.3 Map of the Grand Train Tour of Switzerland (© Switzerland Tourism)

Case Overview

As part of the third film production for Switzerland Tourism in 2023, Roger Federer acted as a global ambassador for Switzerland as a destination, this time alongside comedian Trevor Noah. The film, which is part of the campaign and promotes the Grand Train Tour of Switzerland, was released worldwide on 30 March 2023 and targeted foreign guests.

The campaign achieved considerable success, which can be demonstrated by several factors. For example, a total of 83 million views were recorded on the YouTube platform by the end of 2024. In addition, a significant increase in the number of Swiss Travel Passes sold was observed and over 800 million marketing contacts were achieved.

Case Organisation

Switzerland Tourism is the national organisation that promotes Switzerland as a travel destination worldwide. Based in Zurich, its goal is to implement innovative marketing strategies and co-operate closely with partners from the tourism, transport, and cultural sectors. The aim is to establish Switzerland as a first-class travel destination. Through campaigns that focus on digital innovation and emotional appeal, the organisation reaches millions of potential travellers worldwide.

Switzerland Tourism stands for sustainability, high-quality offers, and a unique travel experience that is attractive to both individual travellers and group travellers.

Initial Situation

The initial situation and challenges for this case were complex.

Addressing Young Travellers

Switzerland is often perceived internationally as an expensive destination, which discourages younger target groups aged 25 to 35 in particular from travelling to Switzerland. This age group shows a preference for affordable and flexible travel options that cater to their lifestyle and offer digital solutions. The challenge is therefore to make Switzerland more attractive to this target group by providing emotional and modern content that emphasises the unique experience of nature, culture, and comfort. In addition, relevant platforms and channels must be used to reach and appeal to this target group in a targeted manner.

Sustainability

There is an urgent need to establish public transport as a sustainable and essential part of Switzerland's travel offer. Especially because the infrastructure in Switzerland is considered to be reliable and of high quality. Younger travellers in particular are often looking for cheaper alternatives that seem quicker and less complicated. The challenge is therefore to communicate rail travel in Switzerland as an authentic, environmentally friendly, and unforgettable experience that stands out significantly from other forms of travel. It is essential to raise awareness of sustainability and integrate the benefits of public transport into the core message of the tourism offer.

To address these issues, a comprehensive and creative cross-media campaign was developed. The aim of the campaign was to combine the traditional values of Switzerland, such as safety, natural beauty, and quality, with modern and emotionally appealing experiences and to establish rail travel as a sustainable, comfortable and impressive experience.

The Campaign: 'The Ride of a Lifetime'

The campaign pursued two objectives: On the one hand, Switzerland was to be made more visible internationally and, on the other, it was to be established as an attractive, sustainable travel destination. To this end, digital content was to be utilised to a greater extent to increase the engagement of the target groups and significantly increase interaction with the campaigns. The aim was to appeal to younger, tech-savvy travellers who can be reached through digital media and immersive experiences. At the same time, Switzerland's traditional values such as reliability and hospitality were to be combined with innovative offers such as virtual reality experiences and personalised itineraries.

Another objective was to increase bookings for the Swiss Travel Pass. This measure not only served to increase sales, but also to anchor public transport as a central component of the tourism offering. Finally, a key aspect of the campaign was to also establish Switzerland as a pioneer in sustainable mobility.

Development of the Campaign

The campaign comprised various measures to achieve its objectives.

Switzerland Tourism worked with world-famous personalities Roger Federer and Trevor Noah in the area of 'ambassador marketing'. The story focuses on Roger Federer's renewed attempt to shoot a commercial for Switzerland. After the 'unsuccessful attempt' to secure Robert De Niro to make a commercial (2021) and the 'unsuccessful attempt' with Anne Hathaway (2022), he now tries his luck with Trevor Noah, who is known as a comedian and bestselling author (The 'unsuccessful attempt' is part of the campaign storyline). Unfortunately, he fails again as the two co-stars get on the wrong train. However, this proves to be a stroke of luck, as the 'Grand Train Tour of Switzerland' is a great experience even if you are travelling it involuntarily. The central message of the film is that you are never on the wrong train in Switzerland. The emotional and personal film shows Switzerland at its best. The collaboration with the two internationally renowned stars with close ties to Switzerland made it possible to combine a global reach with local authenticity.

In addition to the main advert, which was published and promoted on YouTube, a variety of other advertising materials were used under the motto 'I need the ride of my life. I need Switzerland.' These advertised various offers and experiences related to travelling by train. The campaign, which focussed on digital moving images, was rolled out globally, with a focus on the USA, India, Korea, Southeast Asia, China, the UK and Germany.

As part of performance marketing, the specific needs of users were addressed using targeted advertising campaigns via Google Ads, YouTube, and other social media platforms. A/B tests were used to continuously optimise and adapt the campaigns. In cooperation with tourism partners, tourist offers were advertised that made the Grand Train Tour of Switzerland directly bookable.

In the area of content strategy, an interactive web platform was developed that included travel routes, direct booking options, and inspiring stories. The platform focussed on the presentation of Switzerland's diverse tourist attractions and offered users the opportunity to plan their individual trip.

Image C.1 An app developed for the Grand Train Tour of Switzerland (© Switzerland Tourism / André Meier)

Figure C.4 Report on Switzerland Tourism's campaign (reprinted with permission from Brandadvertising)

Source: Martinez, Eloy (2023): Exploring Switzerland's Grand Train Tour: Roger Federer and Trevor Noah's latest advertising campaign by Switzerland Tourism, *Brandadvertising*, April, www.brandvertising.ch/2023/04/switzerland-tourism-grand-train-tour-roger-federer/.

The publication of social media contents also played a decisive role. Numerous organic posts were published on Switzerland Tourism's social media platforms, which further amplified the messages.

Results and Findings

The results and findings of the campaign are impressive and can be located along the entire customer journey. The following results were achieved in just six weeks of the campaign:

- The campaign reached over 800 million marketing contacts in the period 2023/24.
- The Grand Train Tour of Switzerland recorded an increase in awareness of 31.8%.
- Train ticket sales increased by +59%, resulting in an overall positive return on marketing investment.
- Switzerland has established itself internationally as a safe, sustainable, and diverse travel destination.

The efficiency and impact of the campaign led to a significant increase in Swiss Travel Pass sales (33% above target expectation) and a record number of guests in Switzerland, revitalising the country's image as an attractive travel destination.

Student Questions

Discuss the following questions in your class, in your group or assignment:

Strategic Action Field 'Customer Centricity':

1. How well does the marketing strategy of Switzerland Tourism reflect a customer-centric approach?
2. Develop a customer persona based on a summarised persona description of a typical segment which would/might visit Switzerland.
3. Develop the customer journey for the campaign before a tourist would visit Switzerland: what steps will the tourist take, and what channels will be used to obtain information, and communicate with businesses (e.g., travel agency, airport, train)?
4. How is the digitally enabled customer journey reflected in the multi-channel marketing campaign?
5. Evaluate the choice to integrate world-famous personalities Roger Federer and Trevor Noah into the campaign: in your opinion does this speak to a customer-centric mindset at Switzerland Tourism?
6. How do you think digitally enabled customer centricity could be further enhanced in the customer experience of tourists that become aware of Switzerland as a destination after watching the campaign?

Strategic action field 'Digital Marketing':

1. Which activities were particularly successful in improving the perception of Switzerland as a holiday destination? How could these activities be further optimised?
2. Was the campaign executed using Web 1.0, Web 2.0, or Web 3.0 digital technologies?
3. How could virtual reality add-ons (e.g., virtual tours of Switzerland) be developed to improve the user experience?

4 What are the success factors of influencer marketing with stars (ambassador marketing), and how could this marketing approach be used in the future?
5 What recommendations do you have to other organisations in utilising influencer marketing / ambassador marketing?
6 How could specific target groups be addressed even better in order to take cultural and regional differences into account?
7 What other digital approaches could be used to strengthen public transport as part of the travel experience?
8 What does a possible marketing and sales funnel look like, and what are the key online metrics which Switzerland Tourism should use?
9 Which technologies could help to personalise the travel experience and further increase Switzerland's attractiveness as a travel destination?

Additional Information

Suggested further information can be found at the following:

- Roger Federer and Trevor Noah (2023): www.YouTube.com/watch?v=5JK7vjValvo
- Grand Train Tour of Switzerland: www.myswitzerland.com/en-ch/experiences/experience-tour/highlights-by-train-bus-and-boat/grand-train-tour-of-switzerland/
- Switzerland Tourism: www.myswitzerland.com/en-us/
- Roger Federer and Robert De Niro (2021): www.YouTube.com/watch?v=wXcBGfXXL4w
- Roger Federer and Anne Hathaway (2022): www.YouTube.com/watch?v=IyhpSZBuYoE
- Roger Federer and Mads Mikkelsen (2024): https://www.youtube.com/watch?v=dRID-0fo-2FQ
- Roger Federer and Halle Berry (2025): https://www.youtube.com/watch?v=1Kzf9YZkXSc

Author

Dominic Stöcklin, Head of Marketing at Basel Tourismus and former Head of Media at Switzerland Tourism, Switzerland

Acknowledgements and Authorisation

The book's authors would like to thank Dominic Stöcklin, Head of Marketing at Basel Tourismus and former Head of Media at Switzerland Tourism, for this case study. The case study 'Switzerland Tourism – cross-media campaign "The ride of a lifetime"' and the use of artwork/logos/illustrations was authorised by Switzerland Tourism on 6 January 2025.

CASE STUDY D: VALUU, A CORPORATE START-UP FOR DIGITAL BUSINESS MODEL INNOVATION

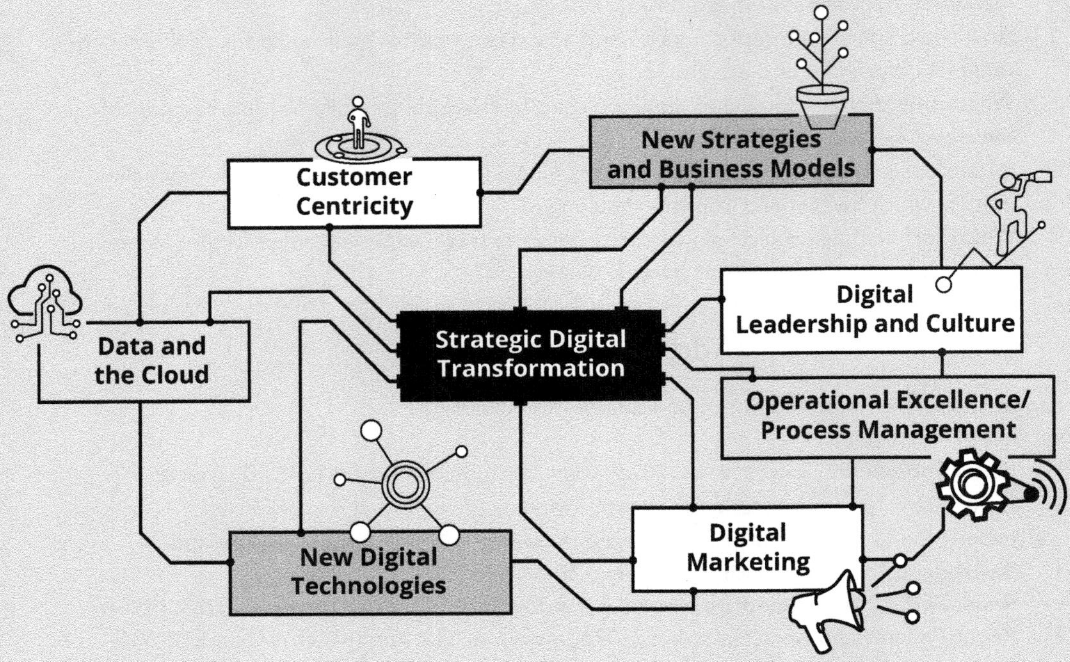

Figure D.1 Valuu seven action fields

Figure D.2 Valuu logo

Case Organisation Profile

- Organisation name: PostFinance
- Country: Switzerland
- Description: Valuu is a digital corporate start-up of Swiss retail bank PostFinance that has revolutionised digital end-to-end mortgage processes between 2019 to 2024.
- Number of employees: 3,340
- Website: www.postfinance.ch

Case Overview

Valuu is a digital corporate start-up of Swiss retail bank PostFinance that has revolutionised digital end-to-end mortgage processes between 2019 to 2024. Throughout the five years of constant digital business model innovation (with investments totalling CHF 50 million according to Zulliger, 2024), it has emerged from a start-up driven by the two intrapreneurs (managers within a company who drive innovation) Thomas Jakob and Michael Gaschen to a digital platform in a banking ecosystem and finally to a provider of digital technology to drive the IT infrastructure of the leading mortgage broker platform in Switzerland.

Background: Retail Bank PostFinance

PostFinance is one of Switzerland's leading financial institutions (PostFinance, 2024), a diversified, innovation-driven financial service provider that offers its 2.5 million customers modern banking solutions. The financial institution has around CHF 104 billion in customer assets and processes more than 1.3 billion payment transactions a year. PostFinance has 3 340 employees and generated profits of CHF 164 million in 2023. The financial institution distributes its banking products via the Swiss Post's 700+ post offices, its own 30 consulting centres, and digital channels. PostFinance is a member of the Swiss Post with an annual revenue of CHF 7.3 billion, operating profit of CHF 323 million and 35,000 employees in 2023 (Swiss Post, 2024).

For over 100 years, PostFinance has been an innovation pioneer and it has a long tradition of innovation and digitalisation going back over the past decades: it was the first financial institution that launched ATMs in 1978 in Switzerland; ten years later, an electronic payment solution followed, and, 20 years later, in 1998, the bank's e-banking platform was introduced. In 2002, PostFinance became the first bank to launch an e-invoicing and settling solution so customers could load admission tickets and user authorisations for sports and cultural events onto their RFID (Radio Frequency Identification) enabled debit card. In 2010, it was again the first Swiss bank to launch a banking app. In 2017, it embarked on a new digital strategy (the 'Digital Powerhouse') to support its digital transformation and remain competitive in the national banking market (Peter, 2019).

PostFinance recognised that 'traditional banking services face a substantial threat if we do not take appropriate measures. We will, therefore, focus more clearly on the digital world in the future and develop PostFinance from a traditional financial service provider into a digital powerhouse. We are convinced that this transformation will help us to better meet the challenges of the future' (PostFinance, 2017, p. 3).

In 2017, a project team initiated the Valuu strategic project, a corporate start-up, to build a digital mortgage platform that would help PostFinance to establish a platform economy in an ecosystem and, with that, a new digital business model. (As PostFinance is a state-owned financial institution as part of the Swiss Post, it has restrictions regarding the establishment of its own mortgage business; it supported the identified opportunity to drive a new digital business initiative.) The team's vision was to establish the leading online mortgage platform in Switzerland that would provide end-to-end digital processes for mortgage comparison, application, and deal-closing without the need for human interactions (no personal contacts or meetings with a financial advisor would be required). The initial business model had a B2B2C (business-to-business-to-consumers) structure, where financial institutions (e.g., banks) would offer their mortgage products to Valuu, which in turn would promote/sell them to their customers/consumers.

Valuu's 2030 Vision

PostFinance defined three strategic pillars for Valuu's 2030 vision (internal presentation, 2019):

- *#1 Platform*: with its independent platform, PostFinance is the top 1/top 2 comparison, brokerage and deal-closing (digital) platform in the Swiss market.
- *#2 Products*: in addition to mortgages, loans, insurance, and retirement solutions can be compared and obtained digitally. Value-added services will also be offered.
- *#3 Ecosystem*: the Valuu platform is at the core of an established and open ecosystem and drives non-interest-based revenue for PostFinance.

The Launch (2019)

PostFinance spent ten months building the digital mortgage platform with a team of 20 employees in 2018 and, in January 2019, announced that its new app was the first fully digital mortgage brokerage platform (Bönzli, 2019). It provides mortgage-seekers with easy, quick, as well as time and location-independent, access to the best mortgage from different providers (lenders such as banks, pension funds, and insurance companies) when purchasing a home or refinancing an existing mortgage. The Valuu app/platform (available for Android and iOS devices) allows users to compare mortgage products/offers from various providers, check financing options, submit documents, and complete the entire process online (via mobile phones). The digital platform provides an end-to-end experience to its customers and strategic partners (the mortgage suppliers) alike. Users enter their property details and instantly receive financing options. They can review the product offerings and then submit the loan application. A rules-based algorithm (machine learning AI) matches customers and suppliers and presents users with not necessarily just the cheapest mortgage offer but the one that is most suitable for them (in addition to the interest, the amortisation terms or the maximum amount of financing can also be important criteria for borrowers). Users can go through all required steps independently and without a (human) consultation appointment directly in the app. At every step, users can contact Valuu's telephone support centre for technical assistance or additional information.

For PostFinance, Valuu will provide a new revenue stream. Banking expert (and board member of another bank) Andreas Dietrich stated in an interview (Millischer, 2019), that:

'The lender transfers around half of the margin to the broker (platform) in the first year of the mortgage.' This, however, provides challenges, as 'all intermediaries say that they are independent, but that is only partially true, as only those providers will appear on the (platform's) comparison who are prepared to share the (profit) margin with the intermediary'.

The strategic intent of PostFinance was to satisfy a new customer need: 'We looked intensively ahead to pick the right business model', said Thomas Jakob, head of Valuu and Chief Business Unit Officer Platform Business at PostFinance in 2019. 'The traditional customer-provider constellation, a 1:1 relationship, is likely to be a customer need for only a limited time in the future' (Bönzli, 2019). In the spirit of the platform economy business model (see chapter 7), Valuu provides value by bringing together potential buyers and suppliers on the same platform (like Airbnb, eBay, or Uber). Unlike existing platforms, Valuu provides an additional value proposition: the app/platform not only simplifies mortgage comparison and the application process but provides a complete and digital end-to-end process (see Figure D.3). While there were mortgage competitors in the market – such as MoneyPark (with access to 100 financing partners), Hypoguide (30 financing partners), Key4 of UBS and Finance Scout (Scout Group) – Valuu was the first and only fully digital mortgage brokerage platform (it was assumed that the mortgage process could be standardised and automated for nearly 30% of all deals).

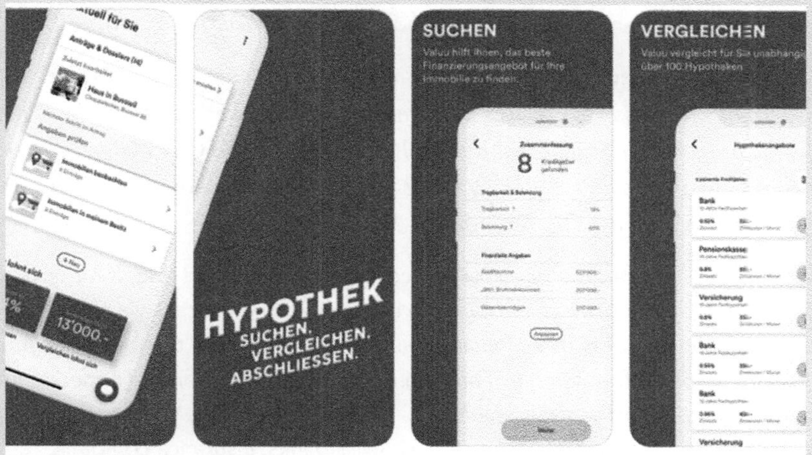

Figure D.3 Screenshots of the Valuu app

The Valuu platform not only has advantages for the mortgage-seeker, but also for the various lenders: with Valuu, they can expand their reach/distribution capabilities, reduce the costs of acquiring new customers and accelerate their own digital transformation and digital processes. As PostFinance already provided mortgages to its customers and tried to lift its market offers in the value chain of the industry to become a platform for all market participants (see chapter 7 for a definition of the digital value chain), Thomas Jakob of PostFinance assured the market that, 'Valuu takes on the "match maker" role in this brokerage model: to achieve this, the Valuu team has concluded contracts with a wide range of banks, insurance companies and pension funds, and in order to ensure independence as the operator of the platform, no PostFinance mortgages will be available on Valuu' (Bönzli, 2019). The financial benefit to PostFinance will not come from the Valuu users, i.e., borrowers, but via the fees that the lenders pay to PostFinance for completed transactions; i.e., successful mortgage contracts. In 2020, mortgages worth CHF 4.5 billion (around EUR 4.8 billion or USD 5.3 billion) were issued via brokers (Dietrich, 2021).

Considering the established competition, Andreas Dietrich (Millischer, 2019) was sceptical about the new PostFinance product: 'Valuu is the fourth intermediary (on the market).' While there are differentiating (digital) features available compared to existing market offers, the banking expert considered these unique value propositions (UVPs) to be weak: 'The market for (digital) mobile mortgage offers is challenging because experience has shown that customers ultimately look for a personal contact (with a financial institution) when making a major financial decision such as taking out a mortgage.'

Valuu's Market Pitch

Valuu (2022) posted the following pitch to promote its platform:

> *Buying a home is one of life's largest investments. Online mortgages promise great savings potential compared to traditional mortgages. There is a large selection of the best mortgages on PostFinance's Valuu comparison and deal-closing platform.*
>
> *The digital route to a mortgage is relatively new. Valuu has been around only since 2019. However, tens of thousands of Swiss consumers have now used the platform. During this time, Valuu brokered mortgages with a total volume of around CHF 600 million (around EUR 650 million or USD 700 million). Valuu is one of the most popular platforms on the Swiss online mortgage market. And for good reason:*
>
> - *Valuu has considered the need for advice right from the start and, if requested, supports mortgage borrowers through the entire financing process via telephone consultants. This service is free of charge, as is the entire use of the platform. Important tips and helpful information can also be found in simple, clear and understandable language in the app or Valuu guide.*
> - *Valuu has a partner network of over 100 Swiss banks, insurance companies and pension funds. Valuu negotiated the best interest rate for its users with these lenders. The personal offers can be easily compared. If you choose the best one, you can save a lot of money because the mortgage interest rates are often several tenths of a percentage point below what the house bank offers. That's why it's worth comparing and closing a mortgage with Valuu.*
>
> *Valuu guarantees the highest level of data security. The platform is even obliged to do this: as part of PostFinance, Valuu is subject to banking customer confidentiality. This is different to many other mortgage brokers. This basis of trust is a particularly important factor for mortgage borrowers. Online mortgages with Valuu combine so many advantages that one in three people can now imagine obtaining a mortgage online – whether for existing or new property.*

The First 100 Days on the Market

The market for mortgage brokers has reported some impressive growth rates over the past three years (2015–2018). However, according to a survey (Dietrich, 2019), around three out of four consumers surveyed cannot imagine themselves signing up to a mortgage through an intermediary (e.g., a platform). But this also means that 24% of those surveyed might sign up to a mortgage deal via an intermediary. Dietrich (2019) interviewed Thomas Jakob, head of Valuu and Chief Business Unit Officer Platform Business at PostFinance, three months after the launch of the Valuu platform, and in his blog post provided a summary of the key achievements to date:

- The app has been downloaded 15,000 times so far, a remarkable achievement for the first 100 days in the market, according to Dietrich (2019).
- A 'four-digit number' of users have registered on the platform so far.
- The platform has already recorded deals (closed contracts) in the low double-digit range.
- Valuu currently has 11 lenders as partners.
- So far, users have mainly chosen the offers from two pension funds and an insurance company. This is not surprising, as customers are currently leaning towards long-term, fixed-interest mortgages and insurance companies and pension funds are currently making attractive offers for long-term mortgages.
- Valuu had prepared in advance for many enquiries from (potential) mortgage customers. In fact, none of the customers who has closed a mortgage to date has called during the process: people either get along with the app and have confidence in a digital deal – or they play around a bit and then leave the app again.
- Most customers have extended or replaced their existing mortgage, and users who take out new mortgages apparently show a lot of activity on the platform but are then hesitant to close the deal.
- Customers with completed mortgage transactions are interest rate sensitive (so they went for the cheapest mortgage) and usually have good credit ratings.

According to Dietrich (2019), Valuu will now implement the following projects:

- First, as the app was offered only on mobile devices, and as some users prefer the 'desktop version' for their laptops/computers, Valuu will now build a web solution, available in the foreseeable future (originally, the use case focused on a customer experience without human interaction; however, following early 'friends and family' platform tests, it was clear that that a desktop version had to follow, including a hybrid customer journey with optional sales support).
- As there was some negative user feedback about the ease of use when signing up for a mortgage, Valuu will improve the app's customer experience. With its monthly release cycles, this will be implemented shortly.

One year into the New Venture (2020)

Within the first year of the launch, in 2020, Valuu completed the web version of its app and provided a French version of the platform. Within a year, Valuu attracted 6,000 active users and brokered mortgages with a volume of CHF 100 million (Fintech News, 2021a).

Go-to-Market Activities in 2020

Advertising agency In Flagranti (2021) supported Valuu's go-to-market activities and posted the following success metrics on its website:

- The use of TV spots, outdoor (digital out-of-home) advertising, and online display ads led to Valuu's un-aided brand awareness rising to 20% after just one year in the market. This means that the brand is already a market leader.
- As mortgages always involve a lot of money, before investing, customers want to feel safe. Valuu's awareness campaign ensures brand awareness, and the multifaceted content marketing activities supported trust building.
- All customer journeys – especially breakpoints – were meticulously analysed and all measures, channels, creatives, etc., from the time at user registration on the website to the completion of a mortgage application on the app, were continuously optimised.

You can watch a Valuu TV spot on YouTube: www.YouTube.com/watch?v=O_5iksAWf64.

Two Years into the New Venture (2021)

PostFinance (2021) celebrated Valuu's second birthday with a media statement, announcing that the platform was able to triple the brokered mortgage volume to CHF 500 million, had around 12,000 registered users and secured 29 lenders for its platform. It concluded that the concept of a digital comparison and deal-closing platform for mortgages was successful and very well received in the market. Valuu wanted to use this momentum and further expand its offering. The media statement concludes:

> *'For two years now, Valuu has provided users with easy, quick, time and location independent access to the right mortgage from various providers – be it for a new deal or a replacement. And that's just the beginning: Valuu wants to become the leading Swiss comparison and deal-closing platform in the medium term and is expanding its offering with additional services this year.*
>
> *Since launching in January 2019, Valuu has already financed mortgages worth several hundred million Swiss francs (CHF).'*

Valuu manager Thomas Jakob was pleased with the strong growth (PostFinance, 2021): 'We wanted to prove that we can survive in this very competitive market. We have more than succeeded in tripling the volume and doubling the number of users. More and more consumers are understanding the opportunities offered by a transparent comparison and digital mortgage platform – and how much money they can save with it.'

Valuu concluded that most users complete the digital process independently, without a human interaction via an advisor, and without any problems, confirming that the app is customer-centric and provides a full end-to-end process, as expected from a digital platform.

Dietrich (2021) summarised the two-year milestone in a blog post as follows:

- *The company has grown significantly in the past year and now employs around 50 employees [see Figure D.4]. Valuu currently works with over 100 partners and has around 50,000 visits to the website per month (website, including app).*
- *Since its launch in January 2019 up to August 2021, a mortgage volume of around CHF 500 million has been transacted via the platform (by January 2020, after a year in the market, the brokered volume was only at CHF 100 million).*
- *The average mortgage stood at CHF 523,000.*
- *The proportion of completed transactions via a mobile device was only around 9%. For this reason, since July 2021, transactions are now only possible via the desktop or tablet version. This development is particularly interesting because at the beginning of its launch, Valuu was designed exclusively as an app.*
- *The Valuu app has been revised accordingly and focuses now on user onboarding, comparing personal interest rates and quickly and easily uploading documents to the platform (e.g., to take a photo via the mobile phone and upload it to the app).*
- *The most popular online mortgage is the ten-year fixed-rate mortgage. More than half of all deals come from this product. 40% of mortgages taken out digitally are fixed-rate mortgages with terms of less than ten years. Fixed-rate mortgages with a term of eleven or more years account for 4%.*
- *58% of all online mortgages taken out via Valuu are from a bank, pension funds account for 31% of online mortgages, and 11% are financed by insurance companies.*
- *Around 60% of all deals are mortgage replacements, and 40% involve new buyers.*
- *The average age of a Valuu customer is 47 years. For new buyers, the age of 41 is unsurprisingly lower than for people who are paying off mortgages (average age: 53 years).*
- *According to a market research agency, Valuu has the highest brand awareness among mortgage brokers in terms of un-aided brand awareness.*

In August 2021, a user with the name of Adrian posted on Dietrich's (2021) post that it is great that Valuu's advertising investments are making an impact. However, earning CHF 500,000 annually from a 0.1% commission on CHF 500 million in closed mortgage deals won't cover all advertising costs or pay 50 employees, whose costs likely exceed CHF 5 million. It would be interesting if HSLU (Dietrich's university) could estimate the actual economic success and ask Valuu how long PostFinance will invest millions in a project that may never be profitable.

Product Range Extension in 2021

In June 2021, Valuu launched a new product (Valuu Pro), an advisory tool for mortgage brokers. It can be seen as an extension of its business model (and value chain, see chapter 7), by providing a software solution to mortgage brokers. On Valuu Pro, mortgage and financial advisors can register as sales partners and use all the features of the digital platform for their customers, including easy and quick searching, applying and closing of mortgages (Fintech News, 2021b). Thomas Jacob of PostFinance promoted the offering by saying that, 'With Valuu Pro, we provide mortgage and financial advisors with an effective and efficient tool to

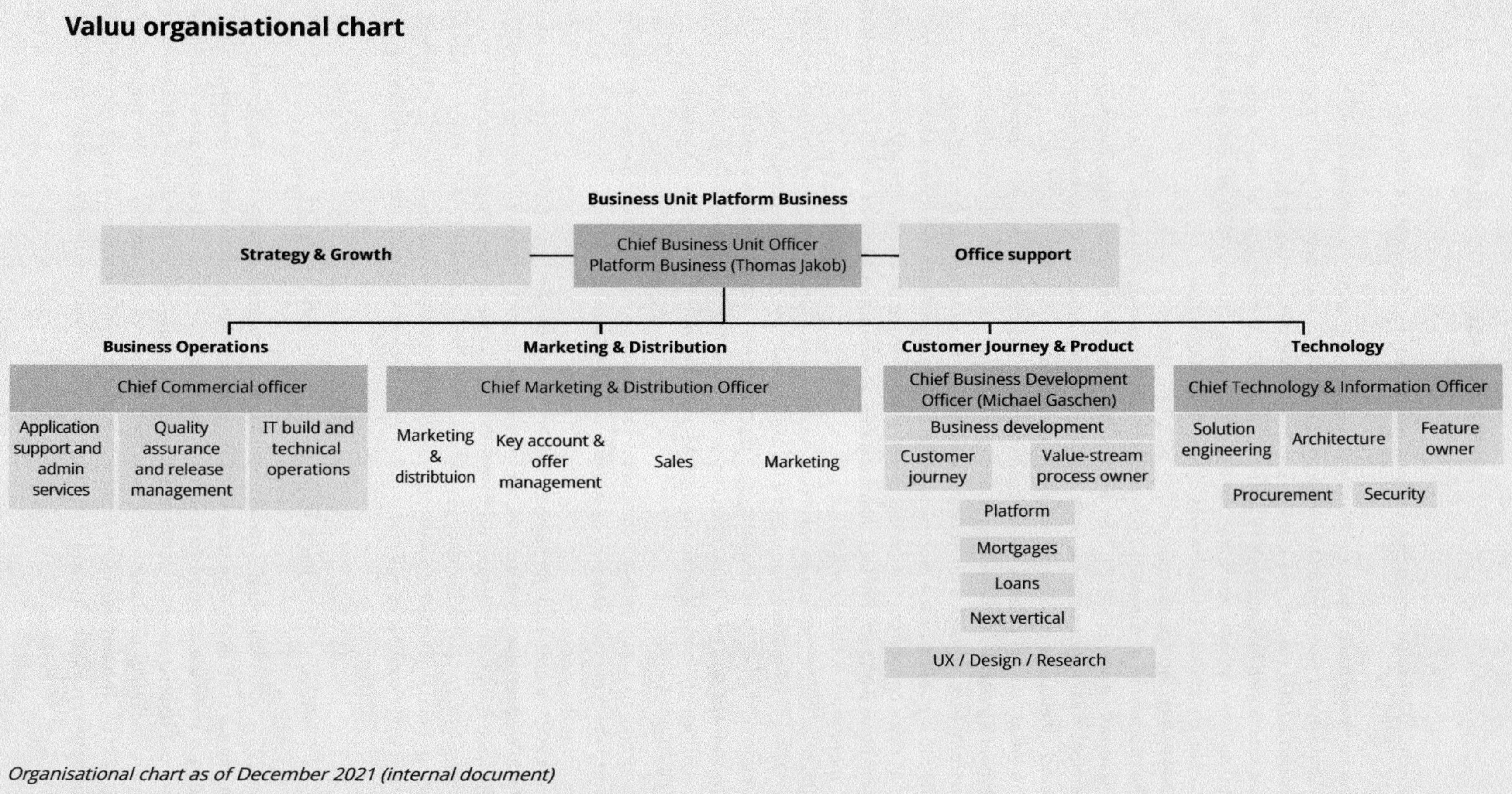

Figure D.4 Organisational chart as of December 2021 (internal document)

better serve their customers.' By the end of 2021, Valuu reached another milestone: many small and large financial advisory firms registered as sales partners, and other brokers such as real estate agents were showing great interest.

In August 2021, Valuu added an additional product offering to its Valuu app: via its various financing partners, users can now apply for personal loans. The fully digital application process takes only ten minutes.

Three Years into the New Venture (2022)

After three years on the market, Thomas Jakob, who ran the platform business at PostFinance, reviewed the journey to date in an interview with a Swiss IT magazine (Landis, 2022).

Together with the TWINT payment app (a market leading payment app in Switzerland, launched in 2017), Valuu was described as another 'prime example of a corporate start-up from PostFinance'. While many providers compete in the market, Thomas Jakob stated that, 'It is clear that not all platforms will be successful or survive. The platform market in the mortgage sector is a winner-takes-it-all-or-most market.' This means that only the number one and number two platforms will survive. In this respect, he expects consolidations and withdrawals of platforms. 'Valuu is now part of the digital comparison and sales business of mortgages and is one of the leading platforms in Switzerland.'

As of February 2022, Valuu reported the following metrics (internal presentation, 2022):

- 2.4 million visits on the Valuu platform to date
- 26,000 registered users
- CHF 750 million of closed mortgage deals.

The Platform Economy Business Model

The article from Landis (2022) explains that 'when financial institutions participate in ecosystems or, like PostFinance, launch their own platforms with Valuu, this is a remarkable step in a traditional sector such as the banking industry. The platform economy business model is often new territory for banks. But there are few alternatives, because the banks' business base has come under severe pressure over the past ten years due to negative interest rates, eroding earnings and falling margins due to increasing competition.'

Digitalisation and, in particular, the increasing use of digital channels have also led to customers increasingly making financial decisions on their mobile phones or computers at home. The mortgage market alone is gigantic, with a total volume of over CHF 1,000 billion and is, therefore, inherently interesting for banks. At the same time, mortgages are one of the anchor products in a financial institution's portfolio.

'If the market in this area becomes increasingly digitised or redistributed, your own position will have to be reconsidered,' said Thomas Jakob from PostFinance. 'The fact that other financial institutions also recognise that the market is changing naturally stimulates the development of business models.'

The platform business and participation in ecosystems also pose risks for financial institutions: the individual players (organisations) must open up to each other to a certain extent so that the network effect can play out. They also must develop a new self-image for their respective roles. 'You may then take on the role of an "expert" in an ecosystem and not that of the orchestrator or the "top dog". This is unusual, but essential in the digital world,' says Thomas Jakob. In principle, any form of participation in platforms is also possible for PostFinance. 'Of course, the focus must always be on economic benefits. In any case, collaboration only makes sense if the sum of the individual parts is greater than the individual parts.'

With Valuu, PostFinance wants to create an ecosystem in which customers 'feel comfortable when it comes to financing, loans and insurance', says Thomas Jakob. 'Uploading the data once to a secure Swiss platform and being able to obtain the required services from there simply, digitally and transparently – that is the goal. And since this goal cannot and should not be achieved alone, networks are needed that provide precisely this added value offer' (Landis, 2022).

Four Years into the New Venture (2023)

By the end of 2022, Valuu's digital technology capabilities and achievements were highly regarded in the market, and the number of registered online users and participating partners grew. However, the commercial success lacked behind initial business plan expectations. As a result, PostFinance added its own mortgages to the Valuu platform, trying to utilise the digital channel for its own direct sales activities (this company decision did not align to the original value proposition to be a neutral platform, and not to sell mortgages from its controlling entity PostFinance). At its height in 2023, Valuu had about 80 employees (60 internal and 20 external) and achieved a mortgage volume of around CHF 1.2 billion, with half being via its new B2B (business-to-business) business model Valuu Pro.

In 2023, Valuu's strategy roadmap was updated to reflect the limited volume acquired from online users in relation to business expectations, but ongoing success from B2B activities via associated mortgage brokers (around 120 brokers used the platform to run their own mortgage activities). Valuu's digital technology platform was so powerful, driven by investments from PostFinance in the previous four years, that a strategic shift towards Valuu as a SaaS (Software-as-a-Service) platform was agreed on. Fintech News (2023) reported Valuu's success in B2B in August 2023, together with the announcement of a strategic collaboration with CredEx (Credit Exchange AG), a B2B marketplace for mortgages in Switzerland that, as of 2024, issued mortgages totalling over CHF 2.5 billion (Credit Exchange, 2024).

In this business deal, PostFinance acquired a stake in Credit Exchange (CredEx) and its digital technology platform Valuu was utilised by CredEx for its business operations from that moment. By 2023, CredEx pooled the brokerage business under the Valuu brand and continued operating the B2B (intermediary) business. Thomas Jakob, head of Valuu and Chief Business Unit Officer Platform Business at PostFinance, saw major opportunities in the joint venture: 'Both platforms are market leaders in their respective customer segments. By working closely together, broker partners can benefit from a one-stop solution – in other words, they can find the best mortgage offer on the Swiss market and take it out there and then with ease' (PostFinance, 2023).

In parallel, PostFinance integrated the Valuu framework and technology in its retail banking business unit. It is the software solution that provides PostFinance sales consultants with the mortgage options and mortgages, be it from CredEx or other providers (which do not want to participate on the CredEx platform). The only difference to the initial business model is that new distribution approach, where the sales consultant, but not the online user, will see the various mortgage options and present them to the customer.

All 60 internal team members of Valuu were able to find new roles within PostFinance, as their skill set and experience from the Valuu corporate digital start-up was invaluable.

Valuu's former head of marketing, Marco Chini, described the strategic shift as a result of Valuu's digital technology expertise and success in the B2B market, in combination with the gained market knowledge since the launch of Valuu that would highlight the limited market opportunity in the B2B2C segment: it confirmed that only 10% of consumers would want to secure a mortgage via a digital platform in the mid-term, while the hybrid market (combining both traditional offline and online channels) would grow. As a result, the B2B2C direct digital mortgage team for online users was closed in early 2023 and the existing Valuu website was used to promote PostFinance mortgages while, at the same time, the B2B business flourished, with many Valuu business partners/financial institutions migrating to the CredEx platform by August 2023 (Interview 1, 2023). Valuu's four-year journey provided PostFinance with a stake in CredEx, with its digital technology platform at the core of CredEx operations.

Lessons Learned

Valuu in the Context of PostFinance and Banking Industry

In August 2023, Valuu's leadership team presented their lessons learned to the board of PostFinance. Their findings are summarised below:

Milestones and Successes

- The 'big bet' of Valuu started with an uncertain outcome and the business model hypotheses were modified, until proved wrong.
- PostFinance demonstrated the ability to build and establish new digital business models.
- PostFinance strengthened its network in the Swiss banking industry through new lender relationships.
- PostFinance took the first steps in the areas of digital marketing and machine learning as a bank.
- It leveraged synergies in the areas of data insights and market comparisons.
- In 2022, PostFinance achieved a great partnership between its retail banking mortgage business and Valuu as a corporate start-up.

Lessons Learned

- A corporate start-up setting is suitable for internal development, but rather a hindrance for partnerships in the market.
- The balance between optimism and realism remains a challenge in the context of new (digital) businesses.
- Looking back, several small 'Valuu's' (ventures) might have resulted in higher chances of success.
- It was difficult to leverage existing 'PostFinance assets' (customer base, distribution channels) in the new business venture in practice.
- Serving the same market/customers with two business models is difficult (traditional mortgages of PostFinance and the Valuu start-up), despite different tactics over the past four years.

(Continued)

- The internal conflict between competing products (traditional mortgages and Valuu's platform strategy) with different profit margins could never be completely resolved.
- Platform partners' fear to lose the direct customer relationship/interaction (because of the platform) led to low market acceptance of the Valuu platform in the retail banking market.

Five Years into the New Venture (2024)

In April 2024, five years into the launch of the Valuu venture driven by intrapreneurs and executive managers, Thomas Jakob and Michael Gaschen, CredEx, sold the Valuu brand to a Swiss regional bank (Thurgauer Kantonalbank) to merge with its own digital mortgage broker platform (www.brokermarket.ch) that had already launched independently in 2021. Schmid (2024) wrote in his post that 'It can be assumed that there will be further consolidation in the mortgage broker market. The number of new contracts has stagnated for several years, and the days of high commissions have come to an end in a generally more difficult market environment.'

A news portal that covers news and opinions of the Swiss banking industry described the Valuu venture as 'now it's the funeral' (Huber, 2024) and as a 'cloudy' project that cost PostFinance millions (estimated to be CHF 50 million (or more, depending on the source), and a national newspaper called it 'a fiasco' (Zulliger, 2024). Andreas Dietrich, whose blog posts were referenced earlier in this case study, said that, 'A few years ago, the industry promised very high growth potential. In Germany, over 40% of mortgages were processed via brokers and platforms, while in Switzerland it is still less than 5%.' The website valuu.ch went offline in July 2024, and PostFinance continues its strategic partnership with CredEx to build digital technology solutions for the mortgage industry.

Michael Gaschen left PostFinance after a successful career of 20 years in 2023 and today (as of 2025), is the senior transformation manager business development at the UPD university hospital. Thomas Jakob (as of 2025) concluded the Valuu business venture by the end of 2023 and was appointed head of sustainability at PostFinance.

Reflection by the two PostFinance Intrapreneurs

Why were PostFinance and the Valuu team so excited about the new strategic digital initiative?

Michael: *The timing back then was perfect. It was aligned to PostFinance's digital strategy (the 'Digital Powerhouse') and the identified market opportunities, and the banking industry was in support of new digital business models. We had a small window of opportunity in the market for a digital mortgage platform.*

Thomas: *Absolutely, it was the right moment to drive a digital innovation. Mike and I were ready to accept the challenge because no one else at PostFinance wanted to kick-start a new project with an unknown trajectory.*

Michael: *Tom and I were able to recruit the project team together – hand-picked individuals who helped us drive this strategic initiative, which is why it was even possible to move forward so quickly.*

Thomas: *It took two people to start such a project – with a handshake at the time – two managers who said 'yes'.*

What were the biggest barriers and challenges during the project?

Michael: *In each lifecycle, these were different. At the beginning, the challenge was to build a team that would drive Valuu forward. We started with a group of 10 team members, all of them with interdisciplinary experiences and skills, covering all business functions. In the second phase, financial challenges were the main barrier. Interestingly enough, at the beginning of the project, the 'honey pot' was almost too big and we had to plan how to invest the available funds. Later on, we had to justify further investments. In the third phase, we were challenged by our own success, the amazing growth (with a large team). We almost grew too fast and had to manage growth. And finally, in the fourth phase, it was the integration back into the operational PostFinance business. We were a forward-looking innovation team and were integrated back into a larger operational organisation.*

Thomas: *Absolutely! We were 60–70 team members with a 'go go' culture and then were suddenly re-integrated into a large corporate. At the beginning of Valuu, there were only two of us, alone in the meeting room. At the end, we had a complete management team and operated as an independent business unit. We could no longer take decisions on our own: there were different opinions and, with that, the need for discussions.*

From my point of view, the biggest challenge was the constant adapting, realigning, finding strengths, and adapting again. This requires a lot of strength and energy from the team. We never had a calm, stable phase – all we had was a restless pushing forward to achieve our goals.

Looking back: what are the most important learnings?

Michael: *From my point of view, there are three main learnings. First, the human factor: people have to be able to work together in a digital start-up to achieve something. It is not about processes, but about collaboration. Without the right chemistry on a human level, Valuu would never have been possible. Second, it is the leadership factor: not only the team, but also the leadership team, the managers, have to be able so successfully collaborate. And, finally, it is the notion of the corporate start-up: it was the right approach, but we should have included the PostFinance executive team more closely into the governance of the start-up. Who could not sleep at night? It was the Valuu leadership team, and not the executive team at PostFinance. By bringing the two groups more closely together, we would have been on the journey together, to both celebrate wins but also to share the risks.*

Thomas: *I would like to add some points to the above. We put everything on 'one card'. today, I would 'bet on multiple horses' and diversify the strategy and our business opportunities in the market. It was a huge burden that we only had one chance. In addition, we never really succeeded, besides PostFinance's financial resources, to*

(Continued)

leverage other organisational assets such as the existing customer base, distribution channels, and sales power to drive the Valuu start-up. And finally, the internal (cultural) alignment was not ideal, as there were tensions between the existing retail banking business with its traditional mortgages, and Valuu's platform business that was based on a different business model and partnered with competitors of the traditional business model. Looking back, I cannot say if internal competition was a good or bad thing.

(Interview 2, 2024)

Image D.1 Thomas Jakob, former Head of Valuu and Chief Business Unit Officer Platform Business at PostFinance

Figure D.2 Michael Gaschen, former Chief Business Development Officer Platform Business at PostFinance and member of Valuu's executive team

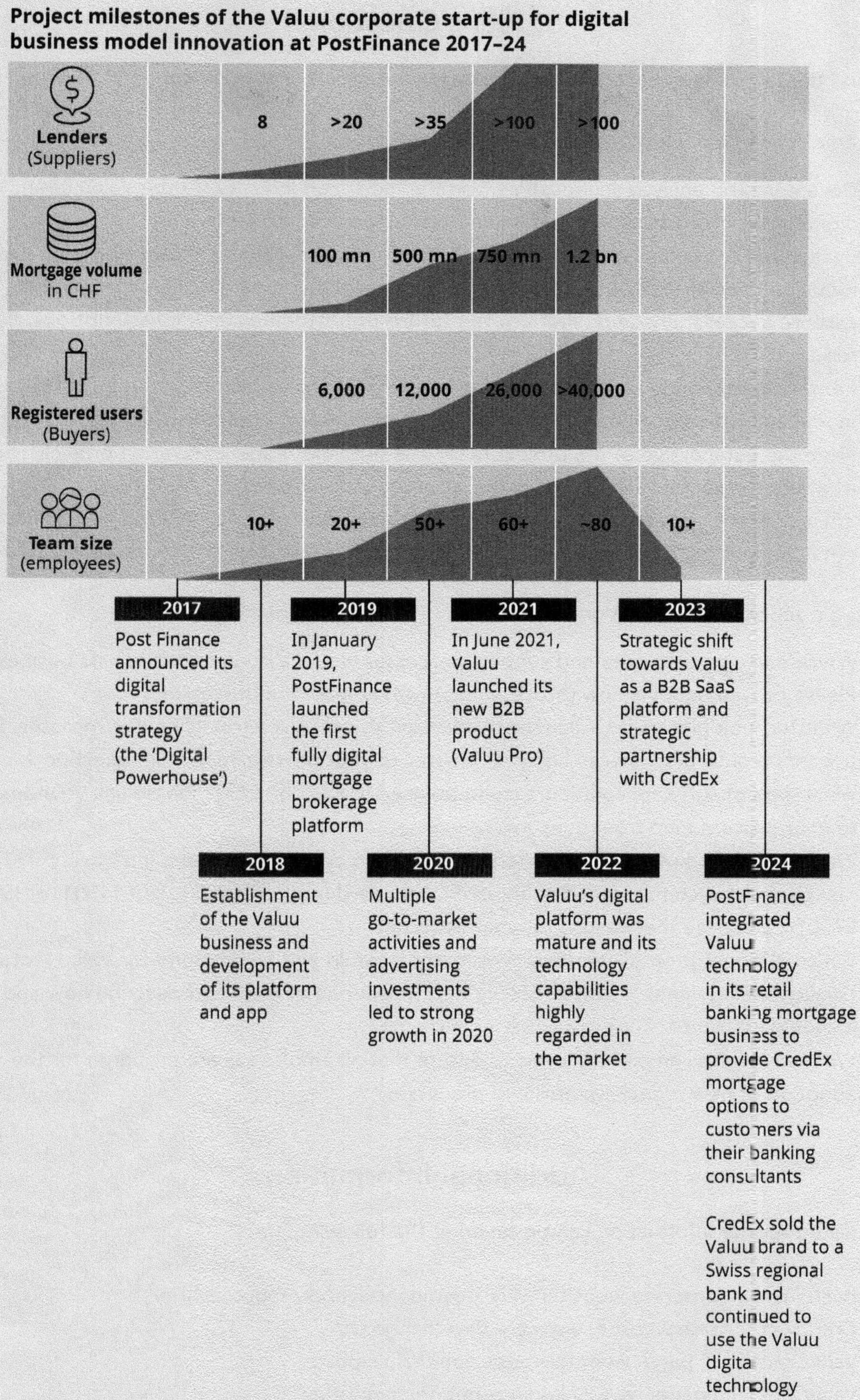

Figure D.5 Project milestones of the Valuu corporate start-up for digital business model innovation at PostFinance 2017–2024 (metrics from public and internal sources as of the end of the year, bar charts not to scale)

Student Questions

Discuss the following questions in your class, in your group or assignment:

Strategic action field 'New Strategies and Business Models':

1. Document and analyse an industry's (use the mortgage industry for the Valuu case) digital value chain and identify data and technology components.
2. Evaluate if the organisation currently covers all digital value chain components (with a focus on data and technology): Which digital opportunities did the organisation capture successfully, and what are the future opportunities (make assumptions, if required)?
3. From a board member's perspective, what are the success factors for a digital business model innovation (a digital ecosystem as part of platform economies like Valuu)?
4. From the perspective of the project team (the business model innovation project team), what are the success factors for digital strategy innovation?
5. What skills are required in a project team to drive a successful digital business initiative?
6. What 'lessons learned' would you consider for your own digital start-up/business venture?

Strategic action field 'Operational Excellence / Process Management':

1. Which management, core and support processes would Valuu need to run its business? Please provide an overview (process map) with at least ten processes.
2. What technologies could Valuu use/implement to optimise/streamline its processes towards digitisation? Please link your answer to your process map from question 1.
3. What type of software solution/s could be used in each process? Please link your answer to your process map from question 1.
4. Would you recommend to Valuu to document and certify its process and quality management systems according to an ISO standard (e.g., ISO 9001, ISO 14001, or ISO 27001)? Describe the reasons for your decision.
5. Which business process improvement method would you recommend for Valuu (Total Quality Management (TQM) or Six Sigma)? Select one or both and describe how and why it should be used.
6. What strategies can be employed to ensure that all employees are prepared for the adoption of new digital systems and processes?

Additional Information

Suggested further information can be found at the following:

- PostFinance corporate website: www.postfinance.ch/en/about-us.html
- CredEx corporate website: www.creditexchange.ch/
- Valuu Facebook page: www.facebook.com/valuuapp/
- Valuu LinkedIn page: www.linkedin.com/company/valuu/
- Valuu TV commercial: www.strategic-digital-transformation.com
- Interview with Valuu CEO Thomas Jakob: www.strategic-digital-transformation.com

Author

Professor Marc K. Peter, HES-SO Valais-Wallis School of Management, Switzerland; Charles Sturt University, Australia; University of Rochester/Simon Business School, USA

Acknowledgements and Authorisation

The authors would like to thank Thomas Jakob (former Head of Valuu and Chief Business Unit Officer Platform Business of PostFinance) and Michael Gaschen (former Chief Business Development Officer Platform Business at PostFinance) for their support in providing this case study.

The Valuu case study and the use of artwork/logos/illustrations was authorised by PostFinance on 12 September 2024.

References

Bönzli, A. (2019). Gastblog: PostFinance lanciert Hypothekenvermittlungsplattform 'Valuu'. Digital Finance Experts, available at: https://digital-finance-experts.blogspot.com/2019/01/gastblog-postfinance-lanciert.html, 22 January (accessed 30 August 2024).

Credit Exchange (2024). Über uns. Credit Exchange AG, available at: www.creditexchange.ch/ueber-uns/ (accessed 30 August 2024).

Dietrich, A. (2019). *100 Tage* Valuu von PostFinance – *erste Erkenntnisse' HSLU Hochschule Luzern*, available at: https://hub.hslu.ch/retailbanking/100-tage-valuu-von-postfinance-erste-erkenntnisse/, 20 May (accessed 30 August 2024).

Dietrich, A. (2021). Valuu erreicht neuen Meilenstein – Fakten zur bisherigen Entwicklung und zur Erweiterung des Geschäftsmodells. HSLU Hochschule Luzern, available at: https://hub.hslu.ch/retailbanking/valuu-erreicht-neuen-meilenstein-fakten-zur-bisherigen-entwicklung-und-zur-erweiterung-des-geschaeftsmodells/, 30 August (accessed 30 August 2024).

Fintech News (2021a). 2 Jahre Valuu: Hypothekar-Volumen verdreifacht. Fintech News Network, available at: https://fintechnews.ch/online-mortgage/2-jahre-valuu-hypothekar-volumen-verdreifacht/42554/, 11 February (accessed 30 August 2024).

Fintech News (2021b). Valuu steht jetzt auch Hypothekar- und Finanzberater:innen offen. Fintech News Network, available at: https://fintechnews.ch/online-mortgage/valuu-steht-jetzt-auch-hypothekar-und-finanzberaterinnen-offen/48498/, 16 September (accessed 30 August 2024).

Fintech News (2023). Online Mortgage Switzerland: Valuu and Credex to grow together. Fintech News Network, available at: https://fintechnews.ch/online-mortgage/online-mortgage-switzerland-valuu-and-credex-to-grow-together/63112/, 16 August (accessed 30 August 2024).

Huber, P. (2024). Der Valuu-Rohrkrepierer der Postfinance. Inside Paradeplatz, available at: https://insideparadeplatz.ch/2024/04/18/der-valuu-rohrkrepierer-der-postfinance/, 18 April (accessed 30 August 2024).

In Flagranti (2021). Mit Tiefzinsen zu Höchstquoten. In Flagranti, available at: www.inflagranti.ch/arbeiten-projekt/valuu/, 30 November (accessed 30 August 2024).

Interview 1 (2023). Discussion on 25 October 2023 between Marco Chini and Marc K. Peter.

Interview 2 (2024). Discussion on 30 August 2024 between Thomas Jakob, Michael Gaschen, and Marc K. Peter.

Landis, Marc (2022). Aus der Position der Stärke lassen sich gute Partnerschaften finden. Netzwoche, available at: www.netzwoche.ch/news/2022-04-27/aus-der-position-der-staerke-lassen-sich-gute-partnerschaften-finden, 27 April (accessed 30 August 2024).

Millischer, S. (2019). Valuu: Postfinance lanciert Hypotheken-Plattform, available at: www.handelszeitung.ch/unternehmen/valuu-postfinance-lanciert-hypotheken-plattform-180266, 17 January (accessed 30 August 2024).

Peter, M. K. (2019). The evolving approach to strategic corporate foresight at Swiss bank PostFinance in the age of digital transformation, in: Schreiber, D. A. and Berge, Z. L. (eds), *Futures Thinking and Organizational Policy*. Palgrave Macmillan, New York, pp. 113–32.

Peter, M. K., Kraft, C., and Lindeque, J. P. (2020). Strategic action fields of digital transformation: An exploration of the strategic action fields of Swiss SMEs and large enterprises. *Journal of Strategy & Management*, 13(1), 160–80.

PostFinance (2017) Annual Report 2016. PostFinance, available at: www.postfinance.ch/content/dam/pfch/doc/440_459/450_01_2016_en.pdf (accessed 30 August 2024).

PostFinance (2021) Valuu verdreifacht das Hypotheken-Volumen, available at: www.postfinance.ch/de/ueber-uns/medien/newsroom/valuu-verdreifacht-das-hypotheken-volumen.html, 4 February (accessed 30 August 2024).

PostFinance (2023) PostFinance mortgage business gets a boost – Valuu and CredEx to grow together. PostFinance, available at: www.postfinance.ch/en/about-us/media/newsroom/postfinance-mortgage-business-gets-a-boost.html (accessed 30 August 2024).

PostFinance (2024) This is PostFinance. PostFinance, available at: www.postfinance.ch/content/dam/pfch/doc/a_d/about_postfinance_2024_en.pdf (accessed 30 August 2024).

Schmid, B. (2024) TKB übernimmt Hypovermittlerin Valuu. *Tippinpoint*, available at: www.tippinpoint.ch/artikel/77353/tkb_uebernimmt_hypovermittlerin_valuu_.html, 17 April.

Swiss Post (2024) Annual Report 2023. Swiss Post, available at: https://geschaeftsbericht.post.ch/23/ar/app/uploads/EN_Post_Finanzbericht_2023.pdf (accessed 30 August 2024).

Valuu (2022) Darum sind Online-Hypotheken die Zukunft. Beobachter (BrandReport), available at: www.beobachter.ch/brandreport/valuu/darum-sind-online-hypotheken-die-zukunft, 4 April (accessed 30 August 2024).

Zulliger, J. (2024) Millionen versenkt: Postfinance zieht der Hypothekenplattform Valuu diskret den Stecker. NZZ, available at: www.nzz.ch/wirtschaft/millionen-versenkt-postfinance-zieht-der-hypothekenplattform-valuu-diskret-den-stecker-ld.1838902, 13 July (accessed 30 August 2024).

INDEX